**Soviet Asian
Ethnic Frontiers**
(Pergamon Policy Studies—44)

Pergamon Policy Studies on the Soviet Union and Eastern Europe

Related Titles

PERGAMON
POLICY
STUDIES

ON THE SOVIET UNION
AND EASTERN EUROPE

Soviet Asian Ethnic Frontiers

Edited by
William O. McCagg, Jr.
Brian D. Silver

Pergamon Press

NEW YORK • OXFORD • TORONTO • SYDNEY • FRANKFURT • PARIS

Pergamon Press Offices:

U.S.A.   Pergamon Press Inc., Maxwell House, Fairview Park, Elmsford, New York 10523, U.S.A.

U.K.   Pergamon Press Ltd., Headington Hill Hall, Oxford OX3 0BW, England

CANADA   Pergamon of Canada, Ltd., 150 Consumers Road, Willowdale, Ontario M2J, 1P9, Canada

AUSTRALIA   Pergamon Press (Aust) Pty. Ltd., P O Box 544, Potts Point, NSW 2011, Australia

FRANCE   Pergamon Press SARL, 24 rue des Ecoles, 75240 Paris, Cedex 05, France

**FEDERAL REPUBLIC Pergamon Press GmbH, 6242 Kronberg/Taunus,
OF GERMANY**   Pferdstrasse 1, Federal Republic of Germany

Library of Congress Cataloging in Publication Data

Main entry under title:

Soviet Asian ethnic frontiers.

   (Pergamon policy studies)
   Bibliography: p.
   Includes index.
   1. Minorities—Soviet Central Asia—Case studies.
I. McCagg, William O.   II. Silver, Brian D., 1944-
HN523.5.S658   1979   301.45'1'0957   79-11796
ISBN 0-08-024637-0

Printed in the United States of America

Contents

Chapter

List of Maps

Preface

This volume on the ethnic frontiers of the Soviet Union in Asia originated in a conference held at Michigan State University, February 25-26, 1977. We would like to express our gratitude to the Russian and East European Studies Program and the Asian Studies Center of Michigan State University, which sponsored the conference, and to the Research and Development Committee of the American Association for the Advancement of Slavic Studies and the Office of External Research of the Department of State, which funded it.

Professors Bernard Gallin and William T. Ross played major roles in maturing the idea for the conference and actively participated in it. Professor Herbert C. Jackson and Mrs. Lillian Kumata, of the Asian Studies Center; Assistant Dean Iwao Ishino of the Institute of Comparative and Area Studies; and Mr. Stephen Hyndman of the Russian and East European Studies Program all played essential roles in the organization of the conference. Mr. Hyndman has helped immensely since the conference in the organization of the published volume. To all of them we owe a special debt.

The active participation of several scholars who attended the conference contributed not only to its success but to the revisions of the papers prepared by the authors of this volume. They are: Professor Alexandre Bennigsen, University of Chicago; Dr. Murray Feshbach, U.S. Department of Commerce; Professor Richard Frye, Harvard University; Professor Larry Moses, Indiana University; Professor Fauzi Najjar, Michigan State University; Professor Karen Rawling, University of Pittsburgh; Professor Mobin Shorish, University of Illinois; and Professor Allen Whiting, University of Michigan.

Among the contributors to this volume, Professors June Teufel Dreyer and Kemal H. Karpat were outstandingly helpful, giving us a good deal of their time in addition to much advice. We are most grateful to them.

Under the supervision of Mike Lipsey, the Cartographic Center of

Michigan State University expertly drafted the maps. Mrs. Jo Grandstaff and Mrs. Berdella Wilkinson typed repeated versions of the manuscript. Without them the volume would never have been completed.

We are also grateful to Dr. Gwen Bell and the editorial staff of Pergamon Press for their help in the final stages of production.

Introduction

Our broad objective in this volume is comparative examination of how major states interact with ethnic minorities living along their frontiers. On the one hand, we study the economic, social, and cultural development of selected minorities in several Asian states and how governmental action has affected their continued viability as national groups. On the other hand, we analyze how the governmental policies toward these minorities may reflect broader strategies of nation building and international relations.

The volume has three major geographical foci. The first is the mountainous Caucasus, where Soviet Georgia, Armenia, and Azerbaijan adjoin Turkey and Iran. The second is the long, predominantly desert, region between the Caspian Sea and the Himalayas - the Soviet-Iranian and the Soviet-Afghan frontier zone. The third is the vast barren steppe that stretches eastward from Kazakhstan and Sinkiang through Siberia and the Mongolian People's Republic to the Amur valley. Our reason for selecting these regions is not only the presence of many ethnic groups, small and great, socially backward and socially advanced, on both sides of the major state frontiers. These regions all involve the largest and most Western state in Asia, the Soviet Union. Furthermore, astride the southwestern Soviet frontiers lies the far-flung world of Islam, still culturally cohesive despite political atomization and the secularizing efforts of Lenin, Ataturk, and Reza Shah. Across the southeastern Soviet frontier lies China, the seat of the world's oldest continuous civilization, now reunited and defiant of Western conquerors, old and new.

Some of the particular questions we ask in this volume reflect the extraordinary political role that frontierland ethnicity has played in the making of the modern world. In Europe, from the very dawn of the modern era in the eighteenth century the incongruence of ethnic and state frontiers provided a motive force to the continent's politics. First the divided German and Italian cultural nations, later on the Greeks, the

South-Slavs, the Rumanians, and the Poles cried for the rescue of their "unredeemed" brothers in other states. The results were the creation of a united Germany and a united Italy, then the complete replacement of the great supranational Ottoman and Hapsburg empires with new national states and the drastic reshaping of the Prussian kingdom and tsarist Russia. The Second World War in Europe and the Cold War over Eastern Europe both began with irredentist demands (first by the Germans, then by the Slavs). Frequently (since 1918) in East Asia, the Middle East, and Africa, irredentism has heralded the end of colonial rule - for example, the Korean and Vietnamese wars and the struggle between Jew and Arab in Palestine.

The potential of ethnic irredentism across the Soviet Asian frontiers commands our attention not only because of the many unsettled claims for political and cultural unification and autonomy by the border nationalities but because of the ambitions of several of the regimes in the region. Consequently, we asked the contributors to this volume such questions as:

1. Is there evidence in the ethnic group under study of political aspiration to change the status quo and to manipulate one of the states in which it dwells against the other?

2. In what ways have the policies of the host country toward this group differed from its policies toward other ethnic groups within its frontiers? Has this group, by its frontierland position, led its host to innovate in political practice or ideology?

3. In what way do direct contacts across the frontier between members of the minority group create problems or opportunities for the foreign policies of the host country?

4. How does the record of the host country's policy toward this group reflect its policies toward its neighbors? Have the policies of the host countries toward one another worked to the advantage or disadvantage of the borderland groups?

Alongside these questions about politics, we have found it relevant to probe deeply into the sociological and even the anthropological character of the frontier groups. The reason again lies in the historical record. Over and over in the past when an irredentist problem was resolved by annexation or through the dissolution of one or another supranational state, the "reunited" have found themselves strangers to one another. In the diaspora they had felt community amongst themselves and acted politically on the basis of that community but they had not recognized the divergences of custom, class, economic development and mass consciousness, and consequently found it often extraordinarily awkward to live together within new "national" frontiers and to build new states representative of all. Cavour's Italy, Bismarck's Germany, interwar Yugoslavia and Rumania, and post-1975 Vietnam all afford dramatic illustrations of how new nation states have exploited the weakness of cultural brothers who once seemed beloved because they were unredeemed. Perhaps, in general, the scars of the diaspora determine the nature of new nation states; and certainly there is no effective way to study the eligibility of frontier-straddling ethnic groups for future national statehood without probing beneath the political surface to perceive the cultural, social, and economic divergences of the national parts.

Accordingly, we put the following questions to the contributors:

1. In what ways has this ethnic group flourished or floundered because of its "betweenland position"? Has the group, or some part thereof, embarked on the path of economic modernization? Has it broken in some degree with its traditional identity? Has its survival been threatened because of its betweenland position?

2. Around what factors has the modern identity of the group and its parts evolved? Do ties of language, religion, territory, or kinship maintain the existence of a unified cultural identity that spans state frontiers? Have some of these factors proved to be more important on one side of the frontier than on the other?

3. Has the group sought means to close itself off from the wider socioeconomic arena on either side of the frontier, or has it sought integration into this arena? Has there been a redefinition of identity or a blurring of distinctiveness?

4. Have there been communications across the frontier? How has the presence or absence of such communications affected the group?

5. In what way do the host countries, through cultural and economic development policies, seek to increase the attachment of this minority group to themselves or to decrease its attachment to neighbors?

6. How well equipped is the host country to have an effect on this ethnic group? What resources of the host have not been (or are not) deployed in its policies towards this group that might be effectively deployed?

Few of the papers in this volume address all the questions posed here. Some of the contibutors have written more about the political aspect, others emphasize sociological factors. One paper examines a single small ethnically mixed mountain valley. Another discusses a large family of ethnic groups - some of which have already achieved statehood. Only some of the papers deal in equal detail with both parts of a nation divided by a state frontier. Furthermore, we make no attempt here at being comprehensive. There is a paper on Turkic peoples who inhabit not only a vast territory inside the Soviet Union and China but also have an independent state outside. Yet there are no comparable papers on the Mongols or on the Persian-speaking peoples who occupy territories almost as large, and who also have states of their own.

We have tolerated such inconsistencies because when first deliberating over the outline of this volume and possible contributors to it, we were struck by the fragmentation of Asian studies. The scholarly community has drawn its own artificial boundaries around disciplinary and area studies specialties so that one who engages in "Soviet studies" seldom converses with one who specializes in "Middle Eastern studies," even though the two might have a common interest in the Turkic peoples of Central Asia and the Near East. By bringing together historians, anthropologists, and political scientists who have ordinarily limited their focus of study to particular regions, we sought to provide a forum for communication that might transcend normal disciplinary and area studies boundaries without creating any new ones. Rather than offer comprehensive detail that might be of interest primarily to the disciplinary or area specialist, we have tried to begin a process of communication and to lay ground work for further collaborative efforts.

Despite the disunity of perspective, a number of conclusions clearly emerged from this volume. Forcible displacement and attempted annihiliation of a troublesome frontier ethnic group by a powerful government by no means necessarily extinguishes the government's problems. The very first paper in our volume, Professor Alan Fisher's study of the Crimean Tatars, shows that autocratic treatment of ethnic problems risks backfire. The case is the more interesting because in the homeland before World War II these Tatars possessed a comparatively inarticulate "national character"; and because those of them who emigrated peacefully to Turkey during the nineteenth and early twentieth centuries have assimilated to the point of disappearance. The Tatars whom Stalin brutally deported in 1944, however, managed to survive in Central Asia and to become in the 1960s (alongside the Soviet Jews and Germans) some of the most potent critics of Stalin's successor regime.

It is clear enough also that some of the smaller border ethnic groups in the Soviet Union and China have succumbed to brutality; for example, the Meskhetian Turks, deported by Stalin in 1944, have disappeared. We may remark incidentally that it is not only Stalinist and Maoist (or the Iranian Shah's repression) that results in ethnic radicalization. Gerard Libaridian's paper on the Armenians recalls that the tolerant social atmosphere of Western Europe, Lebanon, and Egypt has bred a brand of Armenian neonationalist terrorism directed against Turkey. But an overriding lesson of the papers of this volume is that ethnicity is an Achilles' heel of the Communist superpowers because it reveals fundamental limitations to coercive methods of rule.

The so-called Lenin-Stalin nationality policy has achieved extraordinary successes in enabling once "backward" peoples to modernize themselves. Before 1917 the Christian Armenians and Muslim Azeris of the Caucasus and the Muslims of Russian Central Asia were not very different in lack of education or low standard of living from their fellows in the Ottoman and Persian Empires and in Afghanistan or

Eastern China. Indeed, the Sunni Muslims of Bukhara and Samarkand were notorious then for being more ossified in their adherence to ancient tradition than any other group in the Islamic world. Today Soviet Muslim Baku, Tashkent, and Alma-Ata are modern cities and education and electrification have spread throughout Soviet Central Asia. The Ottoman Armenians have on the other hand virtually ceased to exist, and the Muslim villagers of Eastern Turkey, desert Iran, and remote highland Afghanistan are still living in semifeudal squalor.

Of course, Soviet nationality policy has not been gentle. After 1917 separatist and autonomist efforts of nationality leaders in the former tsarist Russian Empire were countered by the violent force of the centralizing Bolshevik party and Red Army. The new regime was uncompromising in viewing all religious dogma as antiquated survivals of the feudal and capitalist past that must be rooted out as soon as possible. Those local leaders who survived to play a role in the first two decades of "socialist construction" were never entrusted with the right to define purely national goals and were eventually liquidated in the Terror of the 1930s, to be replaced by a more docile set of leaders.

But in broad perspective the Soviet regime has seldom been either uncompromising or unresponsive to the existence of ethnic nationality. From the start it promised to spread the benefits of socialist industrialization and agricultural mechanization not only to the Russians but to the non-Russian peoples as well. It gave the latter a nominal political autonomy within a federal political structure. It further encouraged the numerous ethnic groups of the country by promising "a flourishing of national languages and cultures" (and even helped to create the supporting myths of unique origins and great achievements when these might help to define a distinctive culture). In the long run the regime has at times even accepted the need to compromise with the official churches and the popular beliefs of the common man. The results have been impressive. One need not ignore the repressive measures that were frequently taken, or the social and economic inequities that still remain in Soviet Central Asia to recognize that the nationalities there are incomparably better off today than their brothers across the frontier lines. (1) Because of Lenin-Stalin nationality policy, the Soviet Union has been able to retain its colonial empire in an age when the imperial democracies of the West were retreating from theirs.

When convenient, the Soviet government manipulates the ethnic problems of neighboring states, and it uses the Lenin-Stalin nationality policy as a tool of foreign policy in some situations. But in paper after paper in this volume, one learns how hesitant the Soviets have been to use the border nationalities to export Communism. This hesitance is perceptible in Soviet policy even during the present political unheaval in the Middle East.

The most conspicuous manipulation of the border nationalities took place from 1944 to 1946. The Azeris, the Kurds, and the Turkmens of Iran all rebelled at that time, as did the Kazakhs and Uighurs of

Sinkiang, and all apparently received aid and encouragement from across the Soviet frontier. At the same time, Soviet Armenians were demanding over Radio Yerevan the recovery from Turkey of "ancient Armenian lands," the Red Army was supporting the Communists of Eastern Europe by actually arresting their enemies, and the Communists of China were receiving Red Army weapons. Yet even then the Soviet frontiers in Asia remained closed to Soviet non-Russians, who may have thought of joining their brothers across the frontiers. Since then, until very recently, the Soviet Asian nationalities have been literally sealed off from their ethnic brothers and from important elements of their cultural pasts, as if Moscow saw a risk in extending across the frontiers the "fraternal aid" that the Russians are said to bring to Central Asians.

Moscow has tended instead to deal directly with neighboring governments, even when these are autocratic and nonsocialist, and even when as a result of Soviet friendship the ethnic brothers are politically injured. Of course, this has been a general trend in Soviet dealings with the Third World and is hardly surprising given Moscow's drift away from revolution. In the Soviet borderlands, the most conspicuous victims of the trend have been the Kurds, helped in their struggle for independence from Iran (1944-1946), then abandoned in their struggle with Iraq after 1964 and especially after 1975.

On another level of policy, the Soviet Union has exported the Lenin-Stalin nationality policy itself, including it in the modernization package that it recommends to developing states abroad. This policy has included formal recognition of the rights of minority nationalities, the granting of a nominal territorial and cultural autonomy, and a commitment to bringing the fruits of socialist industrialization to the most backward regions and groups. The most notable such export of Soviet nationalities policy in Asia has been to China. After 1949 the victorious Chinese Communist Party instituted the Lenin-Stalin strategy in the new People's Republic, recognizing the rights of Outer Mongolia to independence and those of the "Inner Mongols" and the Kazakhs and Uighurs of Sinkiang to autonomous nationality regions. In the 1970s Iraq also accepted a Soviet-model nationality policy. Thus, in both China and Iraq the lesser nationalities of the frontier zones benefited for a time from Soviet influence in the capitals that ruled them. In the Far Eastern case, indeed, it was the acceptance by the Chinese of the Soviet model that actually enabled Outer Mongolia to achieve the special "betweenland" independence that it has enjoyed since the early 1960s. The trouble has been, however, that Soviet influence in both China and Iraq was temporary and limited in scope. In China, once the Sino-Soviet dispute erupted, the border nationalities suffered because China's concern for fortifying her northern borderlands led to increasing immigration of Han Chinese and curtailment of the ethnic autonomous regions. Correspondingly in Iraq, when the Kurds rebelled a second time in 1975, Baghdad's tolerant nationality policy of the early 1970s was abandoned, and Moscow could do nothing about this.

The events of 1978 and 1979 in Afghanistan, Iran, and Turkey have created an opening for Soviet political influence in the Middle East unprecedented in this century, and have exposed the real difficulties that Moscow faces in dealing with states and nationalities across the Soviet frontiers. In each country Moscow pursued a different policy as the crises emerged. In Afghanistan, as earlier in Iraq and China when the government fell into friendly hands, the Soviets recommended the adoption of the Lenin-Stalin nationality policy. The leftist Taraki government, though dominated by Pashtuns, duly tolerated and encouraged the emergence of cultural institutions among the Uzbeks, Tajiks, Turkmens and (to a lesser extent) the Baluchis of the borderlands. Serious efforts were initiated to recruit non-Pashtuns into government posts. Later, as Muslims (predominantly from the Pashtun community) rebelled against the Kabul regime, Moscow not only introduced weapons and Russian military advisors into the country but also sent, apparently for the first time, large numbers of nonmilitary technical advisors from the Central Asian nationalities to help in economic, cultural, and administrative construction.

In Iran, however, until the very end of 1978, Moscow followed the Americans in supporting the Shah's regime against the general rebellion. This was consistent with a decade-long warming of Soviet-Iranian relations on the economic level, but it did not endear the Soviet Union to the Muslim fundamentalists who emerged victorious in Tehran early in 1979. In Turkey, moreover, the Soviet Union pursued yet a third policy - that of rapprochement with the left-leaning democratic government of Bulent Ecevit, combined with tacit underground aid to Communist elements among the Kurds in the east of the country.

In December 1978 Moscow abandoned support of the Shah and switched to a low-profile policy of support for a left turn in Iran, combined with mild propaganda directed at the Iranian Azeris and Kurds. Then in the spring of 1979, the sheer difficulty of pursuing all these policies at once in adjacent countries came to light. Although the Soviet Union had apparently provided a base in Baku for clandestine anti-Shah radio broadcasts to Iran during late 1978, the Khomeini regime was notably distrustful of Moscow. Though violently anti-American, it was plagued by rebellions among virtually all of Iran's nationalities and tended to blame them on the political left and the atheistic northern neighbor. Moreover, it sympathized with the Muslims of Afghanistan, may have sent military aid to help their rebellion, and openly deplored the Soviet intervention there.

In Afghanistan, on the other hand, the leftist Kalq Party tended to parade its Soviet advisors and was becoming ever more dependent on the Soviet Union for economic and military assistance - drawing the USSR into support of a weak regime against a guerilla movement with a secure base of operations from Pakistan. This enabled the "majority" Pashtun rebels to point to Soviet Samarkand and Bukhara as symbols of the threat that Soviet-style socialism poses to Islam. At the same time, the Soviet Central Asian advisors in Afghanistan were getting a view of the outside world and a sense of their ancestral religion, which they would inevitably carry home. One can only speculate whether the dominant image that they will carry back will be that of a struggle for liberation and enlightenment by their formerly oppressed ethnic brethren to the south, or of a struggle by co-religionists against an atheistic ruling regime that they helped to shore up. But the experience cannot but arouse in them a greater curiosity about the fate of Muslim peoples elsewhere in Asia.

In Turkey, meanwhile, the opposition parties sought to make political capital by attributing the unrest among the Kurds to the Sovietophile policies of the Ecevit government. And the Soviet Union suffered from some broad results of the unrest in the Middle East. For example, there were economic disruptions because the natural gas flow from Iran to the Soviet Transcaucasian republics was cut off; and the murder, in the presence of Soviet "advisors," of the American Ambassador to Afghanistan in early 1979 had adverse effects on the negotiations and impending ratification of the SALT II treaty with the United States.

In sum, as Moscow evidently realizes, manipulation of borderland nationalities can be a useful destabilizing tool. But, especially in the Middle East, such a tool may dangerously boomerang and stymie larger Soviet interests when moments for fundamental political transformation are at hand.

In the Islamic world, traditional methods of handling ethnic problems will no longer be serviceable to the existing states. This is the fourth general conclusion apparent from the articles in this book. Prior to 1978 most Middle East states continued to premise, as in the theocratic past, that within Islam there are no fundamental ethnic-linguistic subdivisions - that only religious differences are important. In 1979, however, a fundamentalist Muslim revolutionary regime came to power in Iran as an alternative to the ethnic centralism of the Shah's regime and as an avowed ally of neighboring Muslim peoples. But it found immediately that Muslims were also Kurds, Azeris, Turkmens, Baluchis, and Arabs. Islam was not a sufficiently unifying bond to overcome the nationalistic claims of peoples whose expectations of liberation or autonomy had been sharply aroused in the campaign against the Shah.

Moreover, the recent concessions to Turkmens and other minorities in Afghanistan may well help to stimulate demands by the Iranian Turkmen minority for greater autonomy. If it is successful, further- more, the Soviet attempt to turn Afghanistan into a demonstration project for the Leninist nationality policy may even provide a more potent stimulus to ethnic demands in Iran and Pakistan than any direct efforts to support Turkmen or Baluchi rebels in those countries could produce. At the same time, the Kurdish unrest in the East of Turkey put an end to the myth that Turkey is an ethnically uniform state - that Kurds are Turks who have somehow forgotten their mother tongue. With the ethnic question contributing to the fragility of Pakistan, Afghanistan, Iran, and Turkey, Muslim rulers can no longer ignore the existence of ethnicity within Islam.

A borderland position, not to speak of actual partition between modern states, is not enviable for an ethnic group. Every group studied in this volume has suffered a great deal because of its borderland location. Quite apart from the danger that they may be deported, there exists a danger of losing identity with brothers beyond the frontier. For example, the Azeris in Iran and the Soviet Union may be developing into two largely different "nations." Further, divided ethnic groups suffer from being unable to mobilize all forces for a national struggle, as is exemplified here by the pitiable history of the Kurds.

Borderland ethnic groups do have an opportunity to become showplaces in which host powers display their tolerance. Estonia and Uzbekistan in the Soviet Union and the Hong Kong and Macao enclaves in China are cited as examples. Soviet Armenia is used as a showcase to impress Armenians from far across the seas. The Soviet Turkic nationalities, as Kemal Karpat points out, have recently (and somewhat reluctantly) been held up as a shining example for the Turks of Turkey. The Mongolian People's Republic is also a showcase. But this last example shows the limitations of this "opportunity." The MPR is a showcase because it is independent of both its great neighbors. Though the Soviet Buriat Mongols remain extant, they have not been offered unification with Mongolia proper, and the Mongols in Inner Mongolia have been swamped by the Chinese, deriving from their borderland position only the prospect of extinction.

Despite the overall peril in which the frontier ethnic groups live, one may perceive factors that determine survival. When a group's cultural development is low, its political development weak, and its numbers few, its chances of surviving a stateless borderland status are poor. But in opposite cases, and especially in those cases where the central governments have been induced to grant a modicum of political recognition to the group, the chances of survival seem high. Of the groups studied, the Assyrians of the Soviet Caucasus and the Kirgiz of mountainous Afghanistan seem examples of the first extreme. On the other extreme one may cite the Soviet Tajiks and other Central Asian nationalities as well as the Outer Mongolians, who all were exceedingly disadvantaged at the time of the Russian revolution but flourish today because for different reasons they were granted a measure of political and cultural recognition by the Soviet regime.

A major factor determining ethnic survival may be the population size of the governing ethnic groups. For some time, for example, the overwhelming numbers of Russians and other Slavic groups threatened to engulf the Kazakhs, especially in the cities of Kazakhstan but also in the countryside. Today, however, it is the high fertility of the Central Asian groups that threatens the Russian numerical majority in the Soviet Union and poses some of the most vexing challenges to Soviet social planners. (2)

In China, the billion Chinese dominate the small minority groups' struggles for survival. In Inner Mongolia, Sinkiang, and Tibet alike, the sheer numbers of Chinese immigrants are threatening to put a close to the native struggles for survival.

Despite the pessimistic outlook that the papers of this volume pose for smaller Asiatic borderland ethnic groups, one final factor must not be lost from view. As Owen Lattimore puts it, for the Inner Asian ethnic individual the desired mobility is putatively "not out but up." Social mobilization is the most important goal for the individual - improvement of his own lot and that of his family, first, and only later improvement of his whole community's lot. It is readily perceptible that this rule works two ways. As long as a governing power in a multinational state can offer individuals more than continued member- ship in an ethnic group can offer, assimilation or at least a subservient political status is likely to be accepted, even if this results in the eventual extinction of the group. But once the balance tips - once the governing power reaches the limits of its benevolence to individual citizens and begins to seem oppressive or unresponsive to their perceived rights or needs - then "disintegration" will predictably occur and spread.

NOTES

(1) For further comparisons along this line, see Alec Nove and J. A. Newton, The Soviet Middle East (New York: 1967).

(2) For a discussion of this problem, see Jeremy R. Azrael, "Emergent Nationality Problems in the USSR," in J. R. Azrael, ed., Soviet Nationality Policies and Practices (New York: Praeger, 1978), pp. 363-90; and Murray Feshbach and Stephen Rapawy, "Soviet Popula- tion and Manpower Trends and Policies," in Joint Economic Committee, Congress of the United States, Soviet Economy in a New Perspective (Washington, D.C.: Government Printing Office, 1976), pp. 113-54.

1

The Crimean Tatars, the USSR, and Turkey

Alan W. Fisher

INTRODUCTION

Although the Crimean Tatars have not inhabited a "borderland" of the USSR since 1944, their traditional homeland lies between the USSR and the Republic of Turkey. They as a people are divided between Turkey and the USSR. These historic relationships are the primary determinants of their present predicament, which is that their existence is often denied.

On the one hand, both the Kazan (Volga and Ural) Tatars and the Soviet officials who decide nationality matters claim that these Crimean Tatars who now live in Central Asia are merely Tatars who happened to live at one time on the Crimean peninsula. The Anatolian Turks, on the other hand, look upon the Crimean Tatars who live in the Republic of Turkey as Turks who, having once lived on the Crimean peninsula, should now be nationally and culturally satisfied by living among other Turks wherever they may be. Neither the present Soviet government nor that of the Republic of Turkey finds the Crimean Tatar "question" an impediment to improving relations; indeed it is hardly even a subject of concern to them.

Even if one uses Stalin's wooden definition of "nation" however, there can be little question that the Crimean Tatars do exist and indeed constitute a nationality of their own. (1) Their community is historically evolved and it is based on a common language, a territory, and a psychological makeup. Though the stability of the community and its common economic life no longer exist, there is a strong surviving community of culture. This paper will recount the history and then review the present dilemmas of this people whose fate has been determined by its borderland status.

1

THE EARLY DEVELOPMENT OF
CRIMEAN TATAR NATIONALITY

It is venturesome to speak of a nationality prior to the nineteenth
century definition of the concept of nationality and indeed before the
people in question saw themselves as a separate entity. But to find
explanations of the predicament of the Crimean Tatars, one must look
at distant history. The Crimean peninsula is divided by a low range of
mountains just north of the Black Sea coast. In the mid-thirteenth
century, the coastline was inhabited primarily by Slavic, Greek,
Armenian, and Jewish populations with a growing minority of Italians in
the city of Kaffa. To the north, the plains were controlled by Turkic
tribes who had remained behind from the periodic nomadic incursions in
the centuries before. In 1241 the entire peninsula was conquered by
Batu Khan, whose East Asian followers were the first Tatars in the
Crimea. (2)

Tatars did not of course displace the entire population of the
peninsula right away. The Christians and Jews of the coastline survived
and even regained a certain independence; but in the wake of the Tatar
conquest, large numbers of Seljuk Turks came from Anatolia to the
Crimea under the direction of the Seljuk Izz ed Din, who received
authority to govern the Crimean peninsula. By the end of the thirteenth
century, Arab travelers in the region reported that the population of the
peninsula was largely Turkish. (3)

During the next two hundred years, Tatars from the Great Horde and
Turks from Anatolia continued to move to the Crimea. It became an
important province of the Great Horde and the city of Solhat, later
named Eski Kirim, became a religious center for the spread of Islam
among the Tatars. Mosques, dervish monasteries, and schools were built
alongside caravansaries. By 1450 almost all of the Crimean peninsula
north of the mountains was Turkic or Tatar. A common language grew
from a combination of the Turkish of the Anatolian Seljuks and the
Chagatay Turkic of the Tatar rulers from the Volga. Culture was
determined by the Sunni Islam of the dervish missionaries from
Anatolia, though from the architecture of the ruined mosque of Sultan
Ozbek in Solhat, it appears that a good deal of Central Asian Muslim
tradition was included. This period came to an end with the creation of
a native Crimean dynasty, the Girays, whose first member was a Tatar
invited from Lithuania by leading Tatar clans in the Crimea to form an
independent government. (4)

Under the leadership of Haji Giray, the first to call himself Khan of
the Crimea, several important Tatar clans emigrated from the Volga
region to the peninsula. In later centuries these clans and the Tatar
Girays provided the bulk of the Crimean upper classes. While they
brought with them their Tatar language and social customs, it is clear
that in time they adopted elements of Anatolian Turkish language and
customs, too. By the end of the fifteenth century the language used by

the Crimean government was apparently neither the Tatar of the Volga nor the Turkish of Anatolia. (5)

A second period of the development of Crimean Tatar identity began before Haji Giray died, with the winning of the coastline from the Europeans by the Ottoman Sultan Mehmet II, the conqueror of Constantinople. (6) From 1475 until 1774 the southern coast of the peninsula was under the direct control of the Ottoman government. The Crimean Tatars ruled the peninsula north of the mountains, and concentrated their political life first in Eski Kirim, and after the 1520s in Bahcesaray. There was no question now of complete Crimean independence; Ottoman power was too great to permit that. But two important factors enabled the Tatars to retain a remarkable flexibility in their relations with Istanbul.

First, the Crimea was important from the geopolitical point of view, and was hotly contested by other states of Eastern Europe. The Ottomans recognized that it was easier here (as in the Rumanian principalities north of the Danube) to rule through local vassals, rather than directly. Some historians claim that during these long centuries the Crimean Tatars were merely the northernmost arm of Ottoman aggression; that they acted as marionettes in the hands of the Sultans; and that in fact they were inseparable from the Turks living under Ottoman rule. (7) Nonetheless, they did have an independent state organization, they continued to maintain their own diplomatic relations with Poland, Lithuania and Muscovy, separate from the Ottomans. They even appeared at Moscow more often than the Ottomans, and this political quasi-independence left them thoroughly conscious that they were not Ottomans. (8)

The second factor contributing to the flexibility of the Tatar-Ottoman relationship - and to the survival of a Tatar consciousness of being different - was genealogy. The ruling Tatar dynasty in the Crimea could claim some measure of direct descent from Genghis Khan and the Mongol-Tatar Empire. The Ottoman Sultans also claimed such a genealogy, which of course carried with it claims to Central Asia, politically significant in dealings with Iran and Moscow. (9) Consequently, to enhance their own case, the Ottomans granted the Tatar sovereigns certain ostentatious prerogatives which they denied to all their other neighbors, independent or subject. The resulting relationship was more advantageous to the Girays and beneficial to a Tatar self-consciousness because the Khans could correctly show direct descent from the Genghisids, while the best the Ottomans could do was to encourage chroniclers to provide legendary connections with Genghis Khan. Both Ottomans and Crimeans understood the difference between direct and legendary.

In their correspondence with the Girays, the Ottomans used the term "cingiziye." Even Suleyman I, in a letter to Khan Mehmet Giray I, called the Khan the "descendant of the Crimean Sultans and of Genghisid Hakhans." (10) As a result of such flattery and despite their really vassal relationship to the Ottomans, never prior to 1783 did the Crimean rulers abandon pretensions to special prerogatives and to possession of the steppe.   On their correspondence with Poland, Muscovy, and the Ottomans, the Khans continued, for example, to use their own Genghisid seal (tamga) which was the most important symbol of steppe sovereignty.

Largely because of their special steppe heritage, the Tatars never developed an exclusive political or cultural rapport with Istanbul. Ottoman chroniclers usually discussed the Crimean Tatars with a combination of awe and strangeness.   Ottoman miniature painters always portrayed the Tatars as Orientals, while depicting Ottomans with distinct Mediterranean and European features.   Tatar chroniclers, on the other hand, in a dialect quite distinct from Ottoman Turkish, emphasized the independent and separate nature of their society and people and rejected the idea that they were just Turks or Ottomans or vassals of either.   If one can assign one major characteristic to all Tatar chronicles it is that they present historical and ideological justifications for considering the Crimeans as a separate people and state with their own institutions derived from the Crimeans' Central Asian heritage. (11)

In 1772 Catherine the Great extracted independence for the Crimean Tatars from the Ottoman Sultan, and in 1783 she annexed them to her own empire.   By the time of this annexation, the Tatars were in considerable disarray.   Economic disasters, civil war, and repeated invasions had decimated the leadership of Tatar society, disrupted social and economic relationships on the peninsula, and left most of the population in a demoralized state.   The best estimates that can be made of their population in the middle of the eighteenth century place the Crimean Tatars at around 500,000.   Yet, except for the Ottoman enclave in the south, the population had produced a culture which represented neither Tatar nor Turkish elements alone.   One can see this most clearly in architecture and language.   The Khan's palace in Bahcesaray, destroyed by the Russian invasion in 1735-36, was rebuilt between 1738 and 1740 along styles distinctly Crimean.   While showing some signs of influence from Topkapi Palace in Istanbul, it remained architecturally a distinct entity. (12)   In literature the chronicle written at the court of Khan Selamet Giray II and the description and analysis of Crimean politics prepared by Said Giray Sultan are both written in a language which is a combination of Ottoman Turkish and Tatar. (13)   The Khanate, even in its last years, represented the political manifestations of a clearly defined nationality.

THE CRIMEAN TATARS IN THE RUSSIAN EMPIRE

In the negotiations between Russian officials and leaders of the Crimean Tatars in the period between 1770 and 1783, it seemed (for the Russians at least) that the Crimean Tatars were quite distinct from both the Volga Tatars, already living under Russian domination, and the Turks in the Ottoman Empire.   Consistently, Russian officials spoke of

Crimean Tatars, Crimean Tatar people, and the Crimean Tatar state. To be sure, their intention was to facilitate the Tatars' severing relations with the Ottoman Empire. But both sides recognized the distinctions to be made between these Tatars and the Turks. (14)

Soon after the annexation, however, the Empress Catherine II ceased to speak much of the Crimean Tatars or to mention them as a people worthy of consideration. Her main interest in the Crimea was clearly economic and political, not national or ethnic. She incorporated the Crimea into the structure of the empire and did not ever consider it a corpus separatum. The keynote of her policy became a certain lack of interest in the Crimea as a special region, different from the rest of the Russian southern frontier. And her precedent set a style. The following characterization of the Crimea at the end of the nineteenth century, written in 1951 by a Soviet apologist for the 1944 Tatar deportation, expresses the prevailing opinion about the Crimea and its Tatars among Tsarist Russians.

> The Crimea in no way may be considered a colony, because the Crimean land was from ancient times Russian land, and therefore the annexation of the Crimea to Russia was not the conquest of foreign land, but was the reunification and reestablishing of the rights of the Russian people to its own land. The economic development of the Crimea was accomplished by Russians, the towns were built by Russian workers, the fields were tilled in the great majority by Russian peasants. (15)

Where are the Crimean Tatars in this description and analysis?

During the nineteenth century, the Crimean Tatars experienced one of the most heavy-handed policies of russification anywhere in the Empire. It is not surprising, thus, that the Tatars living in the Crimea had a difficult time in maintaining or developing their natural culture. In general, after the annexation Tatar society was disrupted by successive political reorganizations and by Slavic immigration.

Right at the start, moreover, the Russians acquired a solid excuse for distrusting the Tatars. After the annexation large groups of Tatars, especially from the upper classes, left the Crimea to live in the Ottoman Empire and along the western shores of the Black Sea. Educated and wealthy, these emigrants found it possible to find new social positions that were comparable to those they left in the Crimea, and in effect they melted into Ottoman society. Many Russian officials clearly believed that this assimilability of Tatars in an Ottoman homeland was dangerous to Russia. At various times during the development of a Russian society in the south the government applied pressures of varying intensity to induce the Tatars to leave the Crimea, not for abroad, but inland away from the strategic coast. These pressures were not very successful, perhaps in part because Tatar peasant inland movement before 1863 would have meant subjection to serfdom. But neither were these governmental pressures conducive to prosperity among the Tatars.

The government also pursued a policy of russianization of the Tatars who stayed. This policy originated from Catherine II's desire to grant the Tatars the very same "rights" which their social counterparts enjoyed in the rest of the Empire. Yet the application of the laws of dvorianstvo to the Tatar mirza stratum, the creation of Russian institutions in the Crimea, and the influx of a growing number of Slavic settlers in the region all combined to create enormous pressure on the Tatars to change their ways of life. To participate fully in the new institutions and to comply with the requirements of dvorianstvo status required a knowledge of the Russian language and an ability to act according to Russian customs. That only some of the Tatars proved willing to adapt shows the strength and persistence of Tatar customs even under inordinate pressure. Tsarist social policies compounded the ruin and uprooting of the traditional Tatar social structure that had taken place before 1783.

With the outbreak of the Crimean War, the St. Petersburg government evidenced real concern about the loyalty of the Tatars in the Crimea. This was a war fought on Tatar land against allies of their religious and ethnic neighbors. In 1855, for security, the governor of the Crimea, Pestel, ordered the local Tatar civilian population transported from the coast and resettled inland. (16)

Then the final straw came just after the Crimean War when Alexander II decided that the continuing presence of Tatars in the Crimea was a nuisance and a danger even in peacetime. He seems to have received faulty information about Tatar collaboration with France and Britain. He is reported to have said: "It is not appropriate to oppose the overt or covert exodus of the Tatars. On the contrary, this voluntary emigration should be considered as a beneficial action calculated to free the territory from this unwanted population." (17)

In 1859 he adopted a policy of facilitating and encouraging an exodus abroad and in the following years a large number of the remaining Crimean Tatar elite emigrated to the Ottoman Empire. This exodus exceeded all those which had taken place earlier. In the years between the Russian annexation in 1783 and the end of the eighteenth century 80,000 may have left. Another 30,000 may have departed during the confusing reorganizations of the political arrangements in the Crimea at the beginning of the nineteenth century. But the emigrations of the reign of Alexander II included large numbers of peasants. After them, in 1876, an Ottoman census listed the Crimean Tatars separately and reported 220,000 of them.   Only some 200,000 or 300,000 Tatars remained in the homeland of their ancestors. (18) The tragedy for this people was greater because the Ottoman Empire, in the throes of a general redefinition of its social classes and governmental functions, found it easier than ever to absorb Muslim Turkic immigrants. The Tatars who fled south quickly adopted Ottoman customs and within a generation largely disappeared as a self-conscious group.

Ironically, however, this same Alexander II also laid the groundwork for the emergence of a Tatar nationalist movement in the final quarter of the nineteenth century. In the period of his great reforms, St. Petersburg established among the Tatars of the Crimea, as elsewhere, a zemstvo system and Western schools. The government presumably anticipated that here, as elsewhere in the Empire, the heavy weight of the traditional social structure would prevent this secularizing measure from having any unfortunate consequences. But since in earlier decades the entire weight of Russian rule had been bent toward destruction of the traditional Tatar secular society leaving only the clergy intact, the results were just the opposite of the government's intent. The clergy had preserved, as if in fossile form, a strong sense of Tatar traditional identity in the population. And thus, when the government undermined its control, there was nothing except time to prevent the rapid emergence of a Westernized intelligentsia free of the old social structures, self-consciously not Russian but Tatar.

The Tatars still faced problems, of course, as is suggested in particular by the career of their first great modern leader, Ismail Bey Gaspirali. Because of the weakness and entrenched conservatism of the leaders of his own society, he had to go outside to the Tatars of Kazan for his training and many of his ideas. During all of his career, moreover, he had to struggle with a great paradox. He feared that complete assimilation and disappearance of the Tatars might result from introducing Russian language education; yet he advocated precisely such a reform as the only means by which his people might escape clericalism. A renewal of Islamic and Tatar society, through the discovery of the West in the Russian language, was Gaspirali's difficult advocacy. (19)

Nonetheless, by the beginning of World War I, the Crimean Tatar community bore almost no relation to that which had existed in 1783. With a large number of Tatar schools pursuing a curriculum modernized under the direction of Gaspirali, a new generation of Tatar leaders was coming of age. Participation in imperial political life in the Dumas and a close association with other Muslim groups in the Empire had given the leaders of the Crimean Tatars a broader horizon from which to view their own predicament. They were not united. Because the Muslim clergy (those Tatar leaders most closely associated with the Tatar traditions) were tied to the interests and policies of the Russian regime, the new intellectuals were forced to search in other directions for their new identity. In this search many fell victim to the quicksand of Western influences and rejected many elements of their past that were necessary for their national identity. (20) But thanks to the peculiarities of tsarist policy in the first half of the nineteenth century which did the work of destroying the Tatar Old Regime, Tatar society and its intelligentsia were more advanced in the national sense in 1914 than many other groups in old Russia.

THE GREAT WAR, THE REVOLUTION,
AND THE GOLDEN AGE

The war of 1914 caused problems for the Tatars. These arose, on the one hand, because a number of Tatar intellectuals were in Istanbul participating in various Turkish and Turkic movements, and on the other hand, because the Russians adopted restrictive policies against what they believed to be a potential Muslim fifth-column supporting the Ottoman foe.

The Tatar intellectuals in Istanbul came for the most part from Crimean student groups who, after completing their studies in Russian Tatar normal schools, continued their education in Istanbul. In 1908, under the influence of the Young Turks, some Crimean students founded a Crimean Student Society (Kirim Talebe Cemiyeti). While this society remained a completely legal organization in Russia until its end in 1917, an illegal offshoot, Vatan, appeared in 1909. Its unabashed goal was an independent Crimean state. Vatan's members engaged in continuous conspiratorial activities in both Istanbul and in the Crimea, and by the beginning of 1917 had succeeded in forming secret nationalist cells in many Crimean towns and villages. After 1910 Vatan issued proclamations against the "Tyranny of Tsardom," and called for the introduction of ideas of "Tatarcilik" in the Crimea to replace Gaspirali's "Turk-culuk." (21)

The Ottoman government was not very interested in this movement. Indeed, there never was any evidence that the Ottomans encouraged a Crimean fifth-column during the War. While a number of the Young Turk leaders, especially Enver Pasa, became interested in the ideas of pan-Turkism, the difficulties of war and the inadequacies of Ottoman resources gave Ottoman leaders no time or energy to spare on such movements. Indeed the Tatars in Istanbul quickly became disillusioned about possible Turkish support and most returned to the Crimea before 1917 to work there for their cause. A major dispute between Gaspirali and the Pan-Turk, Yusuf Akcura, arose at that time in which the Crimean took the position that the Turks in the Russian Empire had a historical destiny separate from Turks in the rest of the world. (22)

The Russian government had a completely different perception of what was going on in the Crimea. Despite the fact that as late as January 1912 the Crimean Tatar leadership had not been in favor of the Pan-Turkic movement, the Russians began to suppress all Tatar activities in the Crimea. The Russian administration took no chances. It pursued a policy of increasing attacks against Tatar cultural and national life. Police agents often interfered with Tatar religious and educational activities. Any discussion of historic Tatar ties with the rest of the Turkic world was prohibited. Newspapers and journals that had achieved such a sound foundation after 1906 were subjected to severe censorship and outright closing.

Yet during the period of the 1917 Russian revolutions, the Crimean

Tatars were able to pursue with some success their nationalist aims. Tatars who had been in Istanbul and the West returned to the Crimea with the fall of the Tsarist government. Tatar intellectuals and politicians worked quickly to fill the political vacuum left by the retreat of Tsarist officials. Their movement passed through three phases during the year 1917 alone. Following the February revolution, from March 25 until the middle of May 1917, the Crimean Tatar leadership struggled to achieve cultural autonomy. Led by Celebi Cihan and Cafer Seidahmet, both of whom had participated in Young Turk and Young Tatar groups in Istanbul, the Tatars chose a Muslim Executive Committee that proclaimed cultural and national autonomy and tried to take charge of all national, cultural, religious, and political affairs in the Crimea. (23)

From mid-May until November the Tatars pressed the cause of territorial autonomy for all non-Russian nationalities. In so doing, however, the Crimean Tatars encountered strong opposition from some other Turkic groups in Russia, especially the Tatars of the Volga and Ural region, because the latter group had no clearly defined territory to claim as their own. The claim of the Crimean Tatars was weakened also by the fact that they constituted only a minority of the population of the Crimean peninsula, which for historic reasons they believed to be their exclusive homeland. Eventually an All-Russian Muslim Congress meeting in late May 1917, in Petrograd, adopted this statement over the Volga Tatars' opposition: "The form of government that is most capable of protecting the interests of the Muslim peoples is a democratic republic based on the national, territorial, and federal principles, with national-cultural autonomy for the nationalities that lack a distinct territory." (24) In this movement the Tatars experienced extreme hostility and opposition also from all-Russian parties - whether monarchist, liberal, or socialist. It soon became clear that any government dominated by Russians would strive hard to preserve the old Russian Empire under new political forms.

The third period of Crimean Tatar revolutionary movement took the form, therefore, of a struggle to establish an independent state. Unable to find support from literally any of the Russian parties for the principle of national or cultural autonomy - the denial of which meant in no uncertain terms a support of the policy of russification - the Crimean Tatars, and a number of other nationalities as well, were forced to push their demands from autonomy to independence.

When the Bolsheviks captured the Crimea in the last months of the civil war, a large number of Crimean Tatars fled abroad, mostly to Rumania, and not to Turkey which itself was undergoing a revolution and internal disruption. Then for a while it seemed as though the Crimean Tatars were going to be able to succeed in establishing, under Soviet rule, what they had worked for during the first period of the revolution, namely national and cultural autonomy. In October 1921, following the advice of the Volga Tatar communist, Sultan Galiev, the Soviet government created in the Crimea (now defined to also include some districts north of the peninsula in the southern Ukrainian steppe) an autonomous republic, the Crimean ASSR, as an integral part of the RSFSR. (25)   The resulting Crimean Bolshevik administration even achieved some autonomy.   Its leader was Veli Ibrahimov, and Tatar exiles now refer to his governance as a Golden Age.

THE ROAD TO DISASTER

With the elimination of national communism in the USSR by Stalin in the late 1920s and early 1930s, Crimean "autonomy" came to an end. By 1933 the Crimean Tatar community had suffered a number of devastating blows.   The sovietization of their cultural and educational life had removed all Tatars deemed untrustworthy from their posts, including Veli Ibrahimov, their most effective Communist leader. Further, a famine had been caused by the attempted collectivization of Tatar agriculture.   The depletion of Tatar leadership continued unabated during the late 1930s.

Then in 1938 the new Tatar Latin alphabet (which was introduced in 1928 and had itself disrupted Tatar cultural life) was replaced with the Cyrillic.   This change had a disastrous effect upon the Tatar language and literature.   It cut off the new generation of Tatar students from the wealth of prerevolutionary and even early postrevolutionary Tatar literature that had been written and published in the Arabic alphabet. It gave the government an easy method of selecting what Tatar literature would be made available to the younger generation. (26)

The number of journals and newspapers published in the Tatar language dropped from 23 in 1935 to 9 in 1938.   Many Arabic, Persian, and Turkish words were excised and replaced with Russian.   The rules for assimilating foreign (Russian) words were changed so that they followed Russian rather than Turkic conventions.   As Gare Le Compte wrote, the russianization of their alphabet "increased both the flow of Russian terminology into the Turkic languages and the facility of Muslims to learn Russian." (27) During Stalin's time, at least, sovietization of native cultures meant no more and no less than russification.

This debacle in the Crimean homeland was paralleled in Turkey where a large Crimean Tatar community continued to reside.   Ever since the war Ataturk had been striving, with mixed success, to create a new Turkish nationality.   A large number of the Turks living in Turkey had ancestors who had come from the Balkans and the Caucasus as well as from the Crimea.   Ataturk himself was a Turk from Macedonia; but one of the hallmarks of his program had been the abandoning of any connections with Pan-Turkism or Pan-Islam, and the redefinition of the territory and people to be included in his new republic.   There was no room for either territories or peoples within Russia in his new nation. Furthermore, Ataturk made it very clear that his new Turkish nationality had no Pan-Turkic aims.   He intended the Turkish Republic to have firm and limited frontiers. He recognized that his new Turks had a variety of cultural and ethnic backgrounds, but he insisted that they would all have to transfer whatever former loyalties they had (religious, territorial, cultural) to the new republic. The adoption of one Turkish language and uniform education throughout the country were his two major instruments for the creation of this new nationality. As a result, most of the Tatars who lived in Turkey were by 1938 well along the way to assimilation into the larger body of Turks. No schools in Turkey taught Crimean Tatar language or literature, except at the university level.

Only in Rumania was the situation of the Tatars hopeful in the late 1930s. Living in the midst of a non-Turkic and non-Muslim people, the large Crimean Tatar community found it easy to retain its ethnic and cultural identity. In Constanta, where a Crimean National Center was established, journals, newspapers, and books were published in Crimean Tatar and about the Crimean Tatars. The political-cultural journal Emel [Hope] was founded in 1930 and continued to be published until the outbreak of the war. Leaders of this Crimean Tatar community were individuals who had played an important role in Tatar politics during the revolution. But their political identification went from communist to right of center, and virtually all were conscious of being grateful to Bucharest. (28)

The defeat of the Soviet armies in 1941 and the occupation of the Crimea by the Germans and the Rumanians led directly to the final debacle of the Crimean Tatars. There can be no question that many of the Tatars now collaborated with the occupation authorities, and it was for this that the entire nationality group was penalized by deportation in 1944. But in judging this "collaboration" one must keep in mind several exculpatory factors. For example, it is worth remembering that for the diaspora Tatars who now came home, the Germans were a last resort. In 1941 several of them - notably Cafer Seidahmet, Edige Kirimal, and a new leader, Mustecip Ulkusal - sought to negotiate help from the Turkish government. This was their first choice; but Ankara proved ever less willing to get involved in Tatar affairs. The Tatar leaders returned from the negotiation empty-handed, and only then did they turn to the Rumanians and the Germans (to whom, it may be recalled, they had reason to be grateful).

One may remark, moreover, that between 1928 and 1941 the activities of the Soviet government had resulted in the destruction of the Crimean Tatar native political and cultural leadership to an extent not experienced by any other Soviet nationality. Almost half of the Tatar population had already been destroyed or deported; and the Tatar masses, that is the peasants, had not experienced a single verifiable benefit from Soviet rule. They had suffered the same fate as their leadership. As Lemercier-Quelquejay wrote: "It was an enfeebled and exhausted Tatar community that encountered the final tragedy, German occupation, and later, deportation." (29)

The word "collaboration" has two distinct meanings: to work

together, as well as to cooperate treasonably. And the word "treason" means violation of allegiance toward one's sovereign or country. In the USSR during the war it was treasonable behavior to act in any way other than to actively oppose the German occupation. But given that a large part of the Crimean Tatar population did not consider the government in Moscow to be their "sovereign" nor the USSR to be their country, the negative connotation of "collaboration" does not completely apply to the Tatar case, except as viewed from Moscow itself.

Tatar "collaboration" with the Germans took the following forms. First, early in 1942 the Germans encouraged the creation of "self-defense" battalions of Tatars to "defend" their villages against activities of Soviet partisans in the Crimea (it must be remembered that the Tatars accounted for not more than one-fourth of the population of the peninsula). According to German records, between 15,000 and 20,000 Crimean Tatars formed these military units. (30) Second, with German aid, Tatars established local "Muslim Committees" to take over the responsibility for most nonpolitical and nonmilitary affairs in those towns which had a substantial Tatar population. These concentrated exclusively on cultural and religious matters. (31)

On the other hand, there is substantial evidence that the Tatars did not uniformly support cooperation with the Nazi occupation forces. As many Crimean Tatars fought in the Red Army on other fronts as participated in the "self-defense battalions." According to Pisarev, "nearly 20,000 Crimean Tatars fought on the front during the war; thousands were given orders and medals of the USSR. Eight were called Heroes of the Soviet Union, and one Crimean Tatar pilot, Ahmet Khan Sultan, was twice awarded that order." (32)

A recent issue of the samizdat journal, Chronicle of Current Events, reported: "Out of the total population (302,000) before the war, there were 95,000 men over 18 years. 53,000 fought in the [Red] army and 12,000 in the [pro-Soviet] resistance and the underground. 30,000 Tatar participants in the war perished." (33)

The deportation, which occurred in May 1944 not very long after the Soviets regained mastery of the peninsula, included not only those Tatars who actually aided the Nazis, but all Tatars, young and old, men and women. Even Tatars who had fought for Soviet victory serving in the Red Army on other fronts, Tatars who were in the first ranks of the Communist Party, as well as Tatars who had been in partisan units, were swept up in the vast deportation net. Some fifty Communist Tatar writers and journalists who had distributed anti-German proclamations and newspapers in Tatar during the war were deported, too. (34) Some 40 percent of the deportees died in the process of resettlement. A year after the deportation, the Crimean ASSR was officially abolished, and the Crimea became the "Crimean Oblast" of the RSFSR (later to be transferred to the Ukraine).

Until today the official justification for the resettlement has been accepted by most observers of Soviet affairs. There can be no question that a large number of Soviet officials believed it.   But this cannot explain the deportation of all of the Tatars, including those who had fought with the Soviet army and partisans, as well as those who had served in the Soviet underground as commissars and political instructors during the occupation.   Such nationalities as the Volga Tatars and the Turkestanis provided military and political collaborators on the same levels as did the Crimean Tatars, and they were not punished in the same collective way.

The answer to this problem seems to lie in Stalin's foreign policy toward the Republic of Turkey.   Recently the deportation of the Meskhetian Turks in November 1944 has come to light.   This has never been officially announced or admitted by Soviet authorities, and with good reason.   The Meskhetian Turks, who formerly resided along the Georgian side of the Soviet-Turkish border, did not collaborate with the German invaders; in fact, they had no contact with them at all.   Yet when the Chechens and Crimean Tatars were removed for collaboration, the Meskhetians also were deported to the Soviet East, primarily to Uzbekistan.   In a recent article, Wimbush and Wixman point out that these Turks were removed from the Turkish border and replaced with Soviet Armenians just before Stalin began making strong claims to increased Soviet influence in the Turkish Republic and even to control of the Straits.

In March 1945 Molotov informed the Turkish ambassador to Moscow that the USSR was renouncing the Turco-Soviet Treaty of Neutrality that had been signed in December 1925, since "this treaty no longer corresponds to actual conditions and to changes brought about by the war that require significant alterations in our relations." (35) On July 7, 1945, Molotov informed the Turkish ambassador that the USSR requested the right to establish military and naval bases on the Straits. In the same conversation Molotov also raised the question of the northeastern Turkish provinces of Kars and Ardahan which had been "ceded to Turkey at the end of the First World War at a moment when the Russian weakness left them with no alternative to acceding to Turkish demands."   These provinces were not to be returned to the USSR.   It is probably no coincidence that the Meskhetian Turks had lived on the border of the province of Ardahan. (36) When he deported them, Stalin made sure that no fifth column of Turkic nationals would stand in the way of such pressure being applied on the Soviet-Turkish border. (37)

Would the same reason hold true for the Crimean Tatars as well? Evidence for this possibility emerges from an analysis of the Geographical Atlas of the USSR, published in 1950, which shows that all of the other non-Slavic minorities in the Crimea (save the Armenians) were removed after 1944 also.   This included Greeks and others who had not aided the Germans in any way.   They were all replaced by Russians and Ukrainians. (38)

CRIMEAN DIASPORAS IN TURKEY
AND THE USSR TODAY

The vast majority of the Crimean Tatars live in the Republic of Turkey. Some Tatar spokesmen there claim that the numbers reach five million, and there may be some truth to this claim. After all, the various Tatar immigrations in the nineteenth century must have left large numbers of Tatars in areas to be incorporated into the new Turkish Republic. Yet today only a fraction of this total views itself as Crimean Tatar; most have been successfully assimilated into the broader Turkish nationality. And herein lies the major problem for those Tatars who retain a sense of Crimean national identity.

As noted earlier, the national policies of the Turkish Republic have been aimed at the assimilation into one Turkish nationality of all Turks who live within its frontiers regardless of their place of origin or original Turkic nationality. Today all Turkish children must attend state-run public schools through the fifth grade; textbooks and teaching materials are uniform throughout the country and are prepared under the direction of the state ministry of education. All Turkish children, whether their parents were Crimean Tatar, Uzbek, Kazakh, or from the Caucasus, became in fact Turks with uniform language and uniform views about their past and heritage. Crimean Tatar, Azeri, Uzbek, and Turkmen are not used in any Turkish school as the language of instruction; books and other teaching materials appear only in the official Turkish language of the state (except at the university level). Virtually no mention is made in these Turkish schools of the history of any of these other nationalities or Turkic ethnic groups. The history texts used in primary schools (and at the lycee level) emphasize the history of the Republic and until recently neglected even the history of the Ottoman Empire. In the last few years, the history of the Ottomans has been taught, too, but the Ottomans are regarded as Turks only, not leaders of the multinational empire that was the reality.

In fact, the vast majority of Turks today do not even admit the diversity of the Turkic nationalities and ethnic groups. Turkish Cypriots are called Turks who live in Cyprus. There are also Turks who live in Thrace (eastern Greece), Turks who live in Central Asia, and so forth. The Turkish adjective turk does not allow the distinction between Turkish and Turkic. The Crimean Tatars are viewed by almost all Turks as Turks who lived at one time in the Crimea (remarkably similar to the view officially put forward today by Soviet authorities).

The nationally aware Crimean Tatars in Turkey are few in number and generally come from the older generation. They have organized a Crimean National Center in Istanbul and pursue a number of national enterprises. Among these are the publication, since 1960, of a bimonthly journal devoted to Crimean Tatar history and culture, Emel, which is published in Turkish, not Tatar. A typical issue (March 1977) includes the following articles: "Those Who Serve The Nation

[Crimean Tatar] Will Not Be Forgotten, Must Not Be Forgotten"; two articles about Selim Abdulhakim, a Tatar leader in Rumania before World War II; an article on the use of fire and its symbolic meaning among early Crimean Tatars; a translation of an article on the struggle of the Crimean Tatars in the USSR written by Peter Potichnyj and originally published in Canada; a first installment of a Tatar epic poem (with Turkish translation); continuation of a Crimean Tatar play translated into Turkish; and a series of news items about Tatars in the USSR. But the publishing run of this journal is less than 500 per issue and the readership is almost totally from the older generation. (39)

The Crimean National Center (Kirim Milli Merkezi) in Istanbul also supports folklore groups which are more popular with the young people. Yet the Tatar youth view these activities as "folklore," not much related to their own nationality. Once a year in Istanbul a "Crimean Tatar Evening" is held at a large casino. In 1977 about 500 attended. But Turkish, not Tatar, was the language in use even among the older generation. The folklore groups presented dances and music; the few talks given were practically devoid of political or national content. Assimilation, not ethnic particularism, was the major characteristic.

In a long conversation with several of the nationally active Crimean Tatars in the fall of 1976 in Istanbul I learned of their problems and goals. The unofficial leader of the group, Bey Mustecip Ulkusal, remarked that "the Jewish people, despite 2,000 years of living without a homeland, were able to retain their national and ethnic identity, so that when the opportunity arose after World War II they could reestablish their nation. The Crimean Tatars in Turkey, after only a few decades of living without a homeland, are already beginning to fall apart and to lose their identity." (40)

The policies of the Turkish Republic towards assimilation of all Turkic peoples living within the state and the relative ease for most of them to adapt makes it highly unlikely that any Tatar national movement will succeed in Turkey. It is perhaps ironic that the relatively small Crimean Tatar community living in the United States is having much more success in preserving its cultural and national heritage than is the much larger one in Turkey. In Brooklyn there is a Crimean Tatar mosque and school where the language, culture, and history of the Crimeans is studied. It is a thriving enterprise with many more applicants than places. To my knowledge, there are no lessons given anywhere in Turkey either in the Tatar language or about Crimean Tatar history and culture (even at the university level).

There are still a number of Turkish towns and villages where the Crimean Tatars predominate. The largest is Eskisehir, a hundred miles southeast of Istanbul in the Anatolian plain. There Tatar cultural activity is still quite strong and youth groups from the city dominate folklore associations for the Tatars in Turkey. But when asked, they identify themselves as Turks "whose parents and grandparents came from the Crimea." I visited one small village in Turkish Thrace, Subasikoy, which had once belonged to the Giray family well before the

Russian annexation of the Crimea. Even a decade ago the town was visibly Tatar. Its mosque was a wooden one built by Selamet Giray in the eighteenth century following Tatar architectural styles, and there was a large wooden palace once belonging to a wife of a deposed Crimean Khan. But in the last two years all vestiges of its Tatar past were removed. The imam of the village mosque proudly said that his village was "now going to have a new mosque that looked like those in the big city [Istanbul]." His hope was that all of the village young people "who had left to live in Istanbul" would thus be enticed back to the village. But one could see that there was no hope for a Tatar future there either.

A completely opposite situation occurs in the USSR for the Crimean Tatars. There Tatar national and cultural identity not only continues to exist but is actually growing in strength and intensity, with the Tatars playing a significant role among the Soviet Union's protest movements. The reason for this is in part the fumbling effort on the part of the Soviet government to repair the injustice of 1944. In June 1954 (the same month in which the Crimea was made an oblast of the Ukrainian SSR), some of the restrictions placed upon the Tatars in Uzbekistan were lifted. In 1956 they were permitted to leave their places of exile, although the relevant decision stated that "the property of the Crimean Tatars confiscated at the time of their deportation will not be returned, and they do not have the right to return to the Crimea." (41) In 1957, when a number of other deported nationalities were rehabilitated by the Soviet government, the Tatars received permission to begin the publication in Tashkent of Lenin Bayragi [The Flag of Lenin] , the first Crimean-Tatar language newspaper since 1944.

These governmental measures do not explain, however, all that has happened. As Sheehy points out, much of the official improvement in the life of the Crimean Tatars was accomplished without national publicity. As late as 1966, after Lenin Bayragi had been operating for nine years, the leading Soviet linguists were unaware of its existence. They wrote in 1966 that the Crimean Tatar language was "in the category of languages without a written form." (42) The key to the Crimean Tatars' revival is the exceptional educational level which they had achieved even before the war, compounded by cosmopolitanism and mobility resulting from the deportations. Indeed it is ironic to note that just as the repressive Tsarist policies in the Crimea during the nineteenth century helped in the long run to make the Tatars a modern nationality, so the extermination efforts of the Soviet regime in the 1940s contributed in the long run to the rebellion of the 1960s.

From 1957 until 1966, the Crimean Tatars collected and forwarded to various Soviet authorities dozens of petitions asking for complete rehabilitation and the right to return to the Crimea "in the light of Leninist nationality policies." By 1961 they were consistently able to procure more than 25,000 signatures for each petition. (43) Then, from 1962 to 1966, they moved in two other directions. First, they organized in each town and village in which they resided Tatar Committees to coordinate protest activity and instruct Tatar youth in their language and culture. Second, they began sending delegations to Moscow to present petitions and demand meetings with Soviet officials. The authorities responded with arrests and trials of Tatar leaders. Yet, like the problem of the sorcerer's apprentice, for each Tatar arrested, the local communities sent three replacements. By mid-1967, there were over 400 Crimean Tatars resident in Moscow as official delegates from the Tatar village and community committees. By threatening to demonstrate in Red Square, these representatives finally obtained word that a group of top ranking Soviet officials would listen to their complaints.

At this point the Soviet regime made a mistake. On July 21, 1967, just after a major Tatar demonstration in Tashkent, the chairman of the KGB, Andropov, Supreme Soviet Presidium Secretary Georgadze, USSR Procurator General Rudenko, and the minister for the preservation of public order, Shchelokov, met with some of these Tatars in the Kremlin. The outcome of the meeting was a promise to issue a full rehabilitation of the Crimean Tatars and a commitment to reconsider the question of their return to the Crimea. (44) In September 1967 the regime followed this up with a decree of rehabilitation:

> After the liberation of the Crimea from Fascist occupation in 1944, accusations of the active collaboration of a section of the Tatars resident in the Crimea with the German usurpers were groundlessly leveled at the whole Tatar population of the Crimea. These indiscriminate accusations in respect of all the citizens of Tatar nationality who lived in the Crimea must be withdrawn, the more so since a new generation of people has entered on its working and political life. The Presidium of the USSR Supreme Soviet (1) annuls the sections of the relevant decisions of State organs which contain indiscriminate accusations with respect to citizens of Tatar nationality who lived in the Crimea, (2) notes that the Tatars living formerly in the Crimea have taken root in the territory of the Uzbek and other Union Republics; they enjoy all the rights of Soviet citizens, take part in public and political life, are elected deputies of working people, work in responsible posts in Soviet, economic, and party organs; radio broadcasts are made for them, a newspaper in their national language is published, and other cultural measures are undertaken. With the aim of further developing areas with Tatar population, the councils of ministers of Union Republics are instructed to continue rendering help and assistance to citizens of Tatar nationality in economic and cultural construction, taking account of their national interests and peculiarities. (45)

The government here admitted publicly that the charges of treason during the war made against the Tatars were in large part false. The government also indirectly agreed that the entire deportation had been a mistake - or at least its causes were different from the official justifications given after the war. The Soviet authorities admitted, finally, the existence of a separate Crimean Tatar nationality. Most of the decree spoke only of Tatars who had lived at one time in the Crimea, implying that they were part of the larger officially recognized Tatar nationality of the Volga and Ural region. But the statements on Crimean Tatar culture gave hope to the Tatar leaders of continued growth and development of Crimean Tatar identity, with the blessings of the government.

The results of this decree on the Crimean Tatar people in the USSR have been profound. Rather than taking the edge off their movement, as the Soviet authorities had probably hoped, it has given added impetus to it. Tatars in large numbers have tried to move to the Crimea; most have been forcibly returned to Central Asia because they "lack proper papers." Tatar leaders have joined the more general Soviet dissident movement, and have gained important allies from that quarter, notably Andrei Sakharov and Petr Grigorenko. The Tatar "lobby" in Moscow has persisted despite all attempts by the authorities to end it. One embarrassment after another to the government has occurred at meetings of the international communist movement. Demonstrations occur with growing intensity in Uzbekistan.

Since August 1969, moreover, Lenin Bayragi has carried a special column entitled "Nobody Is Forgotten and Nothing Is Forgotten," in which reports of Crimean Tatar war heroes have been given. In 1970 it introduced another column, "Immortal Soldiers of the Revolution," which discussed the activities of Tatar Bolshevik revolutionaries during the years 1916 to 1920.

Information appearing in this newspaper indicates that a textbook for the study of the Crimean Tatar language, and several collections of Crimean Tatar literature, have appeared in Tashkent. One article appealed to Tatar youth "to emulate Bekir Cobanzade, a prominent poet and scholar who loved his native language and literature, and who perished during the Stalinist purges in the late 1930s." (46) This newspaper is highly subversive from the Soviet regime's point of view, but it is not samizdat. It is legally published and in fact is available to western readers through the normal Soviet subscription channels.

Aside from Lenin Bayragi, the Department of Crimean Tatar Language and Literature at the Nizami Tashkent Pedagogical Institute, "where the students are mainly Crimean Tatars who have taken courses in their native language in Uzbek secondary schools," is another center for the maintenance of Tatar culture. Related to this department is the section for Crimean Tatar publications in the Gafur Gulam publishing house in Tashkent. Headed by the Tatar poet, Cerkes Ali, with Seitomer Emin as poetry editor, this section in 1969 alone published more than twenty works in Crimean Tatar. Not only works by contemporary Tatar writers, but also those by a number of prewar and even prerevolutionary Tatar intellectuals are being published. Such figures as Gaspirali, Cobanzade, and the poet Cergiyev, who died in a

Stalinist camp, are now represented in the firm's publication list. (47)

The aims of the Crimean Tatars are few and straightforward: complete rehabilitation as a Soviet nationality; the right to return to live in the Crimea; and the wide publication of the government's change of mind about Tatar "treason" during the war. There is no evidence that the Tatar leaders envisage a reestablishment of the Crimean ASSR (though they may dream of it), and indeed this would be difficult. There is probably room for a return - the economy of the Crimea has never regained the levels it achieved before World War II, and there is evidence of a continuing need there for additional labor force. But the peninsula was given to the Ukrainian Republic in 1954 and since then it has been thoroughly slavicized by several large waves of Russian and Ukrainian settlers. Even the limited demands of the Tatar leaders, however, have evidently seemed subversive to the Soviet government.

In the past few years, trials and repression of the more outspoken Crimean Tatar leaders have occurred and the punishments levied have been severe. The most recent trial of such a leader was that of Mustafa Cemilev, in Omsk, on April 14, 1976. The trial was held in Omsk, not Tashkent where the alleged crimes took place, because foreign correspondents could not travel to Omsk. Only because Andrei Sakharov and his wife attended and were subsequently brutalized by the local police did the Western press find the event interesting. Cemilev was sentenced to two and one-half years in a labor camp on the familiar charge of anti-Soviet slander, despite the fact that the only prosecution witness withdrew his testimony after the trial, claiming it "had been extorted from him." On April 19, Soviet historian Aleksandr Nekrich called upon his colleagues to give up their "shameful silence" on Cemilev and other persecuted Soviet dissidents. (48)

More recently it was announced that the Soviet authorities have undertaken a major campaign against the Crimean Tatar nationalist movement, and have threatened to try large numbers of Tatars for the treason during the Second World War for which they were rehabilitated in 1967. In the newspaper Selskaia Zhizn', it was reported on July 24, 1977 that two Crimean Tatars were sentenced to death since it had been "established that each of them personally participated in the shooting of guerrillas, workers in the underground and peaceful citizens. For more than thirty years they were hiding from the law." (49)

In addition, it clearly suits Soviet interests to encourage quarrels among Turkic nationalities in Central Asia. It is often Uzbek authorities who are the instruments of Tatar repression in Tashkent and its vicinity. For example, in the aftermath of a Tatar celebration of Lenin's birthday on April 21, 1968, Uzbek officials such as Major General Sharaliev and Deputy Procurator of the Uzbek SSR, Bocharov, directed mass arrests and detention of Crimean Tatars in Tashkent. (50) "Scholarly" accounts of wartime activities are published by other Turks which emphasize Tatar "treason" in 1941 to 1944. An example of such a book is that by Tsarlik Saginbaev, 300 Dnei v tylu vraga (Frunze, 1969).

Unlike the Soviet Jews, the Crimean Tatars have not been able to attract foreign support for their cause. Their decision to ally their efforts with those of the Soviet dissident movement in general in the late 1960s has not brought the desired results, i.e., Western attention. Furthermore, the most logical foreign ally for their cause, the Republic of Turkey, has had reason to close its eyes. Because the Turkish government, becoming increasingly disenchanted with its Western connections, is making tentative moves in the direction of "normalizing" relations with the USSR, it makes no political sense for that government to "interfere" in Soviet internal affairs. It must also be said that the Crimean Tatars have made serious tactical errors in Turkish internal politics. Their general support of right-wing parties, especially that of Alparslan Turkes which campaign on anti-Soviet and anticommunist platforms, encourages other Turkish leaders to view the Crimean Tatar problem as right-wing in orientation. At the same time, the Tatar leaders deny their cause a fair hearing by the Turkish leaders in power. Ironically, the Crimean Tatars in Turkey would have a much better chance of influence if they instead chose to support political parties which strive for better relations with the USSR. Only parties such as that of Bulent Ecevit, through the normalization of relations with their northern neighbor, could have some influence over Soviet internal policies. Yet even this is extremely unlikely.

The Crimean Tatars are perhaps the outstanding example of what in a certain conjuncture of circumstances might happen to any borderland nationality group in the USSR. They have managed over many difficult centuries to build up a clear modern identity and even to awaken consciousness in a broad stratum of their society. But like the Jews in the past, they have been uprooted entirely; they have lost their land. They have chosen not to assimilate into the greater society in which they live - and from which they even derive certain benefits. As a result they are ostracized. At the moment they are a thorn in the side of their rulers. But barring the disintegration of the Soviet state, they face a grim future there.

NOTES

(1) See Richard Pipes, The Formation of the Soviet Union (Cambridge, Mass., 1957), pp. 37-38. See Alan Fisher, The Crimean Tatars (Stanford, Calif., 1978), for a general survey of Crimean Tatar history.

(2) See P.N. Nadinskii, Ocherki po istorii kryma, vol. 1 (Simferopol', 1951), pp. 58-59.

(3) N.A. Smirnov, Rossiia i turtsiia v XVI-XVII vv. (Moscow, 1946), vol. 1, pp. 18-28; and Ahmed Dede Munecimbasi, Munecimbasi Tarihi (Istanbul, 1973), vol. 1, pp. 273-274.

(4) V.D. Smirnov, Krymskoe khanstvo pod verchovenstvom otomanskoi

porty do nachala XVIII veka (St. Petersburg, 1887), p. 146; Halil Inalcik, "Kirim Hanligi," Islam Ansiklopedisi 6 (1955): 746; and Halil Inalcik, "Hadji Giray," Encyclopaedia of Islam (new edition), vol. 3, pp. 43-45.

(5) See O. Akcokrakly, Tatarski tamgi v krymu (Simferopol', 1927), pp. 10-14, for examples of these early Crimean Tatar writings.

(6) This complex period is most successfully unraveled by Halil Inalcik, "Yeni Vesikalara Gore Kirim Hanliginin Osmanli Tabiligine Girmesi ve Ahidname Meselesi," Belleten 8, no. 31 (1944): 185-229.

(7) Nadinskii, op. cit., pp. 58-65; A.A. Novosel'skii, Bor'ba moskovskogo gosudarstva s tatarami v XVII veke (Moscow, 1948), for negative judgments about Crimean Tatar legitimacy.

(8) "Istoricheskoe i diplomaticheskoe sobranie del proiskhodivshikh mezhdu rossiiskimi velikimi kniaziami i byvshimi v kryme tatarskimi tsariami s 1462 po 1553 god," Zapiski imperatorskago odesskago obshchestva istorii i drevnostei, 4 (1863): 277-278, 379-380; S. Belokurov, O posol'skom prikaze (Moscow, 1906), pp. 78-79.

(9) The Sultans, in their Imperial titles, used the terms Khan and Padisah-i Dest-i Kipcak (Sovereign of the Desolate Steppe). I discuss this more fully in my "Crimean Separatism in the Ottoman Empire," in W. Haddad and W. Ochsenwald, Nationalism in a Non-National State: The Dissolution of the Ottoman Empire (Columbus, 1977), pp. 57-76.

(10) Feridun Bey, Munseat-i Selatin (Istanbul, 1849), vol. 1, p. 502.

(11) See Fisher, "Crimean Separatism," op. cit.

(12) P.I. Sumarokov, Dosugi krymskago sud'i ili vtoroe puteshestvie v Tavridu, 2 vols. (St. Petersburg, 1803-1805) for the most detailed descriptions of the Crimean palace. On the palace at Saray, see R. Balodis, "Alt-Serai und Neu-Serai," Latvijas Universitates Raksti (Riga, 1926), vol. 13, pp. 3-82.

(13) Barbara Kellner-Heinkele, Aus den Aufzeichnungen des Said Giray Sultan (Freiburg, 1975); and Seiid Mukhammed Riza, Asseb o Sseiiar' ili Sem' Planet' (Kazan, 1832).

(14) See Alan Fisher, The Russian Annexation of the Crimea, 1772-1783 (Cambridge, 1970).

(15) Nadinskii, op. cit., p. 168.

(16) Arsenii Markevich, "Tavricheskaia guberniia vo vremia krymskoi voiny," Izvestiia tavricheskago uchennago arkhivnago kommissii 37, (1905), 6-8.

(17) Chantal Lemercier-Quelquejay, "The Crimean Tatars: A Retrospective Summary," Central Asian Review 16, no. 1 (1968): 19; and

Mark Pinson, "Russian Policy and the Emigration of the Crimean Tatars to the Ottoman Empire, 1854-1862," Guney-Dogu Avrupa Arastirmalari Dergisi 1, (1972): 37-38.

(18) Roderic Davison, "Nationalism as an Ottoman Problem and the Ottoman Response," in Haddad and Ochsenwald, op. cit., p. 29.

(19) The best treatments of Gaspirali are to be found in Cafer Seidahmet, Gaspirali Ismail Bey: Dilde, Fikirde, Iste Birlik (Istanbul, 1934); and Edward Lazzerini, "Ismail Bey Gasprinskii and Muslim Modernism in Russia," (Ph.D. dissertation, Univ. of Washington, 1973), and "Gadidism at the Turn of the Twentieth Century: A View from Within," Cahiers du monde russe et sovietique 16, (1975): 245-277.

(20) G.E. von Grunebaum, "Problems of Muslim Nationalism," in Richard Frye, ed., Islam and the West (The Hague, 1957).

(21) For discussions of these nationalist movements see: Alexandre Bennigsen and Chantal Lemercier-Quelquejay, La presse et le mouvement national chez les musulmans de russie avant 1920 (Paris, 1964); Edige Kirimal, Der nationale Kampf der Krimturken (Emsdetten, 1952); and Serge Zenkovsky, Pan-Turkism and Islam in Russia (Cambridge, Mass., 1960).

(22) Kirimal, op. cit., p. 25.

(23) Ibid., pp. 36-37.

(24) Pipes, op. cit., p. 77; Zenkovsky, op. cit., pp. 140-142; N.N. Agarwal, Soviet Nationalities Policy (Agra, 1969).

(25) Pipes, op. cit., pp. 189-190; Kirimal, op. cit., p. 287.

(26) "Cobanzade Bekir Sitki," Emel 46, (1968): 17.

(27) Bennigsen, La presse, op. cit., p. 284; Edige Kirimal, "The Crimean Turks," in Institute for the Study of the USSR, Genocide in the USSR, Studies in Group Destruction (New York, 1958), p. 22; Peter Potichnyj, "The Struggle of the Crimean Tatars," Canadian Slavonic Papers 17, no. 2-3 (1975): 305; and Gare Le Compte, Muslims of the USSR (Munich, n.d.), pp. 8-9.

(28) Mustecip Ulkusal, Dobruca ve Turkleri (Istanbul, 1955), and his article about the early Emel: " 'Emel' ve Kirim Davasi," Emel 76 (1973): 1-14; Mary Ellen Fischer, "Nation and Nationality in Romania," in George W. Simmonds, ed., Nationalism in the USSR and Eastern Europe (Detroit, 1977), p. 514. For a discussion of the Crimea under Nazi occupation, see Fisher, The Crimean Tatars, op. cit., chap. 13, and Mustecip Ulkusal, Ikinci Dunya Savisinda 1941-1942 Berlin Hatiralari ve Kirim'in Kurtulus Davasi (Istanbul, 1976).

(29) Lemercier-Quelquejay, "The Crimean Tatars," op. cit., p. 23.

(30) Patrik von zur Muhlen, Zwischen Hakenkreuz und Sowjetstern, Der

Nationalismus der sowjetischen Orientvolker in zweiten Weltkrieg (Dusseldorf, 1971), p. 60; Norbert Muller, Wehrmacht und Okkupation 1941-1944 (Berlin, 1971), passim. This compares with between 35,000 and 40,000 Volga Tatar "volunteers" and over 110,000 from the Caucasus. Even the Kalmyks provided about 5,000. See Joachim Hoffmann, Deutsche und Kalmyken 1942 bis 1945 (Freiburg, 1964).

(31) Muhlen, op. cit., pp. 123, 184; Necip Abdulhamitoglu, Turksuz Kirim: Yuzbinlerin Surgunu (Istanbul, 1974), pp. 51-52.

(32) S.P. Pisarev, "Iz istorii krymskikh tatar," Politicheskii dnevnik 1964-1970 (Amsterdam, 1972), p. 701. Ironically, in a recent account of Crimean history, the Soviet author provides a photo of the Tatar Ahmet Khan Sultan, without identifying him as a Tatar. Indeed, the general catagorization used in this and other Soviet volumes is: Tatar, when collaborators are meant (whatever their real nationality), and Soviet patriot (even if a Tatar) when partisans are discussed. See L.D. Solodovnik et al., Istoriia mist i sil ukrainskoi SSR: Krims'ka oblast' (Kiev, 1974), pp. 66-67.

(33) A Chronicle of Current Events, no. 28-31 (1975), pp. 147-148.

(34) Kirimal, "The Crimean Turks," op. cit., pp. 26-27.

(35) Feridun Cemal Erkin, Les Relations Turco-Sovietiques et la Question des Detroits (Ankara, 1968), pp. 286-287.

(36) Jonathan Knight, "American Statecraft and the 1946 Black Sea Straits Controversy," Political Science Quarterly 90, no. 3 (1975): 452; and Erkin, op. cit., pp. 300-301.

(37) S. Enders Wimbush and Ronald Wixman, "The Meskhetian Turks: A New Voice in Soviet Central Asia," Canadian Slavonic Papers 18, no. 2-3 (1975): 320-340.

(38) Edige Kirimal, "Kirim Turkleri," Emel 49, (1970): 16; Geograficheskaia atlas SSSR (Moscow, 1950), p. 104.

(39) Two recent books published in Turkey deal with the Crimean Tatars in the USSR: Abdulhamitoglu, op. cit., about the deportation; and Mustafa Nurettinoglu, Kirim Faciasi ve Mustafa Cemiloglu (Istanbul, 1976) about the Crimean dissidents. Some Turkish friends assured me they are just "anti-Soviet propaganda" in both intention and in factual content, although in fact both are reliable accounts.

(40) Bey Mustecip Ulkusal is the former director of the Crimean National Center in Istanbul; he was a Crimean Tatar representative in Berlin during the war.

(41) Ann Sheehy, The Crimean Tatars and Volga Germans: Soviet Treatment of Two National Minorities (London, 1971), p. 12; and Robert Conquest, The Nation Killers: The Soviet Deportation of Nationalities (New York, 1970), p. 185.

(42) Sheehy, op. cit., p. 30, citing a five volume survey of Soviet languages published by the Institute of Linguistics in 1966. On <u>Lenin Bayragi's</u> founding, see Abdulhamitoglu, op. cit., p. 133.

(43) Abdulhamitoglu, op. cit., pp. 135-136.

(44) Sheehy, op. cit., pp. 15-16; Abdulhamitoglu, op. cit., pp. 140-143.

(45) <u>Lenin Bayragi</u>, September 9, 1967.

(46) Kirimal, "The Crimean Turks," op. cit., p. 91.

(47) Kirimal, "The Crimean Turks," op. cit., pp. 92-93; Abdulhamitoglu, op. cit., pp. 227-237; Sheehy, op. cit., pp. 22-23.

(48) <u>Christian Science Monitor</u> (April 15, 16, 20, 1976), written by Elizabeth Pond. The <u>Monitor</u> was the only U.S. newspaper that saw the event as having implications beyond Sakharov himself.

(49) As reported in the <u>New York Times</u>, July 25, 1977, p. 4.

(50) <u>Arkhiv Samizdat</u>, No. 77. It is interesting to note that Lenin remains the Bolshevik "hero" for the Crimean Tatars because of what they believe to have been his nationality policies; they recall that it was he who created the Crimean ASSR.

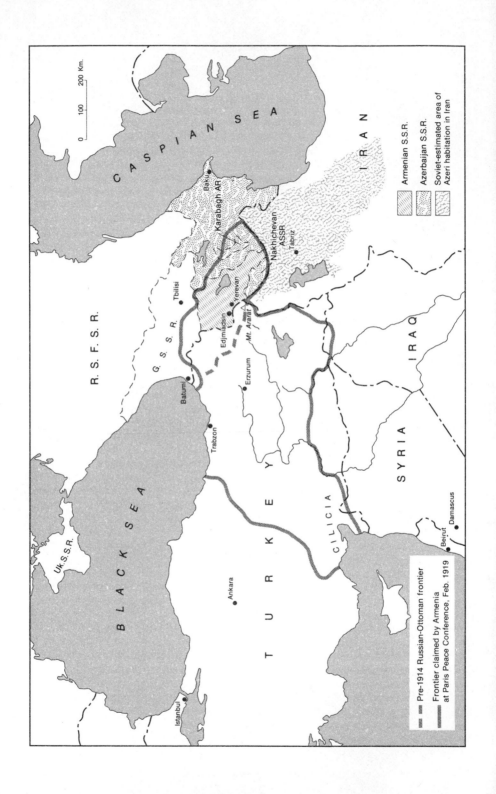

CASPIAN SEA

IRAN

Armenian S.S.R.

Azerbaijan S.S.R.

Soviet-estimated area of
Azeri habitation in Iran

Baku

Karabagh AR

Nakhichevan
ASSR

Tabriz

R.S.F.S.R.

G.S.S.R.

Tbilisi

Yerevan

Edjmiadsin

Mt. Ararat

IRAQ

Erzurum

Batumi

Trabzon

BLACK SEA

SYRIA

T U R K E Y

CILICIA

Damascus

Beirut

Uk.S.S.R.

Ankara

Istanbul

200 Km.

100

0

Pre-1914 Russian-Ottoman frontier

Frontier claimed by Armenia
at Paris Peace Conference, Feb. 1919

2 Armenia and Armenians: A Divided Homeland and a Dispersed Nation

Gerald J. Libaridian

Modern nation-states nail down frontiers in order to legitimize their authority and to facilitate the execution of their policies. Yet the more they do so, the more they force the stateless peoples of the world into struggles to secure territorial footholds of their own. Such has been the case for the Armenians.

This essay will study the role of the territorial imperative in the development of Armenian nationalism. It will contend that the unsuccessful struggle for the liberation of historic Armenia began a century ago for essentially social and economic reasons that are today largely redundant. Even a thawing of the Cold War will not produce the changes presently sought by Armenians in the status and borders of their homeland, divided between Russia and Turkey. However, the fateful process of state formation during the early decades of the twentieth century gave territorial aspirations a dominant function in current Armenian perceptions which tend to divorce Armenian nationalism from consequential realities.

FROM PEOPLE TO NATION

The present border dividing Armenia dates back essentially to a treaty of 1639 between the Ottoman and Safavid Empires, which for a century had been contending for the domination of Mesopotamia and Trans-caucasus. That treaty brought much-needed relief to the Armenian population from the ravages of war, but it also subjugated them to foreign rule, unwelcome because both empires imposed a harsh system of taxation and an oppressive social structure that discriminated against the non-Muslims. Before long, Armenians in both empires started searching for means to alter the status quo. For East Armenians the growing power of the "Christian King of the North," namely the Tsar, offered a viable alternative. (1)

Russian expansion to the Caucasus occurred when modern Western imperialism was becoming the most pervasive force in international relations, and when technologically backward states such as the Ottoman and Persian realms were being integrated into the world market system. What once were issues of local significance acquired implications for major power relations, and decisions taken in Europe affected the lives of peoples in remote areas of the globe.

Modern Armenian political consciousness evolved as a reaction against the suffocating effects of medieval Ottoman and Persian imperialism in the process of disintegration and as a response to new but problematic opportunities for liberation offered by increasing Western and Russian interests in the area. Thus when Russia, a more secular and dynamic state, annexed Persian Armenia in 1828, it transformed the region into a lively arena of inter-European conflict which in turn made the politics of Western powers accessible to Armenians. It introduced new patterns in East Armenian life, and a faster pace of change. (2)

Yet, despite a growing divergence between the Armenian communities on opposite sides of the border by the middle of the nineteenth century, circumstances made it possible to transform the cultural renaissance of the 1840s and 1850s into the common political program of the last quarter of the century. First, both sectors drew on a two thousand-year-old common history to assert a distinctive national identity. Textbooks and poetry published in Constantinople and Moscow revived ancient personalities whose grandeur and heroism contrasted sharply with the prevailing servile mentality and status of most of the Armenian population. Secondly, by the 1860s a liberal intelligentsia among East as well as West Armenians won its battle for secularization of institutions and values. Their use of modern Armenian instead of the classical language was most consequential. Although a different dialect was accepted by East and West Armenians as the norm, it now became possible for them all to understand each other's writing without much effort. (3)

Thirdly, the relative lack of discrimination and oppression in Russian Armenia allowed Armenians to focus their attention on the Ottoman sector, where social and economic conditions had deteriorated considerably and where a clear danger to the physical survival of the Armenian people was seen. This was particularly true during and after the famine that followed the war of 1877-1878. Although the Russian government later decided that another Bulgaria could not be tolerated on its flanks, at the time it did not object to the Russian Armenians' advocacy of West Armenia's liberation, particularly if that meant further tsarist annexations. (4)

The road to a political program for a new Armenian nation was not straight. Circumstances directly related to Armenia's betweenland position - lack of opportunities and protection normally provided by a national government; lack of communication for the joint exploitation of the land's resources; absence of security of property, particularly in the Ottoman sector - produced two Armenian bourgeoisie. In the Ottoman Empire evolved a commercial class, beneficiary of the growing trade with the West; in Russia the bourgeoisie became increasingly industrial and financial. Both flourished in the capitals and in major administrative and commercial centers of the two empires, outside the Armenian heartland where the majority of Armenians lived and which had become backwaters of the Ottoman and Russian territories. By mere economic necessity, and lacking a social basis to exert any political power, affluent Armenians linked their fortunes to the regimes in their respective states. Hence, the two bourgeoisie did not seek, and could not have achieved, a common program solely on the basis of their ethnic background, notwithstanding contacts between the liberal intelligentsias supported by each. Their interest in the improvement of the lot of the common man in Armenia proper did not exceed a mild reformism; under no circumstance did they antagonize the governments that had afforded them economic prerogatives.

Thus, the East Armenian bourgeoisie, which had earlier strongly supported Russian advances into Ottoman territories as a means of freeing the West Armenians, did not protest in 1885 against the closing of hundreds of parochial Armenian schools in East Armenia ordered by the Tsar's government. Furthermore, when Russo-Turkish relations improved in the 1890s, and Russia actively opposed the anti-Ottoman activities of Armenian revolutionaries, the latter were denied any assistance by this wealthy class. Similarly, the West Armenian bourgeoisie lost much of its enthusiasm for systematic reforms in the eastern provinces once Sultan Abdulhamid II revealed his reactionary attitudes toward social change. The Armenian National Assembly in Constantinople limited its activities in this last regard to formal representations to the Porte. Most well-to-do Ottoman Armenians were only too willing to accept the Sultan's occasional paternalistic favors to chosen individuals as a proof that his rule was benevolent and his society harmonious.

In the 1880s it became clear that the reforms advocated by the traditional leadership would not be carried out. By then, the Armenian bourgeoisie and the once powerful Armenian Church associated with them had retrenched from their earlier active participation in the process of political awakening. The Ottoman constitutional movement and Armenian liberalism had failed. Consequently, revolutionary political parties emerged, organized primarily by elements from the lower classes and by the radicalized segments of the intelligentsia. (5)

The ideologies espoused by the new parties were the first in Armenian history to be rooted in the needs of the masses. They all proposed to struggle against the political despotism, economic stagnation, and social inequality of the Ottoman system. The 1892 platform of the most influential of these organizations, the ARF or Dashnaktsutiune (Hay Heghapokhakan Dashnaktsutiune, or Armenian Revolutionary Federation, founded in 1890) called, for example, for the establishment of a popular-democratic government based on free elections. This government would guarantee security of life and right to work; equality of all nationalities and religions before the law; freedom of speech, press, and assembly; distribution of land to the landless; taxation according to ability to pay; abolition of the military exemption fee and replacement of it with equal conscription; establishment of compulsory education and promotion of national intellectual progress; and reinforcement of communal principles as a means to greater production and exports. (6)

The political parties viewed specific demands as means to achieve the larger goal of a dynamic progressive society. The slightly older Hunchakian Revolutionary Party (founded in 1887 and 1888) asserted, for example, that "Political freedom for the Armenian people will be considered as only one of the conditions necessary for the realization of a series of basic and radical reforms in its political, social and economic life. . . that will insure a solid basis and the true path for the moral, intellectual, and material progress of society." (7)   The ARF, too believed that "the liberation of the people from its untenable condition in order that they may enter the mainstream of human progress could only be achieved through revolution." (8)

One feature that distinguished the new organizations from prior advocates of reform was their use of weapons to force the Ottoman state and the signatory powers of the Treaty of Berlin to live up to their responsiblities. But on a larger scale this revolution entailed first and foremost a campaign against the slavish mentality of the Armenian masses. Propaganda was to be reinforced by living examples of valor and martyrdom in situations of armed resistance to oppression. In addition to their psychological impact, the revolutionary parties viewed the acquisition of arms by the Armenian populace as the best means of defense against widespread lawlessness overlooked by the Ottoman government, and occasional pogroms condoned by it. (9)

Mass participation in the liberation movement was low despite an apparently widespread sympathy with the revolutionary activities. Many Armenians continued to believe that any opposition to the existing order would constitute an act of insubordination against God's pre-ordained scheme for the world. Others, in areas sparsely populated by Armenians, were apprehensive of the reaction of their neighbors and overlords. Moreover, the Church, fearful of losing the few prerogatives it had managed to retain, remained aloof from the movement, although a few clergymen were involved in clandestine operations.   The revolutionary parties considered the Church a lethargic and regressive institution. The church, in turn, would not cooperate with parties that called for a struggle against patriarchal institutions and advocated a secular society. It is true that in 1903 the ARF had come to the support of the Church when the Russian government decreed the confiscation of Armenian Church properties; and following massive opposition and large scale demonstrations against the decree the revolutionaries had been able to force its rescision. But all of that was forgotten during the days of the first Russian Revolution when a General Assembly of Eastern Armenians was convened at the Holy See of Edjmiadsin. There most of the delegates elected were members or sympathizers of the ARF; the party felt strong enough to propose the distribution of Church-owned agricultural lands to the peasants who had tilled them for generations. The Assembly was disbanded in two days by the Russian police, most probably at the instigation of high-ranking churchmen. (10)

Relations between the political parties and the Armenian bourgeoisie had a similarly ambivalent character. Notwithstanding their programmatic antagonism toward all exploiting classes, the revolutionaries, especially the ARF leaders, expected the wealthy at least to provide financial assistance since the struggle undertaken had a national character. (11) Their press often criticized the Armenian upper classes for the latter's cowardice and lack of interest in the fate of the common Armenian. The mutual distrust dissipated in the Caucasus during the Armeno-Tatar conflict of 1905 to 1907. Unable to rely on government forces to protect their interests and properties, merchants, financiers, and industrialists turned to the ARF. The ARF accepted the challenge. Its leaders argued, firstly, that Tatar aggression had been instigated by the reactionary Russian government as part of a larger anti-Armenian policy; hence it was as necessary to defend Armenian-owned property as it was to protect helpless Armenian peasants. Secondly, they argued, given employment discrimination against Armenian workers in non-Armenian concerns, the assistance provided to the Armenian bourgeoisie was tantamount to the safekeeping of employment opportunities for Armenian laborers. (12) Paradoxically, this alliance coincided with the ARF's most intense socialist-oriented propaganda and activities in the Caucasus. It also allowed the flow of arms and financial assistance to the struggle in Western Armenia on an unprecedented scale. Yet the ideological inconsistency provided the best opportunity yet to the nascent Armenian Marxist group to criticize the now dominant ARF. (13)

From the beginning, though, the revolutionary parties concentrated their efforts among the artisans, peasants, and petty bourgeoisie of Western Armenia. And here there was no lack of support in provinces and districts where lawlessness and poverty had reached unbearable dimensions. Furthermore, in regions such as Sason, Mush, and Zeytun, where vestiges of the medieval Armenian feudal system remained subject to constant harassment by regular army troops and by Kurdish chieftains, the response to the appeal of the revolutionaries was immediate and overwhelming. Long before any of the parties were founded, local leaders in these mountainous districts had organized self-defense units and individual fighters had taken up arms to protect their families and villages.

The revolutionary parties provided a direction to those elements and attempted to coordinate their activities with newly organized units and within the framework of an overall strategy. Guerrilla fighters came mostly from traditionally devout families, and lacked the sophistication of urban intellectuals in the parties; but they overcame the impediments of religion by supplanting the God of submission and patience preached by most clergymen with the God of justice and retribution, or simply by deifying local saints who could "understand their situation" better.

Moreover, revolutionary parties were readily supported in cities and towns where educational institutions founded during the cultural renaissance had been instrumental in raising the level of political consciousness among the young. In fact, in the cities of Van and Erzerum, young Armenians had attempted as early as 1872 and 1882, respectively, to establish secret organizations devoted to the "salvation" of Armenia. Finally the movement acquired a large number of adherents among provincial Armenians who had moved to Constantinople or emigrated to the Russian Empire, Europe, and the United States to escape misery.

The new parties sought to achieve political emancipation in different frameworks. (14) The Hunchakians advocated the establishment of an "independent" homeland. Although the ARF used the vague expression "free Armenia," its goal was administrative autonomy for Turkish Armenia and the basic concern was for the essence of freedom, rather than for particular forms of political organization. (15)

But regardless of what framework was thought desirable or possible at any given moment, there is no doubt that these Armenian revolutionaries thought of Armenia as a distinct geographic entity. Here lay one of their weaknesses. "Turkish Armenia" referred to the six eastern vilayets of the Ottoman Empire: Erzerum, Van, Bitlis, Diarbakir, Harput (Mamuret-ul-Aziz), and Sivas. According to Turkish sources, during the years immediately preceding World War I 666,000 Armenians lived in those provinces (comprising 17 percent of their total population), and a grand total of 1,295,000 Armenians lived in the Empire. The Armenian Patriarchate of Constantinople claimed there were 1,018,000 Armenians in Ottoman Armenia (comprising 38.9 percent of the region's total population), and that there were 2,100,000 in the whole Empire. (16) Neither set of figures is scientifically reliable, although the latter count seems closer to reality. Thus Armenians constituted at best a plurality in their homeland. Occasional attempts by revolutionaries at cooperation with similarly oppressed non-Armenian elements, which would have neutralized the numerical impediment, were largely unsuccessful. (17) But statistical facts were irrelevant to most Armenians. They simply argued that the depopulation of the Armenian plateau of its native inhabitants was the result of a deliberate Ottoman policy of reducing the number of Armenians (during the widespread massacres of 1894 to 1896 alone a minimum of 200,000 were killed) and a consequence of the lack of security and economic development. Armenians identified themselves with Ottoman Armenia, by far the larger part of the divided homeland, not because of numbers but because of a "force of history." In common usage "Armenia" (i.e., Ottoman Armenia) and "Armenian People" had been interchangeable. Conquerors, however long they lasted, would remain alien to the land on which the Armenian people were born and had built a glorious past.

In popular perception it was the historic past that sustained a sense of identity with the land; and in the revolutionaries' thought this relationship was evolved into a dynamic "force" that would achieve liberation. The practical problems involved in creating an independent state (not to speak of those involved in reuniting Russian and Ottoman Armenia) did not prejudice the new liberators against a deep-seated belief that weaknesses and distinctions predicated by Armenia's betweenland position could be overcome and that the nation would participate in history again. This belief was expressed most pas-sionately at times of crisis, such as in 1903 when the Tsar's government decreed the confiscation of Armenian Church property. Anticipating the worst from the confrontation between tsarist police and politicized Armenian masses, Kristapor Mikayelian, one of the founders of the ARF and its most respected leader, exclaimed:

> Now that, following the massacres in Turkish Armenia, we might be on the eve of pogroms in the Caucasus, it is time to adopt as our general motto the indomitable will to struggle and fuse as one. It is necessary to erase those borders on maps drawn by this or that chief bandit. It is necessary to obliterate those geographic colors which are separating us, which usually are not eternal, and at times are short lived. No oppression, no persecution and no border can separate a people, if that people, inspired by a consciousness of common interests, manifests an unwavering determination to fight as well . . . . (18)

The National Program Thwarted

From his hatred of sultan and tsar alike, Mikayelian had reached the ideal of national union - even though ideals must be pursued within given political realities if they are to remain relevant. Thereupon, during the first decades of this century, the Armenian revolutionary groups experienced disasters. First, the Ottoman Empire proved to be more durable than anticipated. It was sustained rather than destroyed by rivalries among the Great Powers. Secondly, the attempted tsarist governmental confiscation of Armenian Church properties in 1903, and the bloody Armeno-Tatar clashes in 1905 to 1907 in the Caucasus compelled the Armenian parties to take responsibility for reorganizing the East Armenians as well as those of the West, shattering illusions regarding tsarist sympathies for Armenians and their struggle.

The most important development of the period was the emergence of the Young Turk movement in the Ottoman Empire. The beleaguered Armenian parties at first found cause here to renew their hopes for reforms in the Empire and its eastern provinces. They consulted, negotiated, and cooperated with prominent Young Turks, and in 1908 when the latter took control of the Ottoman government and proclaimed the Ottoman Constitution, jubilant Armenians welcomed the dawn of a new era, Armenian guerrillas put down their arms, and the parties made the necessary ideological adjustments. In its 1907 program the ARF had already endorsed democratic federalism as the system most suitable and desirable for the complex needs of Ottoman society. (19) In 1909 the Hunchakian Party renounced separatism and opted for a centralized government that would nonetheless allow cultural autonomy for its ethnic groups. Each party aligned with the Turkish organization closest to its ideas. (20)

The era of Armeno-Turkish cooperation did not last long, however. On the one hand, the Armenian leaders became impatient with the procrastination of the Young Turk CUP (Ittihad ve Terakki or Committee of Union and Progress) in implementing promised reforms. On the other hand, the more liberal democratic elements in the CUP lost control and a new ruling clique gravitated toward extreme nationalism. Turkish or Pan-Turanian doctrines began to supplant religion as the Ottoman state ideology, and the Armenians began to be regarded as a source of irritation for whom there was no room in a Turkish nation defined in territorial and linguistic-religious terms. Moreover, the CUP began to entertain ideas of expansion toward the East, and these also made the Armenians seem a nuisance.

At the end of October 1914, the militant faction of the CUP led the Ottoman Empire into war. In April 1915, systematic massacres and deportations of the West Armenian population began. The overwhelming evidence from a variety of written and oral sources indicates that these pogroms were coordinated, followed a predetermined course, and could not have been realized without the knowledge and resources of the Turkish government. By the end of the War at least one million Armenians had been killed or had perished otherwise. Some of the survivors had fled across the Russian frontier, others had settled in new lands to the south establishing a new Armenian diaspora. (21)

Meanwhile, on the opposite side of the border, the Russian revolutions, the disintegration of the Caucasus Front, and the Civil War temporarily ended Russian rule over the peoples of the Caucasus. In May 1918, following a brief and unsuccessful attempt at federation, the three major groups - the Georgians, the Azeris, and the Armenians - all declared their separate territories independent. (22) The government of the Republic of Armenia, dominated by the ARF, was confronted with the enormous task of caring not only for the native population but also for the tens of thousands of refugees from Western Armenia. Consequently, the inclusion of Armenian-populated areas of the Caucasus in the boundaries of the Republic became a crucial factor in its relations with Georgia and Azerbaijan; and its long-range foreign policy was aimed at extending its jurisdiction over Western Armenia. In 1919 the ARF declared a united and independent Armenia its political ideal, and the government of Armenia officially advanced its claim to Western

Armenia. To realize these goals, the Republic sent plenipotentiaries to the peace conference of the victorious Allies in Paris, there joining a separate delegation of West Armenians. As a result, the treaty of Sevres (August 1920) between the Allies, Armenia, and a defeated Turkey recognized the Armenian Republic and most of its claims. A new era seemed to have dawned for the Armenians. After the horrors of the massacres, the remotest prewar dreams were to be realized.

Then came the final debacle. As the Allied projects for dissolving the Ottoman Empire came to light, revolutionaries established a new regime in Ankara. Turkish leaders, for whom the concept of an integral territorial nation had become as crucial as it had for Armenians, began a campaign against the Republic of Armenia. Western intervention in the Russian civil war lent to an alliance between the Russian Bolsheviks and Turkish nationalists. (23) The resulting military and diplomatic cooperation shattered the Armenian dream. In December 1920, less than five months after the signing of the Sevres Treaty, independent Armenia collapsed. In 1921 the West Armenian lands (denuded by then of most of their Armenian population) returned to Turkish sovereignty; and in East Armenia the Republic began to be sovietized. (24)

The Soviet Armenians: Between Old and New

East Armenia formally entered the Soviet Union in 1922, a year after the dissolution of the independent republic. It was then considered part of the Transcaucasian Soviet Federation (along with Georgia and Azerbaijan), a grouping which survived until the promulgation of the Stalin constitution in 1936. Since then Armenia has figured as the smallest of the constituent republics of the USSR (30,000 km^2). It has a population of 2.5 million, 88.6 percent of which is Armenian. It contains only 62 percent of the 3.5 million Armenians in the USSR, however. Another million (26.3 percent of the total) live nearby in Caucasus, sometimes concentrated in areas such as the autonomous Karabagh province of the Azerbaijan Republic, where 80 percent of the population is Armenian. The final 350,000 Armenians are scattered in the Soviet territories outside the Caucasus. In all, the Armenians constitute 1.5 percent of the Soviet population. (25)

The path of sovietization has been difficult for the Armenians despite early promises by Revolutionary Russia. (26) Soon after assuming power, Lenin issued a decree that has been held up as a model of Russian understanding of Armenian political and territorial aspirations. The decree of December 31, 1917 stated that the new Russia "defended the right of the Armenian people to free self-determination in Russian occupied 'Turkish Armenia,' including even total independence"; it stated further that the realization of this overall objective required the return of all uprooted Armenians to Turkish Armenia and stringent measures to guarantee their security. (27) No practical steps were taken to secure any of the stated goals, however. In addition,

Soviet Russia actively sought the demise of the Republic of Armenia on the eastern part of the land; and, once that goal was achieved in December 1920, the Soviet government lost interest in "Turkish Armenia" and even disposed of territories formerly under the control of the Republic.

At that time Armenia was contesting several districts with its neighbors - with Azerbaijan, the mountainous Karabagh district to the southeast, with its dense Armenian population, (28) and the Nakhidjevan region enclosed between Armenia and the Persian frontier; with Georgia, the district of Akhalkalak, 82 percent Armenian-populated even today; and with Turkey, the provinces of Kars and Ardahan which had been part of the Russian Empire from 1878 until 1917, and the district of Igdir which contains the consecrated symbol of historic Armenia, Mount Ararat. In 1921 its control of the Caucasus in the balance and its relations with Turkey at a critical point, the Soviet government ceded all these districts to their non-Armenian claimants. Then, when the first Bolshevik commissars arrived in Armenia, they proved so thoroughly revolutionist in the poverty and disease stricken land and they so enthusiastically persecuted everyone associated with the leadership of the ARF-led Republic, that on February 21 they provoked a popular uprising, against which Lenin had to send Red Army reinforcements. (29)

Once the revolt had been put down, Lenin contacted Erevan Alexander Miasnikian, a more circumspect and disciplined leader, and advised Caucasian communists to take into consideration specific local conditions and to follow "a gentler, more cautious, and more conciliatory policy toward the petty bourgeoisie, the intelligentsia, and particularly the peasantry . . . . What is feasible and necessary in the Caucasus is a slower, more prudent, and more systematic course of transition to socialism than was warranted in the RSFSR . . . ." (30)

Once settled, Miasnikian's government started implementing programs of modernization in education, hygiene, transportation, and economic reconstruciton. The government also attracted a number of prominent Armenians from Europe and other parts of the USSR to enhance academic, scientific, and cultural development, and it inaugurated a period of material development in East Armenia that may not be disregarded.

Subsequently, of course, there was another turn for the worse. Stalin rose to power. He ignored Lenin's admonitions and started his notorious drive for collectivization of the Soviet Union's agriculture. In Armenia again there was massive resistance. Peasants slaughtered cattle and stock willfully, producing a famine that lasted until 1934. Soon thereafter, the great purges of 1936 to 1939 claimed the lives of hundreds of Armenian intellectuals and a new generation of communist Armenian leaders. (31) It is notable that the most prominent among the latter, the popular first secretary of the Communist Party in Armenia Aghassi Khanjian, was a West Armenian refugee from Van. Khanjian had been 14 years old when the massacres of the West Armenians began; he was a natural ally of the Soviet regime, and yet, like so many others, he was accused of harboring nationalist sentiments, and shot. Then came the war, which was perhaps not Stalin's fault, but in which Armenia was involved because it belonged to the Soviet Union. Over 450,000 Armenians were called upon to fight in the USSR armed forces between 1941 and 1945.

Paradoxically, World War II also opened new prospects for change. An important aspect of the war effort was the Soviet regime's toleration of Armenian national identity and pride. No doubt this was calculated to create enthusiasm for the now-threatened Soviet fatherland. But in 1945 the regime went further. Stalin abrogated the treaty of friendship and neutrality with Turkey which since 1925 had stifled Armenian national territorial aspirations, he called for a revision of the Montreux Convention which regulated the Straits, and he issued demands for the return of Kars and Ardahan. Whatever the Soviet motivations, these developments allowed both Armenians and the neighboring Soviet Georgians an extraordinary new opportunity to express national hopes.

In a memorandum forwarded to the leaders attending the Moscow Conference in December 1945, the Catholicos in Edjmiadsin, Gevork VI, expressed the hope that justice will finally be rendered to the Armenian people by the "liberation of Turkish Armenia and its annexation to Soviet Armenia." (32) The first secretary of the Communist Party of Armenia, Grigor Harutiunian, declared in the electoral campaign of 1946 that "the question of the return of the provinces conquered by Turkey is posed by the Armenian people itself in Soviet Armenia as in Europe, America, the Near and Middle East. These claims are being defended by the government of Soviet Armenia . . . and are of vital importance for the Armenian people as a whole." (33) The speech, interspersed by much applause, also assured that there were no strategic considerations in the Armenian demands. Leaders in Soviet Armenia recalled the enormous sacrifices offered by Armenians in the struggle against fascism - as opposed to Turkey's procrastination. They had thus earned the right to see their fatherland expanded. Armenians also argued that Soviet Armenia had the moral and historical duty to provide a homeland for diaspora Armenians and that the territory of the Armenian SSR could not accommodate the large numbers expected to heed the call for repatriation.

The role of "government of all Armenians" was Soviet Armenia's only for a brief moment in its history of course. The Soviet demands on Turkey were explicitly retracted in 1953, immediately after Stalin's death. But meanwhile there had been a considerable repatriation of diaspora Armenians. Between 1946 and 1948 approximately 100,000 Armenians, mainly from the Middle East, "returned" to Soviet Armenia; (34) and in the diaspora enormous enthusiasm was generated by the Soviet initiative.

So erratic has been the record of sovietization in Armenia that radically different evaluations can be justified. Sovietization has been acclaimed as the salvation of the Armenian people and decried as a new form of slavery. For some it represents the best available defense against Pan-Turanian imperialism and Turkish expansionism which in 1920 could have resulted in the decimation or uprooting of the East Armenian population as well; and by providing for a form of statehood with secure borders, it grants the Armenian people the opportunity to develop economically and culturally. For others this same sovietization forced Armenia back into an orbit where an independent pursuit of national interests has been impossible. It made Armenia's fate subject to the vicissitudes of Russian policy toward Turkey, the degree of autonomy it allowed was conditional upon decisions made in Moscow; and, because of it, Armenian culture fell into the danger of being submerged by the dominant Russian one.

To make sense of such contrasting evaluations, one must seek out realistic measuring tapes, and one is certainly the process of industrialization that has affected Armenia under Soviet rule. Beyond any question there has been great benefit in this respect. Whereas the average increase in production in the USSR has been 113-fold between 1913 and 1973 (117-fold in the RSFSR), Soviet Armenia's production has multiplied 222 times. The war effort accelerated the pace of production especially in the machine and chemical industries. Just between 1950 and 1975, the output in electricity has increased 9 times; chemical and petroleum products, 164 times; machine and metallurgy, 57 times. (35) The rate of urbanization has been equally dramatic. Compared to a 10 percent urban population in 1931, 59 percent of Armenians now live in cities (all-Union average, 56 percent). Soviet Armenia has one of the highest rates of workers in the sciences and professions and skilled workers with higher education in the USSR. (36) However much one weighs this sort of data against the arbitrary planning and the crash methods of the centralized Soviet economy, one must admit that East Armenia has been transformed by Soviet rule in a fashion entirely unparalleled in the other countries of the Middle East.

Population statistics provide an equally sensitive barometer of the benefits and disadvantages of sovietization in Armenia. The Armenian SSR has posted a 41 percent increase in its population between the most recent census years, 1959 and 1970. The average 3.72 percent annual increase constitutes the fourth highest in the USSR, exceeded only by Tajikistan (4.18 percent), Uzbekistan, Turkmenistan, and Kirgizia. Furthermore, during the same period, of all the major ethnic groups in the USSR, the rate of increase in the use of the mother tongue as a first language was highest among Armenians (1.5 percent).

Despite this optimal record, apprehensions concerning the threat of assimilation plague official and nonofficial Armenian circles. (37) To begin with the same empirical evidence, the high rate of increase in population is due primarily to immigration. As a result of inter-republic migrations, 146,000 new residents have come to Soviet Armenia from other areas of the USSR during the intercensus years. (38) In addition, between 1963 and 1970 approximately 16,000 resettled there from the Diaspora. (39) The large increase in the rate of those using Armenian in the ASSR as a first language must also be ascribed to this same phenomenon; and on the other hand one must note that of the 14 non-Russian "union republic" nationalities, Armenians rank lowest in their preference for marital endogamy within their own republic. (40) Also, the tremendous increase of the number of women at work in an expanding industrial economy has led to a reduction in size of the Armenian family.   Since 1928 the birthrate among Armenians had declined steadily from 56 to 22.1 per thousand in 1970. (41) A survey conducted by an enterprising journal in Yerevan has revealed causes for this phenomenon similar to those prevalent in the West: marriage at later ages; and rising concerns for the availability of child care centers, time to spend with children, housing, and the quality of life.   The researchers were thankful that very few mentioned conjugal problems as a factor, and that traditional Armenian marital harmony was still valued. (42)   But this did not reduce the disturbing implications of the phenomenon for the future of the Armenian people.

In this connection one may note also that the percentage of Armenians using their native tongue as a first language varies in different parts of the USSR.   In Armenia it is 97.7; in Georgia, 85; Azerbaijan, 84.   In the province of Rostov (RSFSR), however, it is 71.5, and in the city of Moscow, it is only 35.5.   The use of Armenian seems to decrease with the distance of one's residence from Armenia. The age of a community and its historical relationship to Armenia continue to play an important role as well. Thus, of Armenians in the Autonomous Republic of Nakhidjevan (now only 2.6 percent Armenian in population) and the autonomous province of Mountainous Karabagh (still 80 percent Armenian in population), 98.5 percent and 98 percent respectively consider Armenian their first language. Both are historically Armenian territories.   Ultimately, however, the demographic context and the availability of native language schools will constitute the most decisive factors in the use of Armenian among those outside the Armenian SSR. Most communities outside the Republic lack facilities for the preservation of the Armenian language and culture. Also, for reasons of cultural and political nationalism in some areas, Armenian educational and community institutions are subject to severe local pressures. (These pressures might explain the sizeable recent Armenian immigration from Georgia and Azerbaijan to Armenia.)

The USSR is the heir of the Russian Empire and Russian is the lingual franca of the Union, as it was during tsarist times. To a large extent this is natural, given demographic and geographic realities. More than at any given time, however, opportunities for recognition and promotion on the all-Union level presently require the use of Russian for most professions, while economic interdependence growing out of regional imbalances in natural and manpower resources mandate the universalization of values consecrated and institutionalized in Moscow. Of those emigrating from the Armenian SSR to other parts of the Union, 37.2 percent go to the RSFSR. (43) It is not surprising that there are as many Armenians with higher education living outside as there are

inside the Armenian Republic, and that the absolute majority of
Armenians not knowing or using their mother tongue live in the major
urban industrial centers of the USSR. Assimilation is a real danger to
the Armenian people in the USSR, an unavoidable concomitant of
industrialization.

Since Stalin, the Soviet regime has become more permissive in
Armenia. An early measure in this respect came in 1956 when the
government allowed the election of a Catholicos of All Armenians to
the vacant seat at Edjmiadsin in the Armenian SSR. Since then the new
supreme spiritual leader, Vazken II, has enjoyed a wider margin of
movement and easier access to his people than at any time since 1921.
In 1965, on the 50th anniversary of the genocide of 1915, there were
subdued official commemorations in Yerevan and a monument was
erected to it near the city. Since then the republican leaders have
institutionalized government participation in this most symbolic and
emotional of Armenian ceremonies on each April 24. In recent years,
the new first secretary of the Communist Party of Armenia, Garen
Temirjian, has led the official delegations and masses of marchers to
the monument.

Since 1956 references to places, events, and people tied to the
history of Western Armenia have abounded in Soviet literature and the
arts. Historians have dwelled at length on the human and political
consequences of the Genocide. Earlier the term "liberation" had been
exclusively applied to the activities of Armenian Bolsheviks, the effects
of the November Revolution on Armenia, and the process of
sovietization, while the ARF and the Hunchakians were branded as
reactionary. Now historians have rehabilitated the Liberation Movement in Ottoman Armenia by recognizing its mass appeal, and studying
it in the proper historical context, even though the parties leading that
movement remain subject to severe criticism. A new study published in
1976 has even included a detailed description of the activities of
guerrilla leaders whose names were long known and cherished by the
public through revolutionary ballads. (44) A well-known novelist,
Khachig Dashtents, has based his most recent work on a fictionalized
version of the same theme. (45) The Soviet Armenian language has been
gradually cleared of common words transferred from the Russian.
Academicians have been developing a vocabulary of scientific and
technical terms derived from the wealth of the Armenian language.
Today, though it is in Turkey, Mount Ararat is found on the flag of the
Armenian SSR, and the national soccer team carries its name. (46)

These largely symbolic concessions have not reflected Soviet policy
toward Armenian territorial aspirations. As noted above, the post-
Stalin era opened with Molotov's deliberate retraction in 1953 of the
Stalinist demands on Turkey of 1945. In 1965 Prime Minister A. Kosygin
went further; he suggested a new nonaggression pact to achieve "good
relations" with Turkey. He also stated that the USSR had no territorial
designs against that country. (47) Although Turkey turned down the
offer, Soviet-Turkish relations have since improved. The two governments have cooperated on industrial projects in Turkey, which has

become the largest recipient of Soviet economic aid to any Third World country. Further, an economic cooperation pact signed between the two countries in April 1978 was followed by the visit of an official delegation to Turkey led by Marshal N.V. Orgakov, chief of staff of Soviet Armed Forces. The delegation intended to discuss a new nonaggression treaty. (48)

Unusual manifestations of Armenian nationalism are in part reactions against these overtures to the traditional antagonist. In 1965 the official commemoration of the 50th anniversary of the Genocide was interrupted by violent outbursts of young demonstrators in Yerevan. They demanded action "to recover their lands" rather than ceremonies to honor the victims. (49) It is probable that the major reason for the removal that year of Y.N. Zarobian as first secretary of the Communist Party of Armenia was his inability to prevent and to deal effectively with these demonstrations. (50)

Subsequently, illegal activities were carried on secretly. In 1969, 1970, and 1973 to 1974 Soviet Armenian courts tried, convicted, and imprisoned a number of activists - grouped under a "National United Party" - for having advocated the idea of a united and independent Armenia and for having formed cells to achieve their goal. (51)

Historically related to the territorial claims against the Republic of Turkey is the issue of Mountainous Karabagh within the USSR. This district remains under the jurisdiction of the Azerbaijani SSR despite a decision in 1920 by the Soviet Azeris to return it to Soviet Armenia. (52) Armenians have consistently charged that the Azerbaijani authorities have pursued a policy of cultural oppression, economic discrimination, and ethnic disadvantages against the overwhelmingly Armenian population of the district. (53) This policy reached such proportions in 1969 that the Soviet Armenian republican leaders reportedly went to Moscow to register their complaint and request the incorporation of the district in the Armenian SSR. The request was denied. (54)

In 1975 many Armenians were ousted from the Party in Karabagh or imprisoned on charges of nationalist agitation contrary to "the principles of Leninist friendship of peoples and proletarian internationalism." (55) Having silenced all local opposition to the status quo, authorities in Karabagh and Azerbaijan declared the issue resolved to the satisfaction of all concerned. (56) These declarations, printed in an official publication and including derogatory statements toward the Armenian SSR, prompted one of Soviet Armenia's most respected novelists, S. Khanzatian, to dispatch a letter of protest and indignation to L.I. Brezhnev. Khanzatian, a member of the Communist Party since 1943, reminded Brezhnev that "nothing hinders the development and strengthening of the solidarity between proletarian classes more than injustice against a people." He reiterated the demand for the return of Karabagh in the name of the same principles that had been called upon to justify the current situation. A commentary that accompanied a copy of the letter to the diasporan press asserted that the systematic policy of forcing Armenians to leave the region through social, economic, and other forms of oppression is tantamount to genocide according to one definition in the U.N. Convention on Genocide to which the USSR is a signatory. The unknown author further revealed that according to an unofficial survey, Armenians in Karabagh wanted nothing more than to see their land under the jurisdiction of the Armenian SSR. (57)

To achieve a modus vivendi between official policy and Armenians' expectations, the Soviet state has relied largely on bureaucratic methods of oppression rather than the massive violence of the past. At times it has even taken conciliatory steps to avoid large-scale, active opposition to the government. Most recently, for example, the draft submitted for final approval of the new Constitution of the Armenian SSR had deleted the provision in the previous law which had recognized Armenian as the official language of the republic. Following demonstrations against a similar proposal in Tbilisi for the Georgian SSR, the government reinstated the language provision in the new version. (58)

The change from Stalinist practices could be ascribed to the Soviet government's expectation that the emerging technological society will induce historical amnesia; or, conceivably, it might stem from calculations that Armenian irredentism against Turkey can be used to legitimize future annexations from that country. The relative leniency might also reflect the price Soviet leaders are willing to pay for the success of their overall policies.

But still the Soviet government has difficulty in determining when nationalism is harmless in extent or form. Hence it has not hesitated to press the full power of the state against such manifestations it considers threatening. There has been a barrage of criticism aimed at Armenian chauvinism, nationalistic tendencies, and disregard for Marxist-Lenist principles in the interpretation of Armenian history. The guardians of the faith have not spared writers and artists who have deviated from the norms of "socialist realism." (59) In addition to those already mentioned, the list of political prisoners included the film director Sergei Paradjanov or Sargis Paradjanian, whose talent has been recognized within and without the Soviet Union. (60) Others have been subjected to varying forms of censorship and silence. The interesting fact regarding this last wave of repression against intellectuals is that the works of these victims have displayed more humanism than nationalism.

It is true, nonetheless, that national aspirations have not retreated since the Revolution; and territorial aspirations formulated at the beginning of the century survive among East Armenians, many of whom trace their roots to historic Armenia outside the boundaries of the present Republic. Moreover, a half-century of oppression and abnegation within the new empire has strengthened that nationalist sentiment. As a consequence, there seems to be a growing cooperation between activists in Armenia and other parts of the Union, especially Russia and the Ukraine; and, at least for some, the national issue has been reintegrated within the larger sphere of problems faced by Soviet society. An Armenian samizdat has proliferated in Yerevan and a committee has been formed there to monitor the implementation of the Helsinki accords. (61) In addition, a number of Armenians have been involved in dissident activities in the Soviet Diaspora. (62) Even the National United Party, once an adherent of an exclusive nationalism, has eliminated from its program the strict ideological opposition to communism to pursue its goal of independence within the context of other forms of opposition to the present Soviet state. (63)

Soviet Armenian nationalism embodies, then, an unwillingness to accept the injustices of the past as well as resentment of present oppression. In its extreme form it probably detracts from the ability of its adherents to deal effectively with the challenges of a changing, modernizing society. It remains, nonetheless, less abstract and far less idealized than that among the Diaspora Armenians.

Armenians in Turkey: A Silent Minority

An estimated 60,000 Armenians now live in the Republic of Turkey; a majority of these are concentrated in Istanbul. This estimate does not include perhaps an equal number of partially assimilated Armenians in distant provinces who, at best, preserve a blurred sense of their origins through rituals and symbols, since the former Armenian provinces were thoroughly islamicized and turkified during and after the massacres. In central and western Anatolia there are a few recognizable communities of Armenians. Some of these have churches at their disposal; but only three - Iskenderun, Kayseri, and Diyarbakir - have parish priests (all of the Apostolic or Gregorian faith); and the general demographic tendency in these provincial communities has been to move to Istanbul. For most Turkish Armenians, reaching that ancient city remains the only hope against total loss of identity. (64)

The leader of the Turkish Armenians is the Patriarch in Istanbul, even though the Armenians of that city belong to more than one religious denomination. Once all-powerful over the whole Armenian population of the Ottoman empire, the Patriarch is now little more than a local prelate. His duties still include the representation of the interests and needs of the Anatolian flock and, with leaders of smaller Catholic and Protestant communities, the maintenance of various Armenian religious, educational, and charitable institutions. But for some time now his main practical responsibility has been to bring Armenian children from the provinces to Istanbul and to provide them with adequate health care and an education.

Outwardly, harmony reigns between the Armenians of Turkey and the Turks. Ataturk's revolution separated state and religion, and the constitution of the republic explicitly prohibits religious and ethnic discrimination. The mushrooming Turkish middle class is in fact highly secular and assumes a tolerant attitude towards religious minorities.

Archbishop Shnork Kalustian, the Istanbul Patriarch, himself asserts that Armenians enjoy "total freedom of worship" in Turkey. (65) Those who live in Istanbul are involved primarily in trade, industrial production, the liberal professions, and crafts - social areas where secular views are likely to prevail. Although reduced in scope and prestige, the Armenian press and cultural societies continue to provide a forum for cultural activities. Nonetheless, there is strong evidence of both official political and social discrimination against the country's Armenians, and of harassment of their institutions.

This particularly affects the opportunity of Armenians to send their children to community-owned schools. The Turkish Ministry of Education requires that the identity card of an Armenian child bear official recognition of his Armenian origin before he or she is allowed to attend an Armenian school. This is not only contrary to the Turkish constitution, but the office granting these identity cards has in recent years ruled against the use of such notations. As a result, the proper certification is difficult to obtain, and an increasingly large number of Armenian children are forced to attend public schools where they will be denied any instruction in Armenian language, culture, or religion. Comparable vicious circles regarding the issuance of permits necessary for the restoration or relocation of Armenian community buildings exist. (66) Furthermore, there have been arbitrary administrative actions affecting Armenian culture. For example, in the summer of 1977, the newly refurbished Apostolic Church of Kirikhan (Hatay Province) was closed without explanation by order of the Interior Minister who had earlier expropriated property belonging to that community. (67) Often travelers in eastern Turkey have found ancient and medieval monuments of Armenian architecture in a process of decay, at the mercy of the natural elements and marauders, and occasionally subject to willful destruction. (68)

In his most recent annual report the Patriarch disclosed that through unlawful taxation, bureaucratic procrastination, and administrative roadblocks the government was in fact discriminating against Armenian educational and charitable institutions, making it increasingly difficult for Armenians to use and ultimately to sustain them. He suggested that authorities were denying Armenian citizens essential human rights - rights which were routinely granted to noncitizen residents of Turkey - otherwise guaranteed by the Turkish constitution as well as by Articles 37 through 44 of the Treaty of Lausanne. The report concluded:

> For the last 10 to 12 years, we have duly reported these restrictions, discriminations and restraints to the respective departments of our State. But we confirm painfully that neither a positive nor a negative reply has been received. This means, that the demands are so well-founded, legal and rational, that nothing can be said against them. Nevertheless, we have never ceased hoping, because in the final resort justice and law shall prevail. (69)

A former Belgian representative on the United Nations Commission on Human Rights has been much less restrained in accusing the Turkish government of systematic discrimination against Armenians. (70)

All this must be supplemented by mention of the social pressures that discourage the use of the Armenian language in public places in Turkey and persuade Armenians who wish recognition and advancement in business and professional circles to adjust their family name endings to Turkish patterns.

Faced with these conditions the Armenians of Turkey abstain consciously and massively from political life, constraining the Patriarch to reaffirm from time to time the total allegiance of his flock to the Turkish fatherland and state. Armenians in Turkey manifest none of the concerns evident elsewhere for the political, territorial, or moral issues emanating from the massacres and deportation of their people during World War I. The fiftieth and sixtieth anniversaries of the Genocide, ostentatiously commemorated in the ASSR and the Diaspora, were ignored by Armenians in Turkey. They are subservient to any and all governments lest any criticism be interpreted as unfaithfulness.

The return to power in June 1977 of Bulent Ecevit's Cumhuriyet Halk Partisi or Republican People's Party raised hopes that the most obvious of the transgressions against the rights of Armenian citizens of Turkey would be eliminated. During the electoral campaign Ecevit had charged the neofascist National Action Party with terror against non-Turkish minorities such as Kurds and Armenians. When he took office as prime minister, Ecevit rescinded the order of the previous government to restrict the entry into Turkey of foreigners of Armenian extraction regardless of their citizenship. (71) More importantly, he and other ministers of his cabinet met with Patriarch Kalustian to discuss the legal and bureaucratic difficulties encountered by the Armenian community. Ecevit promised to end bureaucratic abuses and to study cases of legalized discrimination. The meetings took place at the end of March 1978, on the eve of annual commemoration of the Genocide in the Diaspora. This could hardly have been accidental. Ecevit and his colleagues suggested to the Patriarch that their promises hinged on the Patriarch's willingness to convince Armenians in other parts of the world to end anti-Turkish demonstrations, although the Patriarch has no administrative or legal authority outside Turkey. (72) Following the meetings the Patriarch issued an appeal to the Diasporan press inviting Armenians to refrain from political activities related to "past events" and to remember the dead only as a religious and spiritual duty. (73)

Since then the only positive development has been the return of the Kirikhan Church to the local community. On the other hand, a ruling by the ministry of education in December 1977 decreed that private schools, such as those under the jurisdiction of the Armenian Patriarchate, could close only on days officially designated by the government and would have to remain open during the traditional Christmas and Easter holidays. (74) In January 1978, moreover, bombs exploded in the Armenian Cathedral of Istanbul, in the chancellory of the Patriarchate, and in one of two Armenian orphanages in the capital. A secret Turkish organization claimed responsibility for the acts that were reportedly undertaken in revenge for similar attacks by Armenian groups against Turkish government offices in Europe. (75)

Armenians in Turkey have been reduced to a cultural group that can no longer acknowledge its own roots. Many find emigration to Europe or North America a better alternative.

THE DIASPORA: DILEMMAS AND DANGERS
OF LANDLESSNESS

Land has been an essential component of the Armenian ethos. The defense of the motherland provided chroniclers the raw material from which heroes and villains were created. Love of land permeated ancient Armenian mythology as well as the ideologies of the modern era. Yet paradoxically a history of just that land can in no way adequately cover the history of the Armenians. Particularly since the eleventh century, Armenian communities were to be found in places as far off as India and England, Egypt, and Eastern Europe. Frequent domestic and foreign pressures have forced waves of Armenians to seek security and prosperity beyond the boundaries of a homeland that lacked peace and an indigenous government. Starting in the eighteenth century, these communities played a significant role in the transmission of secular and western ideas of the Enlightenment to the Armenian people. Expatriates in Madras, Venice, Constantinople, Moscow, and Tiflis drew the contours of the nineteenth century cultural renaissance. They also played an important political role. Until the nineteenth century, merchants and clergymen in London, Moscow, and Paris contributed to the plans to reestablish an Armenian state and attempted to insure the help of powerful western monarchs for the realization of their endeavors. By the end of the century the ranks of older communities had been swelled and new ones had been developed by the emigration of thousands of West Armenians of humbler origins. When the revolutionary acitivites erupted in Ottoman Armenia, communities in Egypt, Europe, the United States, and Russia provided essential organizational, logistical, and financial support. During World War I, many from Europe and the United States joined the Allied forces hoping to minimize the extent and effects of the massacres and deportations. (76)

At the present time, as in the past, the Diaspora plays an inordinately important role in the life of the world's Armenians, more than compensating for the withering historical memory of the Armenian community in Turkey. There are presently about 250,000 Armenians in Europe, 450,000 in North America (primarily in the United States), some 100,000 in South America, and about 100,000 in Africa and the Far East. (77) But Diaspora Armenians have long regarded communities in the Near and Middle East as the more important because of their compactness, proximity to the historic lands, cultural facilities, and ability to resist assimilation. Close to 200,000 live in an ancient community in Iran. Another 200,000 are in Lebanon, 100,000 in Syria, and a final 100,000 are scattered in Egypt, Iraq, Kuwait, Jordan, Israel, Cyprus, and Greece. Diaspora Armenians are, to a considerable extent, people or the offspring of people who survived the genocide by fleeing to other former parts of the Ottoman Empire. They carry on the impassioned political heritage they brought with them.

Between the two world wars several factors tended to inhibit the emergence of Armenian political activism in the Middle Eastern Diaspora. The most obvious is that as refugees their immediate concern was economic survival. In addition, they were preoccupied with the enormous task of creating, with meager resources, a community infrastructure of schools, churches, and community organizations in an alien environment.

An equally important factor was a matter of administration. The newly mandated Arab states of the 1920s preserved for a while in the sphere of civil law and religious affairs the institutions they inherited from the Ottoman Empire. As a result the Church became the primary forum of social organization as was the case in the Ottoman millet system. In 1921 the Catholicossate of Cilicia was evacuated from Turkey and established in Lebanon. Originally established when the medieval Armenian kingdom had its center in Cilicia, this see had since 1375 lost much of its glamour. But now, with the Soviets in control of the Catholicossate of Edjmiadsin and the Constantinople Patriarch's power limited to Turkey itself, the Catholicos of Cilicia settled in Antelias, a suburb of Beirut, and assumed jurisdiction over Apostolic Armenians in Lebanon, Syria, and Cyprus. By definition and by tradition, the Church has functioned as an agent of "conservation" under circumstances created by nonindigenous forces. Within the conditions of the Diaspora that tradition acquired a new impetus and significance.

Finally, the revolutionary ARF and Hunchakian parties, which had struggled to raise the political consciousness of the Armenian people, had suffered greatly during the disasters of West and East Armenia. For them, the technical task of reorganization in new countries proved much easier than digesting the events and experiences of the past decade. Even then they spent their energy dealing with the immediate problems that the communities faced. In this they were assisted by a reinvigorated third party, the ADL (Ramkavar-Azatakan or Armenian Democratic Liberal Organization). (36) The ADL was founded in the Ottoman Empire in 1908 and reorganized in 1921. Based on upper and middle class elements, it was committed to the free enterprise system and its mission was to offer Armenians an alternative to the revolutionary, socialistic parties. (78) For the ADL the Church was an integral and essential part of Armenian culture. Diaspora conditons favored such an outlook and the ADL soon replaced the Hunchakian Party as the prime adversary of the ARF, which remained the strongest party. Nonetheless, within the Diaspora the ADL strengthened the inclination toward acceptance of reduced political goals and lowered expectations.

Generally speaking, these interwar arrangements in the Middle Eastern Diaspora provided quasi legal recognition of Armenianness and a form of extraterritorial self-management; at the same time they fostered conservatism and created obstacles to cultural and political integration of the refugees into their new environments. Attachment of the refugees to their old homes and a continuing, pietistic hope of return enhanced the feeling of Armenian separateness and temporariness in the Arab states. But since World War II there have been marked changes in this process of adjustment.

First, the rise of Arab nationalism has provided a sharper focus to the cultural and political identity of peoples in those states. Second, the emergence of statism in the developing societies of the Near East, especially in Syria and Egypt, has changed the relationship between citizen and state. The success of the new state policies has required control and planning in the economy and to some extent in social relations. The impact of these changes on Armenians has been manifold. For some it has meant the loss of prominence in industry, trade, and various professions, and often an end to prosperity. All have been confronted with the need to formulate a more integrative concept of national identity to replace the self-containment of the past; and a problem of assimilation has emerged. The new generations born in the new milieu are far better integrated than their parents could be. Enjoying conditions far less trying, and an environment far more conducive to a normal life than was the fate of the refugees, the Diaspora youth tend to know the local languages and feel more secure in their legal and social standing.

The same factors that provide a degree of permanency have caused a rise in the political consciousness of the youth and in their interests in Armenian affairs. If the passing generation defined its Armenianness within the context of a helpless victim, and remembered longingly but passively the ancestral lands, the new generation tends to come forth as the vindicator and consummates a rediscovered idealism in its role of claimant. The dual phenomena of integration and "activism" have thrust a new life as well as new burdens on the two institutions of leadership - the political parties and the Church.

The process of adjustment by the political parties to new, unfavorable realities started before World War II. The quasi Marxist Hunchakians - the oldest but weakest of the groups - laid aside their erstwhile dreams of territorial grandeur and independence to adopt a sovietized Eastern Armenia as the realization of their program. The liberal ADL also gradually accepted the status quo in Soviet Armenia and professed satisfaction with the technological and cultural progress taking place there, though this policy was adopted largely on pragmatic considerations and could not have emanated from their ideology. (79) The two made a coalition with the small number of Soviet-oriented Armenian communists in the Diaspora to support the USSR's claims against Turkey at the end of World War II. Further, they believed that the Soviet Union would respond more readily to avowed sympathizers than professed enemies and thus, subsequent to the War, they refrained from any activities that could have jeopardized Soviet goodwill toward Armenians and their claims.

Meanwhile the once socialist ARF, still soured by its experiences with the Soviet state in 1917 to 1921, remained more sensitive to antinationalist elements in Soviet practice and ideology. Hence it continued to insist on a free and united Armenia independent of Soviet influence and Turkish domination. (80) During the hopeful years of 1945 to 1947, nonetheless, the ARF declared that in relation to territorial demands the political question of Armenia's regime was of secondary importance. Along with all other factions, the anti-Soviet organization announced its readiness "to assist the USSR if that country took upon itself the defense of the Armenian Case." (81) But then, during the cold war, the ARF became aggressively anti-Soviet.

The year 1956 turned these differences between the political parties into a deep dissension. In that year the Soviet authorities allowed the election of a new Catholicos to the vacant seat of the see of Edjmiadsin. He proceeded to reassert his authority over other administrative centers of the Apostolic Church as spiritual leader of all Armenians. The same year the see of Cilicia began increasing the number of Diaspora communities under its jurisdiction. Conflict between the two centers developed inevitably. Even though the programs of the political parties demanded dynamic secularization of Armenian values, they could not avoid involvement in the conflict of these traditionalist ethnic and religious centers. The Cilician see came under ARF control. The cause of Edjmiadsin was taken up by the Hunchakian-ADL bloc. Passions came to the surface that are best described as symptomatic of parties in exile. During the 1958 civil war in Lebanon the Armenian community there split asunder. The parties raised cold war banners, supported opposite sides, and conducted their own miniwar against each other.

Since 1960, relations between the opposing factions have improved. The political parties realized that neither the USSR nor the West is as attractive and trustworthy as earlier rhetoric had made them appear. It became clear that the polarization had placed the national leadership, both religious and political, in direct contradiciton with their professed concerns for the general welfare of the Armenian people. Irrelevance in the eyes of a new, politically conscious generation was an important factor in forcing the factions to reevaluate their mutual hostility in terms of Armenian needs. The ARF recognized that, considering the total alienation of West Armenian territories and the threat of assimilation in the Diaspora, Soviet Armenia is a most positive reality. The ADL-Hunchakian bloc recognized, on the other hand, that Soviet Armenia far from embodied the political and territorial aspirations of the Armenian nation. In 1965 joint commemorations of the fiftieth anniversary of the genocide inaugurated an era of partisan rapprochement. A manifestation of the rising spirit of cooperation was the attitude of Armenian organizations toward the recent civil war in Lebanon. During 1975 and 1976 the three Armenian groups agreed on a policy of "positive neutrality," combined their efforts to minimize the inescapable loss of life and property within the Armenian community, and even tried to mediate between the fighting elements.

Since the two segments began to perceive a commonality of interests, links between the Diaspora and Soviet Armenia have multiplied. Soviet Armenian artists, performers, and writers tour the communities abroad. Diaspora Armenians visit Soviet Armenia by the thousands yearly. Groups of teachers, students, and often individual performers are invited to spend time in that country. Through these contacts have emerged not only an appreciation by each of the problems and concerns of the other, but also a realization that some of these problems are common. Furthermore, each has contributed to their solution in its own way. Soviet Armenia's cultural viability has infused fresh blood into a stagnating and disintegrating Diaspora, although to satisfy the masses there and to support the claim that Soviet Armenia is a home for all Armenians, authorities in Moscow and Yerevan have had to make serious concessions to Armenian cultural nationalism.

The improvement in the political climate has also produced a rapprochement between the two Catholicossates. As a gesture of goodwill the Catholicos of All Armenians in Edjmiadsin sent an official delegation to represent him at the election and anointment in May 1977 of a coadjutor Catholicos to the see of Cilicia. Karekin II, now the co-ruler with the ailing Khoren I, had been instrumental as a bishop in promoting a tacit agreement between the two sees on the most crucial issue dividing the Armenian national Church - the elimination from the statute governing the see of Cilicia of those provisions which had allowed extension of its jurisdiction over communities in the Diaspora formerly under Edjmiadsin.

Yet the most characteristic development in Diaspora politics has been the adoption of a united front by the Hunchakian Party, the ARF, and ADL regarding the territorial claims against Turkey. In a memorandum submitted to the United Nations in 1975, and in other related documents, the three demanded "the return of Turkish-held Armenian territories to their rightful owner - the Armenian people." (82) The deliberate vagueness of the formula accommodates differences of opinion beyond the crucial idea itself, provides for any eventuality in future international developments, and yet stresses the fundamental rights of the Armenian people as a nation. The document fails, however, to specify the exact boundaries of historic Armenia, although reference to the Sevres Treaty suggests that these encompass the six eastern provinces of the former Ottoman Empire. (83)

Primarily by peaceful means, Diaspora Armenians have multiplied their efforts on behalf of these claims. They have propagated documentation of the genocide and its effects. They have organized public demonstrations, erected memorial momuments, made anti-

Turkish propaganda through various publications, and approached the diplomatic missions of various countries and international agencies regarding moral, financial, and above all territorial reparation by the Republic of Turkey. (84) Yet it is altogether clear that if acquisition of a national territory is the national goal, none of these activities provides more than momentary respite. The centuries-old partition of Armenia will not be ended by public opinion drives. No Turkish government will willingly relinquish any part of its territory. No Western power has any interest in placing the Armenian case on the agenda of nations as "unfinished business." The more the rivalry between the superpowers abates, the less the chance that the USSR will challenge the legitimacy of Turkey's frontiers. The frustration growing out of the impasse is largely responsible for the nonpeaceful means adopted by some Armenian groups. During the last few years such groups have claimed responsiblity for the assassinations of three Turkish ambassadors and attempts on three others, for the bombings of Turkish government offices in Europe, and two explosions in Istanbul itself. (85)

The territorial nationalism in the Armenian Diaspora is at least partially a reaction against the increasing threat of assimilation. A recent study has shown that even in Lebanon, the state with the highest concentration of Armenians in the Middle East, there has been a detectable erosion in the ethnic orientation of Armenians during the past two decades; (86) and the ethnic orientation has been proven to be highest among those involved in the activities of the political parties. (87) In the unsettled world of the diaspora, nationalism - the vision (however vague) of a territorially integral Armenia - satisfies two basic needs. First, it establishes an immediate link with the past through the most material of the elements of the past - land. Secondly, it offers a mental framework within which Armenians can continue to perceive themselves as Armenians in foreign lands.

While it is true that not all Armenians in the Diaspora share the vision of a united Armenia as a political program, territorial aspirations are sustained, nonetheless, by the deep sense of injustice that Armenians generally feel. Turkey continues to deny the events of the past that caused the formation of a Diaspora; its government has refused to compensate in any way the losses suffered during World War I; and, occasionally, its diplomatic representatives have used their influence with foreign governments to hinder activities by Armenians that might result in an unfavorable world public opinion toward their country. Consistently adhered to by successive Turkish governments, this policy has been more effective in perpetuating Diaspora nationalism among Armenians than any program the political parties could devise.

But this nationalism is also increasingly divorced from the social realities in which Diaspora Armenians presently live. Under these circumstances, those who still carry the burden of the past tend to transform political concepts into abstract, moralistic values; and while the latter can provide a positive frame of identification for a threatened ethnic group, it can hardly bring any changes in the political futures of a dispersed nation and their divided homeland.

NOTES

(1) For a comprehensive and detailed view of developments in Armenia between the fourteenth and eighteenth centuries, see Ds. P. Aghayan et al., eds., Hay Zhoghovrdi Patmutiun History of the Armenian People (Yerevan, 1967), vol. 4; L. S. Khachikian et al., eds., Hay Zhoghovurde Feodalismi Vayredjki Zhamanakashrdjanum, XIV-XVIII DD The Armenian People during the Period of the Decline of Feudalism, XIV-XVIII centuries (1972); similarly, vol. 5 of the same eight-volume series published by the Institute of History, Academy of Sciences of the Armenian SSR, Ds. P. Aghayan et al., eds., Hayastane 1801-1870 Tvakannerin Armenia during the years 1801-1870 (1974), provides the most adequate history preceding the rise of modern political nationalism. See also H. Pastermajian, Histoire de l'Armenie depuis les origines jusqu'au Traite de Lausanne (Paris, 1949); A.K. Sanjian, The Armenian Communities in Syria under Ottoman Dominion (Cambridge, 1965). For an introduction to the modern era in Armenian history, see R.G. Hovannesian's Armenia on the Road to Independence (Berkeley and Los Angeles, 1967), pp. 1-68. The period discussed in this article is covered in S. Atamian's The Armenian Community (New York, 1955), an informative but biased study; and A. Ter Minassian's valuable and concise "La Question Armenienne," Esprit, April 1967, pp. 620-656.

(2) For the process of Russian expansion into the Caucasus, see W.E.D. Allen and P. Muratoff, Caucasian Battlefields: A History of the Wars on the Turco-Caucasian Border, 1828-1921(Cambridge, 1953). See also V. Gregorian, "The Impact of Russian on the Armenians and Armenia," in Russia and Asia, ed. W. S. Vucinich (Stanford, 1972), pp. 167-218.

(3) See J. Etmekjian, The French Influence on the Western Armenian Renaissance, 1843-1915 (New York, 1964); and A. Abeghian, "The New Literature of the East Armenians," The Armenian Review 3 (1977): 256-264.

(4) For what came to be known as the Armenian Question, see W. Langer, The Diplomacy of Imperialism, 1890-1920, vol. 1 (New York and London, 1935), pp. 145-166, 195-211, and 321-354; A.O. Sarkissian, History of the Armenian Question to 1885 (Urbana, 1938); A. Beylerian, "L'Imperialisme et le mouvement national armenien," Relations Internationales 3 (1975): 19-54; and G.H. Cloud, "The Armenian Question from the Congress of Berlin to the Massacres, 1878-1894" (M.A. thesis, Stanford University, 1923).

(5) Political attitudes among the Armenian bourgeoisie are discussed in V. Rshtuni, Hay Hasarakakan Hosankneri Patmutiunts Of the history of Armenian social trends (Yerevan, 1956), pp. 1-374; D. Ananun, Rusahayeri Hasarakakan Zargatsume The social develop-

ment of Russian Armenians vol. 1 (1800-1870) and vol. 2 (1870-1900) (Edjmiadsin, 1916, 1922); L. Megrian, "Tiflis during the Russian Revolution of 1905" (Ph.D. diss., University of California at Berkeley, 1975); M.G. Nersisian, Hay Zhoghovrdi Azatagrakan Paikare Trkakan Brnatirutian Dem, 1850-1870 The liberation struggle of the Armenian people against Turkish despotism (Yerevan, 1955), pp. 266-273; H.G. Vardanian, Arevmtahayeri Azadagrutian Hartse The question of liberation of Western Armenians (Yerevan, 1967), pp. 266-273; and L. Etmekjian, "The Reaction and Contributions of the Armenians to the Ottoman Reform Movement" (M.A. thesis, University of Bridgeport, 1974). For developments leading to the formation of revolutionary parties, see M. Varandian, Haykakan Sharzhman Nakhapatmutiun Prehistory of the Armenian movement 2 vols., (Geneva, 1912, 1913).

(6) Hay Heghapokhakan Dashnaktsutian Dsragir (henceforth HHD Dsragir) Program of the Armenian Revolutionary Federation (Vienna, n.d.), pp. 17-19; this program was devised during the first General Congress of the party in 1892. M. Varandian's H.H. Dashnaktsutian Patmutiun History of the A(rmenian) R(evolution-ary) Federation 2 vols., (Paris, 1932 and Cairo, 1950), still provides the best overview of the ARF's history despite its romanticized approach and polemical style. For an introduction to the early history of the political organizations, see L. Nalbandian, The Armenian Revolutionary Movement (Berkeley and Los Angeles, 1967). See also J. M. Hagopian's "Hyphenated Nationalism: The Spirit of the Revolutionary Movement in Asia Minor, 1896-1910" (Ph.d. diss., Harvard University, 1943). Many of the following observations are drawn from this writer's doctoral dissertation in progress, "Ideological Developments within the Armenian Liberation Movement, 1885-1908" (University of California at Los Angeles).

(7) Hunchak (Organ of the Hunchakian Revolutionary Party, Geneva), November (actually December), 1887, p. 1 (my translation). The Hunchakians later adopted the "social democratic" label. For their history, see L. Nalbandian, "The Origins and Development of Socialism in Armenia. The Social Democratic Hunchakian Party 1887-1949" (M.A. thesis, Stanford University, 1949); A. Kitur, ed., Patmutiun S.D. Hunchakian Kusaktsutian 1887 - 1962 History of the S(ocial) D(emocratic) Hunchakian Party 1887-1962 2 vols. (Beirut, 1962-1963). Unfortunately this latter work falls short of fulfilling the promise of its title.

(8) HHD Dsragir, p. 16.

(9) Ibid., pp. 19-20; "Dsragir Hunchakian Kusaktsutian" Program of the Hunchakian Party Hisnamiak Sotsial Demokrat Hunchakian Kusaktsutian 1887-1937 (Providence, 1938), pp. 38-39.

(10) Varandian, H.H. Dashnaktsutian Patmutiun, vol. 1, pp. 468-472.

(11) This was clearly stated in the first manifesto of the ARF published in 1890; see Divan H.H. Dashnaktsutian Archives of the ARF S. Vratsian, ed., vol. 1 (Boston, 1934), p. 89.

(12) M. Hovannisian, Dashnaktsutiune ev nra Hakarakordnere The (AR) Federation and its Adversaries (Tiflis, 1906-7), pp. 54-83.

(13) For the rise of Marxism among Armenians, see V. A. Avetisian, Hay Hasarakakan Mtki Zargatsman Marks-Leninian Puli Skzbnavorume The beginnings of the Marxist-Leninist phase of the development of Armenian social thought (Yeveran, 1976). This study includes a critique of other Armenian parties from the point of view of Soviet Marxism.

(14) Hisnamiak, p. 38.

(15) HHD Dsragir, p. 17.

(16) Hovannesian, Armenia on the Road, pp. 34-37.

(17) See Varandian, H.H. Dashnaktsutian Patmutiun, vol. 1, pp. 254-264 and G. Sassuni, Kurt Azgayin Sharzhume ev Hay-Krtakan Haraberutiunnere The Kurdish national movement and Armeno-Kurdish relations (Beirut, 1969), pp. 153-191.

(18) Droshak Organ of the ARF, Geneva July 1903, pp. 97-98 (my translation).

(19) H. H. Dashnaktsutian Dsragir Program of the ARF , (Geneva 1907), pp. 18-19.

(20) Hunchak, August-September 1910, p. 2. The resolution was passed during the Sixth General Congress of the Party held in Constantinople, November 1909.

(21) For sources on the genocide of the Armenian people, see R.G. Hovannesian's The Armenian Holocaust: A Bibliography Relating to the Deportations, Massacres, and Dispersion of the Armenian People, 1915-1923 (Cambridge, Mass., 1978). There has always been a tendency among some historians to bring the academic view on the Genocide of the Armenians into harmony with the official position held on the subject by the Ottoman and Turkish governments - to deny that a Genocide ever took place, and to blame the victims for whatever tragedy befell them. This tendency has been particularly strong among Western historians since Turkey joined the NATO Alliance. The most recent example of this sort of scholarship is S.J. Shaw and E.K. Shaw's History of the Ottoman Empire and Modern Turkey. Vol. II: Reform, Revolution, and Republic: The Rise of Modern Turkey, 1808-1975 (Cambridge, London, New York, Melbourne, 1977), esp. pp. 124-127, 188-191, 200-205, 238-247, 262-267, 276-281 and 298-333. For a critical appraisal of the volume, see R. G. Hovannesian, "The Critic's View: Beyond Revisionism," International Journal of Middle East Studies 9, no. 3

(August 1978): 379-388. The same issue of this journal also offers a response by the authors of the volume to Hovannesian's criticisms in pp. 388-400.

Reasons for the disparity between views held on the subject by Turkish, Western, and Armenian historians are explored in this writer's "Objectivity and Historiography of the Armenian Genocide," The Armenian Review 31, no. 3 (Spring 1978): 86-93.

(22) For the history of theArmenian and other Caucasian republics, see R.G. Hovannesian, The Republic of Armenia, Vol. I, The First Year, 1918-1919 (Berkeley, Los Angeles, London, 1971); J.B. Gidney, A Mandate for Armenia (Kent, Ohio, 1967); F. Kazemzadeh, The Struggle for Transcaucasia (New York and Oxford, 1951); and R. Pipes, The Formation of the Soviet Union (New York, 1968), pp. 7-21, 93-107.

(23) See R.G. Hovannesian, "Armenia and the Caucasus in the Genesis of the Soviet-Turkish Entente," The Armenian Review 27, no. 1 (Spring 1974): 32-52.

(24) Pipes, The Formation of the Soviet Union, pp. 193-241. See also A. Caprielian, "The Sovietization of Armenia: A Case History in Imperialism," The Armenian Review 20, no. 3 (Autumn, 1967): 22-42; and S. Vratsian, Hayastani Hanrapetutiun Republic of Armenia (Beirut, 1958), pp. 445-507.

(25) Unless otherwise indicated, statistical information regarding Armenians in the Soviet Union and Soviet Armenia is derived from the latest All-Union Census in the USSR in 1970. As usual, one must approach any statistical information, particularly from the USSR, with caution.

(26) For a detailed study of the early decades of Soviet Armenia, see M.K. Matossian, The Impact of Soviet Policies in Armenia (Leiden, 1962).

(27) J.S. Kirakosian, Hayastane Midjazgayin Divanagitutian ev Sovetakan Artakin Kaghakakanutian Pastateghterum Armenia in the documents of international diplomacy and Soviet Union foreign policy (Yerevan, 1972), pp. 418-419.

(28) The background of the conflict is discussed in R.G. Hovannesian, "The Armeno-Azerbaijani Conflict Over Mountainous Karabagh, 1918-1919," The Armenian Review 24, no. 2 (Summer 1971): 3-39. See also A.H. Arslanian, "Britain and the Question of Mountainous Karabagh," paper presented at the Eleventh Annual Meeting of MESA, Los Angeles, 1977.

(29) S. Vratsian, Republic of Armenia, pp. 524-568. In Soviet Armenian historiography the event is known as the "February adventure" and presented as the attempt of a power-hungry ARF to regain control of the government. See, for example, Ds. P. Aghayan et al., eds., Hay Zoghovrdi Patmutiun 7 (Yerevan, 1967): 136-154.

(30) G. Lazian, Hayastan ev Hay Date - Vaveragrer, Armenia and the Armenian Case -- Documents (Cairo, 1946), p. 306. The same document is discussed in conjunction with the New Economic Policy in Hay Zoghovrdi Patmutiun, vol. 7, p. 176.

(31) The great purges in Soviet Armenia between 1936 and 1939 are covered with much detail in A. Atan's "Sovetahay Kiank" Soviet Armenian Life monthly chronicle in Hairenik Amsagir (Boston, an ARF monthly review) throughout the same period.   For an eyewitness account, see A. Haroot, "The Purges in Soviet Armenia," The Armenian Review 4, no. 3 (Autumn 1951): 133-139.

(32) Lazian, Vaveragrer, pp. 346-350. See also S. Torosian, "Soviet Policy in the Armenian Question," The Armenian Review 11, no. 2 (Summer 1958): 27-39.

(33) Lazian, Vaveragrer, pp. 371-372 (own translation).

(34) A.M. Hakobian et al., eds., Hay Zoghovrdi Patmutiun, vol. 8 (Yerevan, 1970), p. 254.

(35) Sovetakan Hayastan Amsagir Soviet Armenia Monthly (Yerevan), no. 6 (1976), p. 4.

(36) For these and other comparisons see B.D. Silver, "Levels of Socioeconomic Development Among Soviet Nationalities," American Political Science Review 68 (1974): 1618-1637.

(37) See M.K. Matossian, "Communist Rule and the Changing Armenian Cultural Pattern," in E. Goldhagen, ed., Ethnic Minorities in the Soviet Union (New York, 1968), pp. 185-197.

(38) V.E. Khodjabekian, "HSSH Bnakchutiune, Erek, Aysor ev Vaghe" The population of the A(rmenian) S(oviet) S(ocialist) R(epublic) yesterday, today and tomorrow , Lraber (Yerevan), no. 12 (1972), p. 53.

(39) Computed from related data in Khodjabekian, "HSSH Bnak-chutiune," and R. Ezekian, "Hamayn Hayutian Hayrenike" The Fatherland of all Armenians , Garun Amsagir (Yerevan, monthly), no. 11 (1970), pp. 88-93.

(40) L.V. Chuiko, Braki i razvodi (Moscow, 1976), p. 76.

(41) Khodjabekian, "HSSH Bnakchutiune," p. 48.

(42) L. Davtian, "Amusnanal: Erb. Erekhaner unenal: Kani" To Marry: When? To Bear Children: How Many?, Garun Amsagir, no. 10 (1971), pp. 73-77.

(43) Khodjabekian, "HSSH Bnakchutiune," p. 53.

(44) Ds. P. Aghayan, Hay Zhoghovrdi Azatagrakan Paykari Patmutiunits Of the History of the Liberation Struggle of the Armenian People (Yerevan, 1976), esp. pp. 93-296.

(45) Kh. Dashtents, "Ranchbarner" Peasants, Sovetakan Grakanutiun Soviet literature (Yerevan, monthly), no. 7 and 8 (1976), pp. 20-74 and 12-73.

(46) For a detailed study of all this material, see V.N. Dadrian's "Nationalism in Soviet Armenia - A Case Study of Ethnocentrism," G. Simmonds, ed., Nationalism in the USSR and Eastern Europe in the Era of Brezhnev and Kosygin (Detroit, 1977), pp. 202-258.

(47) New York Times, June 26, 1965.

(48) Christian Science Monitor, April 27, 1978.

(49) Dadrian, "Nationalism in Soviet Armenia," p. 247. Less violent, nonetheless unusual demonstrations occurred in Moscow as well; see V.N. Dadrian's "The Events of April 24 in Moscow - How They Happened and under What Circumstances," The Armenian Review 20, no. 2 (Summer 1967): 9-26.

(50) M.K. Matossian, "Armenia and the Armenians," Z. Katz, ed., Handbook of Major Soviet Nationalities (New York, 1975), p. 158.

(51) Cited in Azdak Shabatoriak, no. 17 (1971), pp. 272-274; no. 26 (1974), pp. 419-421. For a statement by the leaders of this group containing the objectives and by-laws of the party, see "Le Parti National Unifie en Armenie sovietique," Haiastan (Paris, monthly), no. 391-392, April-May 1978, pp. 38-40. The renewed national fervor might have caused the removal of yet another first secretary of the Communist Party in Armenia, A. Kochinian. See "Soviet Armenian Chronicle," The Armenian Review 27 no. 1 (Spring 1974): 102-103; no. 3 (Autumn 1974): 325; no. 4 (Winter 1974): 435-437.

(52) Pravda, December 4, 1920.

(53) New York Times, December 11, 1977.

(54) Azdak Shabatoriak, no. 6 (1969), p. 95.

(55) New York Times, December 11, 1977.

(56) Sarada Mitra and Adel Haba, "We Saw the Brotherhood of Nations," Problems of Peace and Socialism 20, no. 6 (June 1977): esp. 18-19, 25.

(57) Both documents were first published in Zartonk (Beirut daily, organ of the Armenian Democratic Liberal Party), October 15, 1977.

(58) Sovetakan Hayastan (Yerevan daily), April 15, 1978; Christian Science Monitor, April 28, 1978. On the question of minority languages see also S. Grigorian, "A Note on Soviet Policies Toward the Armenian Language," The Armenian Review 25, no. 3 (Autumn 1972): 68-76. For two contrasting views on the impact of language reforms in 1958-59, see H. Lipset, "The Status of National Minority Languages in Soviet Education," Soviet Studies 19, no. 2 (October

1967): 181-189; and B.D. Silver, "The Status of National Minority Languages in Soviet Education: An Assessment of Recent Changes," Soviet Studies 26, no. 1 (January 1974): 28-40.

(59) The most vehement criticisms have come so far from the first secretary and secretary of the Central Committee of the Communist Party in Armenia, K. Demirjian and K. Dallakian, in speeches delivered to the Central Committee on January 30, 1975 and October 19, 1975; see Grakan Tert Literary newspaper (Yerevan), February 7, 1975 and Sovetakan Hayastan, October 21 and 22, 1975.

(60) See Le Monde, June 23, 1977; Liberation (Paris), April 8, 1977; and Haiastan, no. 383, July 1977, pp. 9-15.

(61) Haiastan, no. 381, May-June 1977, p. 19.

(62) P. Reddaway, ed., Uncensored Russian - The Human Rights Movement in the Soviet Union (London, 1972), pp. 103, 151 passim; comp. P. Litvinov, The trial of the Four, (New York, 1972), pp. 399-405; and G. Sanders, Samizdat - Soviet Opposition (New York, 1974), pp. 368, 372.

(63) "Le Parti National Unifie," Haiastan, pp. 38-40.

(64) Sermon delivered by Archbishop Shnork Kalustian, Patriarch of Armenians in Turkey, on October 24, 1976 in Paris; see Asbarez (Los Angeles, semi-weekly), December 9, 1976. See also R.P. Jordan's "The Proud Armenians," National Geographic 153, no. 6 (June 1978): 846-853; this article provides one of the rare instances in western literature where reference is made to the status of Armenians presently living in Turkey.

(65) "Annual Report for 1976 of His Beatitude, Archbishop Shnork Kalustian, Patriarch of the Armenian Apostolic Church in Turkey," The Armenian Review 30, no. 2 (Summer 1977): 177.

(66) Ibid, pp. 178-182. See also "Statement on Conditions (1974) by the Chancellory of the Armenian Patriarchate in Turkey," The Armenian Review 30, no. 3 (Autumn 1977): 302-305.

(67) The Patriarch's telegram to Mr. Porkut Eozali, Director of the Ministry of Interior, Turkey, in Asbarez, September 19, 1977.

(68) London Times, April 20 and 25, 1963; see also H. Dasnabedian's introduction, esp. pp. xii-xiv, to Monuments of Armenian Architecture (Beirut, 1972), published by the Central Committee of the "Hamazkaine" Cultural Association.

(69) The Patriarch's Annual Report, p. 182.

(70) J. Wolf, "Les Minorites en Turquie," Notre Temps (Brussels), January 21, 1977.

(71) Christian Science Monitor, July 20, 1977.

(72) <u>Marmara</u> (Istanbul), March 30 and April 1, 1978.

(73) Ibid., April 10, 1978.

(74) <u>Hurriyet</u>, December 14, 1977.

(75) <u>Marmara</u>, January 7, 1978; <u>Asbarez</u>, January 27, 1978.

(76) A major attempt at providing a general picture of Armenian communities outside the homeland throughout the centuries is A. Alpoyajian, <u>Patmutiun Hay Gaghtakanutian</u> History of Armenian Emigration , 3 vols. (Cairo, 1941-1961). For an example of eighteenth century Diaspora-Armenia relations, see A. Hamalian, <u>The Armenians: Intermediaries for the European Trading Companies</u>, University of Manitoba Anthropology Papers, no. 14 (Winnipeg, 1976). Some of the problems in covering the most recent period are discussed in R. Mirak, "Outside the Homeland: Writing the History of the Armenian Diaspora," <u>Recent Studies in Modern Armenian History</u> (Cambridge, Mass., 1972), pp. 119-125.

(77) These figures are generally accepted approximations, as there are no reliable statistics on this subject.

(78) For the 1908 program of the ADL, see A. Darbinian, <u>Hay Azatagrakan Sharzhman Oreren</u> Of the Days of the Armenian Liberation Movement (Paris, 1947), pp. 198-204; and Lazian, <u>Vaveragrer</u>, pp. 323-328.

(79) H. Ervand, <u>Ramkavar Azatakan Kusaktsutiun--Ir Aysore ev Vaghe</u> Democratic Liberal Party - Its Today and Tomorrow (Boston, 1927); "Davanank ev Oughegids Ramkavar Azatakan Kusaktsutian" Credo and Conduct of the Democratic Liberal Party , G. Aharonian and H. Vahuni, eds., <u>"Zartonk" Batsarik</u> "Zartonk" Special (Beirut, 1962), p. 37.

(80) See A. Caprielian, "The Armenian Revolutionary Federation: The Politics of a Party in Exile" (Ph.D. dissertation, New York University, 1975). For a Soviet view of Diaspora politics, see L.A. Khurshudian, <u>Spurkahay Kusaktsutiunnere Zhamanakakits Edabum</u> The Parties in the Armenian Diaspora in Their Contemporary Phase (Yerevan, 1964).

(81) Lazian, <u>Vaveragrer</u>, p. 352.

(82) The National Council for the Sixtieth Anniversary Commemoration of the Genocide, <u>Armenian Memorandum to the United Nations: April 24, 1975</u>, (Beirut, 1975). See also "Two Memoranda on the Subject of the Sixtieth Anniversary of the Turkish Massacres of the Armenians," <u>The Armenian Review</u> 28, no. 1 (Spring 1975): 7484.

(83) Legal aspects of Armenian claims as discussed in Sh. Toriguian's <u>The Armenian Question and International Law</u> (Beirut, 1973).

(84) See K. Donabedian, "Armenians Abroad," The Armenian Review 28, no. 1 (Spring 1975): 85-99.

(85) Le Monde, June 11, 1978.

(86) A. Der-Karabetian and L. Melikian, "Assimilation of Armenians in Lebanon," The Armenian Review, no. 1 (Spring 1974), pp. 65-72.

(87) A. Der-Karabetian, "A Study of Assimilation in the Pluralistic Society of Lebanon: The Case of the Armenians," paper presented at the Tenth Annual Meeting of The Middle East Studies Association, Los Angeles, 1976.

3 Divided Azerbaijan: Nation Building, Assimilation, and Mobilization Between Three States

S. Enders Wimbush

THE "AMONGLAND"

The territory called Azerbaijan lies between two large and powerful states: Iran, which gives to nearly all of the inhabitants of the entire territory its culture and religion; and the Soviet Union, which inherited its half from the tsarist Russian Empire and then reconquered it in the early 1920s. A distinct set of ideas governs the daily life of each half of this territory - Marxism-Leninism in the north and Shi'a Islam in the south. These ideas prescribe two distinct systems of economic, cultural, and political development. Ethnically and linguistically, the majority of the population both of northern and southern Azerbaijan is Turkic. Turkey, in turn, shares one border with Iranian Azerbaijan and another with the Soviet Union, thereby lending a certain immediacy to the mixed national loyalties, obligations, and sentiments of the Azeri population. It would be overly pedantic but not ungrammatical, therefore, to refer to Azerbaijan not as a "betweenland" but as an "amongland," if only to underscore that the forces which shape its people and its politics originate at three points, not two.

Azerbaijan was divided into two distinct territories which fell under the jurisdiction of different states in the first half of the nineteenth century, when Russian armies conquered the northern Iranian principalities of Derbent, Baku, Nakhidjevan, and Ganja. Before this, the territory of Azerbaijan simply was another part of the Persian Empire. This "land of fire" (the territory's name comes from the Iranic word adhar, meaning "fire") was visited by the Seljuk Turks in the eleventh century. Settling mostly in what is now northwestern Iran and southeastern Transcaucasia, the Seljuks set in motion the ebbing, flowing, and relentless process of turkification which came to distinguish the inhabitants of this region from the rest of Iran.

Turkification did not create "Azerbaijanis"; that is, it did not impart a distinct national consciousness to the turkified peoples based upon ethnic rivalries, linguistic differences (Azeri Turkish, a variant of standard Turkish, became their primary language), or the setting apart of this group on its own territory. Instead, "Iran . . . conquered the Seljuks culturally." (1) The Turks of Azerbaijan, like most other Iranian minorities, came to understand that "intangible feeling . . . that Persian culture - traditions, outlook on life, and the like - will always service political domination and the onslaught of new ideologies, and that it is a privilege to partake of this culture." (2) The attachment of Azeri Turks to the Iranian state is a matter of record. Since the late fifteenth and early sixteenth centuries, when Safavid-Ottoman conflicts began, the Turks of Azerbaijan always have sided with and actively supported their religious and cultural brethren in Iran rather than their coethnics in Turkey. Largely this is because Azeri Turks adopted Shi'a Islam - the religion of all Iran - and not the Sunni ritual practiced by most other Turkic peoples; and this had the effect of drawing them closer to the Persian cultural tradition and the Iranian state. To the Shiite, Sunni Islam is heresy, its adherents moral outcasts and implacable enemies.

Although possessing many of the prerequisites which social scientists consider to be the foundations of modern nationhood, Azeri Turks did not evolve a distinct national consciousness nor the idea that the territory of Azerbaijan constituted a national homeland until the early twentieth century, and then only under some unique conditions which will be discussed later. There can be little doubt that Azeri Turks saw themselves as distinct from Ottomans (for religious and cultural reasons) and from Persians (for linguistic ones), very early on. Knowledge of these differences, however, did not lead Azeri leaders to urge that their territory be classified as a national homeland, as the term now is understood. In part, this may be due to the absence of a "modern nation" theory in the Turkic-Mongol tradition. This tradition bequeathed to Turkic peoples a somewhat different notion of primordial affiliation, the notion of ulus. Ulus translates into land, state, and nation simultaneously, and it is impossible to separate one from another spiritually or symbolically. When a Turkic people moves, it takes its land with it; that is, the land on which it settles becomes part of the ulus, provided that the entire community moves together. "Motherland" for a Turk is where he can live among a Turkic majority. Unlike the Armenian or Georgian, whose national sensitivities and identities are bound inextricably with a territory or a historic landmark which stands as the symbol of his national community, the Turk is at home wherever a Turkic majority surrounds him.

It should be noted in this regard that neither Soviet Azeri Turks nor their counterparts in Iran have advanced irredentist claims on the other territory, although the Russian conquerors annexed only half of the original territory of Azerbaijan. Georgia and Armenia, on the other hand, both of whom lost less substantial parts of their motherlands to Turkey during World War I, persisted in their irredentism until Molotov finally renounced these claims officially in 1953 (thereby ending the official controversy but certainly not the immutable propensity of Armenians to gaze at the magnificent summit of Mt. Ararat just across the Turkish border and wish that it were once again their mountain).

Moreover, there would seem to have been little reason for Azeri leaders to seek a real or symbolic separatism from the Iranian state prior to the Russian conquest in the nineteenth century. Since the revival of Iranian statehood by the Samanids in the ninth century, state ideology has been based on three principles. The first is the abstract non-Muslim and non-Turko-Mongol principle of monarchy, in which the ruler may be of any ethnic origin (provided that he meets the second two criteria), and from any dynasty. Second, a state culture and one literary and administrative language are obligatory. Third, there must be a state religion, which in Iran since the fifteenth century has been Shiism.

Azeri Turks satisfied all of these conditions. With the exception of the present Pahlavi dynasty, no purely Iranian dynasty ever has governed the Iranian state. In fact, the majority of the dynasties, including the greatest - the Safavid, and the most recent - the Qajar, have been Turkic. All have been "foreign" dynasties that adopted the Persian language and Persian culture and were Shiite. Over the centuries there was no discrimination toward the Azeri Turks because both Persians and Azeri Turks were Shiite and, therefore, had equal claim on the powers and perquisites of the state. (The birthplace of Iranian state Shiism, moreover, was in the city of Ardebil, in Azerbaijan.) The Azeri Turk nobility even held a slightly more favorable position than the Persian nobility.

AZERBAIJAN DIVIDED

Early in the nineteenth century the Russian Transcaucasian army occupied much of northern Iran, including Tabriz, in one of Russia's recurring efforts to find a southern outlet to the sea. In 1828, according to the terms of the Treaty of Turkomanchai, the present boundary between Iran and Russia was fixed; but in the course of this agreement, the Tsar's representatives secured the northern Iranian principalities of Derbent, Baku, Nakhidjevan, and Ganja - half of the territory of Azerbaijan. Within the Russian Empire, Azeri Turks were granted a social status that was unique among Russia's Muslims. Their feudal lords were accepted into the Russian nobility with privileges and wealth. Many held high positions in the military and in the civil service. In 1914, for example, the Khan of Nakhidjevan was the commander of the entire Guard Cavalry Corps and the Khan of Baku held a high position in the Russian court. (The last Khans of Baku, Nakhidjevan, and Khoy are now United States citizens, and the first is chairman of the Coca-Cola Company for Europe and Asia.)

Following this division, Iranian Azerbaijan changed very much in step with the rest of Iran. The period from the mid-nineteenth century until 1907 was marked by the penetration of Western ideas, economic inroads by foreigners (especially by the British and the Russians), the rise in popularity of syncretistic faiths that challenged Shiism, and the decadence of several luxury-loving autocratic Shahs. These changes, plus the impact on many educated Iranians of the Japanese victory over Russia in 1905, precipitated a constitutional crisis in 1906. Continued instability led the British, who favored a constitution, and the Russians, who bitterly opposed one, to divide and occupy the country (much as they would in 1942). To Russia went all of north and central Iran, including Azerbaijan.

Russian Azerbaijan, on the other hand, from the mid-nineteenth century until 1914, was the seat of an important intellectual and cultural awakening, which was tolerated, if not encouraged, by Russian authorities. It was during this period that the modernist writers Bakikhanov and Fath Ali Ahundzade gained notoriety, and the first Muslim opera by Hacibeyli was performed. Also by 1914, Baku led all cities of the Russian Empire in the number of Muslim periodicals published. This awakening and the accompanying intellectual ferment were indigenous phenomena and not simply the imitation of Russian cultural models, as was the case with the Volga Tatars.

Furthermore, Russian Azerbaijan acquired a modern city in the nineteenth century, as Baku enjoyed an economic boom. A large stratum of native upper-class industrialists grew rich from oil and textiles. From the working class emerged the only genuine industrial proletariat among Russian Muslims. The cultural and economic wealth of Russian Azerbaijan spawned an extremely intense, diversified, and sophisticated political life. All trends were represented, from the staunchly religious right to the Bolshevik-style left. This region became a nursery for political leaders who eventually became prominent in the political life of Kemalist Turkey.

In spite of the separate paths that the two Azerbaijans were taking, even at the end of the century most Russian Azeri Turks saw themselves tied to the Iranian cultural tradition, if not in fact tied in some real way to the Iranian state despite the Russian provincial governors in their midst. "At this time there was not great difference between the Moslems of the Caucasus and Iranians," notes a prominent Iranian who was born in Tabriz, "and Caucasians considered themselves quite as Iranians and sympathized with them, since both were Moslems, and since Ottoman influence had not yet advanced into areas of Shi'a population." (3) The same observer recorded the following story, which he heard from an Azeri traveler in a coffee house on the Russian side of the border:

He said he had gone one day to a nearby village on the Russian side of the Araxes named Yaji, and there, in the square in front of the mosque where the old men of the village used to sit and talk, they had planted plane trees and would watch and water them every day. He said to the old men, "Uncles, you who are so old, what benefit will you get from spending your time on plane tree saplings which require so many years to reach maturity?" When he said this the old men wept and said, "The only desire in our lives is that these trees should grow and this territory become Iranian again and the Iranian tax collectors should come here to collect taxes and we should not be able to pay the taxes and that they should tie us to these trees and beat us!" (4)

But even so, new inclinations were perceptible in Russian Azerbaijan. For the most part, the intellectual leaders in the north had been educated in Turkey and France, seldom in St. Petersburg. Turkish (Young Turk) and French (first liberal and later socialist) political ideas were becoming more influential among them. The Turkic modernist-secular trends, which became especially potent after 1905, argued for a break with the long-held Shi'a, pro-Iranian orientation of the traditional Azeri intelligentsia and for the rapprochement with Sunnite Turkey. Led by Ali Huseyinzade, Ahmed Agaoglu, and Mardan Tapchibashy - all educated in Istanbul and heavily influenced by the Young Turks - the movement advocated a theory of Turkish (not Turkic) solidarity between Azeri Turks and Ottomans, leaving aside the religious distinctions of Shi'a and Sunni in order to forge a more powerful political coalition. For these leaders, both Russian and Iranian Azerbaijan logically should be united to the democratic state promised by the Young Turks. Ethnic and linguistic bonds, they argued, outweighed religious and historical obligations to Iran. The Anglo-Russian partition of Iran in 1907 and the outbreak of World War I made the dilemma of choosing between Turkey and Iran a stark one. Ali Khan Shirvanshir, the hero of Kurban Said's novel Ali and Nino, and his friend and mentor, the wise man Seyd Mustafa, describe what were the feelings of many Azeri Turk intellectuals in Russian Azerbaijan at this time:

I looked at him, shaken. What was right, what was wrong? True, the Turks were Sunnites. And yet my heart longed to see Enver coming to our town. What did that mean? Had our martyrs' blood really flowed in vain? "Seyd," I said, "the Turks are of our blood. Their language is our language. Turan's blood flows in both our veins. Maybe that is why it is easier to die under the Half Moon of the Khalifs than under the Czar's Cross."

Seyd Mustafa dried his eyes: "In my veins flows Mohammed's blood," he said cooly and proudly. "Turan's blood? You seem to have forgotten even the little you learned at school. Go to the mountains of the Altai, or yet further to the border of Siberia: who lives there? Turks, like us, of our language and our blood. God has led them astray, and they have remained pagans, they are praying to idols: the water-god Su-Tengri, the sky-god Teb-Tengri. If these Jakuts or Altai-men were to become powerful and fight us, should we Shiites be glad of the pagan victories, just because they are of the same blood as we?" (5)

This dilemma persisted for many decades. Even today in Soviet Azerbaijan where Ali Khan's side would appear to have the upper hand, there are still those who would answer like Seyd Mustafa: "What shall we do, Ali Khan? I do not know." (6)

These early modernist Azeri overtures to Turkey went largely unrequited. Ottoman leaders before Kemal were interested only slightly in the Azeri Turks, although a few Pan-Turkic dreamers did seek to annex all of Azerbaijan to Turkey. Huseyinzade and other Azeri Turk leaders eventually traveled to Turkey where they invested their energies in the Kemalist cause. Their contributions to the political excitement at home were significant nonetheless, for it was under these modernist influences that northern and some southern Azeri Turks began to evolve something akin to a modern national consciousness - an awareness of themselves as a distinct people living permanently on the same piece of land. This awareness became more concrete when in 1911 the modernist newspaper Azerbaijan first appeared in Tabriz. This was one of the first explicit attempts to reach an "Azerbaijani" audience, that is, an audience that still was politically amorphous but had recognizable territorial and ethnic boundaries.

In 1908, when the Shah ordered an occupying Russian Cossack brigade to disperse the Majlis and its supporters in Tabriz, the people of that city revolted, forcing the Shah to rely on Russian troops to quell the uprising. The brutal massacre of many of Tabriz's Azeri inhabitants at the hands of the Russians only heightened the sense of ethnic isolation and political helplessness felt by many Azeri Turks. The Russian occupation of Iranian Azerbaijan remained in force until 1918. This presence encouraged many Azeri Turks in the north and in the south to cast their eyes on Turkey for deliverance from the infidel. Many were prepared - like Ali Khan Shirvanshir above - to sublimate outstanding differences between Shi'a and Sunni. This sublimation, this leveling, also was a process of self-identification, for to level differences one must first identify what those differences are. To say that religion does not matter is to say that there is a difference. To advocate the annexation of one's own territory by a larger state, in this case by Turkey, is to acknowledge that the territory to be annexed already exists in some sense as a separate, identifiable socio-political unit.

What the Turkic modernists and the Russian Army set in motion, the Bolshevik revolution, the Russian Civil War, and the reconsolidation of the Russian Empire under Soviet rule consummated. Whatever their feelings about their Azeri brethren in Iran or their blood-brothers in Turkey, in April 1918 the Azeri Turks in the north joined the new Transcaucasian federation as a politically distinct and ethnically defined unit. One month later, when this configuration was eclipsed by the Civil War, these same Azeri Turks declared what formerly had been Russian Azerbaijan to be a sovereign, independent nation. When this new nation was reconquered by force in 1920 by the Red Army, Bolshevik leaders first made it a national component of the Federal Union of the Soviet Socialist Republics of Transcaucasia in March 1922, then a part of the Transcaucasian Soviet Federative Socialist Republic in November 1922, and finally a full-fledged Soviet Republic in 1923. Henceforth, Soviet Azerbaijan would fall under Stalin's requirement that communal development must follow a prescribed formula: socialist in content, national in form.

Soviet Azerbaijan soon was assigned a role in the new order of things on the Soviet Union's southern flank; significantly, this assignment was determined not by the Russian Bolsheviks in Moscow but by Muslim national communist leaders in Baku and in other Muslim centers of the Soviet federation. (7) The Muslim national communists, unlike their Jewish counterparts at this time, insisted that the national revolution must precede the social one - that their national territories must be given independence before the internal class struggle could begin. Most Muslim national communists, however, realized that few Muslim national groups possessed a working class and that the feasibility of a class struggle under these conditions was severely limited. Therefore, they concluded, the social revolution was to be put off indefinitely. Instead, their struggle must be devoted to national autonomy within a Russian federation or to outright independence.

For the Muslim national communists, the East appeared as the most fertile ground for national revolution; the West was decadent and incapable of sustaining one. Because of this, they argued, the Muslims of the former Russian empire - given their advanced revolutionary consciousness relative to other colonial peoples of the East - should carry the revolution to the East; their territories should be used as "revolutionary springboards." "The sovietization of Azerbaijan is a highly important step in the evolution of communism in the Near East," wrote the most prominent Muslim national communist theorist, the Kazan Tatar, Sultan Galiev.

> Just as Red Turkistan is playing the role of the revolutionary lighthouse for Chinese Turkistan, Tibet, Afghanistan, India, Bukhara, and Khiva, Soviet Azerbaijan, with its old and experienced proletariat and its already consolidated Communist Party - the Hummet Party - will become the Red lighthouse for Persia, Arabia, and Turkey.... The fact that the Azeri Language is understood by the Turks of Istanbul, the Persians of Tabriz, the Kurds, the Turkic peoples of Transcaucasia, the Georgians, and the Armenians, will increase the international role of Soviet Azerbaijan. (8)

The important literary figure and first Chairman of the Communist Party of Azerbaijan, Nariman Narimanov, predicted that his country would serve as a conduit for Bolshevik-style revolution into "all states

and nationalities professing Islam." (9)   Like Sultan Galiev, Narimanov
emphasized that the Azeri Turk's unique combination of cultural,
linguistic, ethnic, and historical associations made him the ideal
middleman between the Muslims of the new Soviet state and a large
part of the Muslim world abroad.

These events - revolution, civil war, and the consolidation of the
Soviet state - and the influence of the Muslim national communists
firmly established Soviet Azerbaijan as a "nation" and made stark the
distinction between Soviet Azerbaijan and the Azerbaijan in the south.
Indeed, northern Azerbaijan now leaned the more decidedly in the
direction of Turkey, largely because the Muslim national communists --
in whose ranks Azeri Turks were especially influential--were open
advocates of Pan-Turkism.   Furthermore, Turkey now appeared as a
dynamic force - one that could potentially counter the Russians, who
again were tightening their grasp on northern Azerbaijan.   However rash
the behavior of the Turkish troops who had penetrated the Caucasus
during the war, they had penetrated while the Iranians had not.   Turkey
was aggressive; Iran was old and decadent and rooted far to the south.
Or so it appeared.

Hands Across the Border

By 1936 the Soviet regime had purged and liquidated nearly all of the
Muslim national communists, thereby ending any further discussion
concerning the use of nationalist cadres from within the Soviet
federation for mobilizing their ethnic kin across the Soviet border for a
national liberation struggle.   Soviet strategy for its southern flank was
conservative and nonexpansionary.   Even before the new Soviet state
was fully consolidated, Soviet leaders signed treaties of "friendship and
mutual cooperation" with King Amanullah of Afghanistan, Kemal
Ataturk of Turkey, and Reza Khan (the future Reza Shah) of Iran -
governments which by no stretch of the imagination could be thought of
as progressive or socialist in the Soviet sense.

Far from employing Azeri Turks as an advance guard of the
revolution in Iranian Azerbaijan and elsewhere, the Soviet regime
explicitly denied them this role.   The risks of nationalist infection were
high, and what the Soviet regime wanted least at this time was for
Azeri Turks or other non-Russians to recruit support for their own
national causes from abroad.   Undoubtedly it was an appreciation of this
risk that caused the Soviet leaders to send a Bashkir, Sherif Manatov, to
Turkey in 1919 to help organize the Turkish Communist Party.   And it
probably was this appreciation which led Soviet leaders to deny Azeri
Turk support to two southern Azeri movements that presumably could
have benefited from it most: Sheikh Mohammed Khiabani's National
Democratic Party in 1920 and Kuchik Khan's Soviet Socialist Republic
of Ghilan in 1921.   In both of these instances the Soviets employed only
Russian troops to assist the insurgents against the Iranian center, while

at the same time the Soviet government angled for formal treaties with the "reactionary" governments that ostensibly they were seeking to overthrow from within. Once these treaties or other concessions were a fact, the Soviets quickly withdrew their protective troops and, without so much as a backward glance, allowed the Iranian Army to liquidate both Sheikh Khiabani's "democracy" and Kuchik Khan's "republic."

In 1942, when the Soviets and the British jointly occupied Iran, Soviet leaders once again began to meddle in Iranian politics, using an Azeri resistance movement as their lever to gain oil concessions. This was the Democratic Party of Azerbaijan, the creation of a former Ghilanist, Ja'far Pishihvari. There can be little doubt that the Soviets manipulated Pishihvari's movement from the beginning, both through the communist Tudeh Party (the Pishihvari movement and the Tudeh were not from the same root, as has often been argued (10)) and with the assistance of professional agitators from the Soviet side of the border. Nor can there be much doubt of Pishihvari's commitment to securing greater autonomy for the Azeri people within the Iranian state. (11) What is in doubt is the nature of the Soviet commitment to use Soviet Azeri Turks as propagandists and agitators among adherents or potential adherents to Pishihvari's groups.

One observer contends that the border between the two Azerbaijans was left "wide open" by the Soviets in 1946 while the border between Iranian Azerbaijan and the rest of Iran was "partially closed" by Russian troops. The open border, he continues, allowed Russian Azerbaijanis who "had been trained in the technique of agitation" to infiltrate the Pishihvari movement. (12) This account is questionable, if only for the "open border" assertion - which almost certainly did not take place and which the writer could not have observed in any case - but also for the author's claim that "across the frontier was Russian Azerbaijan, speaking the same language with only a difference in dialect." (13) There are, of course, no dialectal differences among Azeri Turks.

Yet another observer speaks of the influx into Iranian Azerbaijan of a number of refugees from the north at this time. (14) It is not clear whether these "refugees" were in fact Soviet Azeri Turks; indeed, the very notion of "refugees" suggests that they probably were not. It is not unlikely that they were former Ghilanists - like Pishihvari himself - who had been trained in the Soviet Union for a suitable opportunity to return to Iran to agitate among the Azeri Turks there. It also is possible that these refugees were Iranian Azeri Turks culled from the many Iranian prisoners of war who were held in Soviet Central Asia, (15) trained in agitation techniques, and promised their release if they followed Moscow's instructions. It certainly is the case that the literature which these propagandists carried across the border with them was of Soviet origin. It utilized words which were current in Soviet Azerbaijan but not in the south. (16) Exactly who the messengers were is problematic.

What is certain - and this lends credence to the idea that Soviet leaders wanted to avoid contact between their own Azeri Turks and any Azeri-led nationalist movement in Iran - is the following. When Russian troops were withdrawn from Iranian Azerbaijan in 1946 and the movement was crushed, as its predecessors had been, from lack of Russian support, a number of Pishihvari's followers fled to the Soviet Union where they expected to find sanctuary among the Soviet Azeri Turks. What they found instead were Soviet prison trains waiting at the border to take them to Siberia for work camp terms of from fifteen to twenty-five years. In this way the nationalist infection was arrested at its source and prevented from spreading to the independent-minded Soviet Azeri Turks, as Soviet authorities knew it would.

The events surrounding the three Azeri resistance movements discussed above (Khiabani in 1920, Kuchik Khan in 1921, and Pishihvari in 1946) prove beyond any doubt that the Soviets are not above stirring up unrest among Iran's Azeri Turks and then controlling it in order to exact special concessions from the Iranian government. These events also prove that the Soviets have little or no interest in the resistance movements for their own sake, and this is why Soviet policy has permitted the callous slaughter of each of the movements when its concession-bearing leverage was exhausted. More significantly, there is little or no evidence to suggest that the Soviet regime ever has chosen to use Soviet Azeri Turks in ethnic ploys along the Iranian border.

Azeri Turks under Soviet Rule

The consolidation of Soviet Azerbaijan as a "Soviet nation" with its own literary language, literary tradition, local press and other media, national schools, universities, and an academy of sciences reflects the Soviet Azeris' "amongland" position. By encouraging the prosperity of its Azeri citizens, the Soviet regime not only intends to erect a showcase to the success of a developmental model that has clear implications for the Middle East and other Muslim underdeveloped countries, but also seeks to integrate Azerbaijan into the Soviet system in order to stabilize a strategic border area. Surely it was with some ideological misgivings - or perhaps a touch of irony - that Soviet state-builders decided that it was necessary to create nations in order to level national distinctions in favor of internationalist ones. But the consolidation of Soviet Azerbaijan as a real nation had the added effect of making permanent the amongland distinctions. Without this division - and the institutional structures that the Soviet regime has created to support it - northern Azeri Turks were likely candidates for absorption into a Pan-Turkic configuration of some sort, to remain simply as Turks attached to a modern Turkey.

Relations between the Soviet regime and Soviet Azerbaijan always have been cautious and unique. There have been few purges of national or nationalist leaders since the major purges of the 1930s, which swept away all of the Azerbaijani Muslim national communist leaders. This attack, like the one that the regime launched against the Azerbaijani national epic, Dede Korkut, in 1951 (which signaled the beginning of an official campaign against all Turkic national epics) (17) was accepted by Azeri leaders in a typical Shi'a manner. They offered no resistance, escaping into the tradition of taqiya - the legal right to apostasy - but launched frequent and skillful counterattacks.

These cautious tactics have earned for Azerbaijanis a greater measure of cultural autonomy than other Muslim groups in the USSR. Much of Azeri cultural patrimony has been rehabilitated - in the case of some purged cultural leaders, posthumously. The Azeri language, written in the Cyrillic, has been culled carefully and many words of Russian origin have been excluded. Following Stalin's death in 1953, some quiet attempts were made to reintroduce several Latin letters, logically as a move to bring Azeri Turkish closer to modern Turkish. There is little open Azerbaijani ethnic dissent and almost no substantial nationalist dissent in samizdat.

Like all other Soviet nationalities, whether historic or newly created in accordance with Stalin's formula, Soviet Azerbaijanis (as they now are called) have been subjected to various social engineering schemes in an attempt to speed Azeri integration. The most recent - and perhaps the most far reaching - emerged from the Twenty-first Party Congress in 1961. It is a two-stage formula that featured sblizhenie, their final "merging" (including biological assimilation). This example of Khrushchev's literal-minded Leninism has been under attack for practical and theoretical reasons for many years. Sblizhenie remains in common usage; sliianie has been replaced quietly by a new term meaning "full unity" (polnoe edinstvo), which emphasizes the propensity of nationalities not to "merge" but to retain some of their crucial ethnonational distinctiveness.

Several indicators suggest that Soviet Azerbaijanis have resisted social engineering of this kind better than most Soviet non-Muslims. In the first place, Soviet Azerbaijanis seldom intermarry with other Soviet nationalities and almost never with Russians, despite the efforts of those responsible for propagandizing the benefits of "merging." Admittedly, data on interethnic marriages in the USSR are rare. Generally they focus on the number of mixed marriages by republic, ignoring entirely the precise ethnic mixture of the union. A 1969 study, however, argued that of all major Soviet nationalities, Azerbaijanis probably have the fourth strongest preference for homogeneous marriage, behind the Kirgiz, Kazakhs, and Turkmen - all Muslim peoples. (18) Data from the 1970 Soviet All-Union Census make this argument more concrete. Between 1959 and 1970, Azerbaijan had the lowest increase in the number of mixed marriages by republic (9.85%); it was the second lowest in the number of mixed marriages per thousand in cities (128); and the lowest in the number of mixed marriages per thousand in the countryside (20). These mixed marriages, moreover, could be between non-Azerbaijanis - between Russians and Ukrainians, for example - and most probably are. The number of such marriages that include Azerbaijanis is probably very low.

The use of the Azeri language also is a good indicator of the ability of Azerbaijanis to resist assimilation and russification. Of the languages of the major ethnic groups in the Soviet Union, Azeri Turkish showed the greatest increase between 1959 and 1970 in the percentage of the nationality who claimed it as a first language among all Soviet nationalities, with the exception of the Armenian language. On the other hand, Soviet Azerbaijanis have demonstrated a significant lack of interest in learning Russian as a second language, both in their own republic and in the USSR as a whole; and in this category they rank near the bottom (with several other Muslim nationalities), at about 15 percent who claim fluency in Russian (compared to 36.3 percent of Ukrainians; 45 percent, Latvians; 62.5 percent, Tatars; and 21.3 percent, Georgians).

From 1920 to 1932, an official campaign encouraged the use of Azeri Turkish as an interethnic language in Dagestan and most of the North Caucasus by making its use mandatory in official media and schools. This "azerification" appears to have been quite successful, and it is probably for this reason that the campaign and the use of Azeri in these forums were arrested in the early 1930s. Instead, the northern Caucasus was divided into fourteen separate language regions, with Russian serving as the interethnic lingua franca. The increasing appeal of Azeri Turkish as a first language lends credibility to the observations of a number of non-Azeri Caucasians who insist that Azeri Turkish slowly is making inroads in other Caucasian republics and smaller ethnopolitical units; and that, in time, it could become the lingua franca of the Caucasus. (19) If this is true, it is a trend with a distinct echo in Iranian Azerbaijan, as I shall show.

A third indicator of the resistance of Soviet Azerbaijanis to social engineering from Moscow is the physical cohesiveness of the national unit itself. According to the 1970 census, 86.2 percent of all Soviet Azerbaijanis live in Azerbaijan proper, while another 9.6 percent live in Georgia, Armenia, or Dagestan. A few of the remainder are dispersed in the RSFSR, but the majority can be found in Muslim Central Asian republics. It is highly unlikely, however, that many of these Central Asian Azerbaijanis are Azeri Turks in fact. The now-dissident Meskhetian Turks - a peculiar conglomeration of turkified peoples who formerly lived along the Georgian-Turkish border - were deported to Central Asia in 1944; and in 1968 all of the members of this group received the new national classification of Azerbaijani. (20) As there may be as many as 300,000 to 500,000 Meskhetian Turks - which could account for as much as 10 percent of the entire Azerbaijani population of 4,379,937 - It is safe to assume that most of the "Azerbaijanis" in Central Asia and Kazakhstan are indeed Meskhetian Turks and not Azeri Turks at all. This number easily could constitute the remaining 4 to 5 percent of the Azerbaijani population not accounted for in the republics of Transcaucasia. Thus virtually the entire population of Azeri Turks lives either in its titular republic or in an immediately adjacent national region.

The tightness of this concentration makes implausible the possibility of Azerbaijani out-migration; as these figures show, if he does leave Azerbaijan, the Azerbaijani seldom goes very far. Recently it has been argued that this pattern is likely to change, that Soviet Muslims are likely to migrate out of their national regions. Cultural ties such as Islam, the proponents of this argument contend, are too vaguely defined to be taken into account as potential deterrents to this movement. Modernization pressures, particularly urbanization and the movement of labor from labor surplus to labor deficit areas, trends which have been observed in the West, are a more reliable indicator of the potential for predicting out-migration. (21) Yet, keeping the above indications of Azerbaijani "closeness" in mind, northern Azerbaijan for at least a century has been under the assault of modernizing influences, providing Baku at the time of the Bolshevik revolution with one of the few native proletariats outside of Petrograd and Moscow. Soviet Azerbaijanis, in fact, are one of the most urbanized Soviet nationalities; 41.2 percent of those Azerbaijanis who live in Azerbaijan live in cities (compared to 22.9 percent of Uzbeks in Uzbekistan, 25.5 percent of Tajiks in Tajikistan, 42.7 percent of Georgians in Georgia, and 45.8 percent of Ukrainians in the Ukraine). These modernizing influences seem to have encouraged few Azerbaijanis to migrate away from their traditional homeland. As we have seen, the number of Azerbaijanis living in labor deficit areas of the Soviet Union is negligible.

The cultural influence that is most responsible for this cohesion is Islam and its accompanying social rituals, prohibitions, and sanctions. Soviet Azerbaijanis have come under heavier religious persecution than other Soviet Muslims, probably because Shi'a Islam is a "real church" with an ecclesiastical hierarchy - in the eyes of the regime, a competitor for power and influence. (Sunnism, the religion of most other Soviet Muslims, has no such hierarchy.) The persecution of Shi'a Islam has not proved fatal to its existence however. While "official" Islam has suffered grievously under the Soviets, "unofficial" (or "underground" or "parallel") Islam thrives as never before. An official of the Muslim Directorate in Tashkent told the author during a recent trip to that city that in all of Azerbaijan there were only sixty-five "official" mosques, compared to the thousands that existed before the revolution. But when in Baku some weeks later, the author was told by a young Azerbaijani that there are more than two hundred "unofficial" mosques in that city alone. (22) The continuous Soviet media campaign against "survivals of the past" (meaning Muslim customs, and against the "cult of holy places," which are usually the tombs of important Muslim clerics or martyrs to which thousands of Muslims make regular pilgrimages) suggests that Soviet officials are extremely concerned lest these unbolshevik practices sidetrack or even derail their own sociological tinkering.

Azeri Turks in Iran

Iran is a modernizing state. Under the Shah, it had ambitions to become a world power. Herein lay, prior to 1979 (and perhaps even since then), both the advantage and the dilemma of Azeri Turks who live in Iranian Azerbaijan. On one hand, they are considered to be citizens possessing all of the rights and most of the privileges of citizenship. On the other hand, they must make some important cultural concessions to the modernizing dynamic, to progress defined by the state.

Unlike Soviet policy which is openly centralist and assimilationist, Iran's traditional integrating formula, Shi'a Islam, is only secondarily so for it is assumed that all Shiites possess an essential attachment to a fundamental and formative set of religiocultural ideas. There is no clash between two cultures in which one must give way. The Azeri Turks of Iran, as noted above, always have shared Persian culture and contributed immensely to it. Thus, for Iran's modernizing elites, the problem of Azeri Turks is not one of forcing them to accept an artificial and alien framework for social mobilization, but of mobilizing them within their existing but changing knowledge of the world, leaving behind those retrograde influences which feasibly can be jettisoned and assimilating those which cannot into the processes of change. For Iran's Azeri Turks, who are Shi'a and Persian in culture but ethnically and linguistically Turkic, this translates into an imperative to accept everything Persian even without assimilating ethnically - one culture, one monarchy, one language, and one state religion.

At present there are approximately 4,625,000 Azeri Turks in Iran, or nearly half (48.3 percent) of all Azeri Turks in Iran and the USSR. Unique to Iranian Azerbaijan is the persistence of nomadic tribal units within the Azeri population, divisions that have disappeared in the north as a result of the Soviets' distinctive mobilization techniques. These tribal units include the Sahseven (18,000 to 200,000), the Karadagly (80,000), the Kemgerlu (35,000), the Karapapakh (20,000), and the Qajar (30,000). (23)

Iranian Azeri Turks share equally with Persians in the rights of citizenship. Moreover, all share in certain "survivals of the past" that are forbidden to Soviet Azeri Turks but are upheld by Iranian law which has assimilated the spirit of the state religion. All share equally as well in the fruits of Iran's impressive economic development. Provided that Azeri Turks do not attempt to oppose other cultural influences, such as their Turkic language, to official Iranian culture, they remain free of economic, social, and administrative discrimination. Azeri social and educational mobility are unimpeded; many Azeris have advanced to the upper social and professional classes, as well as into institutes of higher education and professional schools.

Azeri Turks in Iran do pay some cultural costs, however, for sharing in Iran's prosperity. Specifically, the use of literary Azeri Turkish is prohibited in all of Iranian Azerbaijan. This prohibition extends to the press, radio, and other electronic media, and to the schools. Only

Persian is used. (Although it is possible for some Azeris to listen to Soviet internal broadcasts and to the programs of Radio Liberty in their own language, there are no Soviet broadcasts in Azeri Turkish beamed especially at southern Azerbaijan.) Only "Iranian" history is taught, never the local history of Azerbaijan or of Azeri Turks.

Upper-class Azeri Turks generally are bilingual but not bicultural, a psycholinguist's nightmare. Southern Azeri Turks hence must relate to one another and to their larger environment through one culture - which, as we have noted, is perfectly natural for them anyway - but in two languages. And by a curious paradox, in spite of the prohibition on the use of literary Azeri, this language seems to be replacing Persian and other minority languages as the most widely spoken language not only in Azerbaijan but in the surrounding territories as well. Iranian Kurds, for example, also are bilingual, but their competence lies not in Kurdish and Persian, as might be expected, but rather in Kurdish and Azeri. A recent traveler to Iranian Azerbaijan reported to the author that the linguistic "border" between Azeri and Persian now falls at the bilingual town of Kazvin - a mere fifty miles northwest of Tehran.

Unlike the Soviet regime, Iranian leaders do not offer their Azerbaijan even a symbolic modern nationhood. On the other hand, they offer the Azeri Turks of Iran equal participation in the development of the state, religious liberty, access to world and Islamic culture, and increased economic prosperity. Moreover, it can be no secret to these Azeri Turks that the nationhood of their ethnic kin in the Soviet Union is ersatz and that this pretense is accompanied by limited national sovereignty and limited autonomy, strong official antireligious persecution, and diminishing economic potential due to the exhaustion of Baku's oil reserves. Baku boasts a university, many parks and public places, and an academy of sciences named after one of the greatest Azeri Turk writers (who wrote only in Persian), Nizami of Ganja. But Soviet Azerbaijanis lack access to Ganja's works in the original and must settle for cyrillicized translations. Iranian Azeris read the original. Many examples such as this could be offered, but its significance is clear. Soviet Azerbaijanis, despite their nationhood, have been cut off forcibly from their cultural roots, denied access to their real past.

A Border Between Kin: The Meaning
of a Divided Azerbaijan

Borders divide kindred peoples; they separate different cultures and different political systems; they are symbolic lines between different views of the world; and they create and encourage political and social distinctions that, in the absence of a border, might pass unnoticed or cease to exist at all. The border that splits Azerbaijan does all of these things, so profoundly in fact that it is appropriate to distinguish what has been divided artificially and what has been fundamentally changed as a result of the surgery.

For the Azeri Turks of Iran little has changed. The few separatist movements that have sprung up in southern Azerbaijan are of questionable origin, lacking a popular mass appeal or support from the majority of the Azeri people. Each of these movements was a calculated attempt by the Soviet Union to manipulate a prominent Iranian minority in order to extort concessions from the Iranian leadership, concessions that had little or nothing to do with the welfare of the Iranian Azeri people. Each of these movements prospered initially because of Soviet support, including the use of Russian troops; each collapsed quickly once this support was withdrawn. Not that Iranian Azeri Turks are without ethnic grievances, for if this were true, it would make them virtually unique in a world of interethnic relations. It is plausible to think that some of these movements had more limited objectives than outright independence but that they readily took advantage of Soviet offers of assistance, only to find that the Soviets then controlled the movement's lifeline. Nor would it be inappropriate to suggest that Azeri Turks, like other minorities in multinational states, frame their occasional protests as ethnic ones to reap the full measure of supportive public opinion from a world acutely sensitized to pleas for self-determination.

Thus, while Iranian Azeri Turks may at times exert pressure on the center for greater autonomy in their ethnic affairs (for an official status for their language, for example), in general they are well integrated into the mainstream of Iranian politics and culture. Separated from the Azeri Turks of the Soviet Union and from the Turkish secular-modernist trends that influenced northern Azerbaijanis for many decades, the southern Azeri if anything has drawn closer to his cultural brethren and coreligionists in Iran.   There is no current sentiment among Iranian Azeris for reunification with northern Azerbaijan. It is probable that the southern Azeri Turk no longer feels the same fraternal attachment to his kin in the Soviet Union that he once did. The border between them has created some real differences.

Division has strengthened the focal points of Azeri self-identity in both the north and the south, but in accordance with different criteria. In Soviet Azerbaijan, where religion is attacked and practicing Muslims are persecuted, the focal point is language.   Dialectal differences between Azeri and Ottoman Turks have been exaggerated as a result of the rapid change of alphabets in one decade: Arabic to Latin in 1928 and Latin to Cyrillic in 1939. Many Soviet Azerbaijanis seek to reverse these disparities.   In Iranian Azerbaijan, where Azeri Turkish is forbidden as a literary language and no media or schools are permitted to use it in their daily operations, Shi'a Islam is the foundation on which Azeri identity is based.   These different cultural foci point the two Azerbaijans in different directions: the south toward Iran, where Shi'a Islam is the state religion; the north toward Turkey.

Because of these differences, it is difficult to speak of a unified Azeri cultural identity, an identity that spans the border and is embraced by all Azeri Turks equally. There are no specific "Azeri" customs, nor do Soviet or Iranian authorities seem to be willing to suggest any. Both select only those aspects of Azeri history that are in keeping with their goals of inculcating Soviet and Iranian "ways" of development for presentation to students. In the north this means learning about the pre-fifteenth century Shirvanshah state or about the modernist secularism of the late nineteenth and early twentieth centuries; other periods are ignored or presented perjoratively. In the south the contribution of Azeri Turks to the Iranian imperial tradition is extolled, especially the periods of the Safavids and the Qajars. Many educated or inquisitive Soviet Azeri Turks know of that part of their past which is hidden from them officially, and it certainly is true that Iranian Azeri Turks know well the hardships and successes of their ethnic kin under the tsars and the Soviets. Yet it is impossible to judge how much of a common tradition is preserved in minds when history books ignore it. While Soviet Azeri Turks by no means have assimilated Soviet culture, the failure of Soviet nation builders to cut off ancient peoples from their historical-cultural legacies should not be taken for granted.

Ultimately we are faced with the semantic dilemma of determining just what it was that the border split: a nation - in the modern sense of the term - or simply an ethnic group lacking a strong self-identity as a nation? It is unlikely that the entire Azerbaijan, both north and south, could be considered to be one nation by modern criteria before the Bolshevik seizure of power. In some respects, this was a traditional north-south dichotomy and it begs some cautious comparisons with North and South Vietnam before 1960. They were both separated by the ungovernable placement of natural resources; different patterns, processes, and paces of development that this placement helped to determine; and the different political inclinations and movements that to a large degree were functions of these distinct environments. By the time the Soviet-Iranian border was a fact, both halves of Azerbaijan had been mobilized around different themes, but the mobilization of the northern population around Turkish related themes was particularly intense. While the south remained closely tied to the Iranian state, Shi'a Islam, and Persian culture, the northern population was in the throes of profound social change, moving closer toward a rapprochement with Sunni Islam, a central role in the political activities of Russia's Muslims, and the nationalist-modernist fervor of a dynamic Turkey.

The drawing and sealing of the border, then, split an ethnic group that had not consolidated into a single nation. But this rending forced the consolidation of a nation out of half a people in the north. The act of separation caused many northern Azeri Turks to understand that, while ethnically similar, they differed spiritually from the Azeri Turks in the south; moreover, they were entirely different from the Russian, Georgian, Armenian, and Jewish Bolsheviks who now sought to determine their fate. The drawing of the border added new urgency to two separate but interrelated processes of identification: that of establishing northern Azeri Turks as different from the Azeri Turks in the south, and that of distinguishing the northerners as a distinct nation among the diverse peoples of the Caucasus. Second, because Soviet nationality policy paradoxically called simultaneously for the creation of Soviet "nations" and for the homogenization of all Soviet citizens into a nationally amorphous mass of "new Soviet men," Soviet Azerbaijanis could benefit by supporting the institutions that the new Soviet regime had created to accommodate the Azerbaijani nation, regardless how artificial these props might be. Real Azerbaijani national institutions and structures had not yet come into being, but the ground for the required psychological transformation to nationhood already had been well prepared.

The mobilization of Soviet Azerbaijanis toward Turkey has continued slowly under Soviet rule. They have not become amalgamated into the "Soviet people," and it appears unlikely that they will move in that direction. It might be said that Soviet Azerbaijanis have not yet mobilized into anything; their energies are still to be assigned. It is this potential reassignment which should interest the specialist of this Soviet-Asian ethnic frontier.

Soviet Azerbaijanis in a sense are the elite of Soviet Muslims because their exposure to non-Soviet social, political, and developmental traditions probably is greater than that of other Soviet Muslims. They are surrounded by dynamic peoples with strong traditions of nationalism and statehood - Georgians, Armenians, Turks, Iranians - and by politically active minorities such as the Kurds. It can be expected that some of these groups will have affected them, for the history of nationalisms in the Caucasus is long and bloody. The possibility of becoming infected by nationalism in this region - especially in the face of overwhelming odds - always has been very great.

In addition, economic and social pressures which Azeri Turks have not confronted previously will strain their relationship with the Russian center in the next several decades. Azerbaijan's oil is now considerably depleted, and the jobs and services which an oil-based economy provided for a significant number of Azeri Turks must necessarily decline in the absence of other economic increments of this magnitude. (24) Like the Muslim republics of Soviet Central Asia, Azerbaijan has fallen far behind the state average of per capita national income (-43 percent) and per capita industrial production (-53 percent). Moreover, these gaps have grown wider in the last two decades, not smaller, as the Azeri birth rate has increased. Large surpluses of redundant or underemployed workers can be found throughout rural Azerbaijan, forcing the regime to encourage faster rural-urban migration within the republic and, failing in this (as has been the rule in Muslim Central Asia), to contemplate more rapid regional development. The problems of economic slowdown, insufficient investment, labor redundancy, high birth rate, and rural-urban migration are closely interrelated. Therefore the regime will have to measure carefully the obvious policy tradeoffs for dealing with these issues if it is to avoid creating an environment in which the resulting demands and dislocations assume a (largely anti-Russian) momentum of their own.

The anti-Shah, conservative Shiite take-over in Iran in 1979 poses a special problem for the Soviet leadership and for Soviet Azeris. From the regime's vantage point, this religious victory has a potential resonance in Soviet Azerbaijan. (25) As a result, official Soviet reportage in the Azerbaijan regional media of events in Iran is filtered through the Soviet news agency TASS, which selects, edits, and disseminates news items to the Soviet population in accordance with rigid guidelines established in Moscow. Thus, in the fall of 1978, the protests in Iran were described in Bakinskii rabochi (via TASS) primarily as mass worker demonstrations for social and economic reform and independence from the United States. Almost incidentally, it was noted that some of the opposition leaders were Muslim mullahs and that the demonstrations had a slight religious tinge. In all cases, religious opposition was reported as an adjunct to a more progressive "united national front."

For the Soviet Azeri Turk in Baku or Kirovbad - who undoubtedly learned of the events in Iran and the conservative muslim movement behind them even without official Soviet media acknowledgment - the demonstrations must pose a more complex and troubling dilemma. It is unclear at this point how Soviet Azeris respond to these general entreaties, whether they view events in Iran as antithetical to their long tradition of Islamic modernism, or whether they feel like kindred spirits to their beleaguered Shiite brothers. For them, Shah Mohammad Reza Pahlavi may be the same obnoxious presence he is to Ayatollah Ruhollah Khomeini, but this would require some intense soul searching, if not a touch of duplicity. It is worth remembering that the Shah's trip to Baku in 1956 was cheered wildly by Soviet Azeri Turks who at that time - and perhaps now - viewed him as a symbol of something quite different. Therefore, while it is possible that the resurgence of conservative Islam in Iran and elsewhere may infect Soviet Azeri Turks, it is also possible that this revival may serve to differentiate more clearly their special place in the Muslim world, that is to isolate them, thereby speeding their mobilization in other directions.

At this stage we cannot know with any certainty what these other directions might be. However, it is worth speculating that ethnicity might prove the better of religion in this case. A number of factors suggest that Soviet Azeri Turks are now seeing, and will continue to see, Turkey in a more favorable light. Moreover, Turks now number some 110 million in all Turkic states, including the Soviet Union. Within a few decades, they will become 200 million. That Turks once more are speaking about the spiritual unity of the Turkic world is not surprising under these conditions. Where the Azeri Turks of the Soviet Union fit into this world is yet to be decided, but the attraction is there nevertheless. Their "reassignment," in fact, could begin sheerly by an attraction to numbers.

NOTES

(1) Richard N. Frye, Iran (New York, 1953), p. 53.

(2) Ibid., p. 21.

(3) Seyyed Hassan Taqizadeh, "Document: The Background of the
Constitutional Movement in Azerbaijan," Middle East Journal 14, no.
4 (1960): 461.

(4) Ibid., p. 462.

(5) Kurban Said, Ali and Nino (New York, 1972), p. 74.

(6) Ibid.

(7) For a complete account of the ideology and political activities of
the Muslim national communists see, Alexandre Bennigsen and S.
Enders Wimbush, Muslim National Communism in the Soviet Union:
A Revolutionary Strategy for the Colonial World. (Chicago, 1979).

(8) Sultan Galiev, "Kobiavlenii Azerbaidzhanskoi Sovetskoi Respub-
liki," Zhizn' natsional'nosti, April 9, 1920.

(9) In a letter of Narimanov, quoted in Bor'ba za pobedu sovetskoi
vlasti v Azerbaidzhane 1918-20 (Baku, 1967), p. 20.

(10) Ervand Abrahamian, "Communism and Communalism in Iran: The
Tudeh and the Firqah-e Dimukrat," International Journal of Middle
East Studies 1, no. 4 (1970): 315. But cf. Frye, Iran, p. 85.

(11) Rouhollah K. Ramazani, Iran's Foreign Policy 1941-1973
(Charlottesville, Va., 1975), p. 114.

(12) Edwin Muller, "Behind the Scenes in Azerbaijan," American
Mercury 62, no. 270 (1946): 696-703.

(13) Ibid.

(14) Robert Rossow, Jr., "The Battle of Azerbaijan," Middle East
Journal 10, no. 1 (1956): 18.

(15) Frye, Iran, p. 82.

(16) Ibid., pp. 85-86.

(17) See Alexandre A. Bennigsen, "The Crisis of the Turkic National
Epics, 1951-1952: Local Nationalism or Proletarian Internationalism?" Canadian Slavonic Papers 22, no. 2-3 (1975): 463-474.

(18) L.V. Chuiko, Braki i razvody (Moscow, 1975), p. 76.

(19) Observations made independently to the author by several non-
Azeri Caucasians in Georgia, Armenia, and Azerbaijan (1976).

(20) See S. Enders Wimbush and Ronald Wixman, "The Meskhetian

Turks: A New Voice in Soviet Central Asia," Canadian Slavonic Papers 17, no. 2-3 (1975): 320-340.

(21) Robert A. Lewis, Richard H. Rowland, and Ralph S. Clem, Nationality and Population Change in Russia and the U.S.S.R. (New York, 1976), pp. 354-381.

(22) For a complete discussion of "unofficial" Islam see Alexandre Bennigsen and S. Enders Wimbush, "Muslim Religious Dissent in the U.S.S.R.," in James P. Scanlan and Richard T. DeGeorge, eds., Marxism and Religion in Eastern Europe (Dordrecht, Holland and Boston, Mass., 1976), pp. 133-146.

(23) Turk Dunyasi El Kitabi (Ankara, 1976), pp. 1114-1119.

(24) According to recent figures compiled by the Foreign Demographic Analysis Division of the Bureau of Economic Analysis, U.S. Department of Commerce, per capita new fixed investment in Azerbaijan also has been drastically curtailed since 1961. By 1975, this investment had increased only twenty-five percent - higher only than the per capita new fixed investment in Tadzhikistan - compared to a general increase of fifty percent or more in nearly every other Soviet republic.

(25) See New York Times, November 23, 1978, p. A2; Los Angeles Times, November 30, 1978, p. 7.

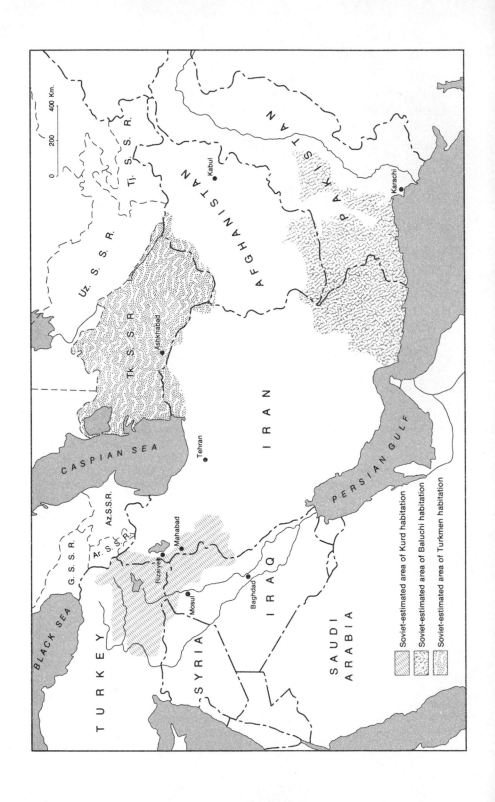

4 The Iranian Frontier Nationalities: The Kurds, the Assyrians, the Baluchis, and the Turkmens

Eden Naby

Straddling the frontiers between Iran and the Soviet Union are a number of ethnic populations, and the Azeris and Armenians discussed elsewhere in this volume are but two of them. Kurds and Assyrians, mainly along the Caucasian border, and Turkmens and Baluchis along the Transcaspian borders together with Persians on both sides of the Caspian, lend the entire frontier a heterogeneous character. (1) In addition, Iran shares some of these ethnic populations with its other neighbors, Iraq, Afghanistan, Turkey and Pakistan. Often in the historic past these peoples have played a critical role in Iranian politics, and as recently as 1944 to 1946 several of them, alongside the Azeris, were manipulated by the Soviet Union in an effort to dismember Iran. Potentially they drew Iran into ethnic conflicts virtually anywhere in the Middle East. This chapter will investigate whether, and to what extent, four of these ethnic populations actually present political problems to the states in which they dwell.

Demographic data about these peoples are hard to find and unreliable (see table 4.1). Iranian census data, for example, mask ethnic heterogeneity under Muslim homogeneity; religious designation in place of linguistic and ethnic identification results in a distortion of the multiethnic nature of the population. Other countries of the Middle East (especially Turkey) indulge in politically motivated engineering of census methods. Afghanistan has yet to complete a modern census. There are great difficulties in achieving uniformity in statistics from countries so diverse as Syria, Turkey, Iraq, Iran, Afghanistan, Pakistan, and the Soviet Union.

Even Soviet statistics are questionable with reference to small ethnic groups such as those discussed here. While recognized as nationalities in the Soviet system, the Kurds, the Assyrians, and the Baluchis are too small to warrant their enjoying territoriality and live in republics dominated by large ethnic groups anxious to guard against any threat to their exclusive control in their republics. In Armenia,

Table 4.1. Population Estimates

	Kurds	Assyrians	Balushis	Turkmėns
USSR (a)	88,930	24,294	12,582	1,525,284
Iran (b)	2,000,000	70,000	600,000	500,000
Afghanistan (c)	--	--	40,000	400,000
Pakistan (d)	--	--	1,000,000	--
Turkey (e)	3,200,000	60,000	--	300,000
Iraq (f)	1,500,000	200,000	--	500,000
Syria-Lebanon (g)	350,000	70,000	--	--
Totals	7,138,930	424,294	1,652,582	3,225,284

(a) Ts.S.U., Itogi vsesoiunznoi perepisi naseleniia 1970 goda (Moscow, 1973), Table 7.

(b) Kurdish nationalists include in the Iranian Kurdish figures Lur
and Bakhtiari tribes that live in or near Kurdish regions but speak
Iranian languages or dialects other than Kurdish. The figures given
here are based on Soviet estimates appearing in Sovremennyi Iran:
Spravochnik (Moscow, 1975), pp. 37-40.

(c) Baluchi estimates appear in Vartan Gregorian's The Emergence o'
Modern Afghanistan (Stanford, 1969), p. 37. Max Klimburg places the
Turkmen population of Afghanistan at the high estimate given here.
See Afghanistan: Das Land im Historischen Spannungsfeld Mittelasie
(Vienna, 1966), p. 126.

(d) A. Rashid, Census of Pakistan Population 1961 (Karachi, n.d.),
vol. I, Table 5.1.

(e) Martin Short and Anthony McDermott, "The Kurds," Minority Grou
Rights, Report No. 23 (1977), p. 6. Assyrians in Turkey are compos
mainly of Jacobite communities in the southeast and in Istanbul. T
figure given here is based on estimates made by Assyrians from that
region and communicated to the writer orally. Turkmen estimates ar
based on figures stated by Turkmens.

(f) Short and McDermott, "The Kurds," p. 6. Soviet estimates of
Turkmen populations are only a fraction of those cited by Turkmens
of Iraq. The Soviets now appear to estimate only about 100,000 in
Iraq. See "Turkmeny," Bol'shaia Sovetskaia Etnsiklopedia 26 (1977)
1091.

(g) Short and McDermott, "The Kurds," p. 6. Assyrian estimates ar
those made by indigenous people.

Georgia, and Soviet Azerbaijan the Assyrians and Kurds are subject to pressure from census takers and the society at large to consider themselves members of the major ethnic group. Many succumb, since belonging to the larger group entitles them to certain social and legal advantages. As a result, Soviet Kurds today officially number barely 100,000, although they are estimated by experts to be three times that number. (2) In using Soviet demographic data, moreover, one must take into account periodic shifts in borders and modifications in the kinds of groups that are recognized for census purposes. For example, the 1926 Soviet census recognized several religious groups such as the Yezidis (members of a Kurdish-speaking heretical non-Muslim sect), which in later censuses are hidden, in this case under the ethnic grouping Kurds.

The total number of Kurds is simply unknown. They are the largest group discussed here and they dwell in a historic homeland now divided between Syria, Turkey, Iran, Iraq, and the Soviet Union. Estimates of their total population vary from the Iraqi government minimum of 5.7 million to the nationalist maximum of 16.5 million.

The Assyrians live in the same general region as the Kurds but since World War I have had a diaspora in the West as well. The world Assyrian population is probably about one million. The Turkmens live primarily in Soviet Central Asia in their own Republic of Turkmenistan, but are also scattered in Iran, Afghanistan, Turkey, and Iraq. Their world pupulation numbers about three million. The Baluchis are the most compact of these people, dwelling primarily in their historic homeland, Baluchistan, now divided between Iran, Pakistan, and Afghanistan, although some Baluchis have migrated to the Soviet Union. The world Baluchi population may hover around the Soviet estimate of a little over two million. (3)

The Kurds, a rapidly growing people both inside the Soviet Union and outside, may be ranked alongside the Palestinians as a major potential disruptive force for almost all of the Middle Eastern states. The Assyrians, the Turkmens, and the Baluchis, though fewer in number, may each objectively be judged suitable material for outsiders meddling in Soviet affairs or Soviet meddling in the outside world. The following pages will examine whether these opportunities are being used or not at the present time.

KURDS

The Kurds for centuries have had to deal with a frontier between the Persian and Ottoman empires, but the fragmentation that affects them today began with the nineteenth century Russian invasion into the Transcaucasus and to a lesser extent, into Transcaspia. As a result of the Turkmanchai Treaty of 1828, Iran lost to Russia all of its lands north of the Arax river. This rearrangement of frontiers separated the Kurds of the Ganja area from those remaining in Iran. Other

Transcaucasian Kurds came under Russian rule following Russo-Ottoman struggles. Still others fled to Russian territory from Turkey during and after the First World War, as unsuccessful Kurdish tribal rebellions produced refugees. Kurdish Yezidis, non-Muslim "devil-worshipers" presently living in the Yerevan region of Soviet Armenia, appear to have sought shelter in Russia from Ottoman religious persecution in the nineteenth century. (4)

In Transcaspia Kurdish tribes, smaller in number and differing from the main body of Kurds by reason of their espousal of Shi'a rather than Sunni Islam, are chiefly descendants of march lords relocated to Transcaspia by various Safavid rulers of Iran to guard Iran's Central Asian frontiers from incursions by Sunni Uzbeks and Turkmens. For centuries these Kurds led a semiautonomous existence, carving out small khanates. The Russo-Iranian border demarcation of 1893 cut through these khanates, leaving some Kurds in Persian territory and others in what has become Soviet Turkmenistan. (5)

But it was the Middle Eastern settlement after World War I that effectively divided the heartland of the Kurdish tribal territory. First the victorious Allies made great promises of a homeland to the Kurds in the Treaty of Sevres (1920). Then under Turkish Republican pressure they completely abrogated those obligations in the Treaty of Lausanne (1923). Kurdish struggles in the Middle East since the 1920s, whether or not instigated by outsiders, have focused on the issue of autonomy or independence for the homeland, which was partitioned then between the Ottoman successor states with practically no regard for ethnic self-determination at all.

The life of Mulla Mustafa Barzani well illustrates the vicissitudes of Kurdish fortune since the disappointment of Lausanne. Born in 1898, the second son of the ruling family of the powerful Barzan tribe, General Barzani grew up in the tribal atmosphere of northern Iraq. Like other Kurdish tribes, the Barzans were often involved in intertribal feuds, which foreclosed the possibility of united action among the tribes. While the General did not hold the leadership position of his tribe, his military nature drew many fighters to him. These he eventually led to Iran where chances for Kurdish autonomy seemed bright in 1945, when Soviet troops occupying northern Iran were sponsoring autonomous or independent ethnic republics on Iranian soil. Barzani became the head of the military arm of the Kurdish Republic, whose center was at Mahabad. In 1946, when Soviet troops withdrew from Iran under political pressure, the Azeri and Kurdish puppet states they had set up both collapsed. (6) Barzani escaped the debacle, and together with about 500 of his followers wound his way through the border mountains separating Iran, Iraq, and Turkey into Soviet Azerbaijan. He spent the next twelve years in a suburb of Baku.

Barzani returned to Iraq in 1958 when the Kassem coup brought an end to the monarchy there, gave amnesty to political dissidents, and promised to increase minority rights. Tribal elements under Barzani, in concert with the more urbanized Iraqi Kurds who had strong leanings toward Moscow, gradually came into conflict with the Kassem regime. In 1961 an open struggle ensued with Barzani at its head, and until 1963, when Kassem was overthrown, Kurdish rebels found sympathetic attention from the Soviets. There were two reasons for this: first, the suppression of the Iraqi communist party by the Kassem regime; and second, the belief that Kurdish rebels could be controlled by Moscow through Barzani and other Kurds who might see Moscow as their only source of aid. In addition, Kurdish autonomy offered the possibility for Soviet influence in the oil-rich region of Kirkuk, a major city in an area of Iraq where Kurds claim to predominate.

In 1963, however, the Ba'ath party reversed the Iraqi state's position regarding the indigenous communist party and also increased the opportunity for the communist party to participate in the Revolution Command Council, the country's decision-making body. Given the opportunity to exercise power in Baghdad, Moscow gradually abandoned its pro-Kurdish position. Barzani coincidentally eliminated the communists from his Kurdistan Democratic Party (KDP) and now sought and received support from Iran. The Kurds continued the struggle to gain the equivalent of nationality status within Iraq and to be recognized worldwide as a distinct ethnic group. (7)

Barzani's battle reached a high point in 1970 when the ruling Ba'athist party of Iraq agreed to a truce and granted on paper very considerable minority rights to the Kurds. Four years later, when the central government unilaterally issued the Law for Autonomy in the Area of Kurdistan, Barzani rejected the Law because it fell short of the autonomy promised in 1970 and excluded Kirkuk from the areas designated as Kurdish. Armed rebellion resumed in 1974. In 1975 at Algiers, the Iranians decided to end their differences with Iraq and entered an agreement regulating Shi'ite pilgrimages and water rights at the Shatt al-Arab and other sites in Iraq. Barzani now lost Tehran's support and his rebellion collapsed. Since Iran may even have threatened to help Iraq quell the fighting, the Kurds were not in a position to negotiate truce terms with Baghdad as they had in 1970. (8) With the Turkish border closed to them, the Syrians unwilling to support them, and the Soviet Union allegedly master-minding the final assault into Kurdistan in 1975, the Kurds lost all the territorial gains they had achieved. Barzani himself initially sought refuge in Iran, but finding the atmosphere there not encouraging, he and splinter sections of the Kurdish autonomy movement established themselves in the West. He died in Washington, D.C., on March 4, 1979. His body was flown to Iranian Kurdistan for burial.

Barzani's activities, since World War II, capsulize the full circle that Kurdish independence movements have taken. From total dependence on the Soviet Union in 1945 and 1946, the Kurdish autonomous movement has come to rely on the Western powers for support.

The Kurds in Iraq

The situation of the Kurds in Iraq brings to light with particular force the dilemmas facing the Kurdish nation today. Although fewer in number than the Kurds of Iran and Turkey, the Kurds of Iraq have one fundamental advantage: they form a far larger proportion of the overall population in that country than they do elsewhere. For this reason, the League of Nations twice (in 1925 and 1932) insisted on regard for Kurdish cultural and regional rights in Iraq. And for this reason also the Kassem constitution of 1958 stated that "Arabs and Kurds are partners in this homeland," and the 1970 Peace Agreement between the Kurds and the Ba'athist government recognized the binational character of Iraq. (9) The demographic strength of the Kurds explains also why Iraq has had so little success in the past in pursuing assimilationist policies such as those of Turkey and Iran. Even with its present relatively stronger central government, and isolation of the Kurds in Iraq from outside sources of support, Iraq will have difficulty effectively dismantling the tribal structure and allegiances of the Kurdish population, restricting absolutely the use of the Kurdish language, resettling the Kurds massively outside their traditional homeland, and reducing their influence in northern Iraq.

Yet if the sheer number of the Iraqi Kurds gains them a relative autonomy, it cannot force the Baghdad government to give them in practice the rights it grants on paper; and this is not to mention the full benefit of the revenues from the oil exported from Kurdistan. According to the peace agreement of 1970, the Kurds are a nationality recognized under the law. (10) Further, the agreement provided for the Kurdish language to have equal status with Arabic throughout the country with one or the other being the language of instruction and the other a secondary language depending on the make-up of the population. A Kurdish-language university was to be established. Politically, the Kurds were to have responsibility in their own regions for elections, education, health and local affairs, representation in the central government proportional to their population, and their own political organization and newspapers. In addition, it was agreed that a Kurd would serve as one of the vice-presidents of the country. Economic agreements concerned compensation for war victims, the allocation of special funds (separately administered) for Kurdish regional development, equal development for Kurdish areas with the rest of Iraq, and the application of the Agrarian Reform Law to Kurdish areas in order to liquidate "feudalist relations." Direct mention of the oil fields and the control of the oil industry in regions substantially or predominantly Kurdish was omitted. The intent of the peace agreement was understood by the Kurds as offering them autonomy within Iraq, a position short of the hopes of some Kurdish circles outside Iraq, but agreeable to General Barzani and his followers.

The Baghdad government claimed in 1974 that it fulfilled the provisions of the 1970 agreement through the Law for Autonomy in the

Area of Kurdistan. (11) In fact, the Law fell far short in several crucial areas and granted Kurds a semi-autonomy without equal status for their culture and language in Iraq.   Politically, the Kurdish institutions described were to a considerable extent subservient to the central government and highly controlled.   No provisions were made for a Kurdish vice-president for the Republic of Iraq and few opportunities are available under this law for the Kurds as a nationality group to influence the Baghdad government. Most objectionable to the KDP was the unilateral decision by Baghdad to base the area of Kurdistan on the 1957 census which grossly undercounted the Kurds. Even before the law was announced, the KDP complained to Soviet representatives that Baghdad appeared to be reluctant to implement, at the minimum, the cultural and economic promises of 1970. (12) Yet no avenue appeared open to the Kurds in 1974 other than rejecting the law imposed by the Ba'athist government. With the abrupt termination of Iranian support, the Kurds for now have lost the opportunity to advance claims in Iraq unless they do so as part of a new Kurdish movement spanning political boundaries with Turkey and Iran. Major disturbance of the stability in either of these states may allow Kurds in Iraq to put forth their demands once again.

The greatest substantive gains of the Kurds' long struggle in Iraq lie in the area of cultural rights. For example, a new university has been established at Suleimaniyeh, in the heart of the Kurdish region. "When possible" it will conduct its teaching and administration in the Kurdish language.   There is also a Kurdish academy at Baghdad, originally projected in the 1950s under the monarchy, but evidently operating only after 1970. Kurdish newspapers and scholarly publications are printed and distributed in Kurdish towns. To counter this, however, Baghdad is actively pursuing the arabization of key cities such as Kirkuk; and it is forcibly resettling Kurdish refugees returning from Iran in southern Iraq rather than permitting them to live in the Kurdish regions of the north.

On paper the nationality policy of Iraq approaches that of the Soviet Union regarding major minorities such as the Ukrainians and the Uzbeks. Indeed there is some ground for believing that Baghdad's policy has evolved under Moscow's tutelage.   Speaking in 1975, Premier Kosygin referred to the USSR's "wealth of experience" with its own Leninist nationality policy and said that Iraq could always be sure of "a deep understanding among Soviet people of a policy directed to the democratic solution of the national question, and to ensuring not only the legal but also the actual equality of nationalities." (13) In deleting from the 1974 law any provision for Kurds as a nationality to exercise power in the central government, the Iraqis have shifted even closer to the Soviet nationality model than the 1970 peace agreement had generously promised. In practice one must admit that the situation of the Kurds in Iraq is far weaker today than ever before. Nevertheless, given the severity with which neighboring countries deal with any sign of Kurdish agitation for the most elementary ethnic rights, the Iraqi policy still is noteworthy for its liberality.

The Kurds in Iran

Unlike other minorities in Iran, Kurds hold a special fascination for Iranian intellectuals, chiefly because the renewed emphasis by the Pahlavi regime (1925-1979) on Iran's pre-Islamic past has strengthened Kurdish claims to being descendants of the Medes and therefore, together with the Persians, to being Iranian in culture. Linguistically, moreover, Persian and Kurdish, though not mutually intelligible, are closely linked and are perhaps as alike as Russian is to Polish. On the other hand, most Iranian Kurds differ from Persians by religious affiliation: they are either of the Sunni or Ahl-e Haq persuasion, while Persians (and Azeris) are followers of the Twelver Shi'ite sect of Islam. But, of all the states among which they have been divided, the Kurds have a closer cultural affinity with the Persians than with any other people.

Despite the special historical and linguistic relationship that links Persians and Kurds, the Iranian government has regarded its Kurdish minority with suspicion in view of their participation in the pro-Soviet Mahabad Republic. These suspicions have been refueled recently by Kurdish autonomy demands following the disintegration of central authority in the winter of 1979. Basically, Kurds in Iran have shared the same position as other Muslim minorities: they are recognized but not counted, allowed to speak their language but not to propagate it through schools or publishing. The Iranian policy aims at assimilation of all minorities into an Iranian identity. Under the Shah, Kurds enjoyed no particular privileges in terms of government representation (unlike the Armenians, Assyrians, Zoroastrians, and Jews) or territorial recognition. The Iranian province called Kurdistan includes only part of the area in which Kurds live. Like the province called Baluchistan, and the two bearing the name Azerbaijan (East and West), the appellation implies no nationality privilege as is the case for Soviet eponymous republics. The only Kurdish language organ circulated widely by Iranians is Choewar Chera (Four Lights), a leftist newspaper issued by the Confederation of Iranian Students in West Germany. (14)

The position of Kurds in Iran has been considerably affected by events in Iraq, however, particularly since the outbreak of fighting there in 1961. While continuing to exercise strict control over its own large Kurdish population, Iran supported the Kurdish rebellion in Iraq, perhaps hoping to gain territorial concessions near its vital oil-rich areas in the south. This led to lasting changes. For example, in the propaganda war against Iraq, Iran used its own Kurdish nationals to encourage Kurdish fighting through media broadcasts. The resulting Kurdish-language radio and occasional television programming continue in Iran today, although the message sent has been altered to suit Tehran's formula for propaganda to its own Kurds. The national Iranian radio broadcasts a total of 26 hours a week of Kurdish cultural materials and Kurdish-language news from Rizaiyeh and other towns with large Kurdish populations. This number of hours appears large when compared with Azeri-language broadcasts presumably serving a larger population.

Iran also aided the Kurdish rebellion by allowing men, military equipment, food and medical supplies, and refugees to traverse its borders with Iraq. Moreover, while large-scale involvement of Iranian Kurds in the fighting in Iraq appears to have been prevented by Iran, the government did not prevent sympathetic tribesmen from contributing financially to the revolt. (15) Hospitals in Iranian towns adjacent to northern Iraq treated civilian and military personnel from across the border. Most of the arms and ammunition bought by the Iraqi Kurds passed to them across the Iranian frontiers. Iranian artillery support played a key role in countering the heavy arms and war planes put into the field by Iraq against the Kurds. Finally, it is estimated that about 250,000 Kurdish refugees fled to Iran, particularly during the last year of fighting. Rather than continuing to care for these Kurdish refugees, Iran has urged them since 1975 to accept Iraqi amnesty. Rations to refugees were halved after 1975 and those who did not return to Iraq (numbering about 40,000) have been relocated to widely dispersed areas of Iran.

But while withdrawing aid from Iraqi Kurds, Iran in the past has allowed a few concessions, even cultural ones, for its own Kurds. Although Kurdish language publications were prohibited in the country, the rule was intermittently enforced in the case of nonpolitical poetry or religious materials distributed locally in Kurdish areas. A few scholarly materials such as dictionaries of Kurdish appeared for wider distribution. Under the monarchy, Kurdish-language schools, like other ethnic Muslim schools of a secular nature, were prohibited, but in predominantly Kurdish areas the stricture against use of the Kurdish language in schools was not, and could not be, effectively enforced. The results of the strict "Iranization" policy enforced under the Pahlavis was twofold. First, some Kurds were attracted into government and cultural circles, thus reducing the ranks of traditional Kurdish leadership. Second, the larger group of traditionally attached Kurds, even when settled in villages close to the urban areas, harbored resentment for the cultural and political restrictions placed upon them. This resentment flared into opposition to the Shah during 1978 in conjunction with other anti-Shah forces. Later, during March of 1979, aspirations for autonomy led to armed revolt against the provisional government controlled by Ayatollah Ruhullah Khomeini. The truce negotiated with the Kurds may prove fragile if the new Iranian constitution offers only cultural concessions (bilingual schools) and not the substantial economic and political autonomy for the Kurds in their own regions.

The Kurds in Turkey and Syria

In contrast to Iraqi and Iranian treatment of Kurdish minorities, the Turks have dealt with potential problems created by Kurds by denying their existence as a distinct ethnic minority. Turkey chooses to call Kurds "Mountain Turks" and the constitution bans the espousal of minority causes by political parties, thus making it difficult for the Kurds to be politically organized or heard through an established party. Paralleling the Uzbek attitude toward Tajiks of Central Asia, Turks claim that Kurds were merely Turks who have forgotten their native Turkish language because they have dwelt in the remote mountains of the east.

This attitude has thawed at times, for example during the mid-sixties. During the thaw, some Kurdish-language publications appeared (in the Roman alphabet) and initial steps were taken toward organizing Kurdology in academic institutions. A reversal occurred in 1970 when it appeared that Iraqi Kurds had gained concessions and that Kurds in Turkey might be infected with the same desires for autonomy and cultural expression. Since 1971, when Kurds became involved in Turkey's political unrest, Turkey's borders with Iraq have been closed and mined to prevent the entrance of refugees or guerrillas. (16) In 1975 many Kurds, hard pressed by Baghdad's army, died trying to cross this border. More recently, Kurds who managed to cross the border have been returned to Iraq. The Turks have signed no agreement regulating seasonal migration of tribesmen over their border with Iran. Kurdish cultural expression, Kurdish political organizations, and any form of aid to Kurdish rebels in Iraq are prohibited.

During the present (1979) Turkish political disruptions, Turkey's eastern provinces, some of which are about 80 percent Kurdish, have been especially susceptible to bloody clashes between rightist and leftist groups. Complicating the political picture is the demand for autonomy put forward by Kurds in the towns and in mountain hideouts. Thus far only the Maoist political faction in Turkey favors Kurdish autonomy while the leftist group, which is pro-Soviet, regards the Kurdish problem as one that should be solved as part of the general socioeconomic realignment of Turkey. Allegations of foreign agitation among the Kurds are rife. (17) Iraqi-Turkish relations cooled during 1978, partially at least, because of the Iraqi feeling that Turkey could have taken firmer action to control Kurdish fighting within its border. In southeast Turkey remnants of pro-Barzani tribal elements have clashed with Iraq-based pro-Soviet Kurdish groups whose leadership has over the past decade formed the core of the communist Kurds. Many Turks suspect that their rebellious Kurds receive encouragement from Moscow through these Iraqi Kurds.

Aside from their minority position as an ethno-linguistic group, the Turkish Kurds also form the chief component of the Shiite population of Turkey. Many belong to the Ahl-e Haq (or Ali Ilahi) sect of Shiism and are identified by other Turks generally as "Alavis," a name which is extended in popular usage to include all Shiites. Therefore the alignment of extreme leftist and Alavis against rightists and, adversely, Sunnites springs to a major extent from the suppression, isolation and alienation of Turkey's Kurds. To prevent the spread of Kurdish resurgence following Kurdish autonomy demands in Iran during April 1979, Turkey and Iraq hastily agreed to cooperate in suppressing Kurdish separatism in their adjacent border areas. This is yet another event proving the Kurdish nationalist motto, "Kurds have not friends."

The Syrian attitude toward the Kurds seems to be similar to the Iranian one - that the best way to improve the position of the Kurds is to assimilate them into the national milieu, in this case an Arab one. Unlike the Iranians, the Syrians have attempted to relocate Kurds away from traditional areas adjacent to Turkey and Iraq in order to minimize the likelihood of parts of Syria being incorporated into a greater Kurdistan. Syrian animosity toward Iraq, when a factor, could potentially lead to greater support for the Iraqi Kurdish dissidents, but at present the chances seem slight for such involvement.

The political organizations among Turkish Kurds espouse social reform and nationalism and often ally themselves with other groups that call for reforms in government to improve the lot of all citizens, not just minorities. This position is consistent with the demands of the moderate faction of the KDP in Iraq as well. Since in Turkey Kurds live in underdeveloped, yet minerally rich areas that are exploited by the central government without benefiting indigenous Kurds, part of the appeal of the underground Kurdistan Democratic Party is based on advocacy of Kurdish economic rights. The aims of the Kurdistan Democratic Party in Syria, where it is legal, are similar to those in Turkey.

Nationalistic Kurds have sometimes entertained exaggerated notions that their homeland should stretch from the Mediterranean Sea through Syria to northern Iraq, eastern Turkey, western Iran, and a small portion of Soviet Azerbaijan. (18) Others are much less radical. But all have had to face a single unpalatable fact. No Middle Eastern state has been willing to grant the Kurds actual cultural autonomy, lest demands by other ethnic groups for similar autonomy lead to disintegration of their as yet fragile cultural identity. The existing states fear also that any concessions to Kurdish minorities could lead to separatist claims and attempts for a unified Kurdistan. The Kurds receive political aid from existing states only as long as these states see Kurdish agitation as beneficial to their own foreign policy. (19)

The Kurds in the Soviet Union

Of all the countries with Kurdish populations, the Soviet Union boasts the longest history of cultural freedom for Kurds. More than any other Kurds, however, those in the USSR have been shut away from the mainstream of Kurdish national activity because of Soviet insistence on undivided allegiance for them. The Soviet border is sealed so that the changing fortunes of the Kurds in Iraq and Iran have not created a flow of recent Kurdish refugees to and from the USSR. The largest concentration of Kurds in the Soviet Union is in the Transcaucasian republics of Azerbaijan (5,488), Armenia (37,486), and Georgia (20,690). Most live in rural areas, with the exception of Georgian Kurds who appear mainly in Tiflis (18,409) and other towns. A second concentration is found in Soviet Turkmenistan (2,933), but these Kurds appear to be undergoing a process of rapid assimilation to the Turkmen milieu. Earlier in the century both Kurds and Turkmens crossed and recrossed the Soviet-Iranian border in tribal groups several times in the hope of finding relief from the centralization on both sides of the border that threatened their life-styles. Such crossing of borders terminated with the end of World War II, and Transcaspian Kurds hold little potential for playing a significant role as border straddlers. Their numbers in Iranian Khorasan are assumed to be small, while members of the community on the Soviet side in some regions refer to themselves as "Turk." (20)

A third group of Kurds has been settled in Kazakhstan (12,313) and Kirgizia (7,974). They were deported from Transcaucasia in 1941, together with the Crimean Tatars. Little is known about them, save that they were not condemned as a group for collaboration and that they have not returned. (21)

Kurdish cultural activities in the Soviet Union center around the Transcaucasian community, which shares religion, language (the Kurmanji dialect), and history with the Kurds of the Middle East. Only 19.9 percent of all Soviet Kurds use Russian as a second language. A higher percentage uses an eponymous republic language for their second language - Azeri or Armenian. Indeed, a majority of Soviet Kurds are bilingual. Nevertheless, overall use of Kurdish among Soviet Kurds remains high. In 1970, 87.6 percent of the Soviet Kurds claimed Kurdish as a native language, a language loyalty that is much greater than that of other Middle Eastern border straddlers within the USSR such as Iranians (44.7 percent), Afghans (71.8 percent), and Assyrians (64.5 percent). (22)

In those rural locations in Transcaucasia where Kurds form a large portion of the population, Kurdish-language schools exist, mainly for instruction at the elementary level, though Kurdish is not used as the language of instruction in courses in math and science. From Yerevan, Kurdish newspapers such as Ria Taza provide another avenue for disseminating Kurdish language and culture. (23) Radio broadcasts from there and from Baku are received south of the border in Iran, Turkey, and Iraq.

Within the Soviet Union, Kurdish has been a published language since the 1920s. (24) The Soviet Union was among the first countries to develop non-Arabic-based writing systems and presses for the Kurdish language. Since the most active Soviet Kurdish center has been and continues to be Yerevan, the first alphabet used for publishing Kurdish in the USSR was the Armenian alphabet. The only recorded publication in this alphabet, however, was a schoolbook called Shams, which was issued in 1921. (25) This book appeared in 1,000 copies only and was followed some nine years later with the next Kurdish book, this time in the modified Roman alphabet. In the 1930s Kurdish language publication expanded considerably to an average of 22.5 titles annually, using this new alphabet. Then it ceased abruptly during the last years of the prewar Stalinist purges when Kurds and other small and large Soviet nationalities lost considerable portions of their intellectuals and leaders.

Kurdish language publication resumed in 1946, using the modified Cyrillic system adopted for all Soviet Muslim nationalities (and some others) and it is in this alphabet that most Soviet Kurdish publications appear today. The number of book titles published between 1946 and 1960 has averaged 5.2 per year although the struggle against illiteracy has presumably increased the demand for books among literate Kurds. Between 1961 and 1972 when Kurdish revolts and politics claimed world attention, the average number of Kurdish books rose to 8.3 titles annually although these were mainly in editions of 500 copies. Moreover, several popular Kurdish books appeared during these years in the modified Roman alphabet again, in large issue, reflecting perhaps the export of such books to Turkish Kurds who became accustomed to the use of the Roman alphabet used for Turkish since 1923. Most Soviet Kurdish books are concerned with Kurdish history, literature, or linguistics. Kurdish poetry volumes employ themes such as Lenin, Moscow, the kolkhoz, and at times comparisons of tribal ("feudal") life with Soviet life. Signs of allegiance to a greater Kurdish cause, crossing present political boundaries, do not appear. Soviet Kurds are evidently not supposed to understand national allegiance in terms of Kurdistan or a homeland for all Kurds. (26)

In contrast to Kurdish publications for Kurdish consumption, Kurdology (the study and publication of materials about the Kurds) has been on the rise since World War II. Centers for Kurdology exist in Yerevan, Leningrad, and Moscow. Several studies in Kurdology have been written by Kurds who were sent to the USSR to study by the Iraqi government, and at least one study was completed by one of Barzani's fellow exiles. (27) Virtually all Kurdological studies are published in Russian but they serve to feed the cultural identity of Kurdish intellectuals, if not the Kurdish common people. Although Kurdology appears to be making some strides in Iran (Tehran and Tabriz) and in Baghdad under the auspices of the Kurdish Academy, in these locations, as in Moscow, the emphasis falls on classical literature, history, and linguistics. Not being a subject for popular consumption, the effect of Kurdology on the consciousness of the barely literate Kurds of the Middle East would appear to be slight. Nevertheless, Kurdology serves as a bridge to connect the Soviets with Kurdish intellectuals outside, especially in Iraq. (28)

Does the Soviet Union still as in 1944 to 1946 directly manipulate the Kurds to undermine the stability of the Middle Eastern states? This was one of the major questions with which this paper began. As observed earlier, the answer is unequivocally that since 1963 Moscow has not done so, but has shown an ever stronger inclination to work within the existing Middle Eastern state system. Now we may proceed to a further conclusion. While a relationship has existed from time to time in the past between Moscow's awareness of Kurdish rebellion abroad and encouragement of Kurdish cultural activity at home, the Soviet Kurds are in no way encouraged to look outside the Soviet Union or to offer material and moral aid to the Kurdish struggles abroad. In deliberately isolating its Kurds from the rest of the Kurdish nationality, the Soviet Union outdoes even assimilationist Iran.

It is probably of some significance that Moscow appears today to be keeping open lines of communication with at least some of the branches of the Kurdish Democratic Party abroad.   That is the organization within each Middle Eastern country which attracts politically involved Kurds.   From 1946 until 1975 the party hinged overwhelmingly on Barzani's charismatic personality, and consequently the Soviet break with him after 1963 minimized Soviet influence over Kurdish nationalism. Whether or not his successors are able to maintain the cohesion and ideological independence of the party, his disappearance from the scene certainly creates new opportunities for Soviet meddling in the Kurdish lands.

For the moment, however, one may recognize that it is because the Soviets have not in recent years directly manipulated the Kurds, that Iran, Turkey, and Syria can get away with the rigidly centralist, assimilationist nationality policies they are all pursuing.

THE ASSYRIANS

Inhabiting the same group of Middle Eastern countries as the Kurds are Neo-Aramaic-speaking Christians who refer to themselves as Assyrians (surayi). The bulk of those who live in Turkey, Syria, and Lebanon are Jacobite by confession. Those of northern Iran, eastern Turkey, and the Soviet Union are Nestorian. Western missionary inspired offshoots of both indigenous churches exist throughout the region, with the most politically significant being the Chaldean (Roman Catholic) one. Chaldean Assyrians live in Iraq and Iran.   As a Christian minority, Assyrians, the ferocious tribal Nestorians of northern Iraq in particular, have traditionally been deadly enemies of the Kurds.

For the Assyrians as for the Kurds, modern history began with the wars between tsarist Russia and Qajar Iran that led to the treaty of Turkmanchai in 1828 and to the partition of the Transcaucasus. But whereas the Kurds were forcibly divided by that treaty, the Assyrians of Iran voluntarily migrated northward after it, seeing in the lands of present-day Soviet Armenia and Georgia a refuge from persecution in their Islamic-ruled homelands.   In such fashion were established significant Assyrian communities in the central Caucasus and Transcaucasus, which to this day form the core of the Assyrian population of the USSR. From the same time, in 1828, the Assyrians even of the south adopted a new attitude toward the Russians. All through the nineteenth century when Assyrians were persecuted - or felt themselves persecuted - by Persian and Ottoman rulers or by Kurdish tribesmen, they turned to the Russian (and Western) diplomats at Tehran or Istanbul, whom they felt were influential protectors. By the end of the century they were turning also with increasing fervor to Russian missionaries who appeared amongst them.

In 1911, when the Russians occupied northwestern Iran, the Assyrians of the region felt confident that the persecutions by the "infidel" were at least ended, and began to behave with some arrogance. They disregarded local Iranian authorities, and aided by Russian troops (some of whom were actually Assyrians from the Transcaucasus) assumed control of Rizaiyeh (then called Urumiyeh) and much of the Persian territory to the west of the lake of the same name. But then when the First World War broke out, the Assyrians of the Ottoman lands began to pay for their reliance upon and alliance with the West. Like the Christian Armenians, they were pro-Russian and unwilling to consider themselves as part of the Turkish nation. They were subjected to massacre.

In 1915 the Nestorian patriarch, Mar Benjamin Shumon, was forced to lead the remnants of his flock from the mountain homelands they had traditionally shared with the Kurds to Iran. There, with ever-increasing visibility, they collaborated with the Russian military authorities, and this brought on new disasters. In 1917 after the revolution, Russian troops evacuated Iran. They left behind many weapons and also those of their number who were of Assyrian background; but these were not enough to hold off the Ottoman troops and Kurdish irregulars who now flooded murderously across the old frontier. In 1917 some of the Iranian Assyrians followed the Russians north. (29) In 1918 many more fled terror-stricken southward to Mesopotamia, which was then held by the British. By the early 1920s, when peace finally returned, the Assyrians were more scattered than ever, and had lost perhaps two-thirds of their numbers in present-day Turkey and Iran. (30)

The Assyrians in Iraq

In 1918 Iranian Kurds assassinated the Patriarch of the Nestorians in Iran. For five centuries that official had come from the same family, the Shumon family, and he was regarded not only by the Nestorians but by most Assyrians as the head of the Church, and by extension, of the national community. The murder led to Assyrian retaliation against Muslims in the Salmas and Urumiyeh region - an act several times avenged since then by the other side - and also to a sharp embitterment of Christian-Muslim relations throughout Iran and Iraq. As a result, in Iraq under the British mandate between the wars, the Assyrians provided levies that helped control the Arab population and sought to gain a homeland where they could exercise autonomy. Later, when the British departed, the Iraqis in their turn retaliated by expelling the

Patriarch. Attempts to re-establish his seat in Iraq have met with Iraqi resistance and he remains in Tehran today.

In recent decades the tenseness of the relationship between Assyrians and successive Baghdad governments has been sustained because of Assyrian support for the Kurdish autonomous movement. Some of the Assyrian tribesmen of the north fought throughout the 1960s at the side of their age-old Kurdish enemies against the central government. During the years when Tehran was also backing the Kurdish rebellion, special radio programs were instituted in the Assyrian language from Rizayeh that were beamed at the Iraqi Assyrians in order to incite them against the government. Vitriolic claims of Iraqi brutality against Assyrians, and of course boasts about the good treatment of Assyrians in Iran, were made. (Iraqi radio beamed back programs making similar allegations and claims about the Iranians.) Iraqi feelings were further ruffled by the Assyrians as large numbers of refugees fled the disruptions caused by the fighting. The confusion of war offered the opportunity to those who would settle scores with the Christian Assyrians. Many refugees arrived in Iran, generally en route to permanent destinations in Europe and the United States.

Despite the continual strife between Assyrians living in northern Iraq and the government, Iraq continues to be the home for the largest Assyrian community in the world. Urban Assyrians, particularly those following the Chaldean Patriarch, have cooperated with the central government; and those who have joined the Ba'athist party have achieved relatively high positions. At the same time that it was offering Kurds a measure of cultural autonomy, Baghdad was also acting on certain promises to the Assyrians. An Assyrian Academy has been established in Baghdad itself and Assyrian language broadcasting and publishing continue.

The outlook for improvement in the lot of Assyrians in Iraq is clouded by two problems, one internal and the other external. Internally, Assyrians allege that they are being coerced to renounce their Assyrian heritage in favor of an Arab one. They feel particularly harassed by census takers who promote the central government's attempts to reduce the proportionally high Kurdish population in key cities by recruiting "Arabs" among the minorities. Externally, a significant portion of the Assyrian community in the diaspora continues to pursue the fulfillment of aspirations for a national homeland that would be carved out of portions of northern Iraq. Such agitation stirs mutual dislike between Assyrians and the Iraqi government. The new Nestorian Patriarch, elected in 1976 and Iraqi-born, has begun negotiating with the Iraqi government to return the patriarchal seat of Iraq not, as was traditional, in the northern mountains, but at Baghdad. (31) His efforts have thus far been fruitless. But such a rapprochement might entail significant improvement in the status of the entire Assyrian community in Iraq.

Assyrians in Iran

The Assyrians in Iran are considered a religious group, and consequently enjoy a position shared by the other religious minorities, the Armenians, Zoroastrians, and Jews, but not by Muslim ethnic groups such as the Kurds, Azeris, and Baluchis, nor by the Bahais, a religious group considered heretical by Muslims. Because the religious minorities are deemed to require publication in their own religious languages to practice their religious beliefs, all four conduct their own schools, presses, and cultural organizations as well as religious institutions. In addition, they have political privileges. These four religious groups even have the right to elect one or two of their own representatives to the Iranian parliament. (32)

Tehran, together with Beirut and Baghdad, is among the publishing centers for the Assyrian language. As noted earlier, Assyrians in Iran have radio broadcasts in their own language. Moreover, they are able to join and send representatives to international Assyrian bodies such as the Assyrian Universal Alliance. Nonetheless, the Iranian Assyrians have faced major problems ever since the end of the First World War. For example, as a consequence of the measures taken by the Iranian and Soviet governments, the contacts across political boundaries that had enriched the Assyrian community of Iran materially and spiritually before the war ceased after 1921. For a number of years the Iranian government would not even allow Assyrians who had fled Urumiyeh to return, fearing that they would again prove a threat to the territorial integrity of Iran. This restriction was eventually relaxed for those who had not left Iran during the massacres. But suspicion persisted about Assyrians who had fled to the Soviet Union and returned during the 1920s as Iranian citizens, and they were not allowed to resettle in Urumiyeh. This policy resulted in permanently assuring the geographic disunity of Iranian Assyrians and over the past fifty years has led to the decline of Rizaiyeh as the cultural center of Iranian Assyrians, to be only partially replaced by Tehran.

Both the Iranian and Soviet governments have acted over the decades to make visiting and immigration between the two countries virtually impossible for Assyrians. The splintered groups, one on either side of the border, know little about each other. Just as Soviet Assyrians are confident that Iranian Assyrians are economically backward (when in fact the community has prospered as a result of the general economic development in Iran), so the Iranian Assyrians are ignorant of the existence of an active Assyrian community in the Soviet Union.

Finally, one must take note that the monarchist Iranian government used its Assyrian minority to bolster its foreign policy with regard to Iraq. After the 1975 rapprochement on that border, the Assyrians of Iran found their activities (particularly regarding the acquisition of a homeland) more restricted. Even so, the Assyrians in Iran benefited by the freedom from sectarian strife that in the past had plagued their relationships with their Muslim neighbors. For this reason, many openly and loudly supported the Shah. His approaching removal seemed to many of them a threat to the existence of the community. They feared both retaliation for the support they had given him in the past and second citizen status under a theocratic government.

Assyrians in the Soviet Union

In the decades immediately after the revolution, the Assyrians in the Soviet Union flourished. They did not obtain an autonomous district or region as did the Kurds and Ossetes of the Caucasus, but their nationality (narodnost') was recognized officially with attendant privileges. During the twenties and early thirties they had a large number of schools conducted in their own language, and they published language textbooks, as well as histories, poems, plays, and short stories translated or originally written in Assyrian. Like the other Soviet nationalities, they were compelled to shift alphabets, going from the missionary-developed adaptation of the Nestorian script to a modified Roman alphabet. But not having been uprooted, they enjoyed a continuity of cultural centers and even of leadership. Tiflis and Armavir in particular served as centers of Assyrian culture.

Even then, however, the Soviet regime exerted intense pressure to force a new basis of group identity on the Assyrians. Until the revolution they had always been held together by their religion, and this of course is the basis for their identity even today in the Muslim countries discussed above. The Soviet regime proceeded to denounce all forms of religious activity. It brutally attacked all religious leaders. The press denounced the Patriarch (then living in the British mandate of Iraq) as a tool of the British and the French (and, paradoxically, also of the Arabs!). By the 1930s secular history, secular culture, and especially language were becoming the only tolerated basis for Assyrian identity in the Soviet Union. The anti-religious indoctrination of the Soviet Assyrians reached such proportions that today none of the once-flourishing churches of the Tiflis community remains, and the few in Armenia are in total disrepair with little prospect that after the death of the old people, brought up before the Soviet period, the present attempts to restore them will be allowed to continue. Today in the Soviet Union many Assyrians have lost all but the most hazy understanding of the role of the Patriarch, confusing him with Assyrian tribal leaders called maliks and so referring to him as "king." (33)

Beginning in 1934, the Assyrians, like the other peoples of the Soviet Union, were subjected to massive purging. The leaders of the past and the new Soviet intelligentsia alike were virtually annihilated. If they were not shot, they were deported to the Far East, from which only a few were able to return. Moreover, Soviet patronage of Assyrian culture fell off. Assyrian language publications ceased to appear in the Soviet Union. After World War II there was a slight recovery. The attempts to oppose the Nestorian alphabet were abandoned. The Syriac tongue was allowed to be taught in a number of local schools, and in 1975 an Assyrian grammar book was published in Moscow.

In addition other factors have led to a far greater disintegration of the Assyrian communities in the Soviet Union than to those, for example, of the Muslim Kurds. Precisely because the Assyrians had high hopes, because they expected a better life in Christian Russia than among the Muslims who had governed them for centuries, they were not prepared to resist assimilation. They even welcomed Russian culture, tending (because of past experience) to regard the Russians as benevolent. In the Soviet decades, therefore, and particularly with the great mobilization of peoples into urban centers, the Assyrians have been unusually apt to move away from the Caucasian regions into other parts of the USSR, to become scattered and to lose their identity entirely. Even in Armenia they have tended to assimilate. There is a pattern of intermarriage between Assyrians and Armenians, and especially in urban environments the children and parents alike tend to speak Armenian and Russian because of the cultural advantages involved and because these are the languages taught in urban schools.

In this bleak picture there has only been one spark of hope. In 1975 the Soviet government sent the Assyrian Academy in Baghdad three pieces of sculpture by an Assyrian from Yerevan on behalf of the Assyrians of Armenia. (34) This represents the first time since at least World War II that the Assyrians have been allowed to communicate officially with a community outside the Soviet Union. It is also the first time since the 1919 Paris Peace Conference that Soviet Assyrians have participated in activity that would foster general Assyrian welfare rather than specific Soviet policy. If such contacts between Iraqi and Soviet Assyrians are continued, it is possible that Soviet Assyrians may gain opportunities to expand international contacts and thus to resist the pressures to assimilate that overwhelm them in the great multinational empire in which they dwell.

Granted the age-old hostility between Christian Assyrian and Muslim Kurd in the ethnic mosaic of the Middle East, it is somewhat surprising to discover that the fate of the two peoples in recent decades has not been dissimilar. The Middle Eastern states have in general feared and resented them. Iraq (where the bulk of the Assyrians live) has granted them, as well as the Kurds, nationality rights primarily on paper. In Iran they have flourished, albeit for reasons different from the Kurds, above all because it has served the purposes of Iranian policy to tolerate them. In the Soviet Union, though they have had the benefits of modernization, they have been exposed also, far more than the Kurds, to its perils - to assimilation. Though demographically small within the Soviet Union, Assyrians, like other minorities shared with the Middle East, offer a potentially usable Soviet foreign policy tool. Even if they are not thus used, the recognition of this potential by Muslim governments in the south could make the Assyrian minorities there, in particular during unstable periods, susceptible to persecution.

THE BALUCHIS

The Baluchis, like the Kurds, were first fragmented by the intrusion of nineteenth-century imperialists into their traditional lands. Even prior to the British colonization of the subcontinent of India, however, Baluchis frequently faced threats to their independence from powerful kingdoms based in Iran, Afghanistan, and India. From the point of view of these countries, the Baluchis were and continue to be disruptive and unsteady allies. Aspirations for a separate Baluchi homeland blossomed during the latter half of the nineteenth century as Baluchi tribes bitterly opposed British advances into the Sind. (35) The most recent attempt to achieve autonomy came in 1974 when Afghans, Pakistanis, Iranians, and the Soviets all became involved to varying degrees in helping or hindering Baluchi resistance to Pakistan's centralization policy.

Baluchis in Pakistan, Afghanistan, and Iran

The largest Baluchi populations dwell in Pakistan which appears to be the only country in which Baluchis have an opportunity to flourish culturally and politically. Baluchi-language schools in the province of Baluchistan educate the young, and such cultural organizations as the Baluchi Literary Society and the Baluchi Language Association contribute to Baluchi publishing. These facilities have existed with fluctuating success for nearly three decades. (36) Iran treats its Baluchis the same as other Muslim ethnic minorities - it allows no facilities for the propagation of the culture, and no ethnic political institutions.

For the Afghan state, the Baluchi problem takes second place to that of the Pashtuns (Pathans) living in Pakistan. Within Afghanistan the Baluchis have enjoyed no particular rights as a minority in the past although they have not been as discriminated against as some other minorities such as the Hazaras. The tolerable position of the Baluchis may be explained in part by their adherence to the Sunni branch of Islam, which is also subscribed to by most Afghans and Pakistanis. The lack of special cultural rights, especially regarding the teaching or publishing of their own language, reflected primarily the general underdeveloped condition of Afghan education, particularly in remote regions, and secondarily Afghan language policy, which has in the past recognized only two official languages, Pashtu and Dari (Persian). The Afghan situation appears to be changing rapidly under Khalq (People) Party leadership. Baluchi, together with other minority language publishing, is now promoted through the Ministry of Information and Culture. A weekly newspaper, Soub (Victory), began to appear in September 1978. Thus far it features Khalq Party propaganda aimed in particular against the anticommunist Muslim moderate party (The

Muslim Brotherhood), now underground. Government plans currently call for the introduction of Baluchi-language schools in predominantly Baluchi areas. Without census data however, such plans may continue to function merely as propaganda with which to stir dissent among Iranian and Pakistani Baluchi populations.

One may question whether Islamabad would continue to allow cultural expression to its ethnic minorities (such as the Baluchis and the Pashtuns) were there no pressure to do so from neighboring governments willing to use these minorities to gain concessions from Pakistan. In recent years Afghanistan has pressed Pakistan to grant autonomy or independence to Pashtunistan and Baluchistan and thereby theoretically give land-locked Afghanistan easier access to Indian Ocean ports controlled by Pakistan. As part of the pressure on Pakistan, Radio Afghanistan mounted a Baluchi-language propaganda campaign during 1974 aimed at instigating and encouraging ethnic dissent. The government of Daoud Khan (who was killed in the coup in 1978) addressed several letters to the Secretary-General of the United Nations, drawing attention to Baluchi refugees fleeing into Afghanistan to escape Pakistani bombing of tribal strongholds. (37) Pakistan attempted to minimize the struggle in Baluchistan, characterizing it as resistance to its efforts to dismantle feudalism in the area. Moreover, it claimed that Baluchi autonomy and an independent Baluchistan were issues raised by the Afghans in collusion with the Soviet Union. (38) The overthrow of Daoud, and his replacement by a regime more firmly associated with the Soviet Union, could usher in a period of even more intense agitation on behalf of Baluchi rebels in Pakistan.

Iran unequivocally favored the Pakistan government on the Baluchi-stan issue. Any successful Baluchistan separatist movement would affect Iran's southeastern provinces, where Baluchi tribesmen roam in large numbers. Like Pakistan, Pahlavi Iran tried to break the power of Baluchi tribes by eliminating their sardars or chiefs. Some efforts, too, were made to integrate the Baluchi areas into the socioeconomic structure of the rest of the country by building roads and developing the southeast coast of the country principally through the addition of a naval base at Chah Bahar. Iran stands to gain even today by continuing to support Pakistan on the Baluchi question and exerting effort to maintain the "territorial integrity" of Pakistan as the Shah did during the 1974 crisis. (39)

The Shah's plans appear to be in abeyance while Iran struggles to consolidate itself as a republic. Nevertheless, the poverty and neglect of Iranian Baluchistan together with ethnic factors have led to ominous rumblings during the first months of the republic. It is conceivable that the Khalq party in Afghanistan, faced with widespread dissent internally and armed tribal rebels operating from camps in Pakistan, will find reviving an armed Baluchi rebellion a distraction from its own problems and leverage to use against Pakistan and Iran in order to decrease pressure from foreign-based rebels. Escalating Soviet embroilment in Afghanistan would be a factor in involving Russians in this ethnic struggle so dangerous to peace in the Indian Ocean.

In the opinion of one leader, Mohammad Akbar Bugti, a Bhutto follower and former governor of Baluchistan, Baluchis would fight for Pakistan if it were threatened from outside, as it may have been in 1974 by Afghanistan and India. "Should any harm come to Pakistan, we Baluchis stand to lose our identity." (40) But the political situation north of the Arabian Sea is so volatile that one may hardly rely on such a prediction.

Baluchis in the Soviet Union

Baluchis in the Soviet Union have been much studied by Soviet Orientalists, mainly as a linguistic and ethnic group. (41) While the Baluchis, like other Iranian peoples, migrated through Central Asia to reach their present homeland centuries ago, present-day Soviet Baluchis are very recent immigrants to the region. In the nineteenth century, under pressure from Iranians, Afghans, and the British, a number of Iranian Baluchis migrated northward mainly from the provinces of Sistan and Makran. (42) Some of these settled into villages in the Iranian province of Gurgan. Others moved through the Afghan corridor, by way of Herat, into tsarist lands that now form part of Turkmenistan and Tajikistan. As a result of this migration, by the time of the 1917 to 1920 survey of population in the Turkmen oblast' (of the Turkistan ASSR), 936 Baluchis were recorded living in Bairam Ali. Between 1923 and 1928 another group of Baluchis entered the Turkmen SSR from Afghanistan via Iran, joining the Baluchis already in Soviet Central Asia who had left Afghanistan during the reign of Abdur-Rahman Khan (1880-1901). Most of these Afghan Baluchis have their origins in the southwestern area around the town of Chakhansur. (43) As a result of these migrations, by the time of the 1926 Soviet census, the Baluchi population had increased tenfold in about ten years.

During the Civil War following the Bolshevik revolution, the Baluchis took advantage of relaxed authority to raid Iran and Afghanistan for foodstuffs in short supply in Central Asia. With the establishment of stable economic conditions and agrarian reforms during the 1920s, Soviet Baluchis underwent settlement on lands assigned to them in the districts of Iolatan and Bairam Ali (near Merv) in Soviet Turkmenistan. Like other Central Asian transitional leaders unable to bend to the Soviet yoke, some Baluchi leaders by 1932 had either been eliminated or had taken refuge in Afghanistan. (44)

The Baluchis of the Soviet Union are being rapidly assimilated into the Persian, Tajik, and Turkmen populations around them. Those in Tajikistan, while retaining their customs, are losing their native language. The drop in the official number of Soviet Baluchis between the 1926 and the 1959 censuses reflect three factors: the outmigration to Afghanistan following attempts to settle the nomads during the 1920s and 1930s; the losses resulting from the forced collectivization in the

1930s; and the assimilation of the Baluchis into neighboring Muslim groups. Unlike Azeris living in Turkmenistan, however, the Baluchis prefer the Turkmen language to Russian as a choice of a second language, even though both Azeri and Turkmen are related within the Turkic language family while Baluchi is an Iranian language. (45) A partial explanation for this preference lies in the cultural affinity between the Baluchis and the Turkmens, both groups sharing a nomadic and tribal tradition and both belonging to the Sunni branch of Islam as opposed to the Shi'ite Azeris. A third influencing factor involves location; only one out of ten Baluchis is urban-dwelling, while 90 percent live on collective farms cohabited by Turkmens and Iranians (Persians). The Azeris, Tatars, and other non-Turkmen Turks, on the other hand, are concentrated in towns where Russians and other non-Asiatics dominate. (46)

Given the small number of Baluchis in the Soviet Union, their rapid assimilation into surrounding populations, and the lack of Baluchi-language cultural facilities, the Soviet Baluchi role in future Baluchi movements appears to be minimal. No attempt was apparently made by the Soviet Union to manipulate their own small Baluchi population during the brewing Baluchistan struggle of 1974, nor do there appear to be Soviet Baluchis advising Afghan Baluchis now (as there are Soviet Uzbeks, for example).

Border straddling has worked to the disadvantage of all the Baluchis. The establishment of borders dividing Baluchis has all but destroyed their traditional economic structure. Increasingly, the remaining pastoralists and caravan owners are facing the choice of succumbing either to central government economic development schemes or to poverty. The more ambitious and able members of the group seek to fulfill their hopes in non-Baluchi areas, thereby impoverishing the group and contributing to its assimilation in multiethnic urban areas. Nevertheless, the Baluchi potential for troublesomeness, rebellion, and manipulation by outsiders remains a viable threat to the stability of Iran and Pakistan.

THE TURKMENS

The Turkmens' fragmentation among several countries stems from two factors, their pattern of migration from Central Asia in early Islamic times, and Russian advances into Transcaspia during the latter half of the nineteenth century. Culturally and linguistically the Turkmens east of the Caspian (that is, those located in Iran, Afghanistan, and Soviet Turkmenistan) have much more in common with one another than with Turkmens living west of the Caspian Sea, particularly in Turkey and Iraq. Transcaspian Turkmens subscribe to Sunni Hanafite Islam, while some Shi'ites may be found among those in the west. The language spoken by both groups of Turkmens, however, is basically the same, with some regional modifications in phonology and lexicography. The Turkmen language, like Azeri and Turkish, falls within the western branch of the Turkic family of languages and bears a far closer resemblance to Azeri than the Iranian languages of Iran (such as Persian and Kurdish) do to each other.

The Turkmens of the Middle East

Almost half the world's Turkmen population live in Soviet Turkmenistan where they have experienced religious repression, linguistic specialization, and socioeconomic modernization, just like other Central Asian Turkic peoples discussed in this volume. There, with a capital city of Ashkhabad, they have become an officially recognized "nationality." Outside the Soviet Union, however, the Turkmens are fragmented.

Because of the closeness of the Turkmen language to Turkish, Turkmens of Iraq and Turkey have recently (more than ever) identified themselves closely with Ottoman and Turkish culture. Among the Turkmens of Iraq, except for folktales that reinforce a sense of distinctive Turkmen culture, the cultural orientation is not toward Ashkhabad but toward Istanbul and Ankara. The Turkmens of Iraq publish periodicals in highly turkified Turkmen in which Ottoman expressions are retained. In addition, writings of contemporary Turkish authors are often reproduced in Iraqi Turkmen periodicals in the modified Roman alphabet used for Turkish. (47) Therefore, although the Turkmens are permitted native language schools, publications, and other facilities to promote their culture in Iraq, because of their own background they appear detached from the larger Turkmen question.

The Turkmens of Iran fall into three main tribal groups which in turn are subdivided into the Yamut, who live near the Caspian Sea in the province of Gurgan, but many of whom before the Soviet era migrated seasonally to Russia with their livestock; (48) the Goklan, located east of Gonbad-e Kabus in Khorasan itself; and the Salor, who are situated in eastern Khorasan near the town of Sarakhs.

The period of semiindependence under nominal Kurdish overlordship ended for the Turkmens with the decline of the Qajar dynasty. In the fall of 1925, Riza Shah (Pahlavi) ordered a campaign to disarm and to subdue Turkmen tribes in Iran. Unwilling to submit, the Yamut fled to the Soviet Union with their livestock and remained there until both the collectivization of the 1930s and religious limitations drove them back to Iran. The returning tribesmen were accompanied by many native Soviet Yamuts who have since remained in Iran. In spite of the enforced sedentarization of Iranian Turkmens in the 1930s, some Goklan tribesmen have revered to nomadic life in the aftermath of drought. Most Iranian Turkmens, however, make their livelihood by fishing, cotton farming, and pastoralism.

Soviet occupation of northern Iran during World War II brought about a breakdown in authority in Turkmen areas of the northeast, but Soviet stimulation of Turkmen ethnic separatism was not as intense as it was among the Azeris and Kurds. According to C.P. Skrine, the British Consul in Meshed during World War II, two revolts broke out among Yamut Turkmens, many of whom had immigrated from Soviet Turkmenistan. Of the two revolts, one in February and the other in March 1945, the second was the more serious because the Yamuts were joined by mutinying Iranian army officers. Unlike the situation in northwest Iran where Soviet occupation troops refused to allow the Iranian army to quell the native rebellions, in Khorasan, after delicate negotiations the Soviets permitted Iranian entry. Skrine concludes that both the Azerbaijan coup and the Khorasan revolt were timed to coincide as part of an overall Soviet intrigue in occupied Iran. The lack of popular support for the first Azeri revolt may help explain why the Russians desisted in Khorasan. In any case, Soviet troops withdrew from Khorasan, Gurgan, and Mazandaran in October 1945 and when the second (temporarily successful) Azerbaijan rebellion occurred, they no longer held the military control in the east necessary to instigate rebellion. (49)

During the same period, smuggled Russian manufactured goods and Soviet Turkmen carpets appeared in the Meshed bazaars, indicating that the frontiers were far more open than they have been since. The Soviets attempted to impress Iranian Muslims by bringing into Khorasan a Muslim Soviet Azeri general (Alayar Bekov) and taking local religious notables to Ashkhabad, Samarkand, and Tashkent to witness carefully orchestrated tours of Islamic sites and Central Asian mosques full of worshippers. (50)

Like other Muslim ethnic groups in Iran, the Turkmens are prevented from publishing in their own language. But just as Azeri books inexplicably appear in Tabriz bookshops, Turkmen books are found on occasion in eastern Iran. The subjects of the publications are similar to those of Azeri books: classical and traditional poetry and prose. Two Turkmen books published in Gonbad-e Kabus some years ago are Sayid-Hemrah, the fifteenth- and sixteenth-century dastan (love poem) widely known among the Turkmens and other Turkic peoples, and Divan-e Miskin Qilich, a turn-of-the-century collection by one of the great Turkmen poets who studied in Bukharan and Khivan medreses. (51)

Turkmen publication in Iran, like Azeri, is done in the Arabic alphabet, the way that Turkmen was published in the Soviet Union prior to the eventual switch to modified Cyrillic in 1940. For most Iranian Turkmens, current publications emanating from Soviet Turkmenistan would be unreadable. Iranian radio broadcasts news in the Turkmen language for a half-hour a day in Khorasan, and Soviet Turkmen broadcasts also reach the Iranian side across the Atrak River border.

Only within the past few years have government schools made an inroad into Turkmen villages in Iran. Often these schools are still attended by boys only, perhaps because Persian is felt to be useful for them but not for the girls. Many other boys still attend traditional

Turkmen religious schools located in centers like Gonbad-e Kabus and Gomushan where students are taught the Sunni traditions. Some of the older traditionally educated men of the community recall that their teachers were graduates of Khivan schools of the pre-Soviet period. (52)

The Turkmen community of Iran retains its language, customs, dress, social structure, and religious affiliation. As an ethnic group it appears to have maintained its ethnic identity and vitality. From the 1930s when they surrendered their arms to the Iranian army until the collapse of the monarchy in 1979, the sole political involvement of the Turkmens appears to have been induced by the Soviet presence in Khorasan during the Second World War. With the disintegration of central authority, however, grievances surfaced in this ethnic group as among other Moslem ethnic pockets in the country. In late March 1979 armed revolt broke out in Gonbad-e Kabus, which was complicated by support for Turkmens demands for autonomy coming from the Iranian Marxist guerrilla group, the Fedayeen-e Khalq. This revolt was ended through military force rather than negotiation, as was the Kurdish revolt at approximately the same time. Given the location of Iranian Turkmens next to Soviet Turkmenistan and Afghan Turkmens, the potential leftist-nationalist threat from Turkmens to Iranian stability is higher than their small numbers would otherwise suggest.

Over the past few decades, both Soviet and Iranian scholars have taken interest in Iranian Turkmens as an ethnic group that has preserved its traditional structure and life-style to a large extent. Kinship between Soviet and Iranian Turkmens may be assumed since only thirty years ago some movement along the border was possible. Today, however, no roads connect Soviet and Iranian Transcaspia and the border appears sealed. Despite this barrier, Iranian Turkmens together with their Afghan co-ethnics have a very recent history of contact with Soviet Turkmens. For this reason, the two Central Asian Turkmen groups are more susceptible to political use by their host countries than are those of Iraq or Turkey.

The Turkmens of Afghanistan

The Turkmens in Afghanistan are still organized primarily as tribal pastoralists, composed of tribes such as the Tekke which historically have fiercely resisted Russian (and Soviet) advances. They dwell close by the Soviet Turkmenistan-Afghan border, an area to which some fled as late as the 1930s. Turkmens have contributed to the Afghan export economy through their breeding of karakul sheep and weaving of carpets. Their involvement in the mainstream of Afghan political life, however, has been slow to emerge. But during the 1969 parliamentary elections (the last general elections held in Afghanistan) this Central Asian minority, like its Uzbek neighbor, began to exercise regional political power that it had abdicated to the small numbers of well-connected Pashtuns who had moved north.

Moreover, since the 1978 coup, the pro-Soviet Afghan government has shown signs of giving an increased role to Afghan Turkmens. Despite their compactness and relative economic prosperity, under previous Afghan regimes the Turkmens were not offered cultural opportunities as an ethnic minority. The first Afghan Turkmen periodical appeared only after the April 1978 coup. Like the Baluchi and Uzbek press starting at the same time, Gurash (Struggle) is published in the Arabic alphabet. A late 1978 issue featured an attack on religious leadership, an article on the October Revolution that prominently displayed photographs of Lenin and Brezhnev, and four pages on the Afghan revolution. Indications are that Afghanistan has recruited Soviet Central Asians to plan and to produce cultural materials for its Turkmen minority. The geographic and cultural ties binding the Afghan and Iranian Turkmens make the ethnic arousal of Afghan Turkmens and their pro-Soviet indoctrination a likely threat to the passivity of Iranian Turkmens.

CONCLUSION

Several similarities exist among the minorities discussed here in their relations with the Soviet Union. Over the past century Kurds, Assyrians, Turkmens, and Baluchis have all occasionally taken shelter in the Russian-ruled land to the north to escape persecution in the Middle East. Furthermore, the Turkmens have a modern homeland in the Soviet Union. The Baluchis have recently received concrete expressions of political sympathy from the Soviet Union, and despite disappointments with the Russians in Iraq, the Kurds must remember their Mahabad Republic, established with Soviet aid. Therefore, while Middle Eastern states have regarded the Soviet Union as a threat, these ethnic minorities, blocked from cultural or political rights in their "homelands," are able to view their northern neighbor with sympathy. This sympathy may not always take the shape of active allegiance, but should the situation of the minorities deteriorate and no other avenues for help be opened to them, the Soviet Union will seem a source of hope.

Also, since the 1950s the Soviet Union appears to have changed its strategy in dealing with governments to its south. It has found that instead of currying minority favor as a way of pressuring ruling regimes it does not like, it can instead court favor with majority populations that are drawn to it either because of ideology or discontent with the ruling regime. In Iran, for example, religious minorities like the Assyrians found themselves in 1978 fervently supporting the Shah and vice versa, while Moscow tried to attract Shi'ite Muslim political dissidents. In the same way, during the Kurdish rebellion in Iraq the Soviets found that they could win the friendship of Baghdad by all but abandoning the Kurdish minority.

Despite this apparent shift in Soviet tactics, the mere existence of the Lenin-Stalinist nationality policy north of the frontiers is a latent threat to the ethnocentric regimes to the south, particularly to Iran and Turkey. The emergence of a selectively tolerant nationality policy in Iraq and now in Afghanistan may, if actively implemented, undermine the minority policies of those less pluralistically inclined states. Iran, Pakistan, and Turkey will feel more and more the need to distinguish between cultural rights, autonomy, and independence, the three levels of ethnic demands being made in varying degrees by their ethnic minorities. (53)   If they are to maintain their present borders, ultimately all of these countries, as well as Iraq and Afghanistan, must provide practical evidence of their willingness to recognize the rights of minorities. At the same time, policies aimed at easing them into the social and economic (as well as cultural) fabric of the majority, or of the ruling group, must be implemented.   The potential for the disintegration of one or more of these countries (with or without outside meddling) is not, however, inconceivable over the next ten years.

NOTES

(1) The Persian speakers are a peculiar problem in the ethnic border situation because Persians dominate Iran, and together with Pashtuns, rule Afghanistan. In the Soviet Union they possess the Tajik SSR.   The group identified in recent Soviet censuses as "Iranians (Persians)" (27,501 in 1970) is made up of descendants of Shi'a slaves in Central Asia who were brought there over the past centuries, Iranians who remained in Russia after 1917, and those who fled there following unsuccessful antigovernment action in Iran. This ethnic group has played an occasional propaganda role in Soviet-Iranian relations, but it is at once too insignificant and too complex for inclusion in this paper.

(2) Ismet Cheriff Vanly, La Question Nationale du Kurdistan Irakien (Neuchatel, 1970), p. 30; Alexandre Bennigsen, "Les Kurdes et la Kurdologie en Union Sovietique," Cahiers du Monde Russe et Sovietique 3 (April-June, 1960): 514. Both of these estimates appeared before the Soviet census of 1970 was made public.

(3) The world Baluchi population according to Baluchi nationals is as high as 15 to 16 million. See Mir Khuda Bakhsh Bijarani Marri Baloch, Searchlights on Baloches and Balochistan (Karachi, 1974), p. 20.   Soviet estimates appear in "Beludzhi," Bol'shaia Sovetskaia Entsiklopedia 3 (1970): 162.

(4) "Kurdy," Narody Mira: Narody Kavkaza, vol. 2 (Moscow, 1962), p. 604.

(5) William   Irons,   The   Yamut   Turkmen: A   Study   of   Social

Organization Among a Central Asian Turkic-Speaking Population (Ann Arbor, 1975), p. 11.

(6) For a detailed account, see William Eagleton, Jr., The Kurdish Republic of 1946 (Oxford, 1963).

(7) Kurdish spokesmen blame the loss of "liberated" territory after March 1974 partially on the massive Soviet aid in materiel and personnel given to Iraq.   Specifically they assert that Colonel Alexander Vasiliev helped to supervise attacks.   See Martin Short and Anthony McDermott, "The Kurds," Minority Rights Group, report no. 23 (London, 1977), p. 19.

(8) Ibid. p. 23.

(9) Edgar O'Ballance, The Kurdish Revolt: 1961-1970 (London, 1973), chaps. 4-7.

(10) For the text of the Peace Agreement, see Appendix I of Short and McDermott, "The Kurds," pp. 25-26.

(11) The text appears in Ibid., Appendix II, pp. 27-29.

(12) The USSR and the Third World, vol. 3, no. 3 (1973), p. 173.

(13) Quoted in Ibid., vol. 5, no. 4 (1975), p. 163.

(14) Choewar Chera was the name of the square in Mahabad where leaders of the Kurdish Mahabad Republic were executed by Iranian troops in 1946.   The Confederation of Iranian Students publishes news in Azeri as well as Kurdish and Persian.   Each ethnic language publication is meant to appeal to antiregime factions within that ethnic group and therefore bears a title and carries news of particular interest to that group.

(15) O'Ballance, The Kurdish Revolt, p. 156.

(16) Short and McDermott, "The Kurds," p. 8.

(17) "100 days of death," The Economist, April 29, 1978, p. 62; "The Kurds get into the Act," The Economist, June 24, 1978, p. 55; Bernard Brigouleix, "Kurds seek way as violence rises," translated from Le Monde in The Guardian, August 13, 1978, p. 13; "93 dead, 1,052 hurt in Turkish Clashes," The New York Times, December 27, 1978, pp. 1, 5.

(18) O'Ballance, The Kurdish Revolt, p. 18.

(19) The most striking example comes from the recent support of Kurds by Iran with the intent of weakening Iraq, but possibly also Syrian help to the Kurds since 1975 falls into the same category.

(20) "Kurdy," Narody Mira: Narody Srednei Azii i Kazakhstana, vol. 2 (Moscow, 1963), p. 649.

(21) Reference to this event appears in Ch. Kh. Babaev, Iazyk Kurdov SSSR (Moscow, 1973), p. 7.

(22) Kurds who claim Kurdish as their mother tongue, however, have decreased by 2.3 percentage points since the 1959 census, when 89.9 percent made this claim. The drop is explained by Kurdish assimilation in Central Asia, in particular into Turkmen culture. See Naseleniia SSSR (Chislennost', Sostavi, Dvizhenie Naseleniia 1973: Statisticheskii Sbornik (Moscow, 1975), p. 381.

(23) "Kurdy," Bol'shaia Sovetskaia Entsiklopedia, 14 (1970): 28.

(24) The first Kurdish publication anywhere appeared in Aleppo in 1915, when Zare Kurmandzhi, a periodical, began to be issued. Early Syrian publication was under the leadership of Kamuran Bedir-Khan and his brother Jeladet, who published Hawar and Ronahi, both in Damascus. See Dana Adams Schmidt, Journey Among Brave Men (Boston, 1964), pp. 155-156.

(25) N.A. Aleksanian, Bibliografiia Sovetskoi Kurdskoi Knigi (1921-1960) (Yerevan, 1962), p. 17.

(26) See Vanly, La Question Nationale, pp. 22-23.

(27) Dzhalile Dzhalil, author of Kurdy Osmanskoi Imperii v Pervoi Polovine XIX Veke (Moscow, 1963), is such a Kurdologist.

(28) For example, the Soviet Kurdish philologist, Dr. Adjee Djindi from Yerevan, was elected in 1973 to be a corresponding member of the Kurdish Academy of Baghdad. The USSR and the Third World, vol. 3, no. 3 (1973), p. 98.

(29) Dumbus, "Aisory," Novyi Vostok, no. 3 (1922), p. 70. See discussion in Eden Naby, "Les Assyriens d'Union Sovietique," Cahiers du Monde Russe et Sovietique, no. 4 (1975), p. 450.

(30) For details of the Assyrian diaspora, see John Joseph, The Nestorians and Their Muslim Neighbors: A Study of Western Influence on Their Relations (Princeton, 1961).

(31) Personal interviews conducted with the Patriarch of the Assyrian Church of the East, Mar Dinkha, in Tehran, winter 1977. Iraqi sources confirm the commencement of construction of a Patriarchal site in Baghdad in 1978. See "Slanderous Allegations Denied by Iraq," Voice of Assyrians 6, no. 3 (1978): 7.

(32) Since 1958, the Assyrians have taken advantage of their right to send a representative to the Iranian legislature. This right was given to them as well as to Armenians, Jews, and Zoroastrians in the 1906 Constitution and its later amendments. See Eden Naby, "The Assyrians of Iran: Reunification of a 'millat,' 1906-1914," International Journal of Middle East Studies 8 (1977): 245.

(33) Personal interviews conducted in Soviet Armenia during the summer of 1976 under a research grant from the Institute of Current World Affairs.

(34) Personal interview with Vosgin Isakov, the sculptor, in Yerevan, summer 1976.

(35) Aspirations for independence are reflected in Baluchi literature of the nineteenth and twentieth centuries in the works of Abdu'l-vahid Azat Jamaluddini, the poet; Maulana Muhammad Fazil, the educator; and Gul Khan Nasir, another poet; as well as others. See Dictionary of Oriental Literatures, vol. 2 (London, 1974), p. 184.

(36) Ibid., pp. 56 and 58.

(37) Afghanistan Council Newsletter (New York, Fall 1974), p. 3. The Bhutto and Daoud correspondence via Secretary General Waldheim is reproduced there.

(38) "A Dangerous Triangle," Far Eastern Economic Review, August 2, 1974, p. 24.

(39) When the writer raised this matter with Prime Minister Bhutto in 1974, his response was focused toward diminishing the reasons for the Shah's statement, i.e., claiming that the Baluchis were not involved in resistance.

(40) Kayhan International, July 14, 1974, p. 1.

(41) See, for example, E.G. Gafferberg, Beludzhi Turkmenskoi SSR (Leningrad, 1969), p. 3.

(42) The discovery of the Gurgan Baluchis was made recently by Dr. Sadegh Kia of the Farhangestan-e Zabon-e Farsi, but to my knowledge he has not yet published this information.

(43) Chakhansur today remains the main center of Afghan Baluchis. It lies close to the Pakistan border and was the place to which Baluchi refugees fled from Pakistan.

(44) "Beludzhi," Narody Mira: Narody Srednei Azii i Kazakhstana, vol. 2 (Moscow, 1963), p. 633.

(45) Tsentral'noe statisticheskoe upravlenie, Itogi vsesoiuznoi perepisi 1970 goda (Moscow, 1973), vol. 4, Table 27.

(46) Ibid.

(47) See, for example, copies of the Iraqi Turkmen language magazine called Qardashliq published by the Turkmen Bureau in Baghdad.

(48) Irons, The Yamut Turkmen, p. 12.

(49) C.P. Skrine, World War in Iran (London, 1962), pp. 227-228.

(50) Ibid., p. 230.

(51) I am grateful to Dr. Aman Murat for sharing with me this information and materials published in Iran in the Turkmen language.

(52) Hushang Purkarim, "Turkmenha-ye Iran," Honar O Mardum, new series no. 50 (1345/1966), p. 25.

(53) Recognition of this problem came in a speech by Prime Minister Mehdi Bazargan relayed over Radio Tehran on May 16, 1979.

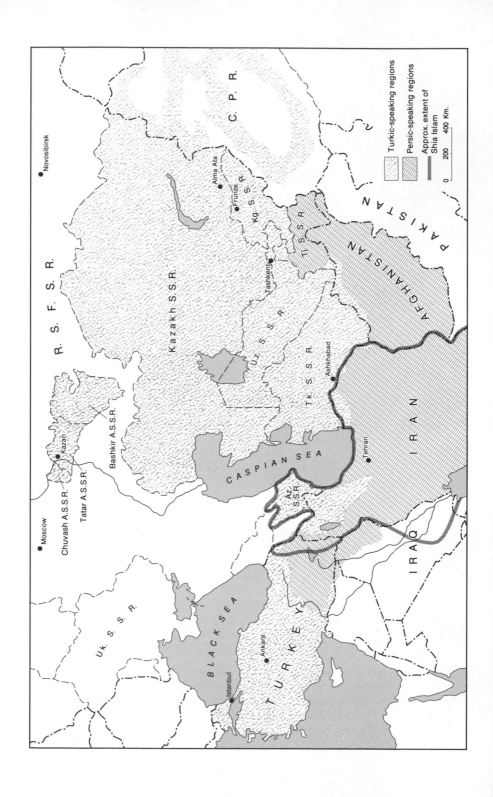

Turkic-speaking regions

Persic-speaking regions

Approx. extent of
Shia Islam

0   200   400 Km.

C. P. R.

Novosibirsk

Alma Ata

Frunze

Kg. S. S. R.

Kazakh S. S. R.

Tashkent

Uz. S. S. R.

Tk. S. S. R.

Ashkhabad

AFGHANISTAN

PAKISTAN

R. S. F. S. R.

Kazan

Bashkir A.S.S.R.

Chuvash A.S.S.R.

Tatar A.S.S.R.

Moscow

CASPIAN SEA

Tehran

IRAN

AZ.
S.S.R.

IRAQ

Uk. S. S. R.

BLACK SEA

Ankara

Istanbul

T U R K E Y

5 The Turkic Nationalities: Turkish-Soviet and Turkish-Chinese Relations

Kemal H. Karpat

Although national revivals arise from many sources, historically they have followed a pattern. In the nineteenth century in the Balkans, merchant-intellectual elites imitated Western models and used Great Power political support to politicize the ethnic and religious communities preserved by the Ottoman government's supranational millet system. More recently in Asia and Africa, a worldwide anticolonialist and antiimperialist movement challenged the colonial powers of the West and directly stimulated the languages and historical-cultural legacies of the native peoples. A Western inspiration has almost always been present in these revivals. The Turkic groups of the USSR seem to have developed national consciousness somewhat differently, however. With minimal Western input (and indeed with minimal elite leadership), they have discovered identities based on similarity of language, religion, tribal background, history, and culture, just by reacting against a colonial status imposed upon them by conquering Russians.

The Soviet rulers of Central Asia of course gloss over this exceptional character of the national revival of the Turkic peoples. They admit that a colonial situation existed in the nineteenth century after tsarist Russia conquered substantial parts of Central Asia. But they deny that it was perpetuated when (under different ideological auspices) they themselves extended central control through intensive administrative bureaucratization, through economic planning, and through industrialization directed largely by Russians and Ukrainians possessing technical skills and higher education. They simply ignore that the (unquestionable) Soviet achievement has created a deep social gap between the Russians and the natives, casting the first into the role of "enlightened" leaders and tutors while dramatizing the position of the second as a "backward," ignorant, and at times despised semifeudal culture. The past sixty years, they claim, has witnessed a revolution and a construction of socialism that was backed by the whole people of

117

the new Turkic republics, save for a few victims of reactionary forces. There has been modernization according to this version of the story. There has been a dearth of Western input, correspondingly. (Soviet Russia has supplied all of the "West" that was needed.) But there has been, in this version, no national revival at all, much less any neocolonialism, even though still today the European minority dominates the higher administrative and political echelons of Central Asia, enjoys a high income and managerial prestige, and lives mostly in modern houses in the urban areas, socially isolated from the natives.

In language, culture, and religion - and in a few cases, in history - most of the Central Asian peoples share common origins with the Turks of Turkey.   There is a natural and mutual interest among all these peoples in one another's fate and achievements. It has been dramatized by the Pan-Turkic movements of the past and is reinforced by the declarations of an important Turkish political party of the present.

In this paper I plan to trace the historical and cultural development of the main Turkic groups in the USSR in a context of Turkey's own modernization in order to underline their originality and their revival of themselves from within.   I shall approach the nationality problem in Central Asia not as a static situation but as a process of constant interaction of the traditional factors of national identity such as ethnic origin, language, religion, and history with the new and dynamic forces such as education, occupational change, and population movements. I shall try to limit my observations to Central Asia. This limitation is extremely difficult to maintain since the problem of Turkic nationalities in the USSR is almost an organic whole, involving all the Turkic peoples of Central Asia, the Caucasus, and the Volga-Kazan area. Most of my observations will apply to the Tatars of the Volga and to the Tajiks of Central Asia, even though the last speak a Persian language, and are therefore different from the Turkic groups. But this paper will deal most specifically with the Uzbeks, Turkmen, Kirgiz, Kazakhs, and Karakalpaks.

THE SOURCES OF TURKIC ETHNIC
AND CULTURAL IDENTITY

The ethnicity of the Turkic groups in Asia may be understood as a sense of identity created originally by a simultaneous biological-cultural act, namely by the birth of individuals into a group and by the crystallization of that group's socioeconomic situation into a culture. In other words, the initial ethnic identity of these peoples resulted from fusion between racial <u>soy</u> ("stock" or lineage) and natural culture without being exclusively either racial or cultural. <u>Soy</u> was in the early stages of tribal life the major bond that brought together the members of one or several related tribes.   Later on, in most cases, a tribe or a confederation of tribes became identified with a specific geographic area and thus the collective identity of the tribe acquired a territorial dimension. Eventually the Turkic tribes and their confederations accepted one or another of the great Eurasian religions. Their original ethnic identity acquired thereby a new cultural dimension, which in some cases was so powerful that it changed totally the group's cultural identity. Indeed, religion played a major role in the identity-devising and identity-changing process of the Turkic groups. For example, the Magyars, still referred to as being "Turks" by Byzantine sources in the nineteenth century, emerged after conversion to Catholicism with a distinct ethnic and cultural identity of their own. The Bulgars also lost their original Turkic ethnic tribal identity through conversion to Orthodox Christianity and their mingling with Slavic peoples and acquired a sense of Slavic identity and language although they kept their original name.

The Turkic groups who remained in Central Asia and converted to Islam followed a markedly different course from these Christian cases. Islam was an integrated sociocultural system which relied on two social units: first, the umma or universal community of believers, and secondly, the family. The Koran and the basic Muslim legislation regulate in detail the relations between the individual and his universal community and family, but barely mention and attach no political significance to the fact that Muslims can be divided into qavim or nations (smaller groups, presumably with distinctive ethnic, linguistic, and social features of their own). Islam, as a result, accepted the new Central Asian Turkic converts into the universal Muslim community as equals but left them free to practice their tribal customs and mores (which in a way were not different from those of the early Muslims, that is, the tribal society of Mecca and Medina). (1) Explained another way, Islam reinforced the tribe's culture or identity by giving it recognition within a well-defined and regulated sociolegal system, yet at the same time superseded it by incorporating it into the global religious-political identity of membership in the umma and by stressing the family. Ethnic and linguistic affinity was secondary to religious and family-tribal attachments. This situation did not change drastically in Central Asia until the twentieth century, and it accounts for the fact that many individuals who belonged to Turkic groups claimed to be Tajik (i.e., Persian) when the first Soviet census was taken in 1926, and vice versa. (2) These Central Asians lacked all sense of the political significance of language differences. Even later, after the Soviet idea of nationality based on language affiliation struck some roots, brothers who belonged to the same family could be found registered as Uzbeks, Tajiks, and Turkmen, respectively. (3)

Some students of Central Asia believe that the Kazakhs have proved less inclined to resist Russian assimilation because they were late converts to Islam, by implication less attached to their faith, and consequently less likely to develop a sense of unity with other Muslims. (4) This opinion stems from a superficial understanding of Islam. If Islam were to operate as a mere theological system spread through indoctrination and missionary effort, one might talk of sufficient and insufficient time for acculturation. Actually, Islam must be viewed as a process of adaptation that operates in a complex fashion. As mentioned above, Islam accepts the social organization and the culture of the converted groups and then subtly reconciles them with the principle of belonging to the community of believers.

In other words, Islam has developed a mechanism that simultaneously preserves, changes, and broadens the sociocultural system of a converted group, superimposing a new identity without forcing it to lose its original ethnic identity or even social organization. Thus the Bosnians who converted to Islam in the sixteenth century cling stubbornly today to this faith, despite the fact that they are Slavs, live amidst Slavic groups in Yugoslavia, and speak Serbo-Croatian. The same is true for the Pomaks of Bulgaria, who have remained Muslims but are Bulgarian-speaking. They remain separated from their Christian kin despite enormous pressure by Bulgarian governments to "bulgarize" them. The Cherkess of the Caucasus, who were converted to Islam by the Nogai mullahs (some as late as the early nineteenth century), preferred to emigrate to the Ottoman state after the tsarist conquest of 1822 to 1878 (just as many Crimean Tatars had) and to forfeit their lands and properties rather than accept the condition imposed by the Russians for remaining, namely, reconversion to Christianity. This attachment of the Cherkess to Islam was not based on strict religious dedication, but stemmed from a new and powerful sense of identification with, and loyalty to, a universal sociocultural system that not only retained but also gave a new force, direction, and meaning to their original sense of ethnic-tribal identity. The proof of this is that later on the Cherkess produced an ardent strain of Turkish nationalism, incorporating into a modern, wholly secular ideology the Cherkess ethos and identity that had been shaped and broadened by islamization.

Conversion to Islam reinforced the basic ethnic identity of the Turkic groups in Central Asia by bringing them into a broader cultural, ethical, and legal system. The distinctions between the normative rules stemming from the adat (custom) on the one hand, and seriat (religious law) on the other became rather meaningless in practice in Central Asia. These normative rules, despite their different origins, converged toward creating one basic pattern of social and psychological behavior and became a dominant feature of the Muslims' cultural characteristics, surviving even after Islamic institutions were formally abolished by the Soviet regime. It is interesting to note that the Soviets, in their unsubtle practice, acknowledge this. They often pose the problem raised by Islam in a rather simplistic fashion - as a choice between the "good" or the "progressive" which embraces all the Russian efforts, and the "reactionary" or "bad" which covers all that can be attributed to Islam. As Geoffrey Wheeler has stated, "Islam is regarded as exotic and inimical . . . and thus as running counter to the mystique of Russian particularism, which has never really been absent from Soviet Communism." (5)

THE MODERNIZATION OF THE CENTRAL
ASIAN TURKS BEFORE 1917

Between the eleventh and the fifteenth centuries the Central Asian Turkic groups were remarkably successful. Within Islam they defended their culture against the Mongols and the Chinese and in the end converted and assimilated many of these invaders. But eventually this Islamic-Turkic society entered upon a long period of quiet and stagnation. Its cultural and religious institutions, faced with no direct challenge to their survival, came to be governed by inert tradition. The original tribal customs survived without any flexibility. Consequently, Central Asian Muslim centers such as Bukhara, Khiva, and Samarkand were not the original foci of the modernization movement among today's Soviet Muslims. This started in peripheral regions, especially among the Tatars of Kazan and the Crimea which (in the one case since the sixteenth century and in the other since the eighteenth) were subject to deadly cultural pressures from their neighbor, the tsarist regime in Russia. By the nineteenth century Kazan in particular had become the seat of a merchant bourgeoisie and an intelligentsia consciously attempting to thwart the Russian onslaught and to avert assimilation. Figures such as Merjani and Musa Jarullah Bigi at Kazan and later Ismail Gaspirali among the Crimean Tatars were aware of the Turkish and Egyptian reformist experiments of the nineteenth century as well as the antiimperialist teaching of Jemaleddin Afghani and later of the Pan-Islamic policies of Sultan Abdulhamid II. It was they who through Tatar colonies in the Central Asian cities eventually started the Turkic groups of Central Asia on the road to mobilization, making them aware of their linguistic and cultural unity.

The modernist-national movements among the Muslims of Russia started in the form of religious reformism early in the nineteenth century, but this early reformism can hardly be credited as having led directly to a modern form of nationalism. This was born chiefly as the consequence of a linguistic and educational endeavor aiming at protecting the Turkic peoples of Russia against Pan-Slavism and russification and at combating illiteracy and underdevelopment. (6) The chief promoter of Pan-Turkism, Crimean Tatar Ismail Gaspirali (Gaspirinski) (1851-1914), regarded all Muslims of Russia as sharing a low level of literacy and an underdevelopment that prevented their national awakening. Consequently, he decided to overcome these difficiencies by cultural as opposed to political measures - by spreading education and intensifying communication. Gaspirali devised a language based in part on Ottoman Turkish and used it as a language of instruction in about 5,000 modern schools opened throughout the Turkic-speaking areas of Russia. Tercuman (Interpreter), Gaspirali's newspaper, became the medium as well as the spokesman for this modernist-reformist linguistic-educational movement known as usulu cedit (new-modern method, reformism) or Jadidism.

Gaspirali might have nurtured political national ambitions but he never defended them openly. His reformist ideas might have been inspired by the Ottoman reforms applied since 1839 and by the ideas of other Muslim modernists in Egypt, Syria, and India. He adapted these ideas to Russian conditions, however, and obtained rather impressive success, despite bitter opposition on the part of the Muslim clergy and conservative elements who defended the status quo. Gaspirali's efforts were instrumental in paving the way for the first, second, and third Russian Muslim Pan-Turkic congresses in 1905 and 1906, and for Muslim participation in the Russian Duma (parliament), mostly in cooperation with the Kadet party.

It seemed to Gaspirali that Jadidism could succeed quickly only by developing among Russia's Muslims a new self-awareness and a new identity capable of encompassing past performance and future aspirations at once. This national awareness began to emerge after the Muslim reformists of Russia placed emphasis on language and culture as the sources of their national consciousness rather than relying solely on Islam. At this point Islam acquired a new importance not only as a religious system but as the chief source of culture, despite the challenge of secularism that nurtured both positivism and even Marxism among the Turkish-speaking intellectuals. Islam enhanced the appeal of nationalism because it provided an emotional and cultural affinity between those who spoke the same language, shared the same faith, and who were treated as conquered people and second-class citizens. In turn, nationalism sensitivized and lifted to a new level the Muslims' religious consciousness by giving it a new political cultural dimension which paradoxically became a major feature of their modernism.

The reformist movement among the Russian Muslims stressed that a change in the Muslims' sociopolitical conditions was possible only by placing their cultural identity in a new frame of reference and thus revitalizing it. All this made a change in one's view of himself, society, the world, and of all social and political institutions almost a foregone conclusion because it gave the Muslim intelligentsia new and subjective criteria for evaluating their sociopolitical situation. This, in effect, made reformism a form of nationalism.

At this point it is appropriate to raise the basic topic of this paper, the influence of Turkey on the Turks of the Russian (later Soviet) Empire. There are obvious cultural, linguistic, and religious similarities between the Turks of Turkey and the Turkic peoples of the Soviet Union and China. Historically, however, most of the Soviet Turkic peoples of today lived outside the authority of the Ottoman state. Further, despite their formal allegiance to the Calif and the existence of a variety of cultural and educational relations with them, the Ottoman state (even at the zenith of its power) made no effort to establish a unitary Turkish state including them because it lacked a national ideology. Language and ethnicity could not be the foundation of Turkish national statehood until the sociopolitical transformation that began during the great Russian expansion southward between the treaty of

Kucuk Kaynarca in 1774 and the Berlin Congress of 1878. Russia acted in a double role, first as the defender of the Christian Orthodox in the Ottoman state, and then as promoter of Pan-Slavism. The Ottoman Empire, lacking a national ideology, reciprocated first through a series of measures designed primarily to reform the Ottoman government apparatus and make it more responsive to the needs of a market economy and the rising middle classes, and second by resorting to Pan-Islamism. (7) In theory this could have appealed to the Russian Muslims, some of whom - Crimeans, Caucasians, etc. - were now former Ottoman subjects. But the Ottomans used it more as a defensive measure against Western imperialism than as an active ideological instrument against Russia. Indeed, Pan-Islamism in the Ottoman state emerged chiefly as a consequence of the territorial losses, Muslim immigration, and the need for a common ideology capable of superseding ethnic differences and of holding together the Arabs whose percentage in the population increased greatly after the 1878 to 1880 period. As far as the nationality of Turkic peoples of Russia and Ottoman states was concerned, Pan-Islamism did not make much difference.

The Ottomans tried to develop their own brand of nationalism based on common citizenship and territory only after they had finally lost the allegiance of their Christian subjects. Only then, after 1908, did they gradually adopt a Turkish nationalism based on affinity of language and culture as a new principle of political reorganization based on national statehood. (The interesting historical parallel between religion and language in the development of nationalism in the Ottoman state and tsarist Russia is too obvious to warrant elaboration; let us note only that the Turks moved from multiethnic statehood to a unitary national state while the Russians adopted the opposite method in the Communist era to preserve what the tsars had conquered through a nationalism based on Christian orthodoxy and Pan-Slavism.)

Relations between the advocates of national revival among Russian Muslims and the Ottoman Turkists failed to reach full consensus until the demise of Sultan Ahdulhamid II (1876-1909). Indeed the Sultan, while sympathetic to a Muslim union based strictly on religious affinity, was opposed to any scheme in which linguistic and ethnic considerations were given priority. He showed sympathy to Russian Turks as Muslims but was cold to their reliance on language as the basis for their national identity, lest this antagonize the Arabs and other non-Turkish Ottomans. Because of this long isolation, one may find among the Muslim thinkers of Russia in Kazan, Azerbaijan, and the Crimea certain reformist ideas that appear to be different from those held by the Ottoman Turks. But a more profound comparison of them shows striking resemblances (though this is a very complex issue that goes beyond the scope of this paper). One fact is certain. Despite different approaches to reform, eventually the Muslim reformers in Russia and in the Ottoman Empire reached the same conclusion at the beginning of the twentieth century - that their ultimate salvation and progress lay in the acceptance of nationalism as a principle of political reorganization.

Thus nationalism, for the Turkic peoples of Russia and the Ottoman state alike, emerged first not so much as a result of cultural, economic, social, and political modernization, but as an instrument of it.

The Young Turks' revolutionary assumption of power in 1908 opened a new phase in the history of the Pan-Turkic movement by tacitly recognizing language and culture as the basis of nationalism. In fact, nationalism was being recognized for the first time as a principle of state organization after the more universal but supranational principles, such as Ottomanism and Pan-Islamism, failed to arrest the disintegration of the Ottoman state or to modernize and to revitalize the Islamic society. Turkish nationalism began to develop formally around the cultural clubs known as the Turk Ocaklari (Turkish Hearths) in 1910 and 1911 and their chief publication Turk Yurdu (Turkish Homeland). It relied on hars as the force capable of bringing together all Turks but without racial connotation. Hars had the meaning of culture in the broadest sense of the word. It involved unity of language, tradition, mores, and religion, though the last is not clearly stated. Eventually, in 1911, the Union and Progress Party, the political organization of the Young Turks, passed a resolution advocating the spread of Turkish as a means of reestablishing Muslim suzerainty and of assimilating non-Turkic elements. Moreover, the party elected Ismail Gaspirali, Ali-Turan Huseyinzade, and Yusuf Akcura (Akcurin) from Crimean, Azerbaijan, and Kazan, respectively, as members of its all-powerful Central Committee.

Thus in 1911 the Pan-Turkic movement departed from its modernist cultural-educational course and adopted openly expansionist and assimilative goals. The Pan-Turkic policy provoked sharp reaction among the Arabs and Albanians. But paradoxically the differences of view concerning the role of the language that thus separated the Ottoman state from these subject Muslims, after the Young Turk revolution of 1908, brought it closer to its distant kin in Russia. Dinimiz birdir (we have a common religion), the old traditional expression of unity, was now complemented by a new expression, dilimiz birdir (we have a common language). Newspapers, books, and reviews printed in Istanbul began to circulate among the Russian Muslims. The language of the Ottoman Turks, and their literature, became a model for developing a common language and common literary themes among the Turks of Russia. The intellectuals from Russia, such as Yusuf Akcura from Kazan and Ali-Turan Huseyinzade and Ahmet Aga Agaev from Azerbaijan, in turn played significant parts in defining the Young Turks' nationalist ideology. For instance, Ziya Gokalp, the ideologue of Turkish nationalism, borrowed some of his basic ideas, especially his views on turkification, Islamization, and modernization (Turklesmek, Islamlasmak, Muasirlasmak) (the three fundamental principles around which the Turkic nationality problem revolved) from the writings of the Azerbaijani writer and journalist, Ali-Turan Huseyinzade. Huseyinzade, following Fath Ali Ahunzade (1812-1878), played a significant part in Azerbaijan's national revival by helping to replace Iranian with Azeri

Turkish as the language of the country.

In Russia the Pan-Turkic ideas spread chiefly among Muslim intellectuals - many student clubs were established there - without reaching the masses. Even among the intellectuals, these ideas had to contend with tatarism, a small movement that did not deny the Turkic character of the Tatar language but claimed recognition for the specific regional culture and history of the Tatars. In the Ottoman Empire the Pan-Turkic ideas played a significant part in the Young Turks' decision to enter the first World War on the side of Germany and to engage in an offensive on the Caucasian front. However, the utlimate Ottoman defeat in the war, the Bolshevik revolution in Russia, and the disintegration of the Ottoman state cut off the relations between Russian and Ottoman Muslims and put an effective end to the Pan-Turkist movement. After the war the Soviets condemned the Pan-Turkist movement as a reactionary ideology and silenced all efforts to revive it in any form whatsoever, a policy enforced with utmost severity until the present day.

The Russian Muslims' efforts at forming independent nation states, notably the short-lived Bukharan Republic and the Azerbaijani and Bashkir experiments in 1917 through 1922, all failed. Indeed, these Turkic republics formed during the Bolshevik revolution, just like the old Muslim khanates of Central Asia, collapsed without much resistance. One may distinguish two basic reasons for their weakness. First and most importantly, the idea of nationality among the Central Asian Muslims, despite the efforts of the Jadids and of the Pan-Turkic reformers (most often they were one and the same), still rested on an ethnic-tribal, religious, and traditional basis. While this identity produced some opposition against the invaders and helped maintain the Central Asians' culture, it failed to generate sufficient mass organizational and technological power necessary to overcome the enemy. The relatively late Russian occupation of Central Asia, the paucity of Russian Christian rural settlers (except in Kazakhstan), the relatively small size of the native intelligentsia, mass illiteracy, the strong authority of conservative traditionalist rulers, and the semi-feudal social structure, all combined before 1919 to keep the Central Asian Muslims' national consciousness at a relatively low level. In fact, there was even considerable tension between the Volga Tatars and the Central Asians (notably the Kazakhs, and to a lesser extent, the Karakalpaks), resulting essentially from their different levels of development.

A second reason for the failure of the first experiment in Muslim nation-building in Central Asia was the almost total lack of material and support from the outside. The expiring Ottoman government had too many problems of its own. Only the ill-organized, conservative Basmachi, who had support in the interior among the traditional elites, received some limited assistance from abroad, mainly from Afghanistan where they live today. They were able to struggle for a decade after the Revolution.

To sum up, before 1917 the Muslim world in general and the Ottoman state in particular (due to their own domination by the imperial powers of the West) provided little material help to the Russian Muslims. Their interest in the fate of the Russian Muslims, and the interest of the latter in the liberation of their co-religionists under colonial rule in Asia and Africa, cannot be doubted. The congress of the oppressed peoples of the East held in September 1920 in Baku; Sultan-Galiev's truly revolutionary ideas concerning the inferior status of the Muslim workers in Russia in relation to the Russians ; and his schemes aiming at the creation of a socialist Turkic state comprising practically all the Muslims of Central Asia and Russia all prove this. But such politically immature efforts were not enough to make a difference when the moment of decision came. By the end of 1920 Kemal Ataturk had made rejection of Pan-Turkism a major plank in his nationalist revolutionary program because it had been so important to the Young Turks whom he had replaced and whose Pan-Turkist dreams had caused such harm to the Ottomans. Thereupon the Soviet government, to cement an alliance with Ataturk, scotched its earlier support of Communist parties in Turkey and elsewhere in the Middle-East and launched a ten-year campaign against Pan-Turkism ("Sultangalievism") in its own domains.

THE SOCIOCULTURAL MODERNIZATION OF
TURKIC ASIA AFTER 1923

The emergence of a nationality is both a demographic phenomenon and a cultural and political act that follows a specific course. Since the revolution the Muslims in the Soviet Union, and especially in Central Asia, have undergone their own peculiar process of nation formation. It was, in fact, the Soviet Union's nationality policy that in a short fifty years forced the Central Asians to abandon their traditional ethnic-religious pattern of organization and to adopt a broader and dynamic sense of national identity. To reiterate, the modern sense of nationality among Central Asian Turks is not the result of a slow and natural evolution of ethnic-tribal affiliation and religious ties. This nationality was born as the traumatic result of a forced interaction between a traditionalist Islamic society and a series of stimuli such as occupational change, education, urbanization, and political indoctrination, introduced mainly by the Soviet regime.

Nor is the modern national identity of the Central Asian nations a recognition of Soviet citizenship. Indeed, their Soviet citizenship is in many ways as much a legalism as was the citizenship of the various Christian nationalities of the Hapsburg and Ottoman states in the nineteenth centuries. This new identity is the composite result on the one hand of the structural transformation of the native tribal-religious communities into nations, and on the other of natives' subjective assessment and reinterpretation of their own historical experiences and present-day status vis-a-vis the Russians. The quantitative or structural transformation of the native society into nations was caused by the changes occurring in occupation, income, leadership, mobility levels, literacy, and other tangible variables. This is an objective situation. But the historical reassessment by the natives of their own past in the light of the mobilization brought by these changes is a subjective process since the actors can maximize the importance and significance of certain past events and achievements and minimize other events, often with future goals in mind.

The revolution in Muslim Central Asia has been neither wholly spontaneous nor wholly misguided. In fact, the Soviets planned and foresaw in advance many of the results obtained so far. For example, right from the start they went about regrouping the tribes and the sedentary population of the region into specific political units, the Turkic republics, and designated as the language of each republic one of the dialects spoken by the natives. In so doing, they wanted to create modern political units to supersede the old clans, villages, tribes, and other communities in which the traditional society was inflexibly anchored. Moreover, they sought from the start to annihilate the traditional religious base of Islamic culture. They brutally suppressed Islamic religious practices and institutions by closing down mosques and medreses and by confiscating the vakfs. Since in the process they wiped out the kadis, who before the revolution had been the main opponents of all change and who more than anyone else had prevented the society's internal adjustment to the modern world, they were remarkably successful. Indeed, the followers of the Alash Orda, the Young Khivans, and other pre-revolutionary progressive groups saw a good many of their own reform plans materialized under the Soviet regime. There was widespread acceptance of many of the reforms. (This was, of course, not least of all because many Bolshevik leaders among the Uzbeks, Kazakhs, and Turkmen attempted initially to persuade their kinsmen to accept the socialist principles of the new regime by equating them with Islam, something which was very shocking to the atheist Central Committee in Moscow.)

The result has been a series of material changes of utmost significance. The Soviet regime increased educational facilities at lower and intermediate levels and greatly reduced illiteracy. It initiated industrialization, the mechanization of agriculture, the building of dams, and the development of a transportation network. All this resulted in increased living standards for a part of the native population, as well as an increased rate of urbanization. The statistical evidence concerning these material achievements is impressive indeed. There is no question that the Central Asian Muslim society at this moment is not only substantially different from the traditional society of the 1920s and 1930s but has a living standard and literacy level higher than most other Muslim countries in the world.

To the successes of the revolution one may attribute also the demographic revolution that is affecting the Soviet Union today, the so-called vengeance des berceaux which is reducing the Russian majority. (8) Because of improved health conditions, the birth rate among the Central Asian Muslims is high (as high as 4 percent among Tajiks), while death and divorce rates are low. The results of the 1970 census show that the population increases in Central Asia in 1959 through 1970 ranged from 36 percent among the Karakalpaks (who are being assimilated by Kazakhs) to 53 percent among Uzbeks and Tajiks, with the Turkmen, Kirgiz, and Kazakhs at 52, 50, and 46 percent, respectively. Moreover, between 60 and 70 percent of the Central Asians are below the age of 30, while in the European part of the USSR roughly only 50 percent are below 30 years of age. Soviet scholars estimate that by the year 2000 the Uzbeks will reach 28 million, the Kazakhs 13.6 million, the Azeris 11.4 million - between two and three times their present numbers. (9) The Russians proper will increase only by 10 percent to 142 million by the year 2000 and will then comprise only 44.3 percent of the population of the USSR, roughly 9 percentage points lower than in 1970.

The success of the revolution has been especially clear in the area language policy. From the start the Soviets favored a policy of eradicating Arabic, Persian, and Ottoman-Turkish words from the native languages both in order to increase the use of the vernacular and to undermine the Muslims' solidarity with their brethren living abroad. At one point the Soviets adopted a plan to introduce one language for all Turkic groups and to use the Latin alphabet to replace the Arabic script, as done by Ataturk in Turkey. (10) But it turned out that this was too much like the policy of the Pan-Turks, who had sought to build a modern Turkish nation in Central Asia around Chagatay, the classical language of the Turks. Consequently, the Soviet regime decided to use the Cyrillic alphabet universally, but to promote one of the major regional dialects in each republic as the "national" language. Thus five or six major Turkic languages, led by Uzbek, Kirgiz, Tatar, and Kazakh, have emerged and each has developed its own literature, poets, and journalists. Actually, each language is intelligible to other Turkic groups and is made easy to read because of the common Cyrillic alphabet. Furthermore, the Uzbeks, Turkmen, Kazakhs, and others (allowed to do research on their national history in order to consolidate their sense of separate nationhood) have discovered that their current language, literature, customs, and tradition had a common origin. Ali Shir Nevai, the most understanding master of this common classical literature, has become a towering figure among all the Central Asian Turks, as well as among the Azeris in the Caucasus area, as have the poet-philosopher Fuzuli and many others. But the idea of Pan-Turkic unity has beyond question been undermined.

Not only successes but difficulties have characterized the revolution in Turkish Central Asia, and the greatest of these arose early on because Moscow's nationality policy deviated from the initial ideas on nationality expressed by Lenin and Stalin and reverted in practice to a policy of assimilation comparable to that of the tsars. More and more the Soviets visualized the process of nation formation among the Turkic groups in the framework of narrow Russian nationalism. Their policy of coping with it was one of russification though it was disguised under various high-sounding ideological slogans. The influx of the Russians (Ukrainians and other Slavs from European USSR are usually included in this) into the Central Asian republics aggravated further a dissatis-faction that had already started with the settlements of Europeans in agricultural areas under Stolypin's reforms in 1906 and 1907. These occupied the leading positions in the party apparatus, industries, administration, and higher education and drew incomes large in comparison with the natives. Living mostly in urban centers (Kazakh-stan excepted) the colonists remained an outside minority, a ruling group in every respect. The dichotomy created by this colonial situation soon became evident in every aspect of life.

Furthermore, in 1927 the modernization drive became a traumatic experience for the population, for the Party leadership decided then to strike at the roots of Central Asian Islam with a cultural revolution imposed from above. The ensuing violent "class struggle" against attachment to religious beliefs, customs, and kinship culminated in the attack on the family. Native women were regarded as the oppressed party and consequently "liberated" to assume social and political power, to have freedom of sex and divorce with total disregard for custom and tradition. The reaction to this "liberation" was so fierce that by 1929 the campaign was brought to an abrupt end. (11) But meanwhile the Central Asians learned to distrust the new regime and developed subtle methods of resistance. This experience sharpened their awareness of their own identity and united them in opposition to forced alienation, in the same way that tsarist tyranny had awakened the resistance of the Volga Tatars centuries before.

To these flaws of the Soviet revolution in Central Asia one may attribute the true "modernization from inside" that constituted the revolution's most extraordinary feature. As noted above, Moscow instituted the Central Asian republics in order to distract Muslims from their religious community and from their membership in the umma, and to destroy that willingness, so evident among Muslims in the past, to leave their homes when these were conquered by nonbelievers so that they might live freely as Muslims under Muslim rulers. To a certain extent this policy was effective. The Turkish word vatan (homeland) before the revolution had a narrow connotation, often simply referring to one's village or tribal territory. Under Soviet rule it came to acquire firmer and broader territorial boundaries corresponding to the limits of the republics. But in Moscow's intent this acceptance of the new connotation of "home" was supposed to be only the first step in the establishment of a "patriotism" corresponding with Soviet citizenship - and this did not happen. Instead, the peoples of Central Asia acquired a mystical identification with their own land of a sort long common among Christian European peasantries but hitherto utterly lacking in the Muslim world. In effect the Soviets brought out among the Central

Asians a wholly unintended counterpart of their own Russian mystical identification of the individual and his territory. This was not the only level on which the revolution backfired. As Alexandre Bennigsen has noted, the suppression of formal religious institutions in general led the Muslims of Central Asia to practice as "national culture" under the Soviet regime everything that they had practiced as Islam in the past.

Worse, from the Soviet point of view, was that this new Central Asian nationalism was not a limitable phenomenon. The modernized languages, the new literatures, and increased literacy enabled millions of newly literate Muslims to read not only official Russian writings but also the history and literature of their lands, usually in their native tongues. The written languages became a major unifying factor among the Muslims living in the republics of Central Asia. Industrialization and education, (12) in turn, produced a new and large native intelligentsia, most of whom came from the lower urban and rural groups, a culture in which Islam, traditionalism, folklore, and the native tongues still prevail. The social experience of other countries has shown that it is this wing of the intelligentsia (rather than the members of the upper classes) who show attachment to their own culture and devise ingenious ways to defend it. A substantial part of this new Muslim intelligentsia in Central Asia serves as teachers in the schools, thus occupying a key role in the education of their own kinsmen.

Moreover, a specific modernization of the traditional culture has occurred in a variety of forms. For example, saints who were worshipped or whose tombs were credited with healing power out of sheer ignorance and superstition in the past lost their magic in the Soviet era and reappeared as national folk heroes or symbols of a folk culture commonly shared by most Turkic peoples. In other words, the partial desacralization of Islam resulting from political indoctrination and increased positivist education transferred into the lay culture elements from the religious culture and made the feudal figures acceptable to the authorities. The secularist native intelligentsia found many such activities and ideas in their own tradition that are compatible with the Soviet regime's outlook. The fact is that the original Lenin-Stalin nationality formula provided the Central Asian Turks with a uniquely legitimate argument with which to defend their own nationality and reject russification without incurring open repression. According to the Lenin-Stalin definition, a nation is "an historically evolved, stable community arising on the foundation of a common language, territory, economic life and psychological makeup, manifested in a community of culture." This is broad and even somewhat liberal. Of course it downplays those subjective elements that give to a nation its distinctive cultural characteristics such as group consciousness, attachment to its history and culture, and the freedom to decide its own political destiny. Using it, the official Soviet understanding of culture rejects the Islamic influences. But Lenin and Stalin could and can always be quoted in defense of the new secular and national culture of Central Asia today.

One can hardly deny that there has been a certain assimilation of Central Asians into official Soviet society over the years. There is always a possibility that rising native elites, inspired by self-interest, Communist conviction, or gratitude for their education, may join the "foreign" minority by making Russian their first language and by adopting their customs and modes of life. The pervasive control exercised by the Communist Party, the periodic "anti-obscurantist" and "anti-bourgeois nationalist" campaigns conducted against the native efforts to defend their religion and national identity, coupled with the rewards bestowed on natives identifying themselves with the system, all lend to such an assimilative trend. One frequently hears of the Kirgiz party leader who attempted to keep a "modern" room furnished according to the Russians' tastes alongside a traditional room for his own Kirgiz visitors. But on the other hand, the very nature of the Soviet elitist bureaucratic system generates and maintains a gap between its members and the masses, who remain consequently imbedded in their traditions, languages, and mores. Furthermore, the present administrative system, based on national distinctions, adds legitimacy to many efforts at defending traditional cultural identities. One may estimate, therefore, that the regime's controls only contain the tensions and conflicts inherent in the colonial situation, without abolishing or even tempering them. Hypothetically, these tensions can last forever, always ready to burst forth when the controls slacken; and meanwhile, one may recall, the demographic factor is having a vital impact on the status quo. The high birth rate among the natives and its far-reaching economic, social, and political consequences are challenging the colonial situation and transforming the elites' role.

It is interesting to note in this connection that in 1970 an average of 98 percent of Central Asians considered their native tongue to be their first language and marriages between Muslims and Russians remain extremely rare. Even though the predominance of endogomy may be imperceptibly weakening, most of the mixed marriages today occur between Central Asian men and Russian women, with a majority of the children of such marriages claiming the father's nationality, often perhaps to draw the benefits associated with the native status, such as easier admission to schools. (Of course, in Central Asia as a whole the overwhelming majority of mixed marriages occur between members of different European nationalities, such as Ukrainians and Russians.)

THE UPSWING IN TURKISH-SOVIET
RELATIONS IN THE 1960S

The Turkish Republic was established in 1923 after a bitter struggle against Allied powers and a victory in which Soviet aid played a crucial role. Relatively friendly relations between Turkey and the USSR ensued because of an agreement that was inserted in the Treaty of Friendship signed in 1921, whereby the two governments formally promised to abstain from activities harmful to each other. This meant that the USSR agreed not to promote Communism in Turkey while the latter promised to abstain from inciting Pan-Turkism among the Turkish peoples of the USSR. That neither country observed this agreement to the letter is proven by the intensive Communist activities in Turkey after 1930 and by the upsurge of Pan-Turkic organizations in Turkey, especially during the 1940 to 1943 period. But a little-known incident concerning the Turk Ocaklari shows that before the war the bargain was kept in general. These organizations functioned normally as nationalist associations until 1929 to 1930, when the Soviets began to put pressure on the Turkish government to disband them since their advocacy of hars, unity of culture, was considered to be a veiled Pan-Turkic propaganda tool aimed at the Soviet Turks. Ankara complied. Subsequently, the Turk Ocaklari were replaced in 1931 and 1932 by "People's Houses," which rejected hars as the basis of culture and instead advocated a territorial, secular, and populist form of Turkish culture and nationalism. In 1951 some Turkish critics advocated the closure of these People's Houses, pointing out that they were inspired by the Soviet Narodnyi Dom.

At the end of the war this relative harmony of Turkish-Soviet relations changed abruptly. In 1945 and 1946 the Soviet Union denounced the Montreux Convention that governed the Bosporus and the Dardanelles, launched repeated propaganda barrages against Turkey, and openly demanded the territories of eastern Anatolia that had been conceded to Turkey under treaties of 1921 and 1925. These pressures, which were maintained until Stalin's death in 1953, played a major role in the start of the cold war and thrust Turkey firmly into alliance with the Western powers. The result was no less deleterious to Pan-Turkism and to contacts between Turkey and the Central Asian Turks than the cooperation of the interwar period had been. For over a decade after 1945 there was virtually no traffic over the Soviet-Turkish frontiers.

All this time the Soviet government pursued its diligent campaign to further the russification of Central Asia, and to indoctrinate the Muslims with the idea that they possess one single socialist homeland, one common class structure, a single world outlook, and a common goal. In 1961, just prior to the Twenty-Second Party Congress, the regime even charged the writers belonging to various nationality groups, including the Central Asian republics, with promotion of the regime's ultimate goal of creating an ideal Soviet personality by merging all groups into one Soviet people within a unitary multinational state. The literatures of the national republics were called to achieve this goal first through convergence or rapprochement (sblizhenie) of all national groups leading eventually to merging or assimilation (sliianie) into one homogeneous monolithic nation which, by all indications, would bear Russian characteristics in language as well as culture. Writers were asked to pour the Soviet (Russian) content of their writings into a local form, that is, into the national language. But then there was a change.

The Party program adopted by the Congress of 1961 pointed out that the abolition of national distinctions, especially language differences, would take a long time. Although sliianie continued to be mentioned, it gradually ceased to be emphasized.

Since then there has been a sustained softening in the Soviet governance of Turkic Central Asia, For example, the Miri Arab medrese of Bukhara, built in 1535 and reopened in 1952 with one hundred students, seems to have more than doubled the number of its students. The Central Asian Muslim interest in pilgrimages to Mecca and in studying Islam in some well-known medrese in the Islamic world has been allowed to grow. Central Asian film directors have been allowed to make films about local celebrities - about Ulugbeg, the astronomer (also, the son of Timur and ruler of Transoxania, a fact which is still seldom mentioned); about Ibn Sina (Avicenna), known as one of Islam's greatest thinkers; about Maktum Kulu, Ali Shir Nevai, and about Firdausi, the Tajik, and many other literary and historical figures. The films extol the great contributions of these thinkers and poets to the civilization of Central Asia and implicitly publicize the cultural unity of the area since these poets and thinkers are claimed by all Central Asian Muslims. Streets, squares, statues in these republics have been named after the same illustrious figures, reminding the people of their common cultural heritage. Local societies have been established by teachers, historians, and the youth to find and preserve monuments and places related to national history, despite official frowning on "mirasism" - preoccupation with historical heritage. The historical, ethnographical, and archaeological reviews of Central Asia have produced articles that stress the achievement of their own people. (13) In 1965 a well-known student of language and literature in Turkey, Agah Sirri Levend, published a three-volume study of Ali Shir Nevai (b. 1441). Even the Dede Korkut, known also as Korkud Ata and by other names among all Turkic peoples (in Turkey it is part of the high school course on literature) and long banned for its praise of the feudal warriors, has been rehabilitated in the USSR. The constant theme behind all these cultural activities promoted by native intellectuals is the originality, creativity, and contribution of the East to world civilization, an indirect refutation of the superiority and exclusive creativity claimed by the "Westerners," who in this case are the Russians.

Meanwhile Muslims have been able to acquire not only some perceptible economic and educational power, but even a recognized political status. The number of native Central Asian Muslims in high administrative positions in their respective republics has increased gradually.

In addition, the past decade has witnessed a spectacular development in Turkish-Soviet relations and in the cultural contacts between the Turks of Turkey and of Central Asia. A rapprochement between Turkey and the Soviet Union, which began in 1964, produced a series of reciprocal visits by prime ministers, other ministers, and parliamentary delegations and led to a series of cultural agreements, including one concerning the exchange of artists and writers. The Soviets insisted on this agreement. The Turkish government accepted it only after considerable hesitation on condition that it be subject to review every year.

The initial contacts involved high-level delegations. Later on Turkish poets, writers, and journalists, usually those with leftist tendencies, repeatedly visited the Soviet Union and the Turkic republics. The visits to the USSR by Turkish statesmen, parliamentary groups, and journalists invariably involve stops in Tashkent, Alma Ata, Bukhara, and Baku. In exchange, scholars and singers from the Central Asian republics and from Azerbaijan, along with many Russian artists, visit Turkey and perform in various Turkish cities. Books published in Turkey are translated into Russian or are adapted for the use of the local Turkic dialects, while the works of many Soviet Turkic writers are translated or adapted to the Turkish spoken in Turkey. Many Turkic songs from the USSR, notably from Azerbaijan, were recorded and sold in Turkey, while much of the cultural and artistic output of Turkey found its way to the Turkic groups in the USSR, especially Azerbaijan. In particular, films from Turkey but also from the Arab countries find great acceptance among the Central Asian Muslims. The film producers from these countries use a script with some social-political content (a strike by factory workers or a peasant revolt) in order to please the Soviet authorities but fill the rest with music, family matters, and love scenes in the Oriental style to please the local audiences. Even films considered in Turkey to be of lower quality find wide acceptance among the Central Asian and Azeri Turks. The more traditional their content, the more they are appreciated.

This exchange program is more significant because it has coincided in time with the reemergence inside Turkey of organized political nationalism. Today there is in Turkey a political party, the Milli Hareket Partisi (National Action Party), which was part of the coalition government in 1975 through 1978. The party, which is led by Colonel Alparslan Turkes, who was known as a Turanist in the past (he was arrested in the crackdown on Pan-Turanists in 1944), is supported by the Turkiye Milliyetciler Dernegi (Union of the Nationalists of Turkey) which includes most of the people with ties to or interests in the Soviet Turks. (14) The party's program defends secularism, socioeconomic development, and peaceful coexistence with neighbors. Although it is fiercely anticommunist, it has not openly espoused Pan-Turkism as its credo. But its definition of the nation and nationalism (Turkculuk) is broad enough to encompass Pan-Turkism. The party, a well-disciplined, tightly organized body, received roughly 3 percent of the popular vote in 1969 and increased its total number of votes in 1973. The increase was mainly the consequence of internal developments, namely the political polarization between the leftists and the rightists, rather than the reflection of an upsurge of Pan-Turanic sentiment. Nevertheless, the background of the leaders and supporters of this party (active even among workers in Europe) and its statements and overall attitude suggest strongly that its commitment to Turkism is deeper than the letter of its program. In the election of 1977 the MHP registered the largest increase in votes and seats in the Parliament; its popular vote and parliamentary seats went up from 3 percent and 3 seats to 6.4 percent and 16 seats, respectively. (15) The party's success may be attributed, among other reasons, to an emphasis on religion rather than race as the basis for culture and unity.

The Soviet decision to permit this broader but controlled contact between Turks of Turkey and the Soviet Union seems to have been based on a series of pragmatic considerations. Above all, the Soviet government has found it expedient to use its Muslims very cautiously to increase its influence among the independent Muslim nations. The Soviet Union's relations with the Muslim countries, notably with a number of Arab countries, have been rather friendly (though one may note that Moscow gave aid to India in the dismembering of Pakistan and the establishment of Bangladesh). The frequent meetings arranged by the Soviets between Central Asians and Muslims living elsewhere, including the Conference of African and Asian writers held in Alma Ata in September 1973 (and Tashkent in 1958), illustrate attempts of the government to capitalize on its Muslims to gain popularity among Muslim states. (16) The Soviets have also been responsive to the criticism leveled by the Muslim students from foreign countries enrolled in Soviet universities. The students criticized the Soviet restrictions imposed on Islam and on Islamic nationalities as incompatible with democracy.

Secondly, the change in Soviet policy is in all probability related to the revolutionary changes that took place in Turkey in 1960 - to the deposition of the Democratic Party - and to introduction of a new and more liberal constitution in 1961. These events led not only to the rearticulation of Pan-Turkist nationalism mentioned above, but also to an outburst of leftist activities. For example, Nazim Hikmet's books, long banned, flooded the market as did a large number of articles and interviews concerning his life in the USSR where he lived after his escape from Turkey in 1951 until his recent death. Nazim Hikmet is considered a great poet even by his political enemies, and is a legend in Turkey. Furthermore, in 1961 the Labor Party of Turkey was organized. It adopted a pro-Soviet attitude, and until its leader Mehmet Ali Aybar denounced the Soviet intervention in Czechoslovakia in 1968 and caused a fatal dispute with the pro-Moscow group, it remained the political bastion of the left in Turkey and promoted the idea of friendly relations with the USSR. Thus the Soviet Union found a suitable ideological ground for establishing a dialogue with the Turkish intelligentsia. Perhaps the Soviets believed that the Turkic groups in the USSR with their recognized national identity and their relatively high standard of literacy and economic development could impress the Turks from

Turkey as the product of a communist regime.

One may note also, of course, that the Soviet Union had much to gain from such overtures to leftist Turks. After 1960 the Turkish intelligentsia showed considerable impatience with the narrow scope of the country's modernization and the low rate of economic development. Moreover, the fast rise of the Third World countries and their ability to devise new developmental methods created interest in Turkey in alternatives to the Western model of development. Consequently, leftist and even rightist intellectuals began to express their disillusionment with the Western methods of slow economic development and their political and cultural biases. Turkey faced a certain political isolation, especially after the Cyprus War of 1974. In search of inner strength in order to counteract this isolation, Turkey took a closer look at her own history and reconsidered her long-ignored Asian heritage, as well as her relations with the Soviets. Rightists and leftists both began to look eastward for special reasons of their own. The Soviet Union took advantage of this situation. Instead of denouncing the Turks' interest in their Central Asian heritage as they did in the past, some Soviet spokesmen actually began to insist that the Turks of Turkey and those of Central Asia had many cultural affinities and that Turkey's future lay in strengthening her relations with the East. I recall vividly an encounter with two Kazakh scholars in Istanbul in 1973, who showed some interest in my work. Our discussion was abruptly interrupted when their "escort," a Turkmen working for the Russian Embassy, appeared and engaged in a long monologue describing the Turks' Central Asian origin and culture, and stating that it was desirable and advisable for them to reassert their oriental heritage and to form ties with the Soviet Turkic groups.

The purpose behind the Soviet-Turkic cultural exchange is thus to detach Turkey from Western orientation in general and from NATO in particular.

The third reason for the conciliatory Soviet attitude toward Islam and the national activities of the Turkic peoples may be the Sino-Soviet conflict. Turkey established unofficial relations with China in 1966 and extended recognition in 1971; but already in earlier contacts with Turkish newsmen the Chinese had stressed the "deep cultural and historical ties" between the two countries and proposed to build friendship on that basis. These "deep cultural and historical ties" regard the Turks of East Turkistan (Sinkiang), which is occupied by China and coveted by the USSR, and the Chinese aim was clearly to enlist Turkish support in stirring up anti-Soviet national feeling among the Central Asian Turkic groups. Both the USSR and China were then engaged in a propaganda war directed to their respective Turkic groups. We may deduce that the relatively benevolent Soviet attitude toward the Central Asian republics was intended in some measure to neutralize the Chinese efforts at exploiting the national issue in these areas and at preempting any mass popular reaction in Turkey in favor of the Central Asians. The members of the Turkic groups in the USSR visiting Turkey are extremely critical of China; on balance, Central Asian Muslims seem so far to prefer living under Soviet rule rather than Chinese.

Turkey has not taken an official position in the Sino-Soviet conflict and has refrained scrupulously from saying anything about the Turkic groups living in either of them. Yet the Sino-Soviet efforts to win sympathies in Turkey continue. Since ideological limitations prevent both the Soviets and the Chinese from openly using the national issue as the focal point of their dispute, they have turned to other tactics. They have directed their propaganda chiefly toward Turkish leftist groups by promoting international proletariansim in the case of the USSR and national communism in the case of China. The ideological war carried out in the Turkish leftist publications began roughly around 1964 with a clear Soviet advantage. But the pro-Soviet wing then proposed to reorganize Turkey's political system on the basis of nationalities. Using the term Turkiye halklari (Peoples of Turkey), they appealed to the minority groups (the Kurds, Tatars, Cherkess, and Lazes) and promised to give them linguistic and cultural autonomy. This did not make them popular, and toward the end of the decade the national communists - or the "Maoists" as they were commonly called - gained the upper hand both in numbers and militancy within the Turkish leftist groups. The Turkish Maoists condemned Soviet "social imperialism," i.e., the policy of russifying the Central Asian Turks, and they were somewhat less obtrusive than their foes about the "nationalities" living in Turkey. In fact, at some point Sultan Galiev's views were in vogue among the Maoists.

Thus Maoism appealed both to the national feelings as well as to the social aspirations of the leftist intelligentsia, especially to those who came from the lower classes and from Anatolian towns. (The pro-Soviet groups included many upper-class intellectuals.) As a result, almost inadvertently, Maoism won the initial struggle within the left in Turkey. Its recently published newspaper Aydinlik (Enlightenment) is sold nationally and seems to enjoy some popularity.

The agitated leftist activity in Turkey was brought under some control after the military intervention of 1971, but it has continued in a subdued fashion until now. Although the pro-Soviet groups seem to have regained the initiative, the others (the leftists are split into five major groups), including the Maoists, seem to have retained their strength. The outcome of the struggle between the pro-Moscow and the pro-Chinese Marxists in Turkey is nebulous at the present time.

PAN-TURKIC CONSCIOUSNESS TODAY

There is no convincing proof that the visits to the USSR converted a large number of Turks to Communism. However, the visits clearly have produced increased awareness among Turks about their kin in the USSR and the close cultural and linguistic similarities between them, despite differences of regime and geographical location. Even though the Turkish Republican government has consistently disavowed any interest in Soviet Turkic groups and refrained from overtly backing any activity likely to weaken Soviet authority over these groups, still the interest of some Turkish intellectuals in the Soviet Turks has always continued. This is the consequence of a great variety of personal and historical ties that exist beyond government control.

Turkey today possesses a miniature union of all the Turkic groups, ranging from a small group of Christian Gagauzes from Bessarabia (Soviet Moldavia) to a multimillion member group of Tatars (mostly from Crimea), and a variety of other groups from the Caucasus and Central Asia. The migration of the Muslims from Russia and Central Asia has continued to our day, the last migrant groups being the Kazakhs from East Turkistan (Sinkiang) in the 1950s. Practically all these groups have organizations and even periodicals and are not shy about engaging in political activity. (17) The educated members of these groups publish books about their history and culture while claiming that they are part of one Turkish nation. Leaders of various Turkic groups from the USSR, such as Cafer Seydiahmet (Crimea), Z. V. Togan (Bashkiria), Sadri Maksudi (Kazan) and Isa Alptekin (Sinkiang), to mention a few, found refuge in Turkey along with thousands of their countrymen, including some army officers. The universities, notably the departments of language, literature, and history, had and still have a number of eminent professors born and raised in Russia or the Soviet Union, such as the late Akdes N. Kurat and A. Caferoglu. Differences in dialect and in physical complexion between the Turks born in Turkey and those migrating from the USSR have proved to be weaker than the religious, cultural, and linguistic similarities that made their mutual adjustment and coexistence easy. Consequently, visits and the endless accounts in the press about Central Asia and the Caucasus area have given the average Turk a new insight into the scope and problems of what may be called the Turkic world.

It is more difficult to pass judgment on the effects of the visits and cultural exchanges on the Turkic peoples of Central Asia. Turkish visitors to these areas do not report having heard any widespread criticism of the Soviet regime itself. On the surface, many natives appear to have adjusted to its philosophy and tend to praise its material achievements. However, the interest in everything Turkish and to some extent Muslim seems to be overwhelming, as a few verified examples prove.

During his visit to Tashkent and Baku in 1967, Prime Minister Suleyman Demirel and his group were met by huge crowds of Turkic people who had come without any official prodding from far away villages to take a took at the Turkish delegation. The road from the airport to the center of both cities was lined with enthusiastic crowds who offered flowers to the visitors and shouted enthusiastically in unison: "kardas, kardas" (brother, brother). On one occasion the Soviet protocol changed the hour of departure and the road to the airport in order to avoid a repetition of the unexpectedly enthusiastic welcome. In Baku a rather trivial incident dramatized the situation further. The Turkish Premier and the Azeri representatives met and exchanged words of greeting in their respective dialects. The accompanying Soviet interpreter attempted to "translate" the Azeri Turkish into Ottoman Turkish but stopped when told by the parties that they understood each other's language. Another case involved the showing of a Turkish film in Baku. The audience forced the Russian interpreter into silence and listened to the Turkish sound, despite the fact that some people did not speak Turkish. The interpreter complained that the behavior of the listeners would damage his reputation in Moscow but was told that because his name was Rashid (a Muslim name), he should not insist on speaking Russian but abide by his national language.

A Muslim professor established in the United States, who participated in a conference organized by the Orthodox Church in Moscow in June 1977, visited Central Asia as part of a group of 130 Muslim participants who were taken to Bukhara, Tashkent, Khiva, and other localities. The observer writes that while Islamic rites were not performed frequently, religion has become personal, and the identity of the Muslims has become strong and manifests itself in efforts to preserve cultural legacy. "Actually," he writes, "far more is being spent by the USSR to reconstruct, maintain and upkeep and propagandize Muslim monuments in Central Asia than any Muslim country." (18) The observer was deeply impressed by the economic advance of Central Asian Muslims and by the desire of their religious leaders to have students study in Islamic universities in Egypt, Libya, Morocco, and Saudi Arabia.

Further significant evidence was supplied by a Turkish folklore team which put on shows in various Central Asian and Caucasus cities in 1976. The halls in all cities were packed to capacity by local crowds who applauded the performers enthusiastically for several minutes. At the end of the show several local people who attended were interviewed. Their reaction was "we liked the music and the dances very much; most of them are like our own and you do many things as we do." When asked to give a criticism of the show the answer was "The only thing wrong with you is that you do not come often enough. Tez tez gelin (come often and oftener)." I myself recall that at a meeting held in Istanbul in 1973 to celebrate the fiftieth anniversary of the Turkish Republic, the late Bobijan Gafurov (the head of the Oriental Institute in Moscow), despite his docility to the system, stated emphatically and angrily that Central Asia had an urban civilization long before the West. His remarks were precipitated by a remark made by a Bulgarian scholar to the effect that urbanization was largely a Mediterranean phenomenon.

In addition to these eyewitness testimonies of the Turkic consciousness of the Central Asian Turks, one may cite a number of quasi-political acts. For example, a few years ago the Soviet Azeris published the celebrated Hophopname of Sabir in Arabic script. The editor explained that this was necessitated by the anniversary of Sabir and consequently that it was appropriate to use the original script, which provided a more accurate spelling and understanding of the words and spirit of the work. At about the same time the poet Anasultan Kekilova from Turkmenistan was sent to a psychiatric hospital because she wrote a 53-page criticism of conditions in the republic and then asked for permission to migrate abroad, presumably to Turkey. Her criticism seems to have been directed against restrictions imposed on Muslim believers.

Finally, one may cite some recent official criticism of the Directorate of Muslims of Central Asia and Kazakhstan that has published since 1968 a periodical in Tashkent entitled Muslims of the Soviet East (in Uzbek, Arabic, French, and English). The review defends the idea that Islam played a progressive part in the life of Central Asian peoples, that it developed as a national religion because of the contribution of local people, and finally that Islam is compatible with progress and modernization. The review has been sharply attacked by other Soviet publications because it showed Islam and the Muslim scholarship to be on the side of science and technology. Officially for the Soviets, Islam is a stagnant and ossified culture destined to disappear some time in the future. Evidently the authorities are afraid that a reinterpretation of Islam is underway in accordance with the needs of contemporary life. They especially fear the view that it is an ingredient of Central Asian nationality. They believe that efforts to make Islam appear compatible with Leninism and Marxism would give it a new lease on life and increase its potential to thwart russification and assimilation. Islam is also attacked for hostility to other religions and cultures which in this case, as mentioned, means hostility to the Russians because they represent the ruling colonial class. Geoffrey Wheeler, who dealt with this Muslim effort to reinterpret Islam and to make it compatible with modernity and Soviet realities, states:

> Even supposing the new trend in Muslim teaching is as important as Soviet propagandists make out, their method of contesting it seems more likely to inculcate pride in the enduring quality of Muslim beliefs and institutions, and in the subtlety of their defense by the hard pressed Muslim hierarchy, than to persuade them to respond to continuing official pressure to abandon them. (19)

In the ultimate analysis Turkey seems to appear to the Central Asian Turks as the only independent political entity in the world with which they can identify ethnically, culturally, and linguistically. Turkey was and remains for the Soviet Turks a haven because of common cultural, linguistic, and historical ties. One cannot study linguistics and the history of literature in Central Asia today without mentioning Mahmut Kashgarli, the Dede Korkut epics, or the Chagatay classical literary language, which are all common to the Turkish Turks as well. (20) There is no reason today to believe that either Turkey or the Turks of the

Soviet Union think of achieving a political union. The time elapsed since the turn of the century, the sociolinguistic differences emerging in each area, and the experiences of each group during the past fifty years have made the Pan-Turkist scheme a remote utopia. Yet the interest of the Soviet Turks in Turkey, especially among the new and educated elites, persists because the population of Turkey out of all the Turks in the world has achieved the highest level of development in the arts, literature, and independent nationhood. Turkey's achievements represent the Turks' contribution to the civilization of mankind and stand also as symbolic proof of the ability and genius of other Turks. (21) Turkic groups everywhere in the world know instinctively that the achievements and fate of Turkey are bound to have deep psychological and political effects of their own destiny. (22)

CONCLUSION

One can say that the development of nationalities among the Turkic groups in the Soviet Union follows a pattern that differs from the process of nation formation in the Balkans and the colonial empires of Western European nations, despite the fact that it contains elements from both. The process of nation formation among the Turkic groups in the USSR consists on one hand of a movement for linguistic and cultural mobilization designed to oppose assimilation by the Russians, and on the other hand of opposition to a colonial situation that forces them to use economic, demographic, and social means to offset the power of the outside colonizers. To an extraordinary extent it has been a "modernization from inside" without the direct input from Western models and Western political power that has characterized other modern national revivals.

Still the West, through Turkey, has consistently made a difference in this internal modernization, and presently, because of the fading of the cold war and the eruption of the Sino-Soviet dispute, is making a much greater difference and will continue to do so. In the distant past the Ottoman Empire was, despite the binding religious and cultural factors, far too distant and aloof a "Western" conglomeration to matter in the cultural and political development of the Central Asian Turks. Even during the revolutionary Pan-Turkic period early in this century, Turkey could serve only as a cultural beacon, unable to give concrete help; and during the Soviet revolution of the twenties, thirties, and forties the frontiers were effectively closed - only memories then kept the influence of Turkey alive in Central Asia. But now all this has changed, and in the immediate future one may anticipate the participation of Turkey in the unresolved and unresolvable nationality problems of Soviet Central Asia.

NOTES

(1) For a discussion of the nationality problem in Islam see Roy P. Mottahedeh, "The Shu-ubiyah Controversy and the Social History of Early Islamic Iran," International Journal of Middle East Studies 7 (April 1977): 161-182. For the cultural transformation of Central Asia see Vasili V. Bartol'di, Histoire des Turcs d'Asie Centrale (Paris, 1945).

(2) See a series of articles on Bukhara in Edward Allworth, The Nationality Question in Soviet Central Asia (New York, 1973), pp. 134-167. A succinct history of Central Asia is in Alexandre Bennigsen, "Tzarist Russia and the Muslims of Central Asia," The Cambridge History of Islam (New York, 1970), pp. 503ff. See also Alexandre Bennigsen and Chantal Lemercier-Quelquejay, Islam in the Soviet Union (New York, 1967); and Michael Rywkin, Russia in Central Asia (New York, 1963).

(3) A similar linguistic-political difficulty occurred among the Christian population of Macedonia beginning in 1885, after the Ottoman government lost its authority and the religiously unifying role of Hellenism exerted by the Orthodox Church was disrupted by the rise of national churches. Serbia, Greece, and Bulgaria laid a claim on the Christian population of Macedonia, and as one learned native witness writes, it was not unusual to see one son of a Serbian father claiming to be a Bulgarian and the other son Greek. Kemal H. Karpat, "The Memoirs of N. Batzaria: The Young Turks and Nationalism," International Journal of Middle East Studies 6 (1976): 276-299.

(4) Serge A. Zenkovsky, Pan-Turkism and Islam in Russia (Cambridge, Mass., 1960), p. 58. Kemal H. Karpat, Turkey's Politics (Princeton, 1959).

(5) Geoffrey Wheeler, "Islam and the Soviet Union," Middle Eastern Studies 13 (January 1977): 42.

(6) For the Pan-Turkist movements see C.W. Hostler, Turkism and the Soviets (New York, 1957), and Zenkovsky, Pan-Turkism and Islam in Russia.

(7) Recent accounts of the modernization of Turkey are Bernard Lewis, The Emergence of Modern Turkey (London, 1961); Stanford J. Shaw and Ezel K. Shaw, History of the Ottoman Empire and Modern Turkey (London, 1977), vol. II; and Niyazi Berkes, The Development of Secularism in Turkey (Montreal, 1964).

(8) In 1969 the crude birth rate for the USSR as a whole was 17.4 per thousand and the death rate was 9.6. But in Uzbekistan the birth rate was 33 per thousand, death was 5.9, and divorce 1.1 per thousand with a net increase of 27.1 per thousand. New York Times,

September 7, 1969. See also Rein Taagepera, "Soviet Demographic Trends," Soviet Studies, (April 1969), pp. 477ff.

(9) G.A. Bondarskaia, Rozhdaemost' v SSSR   Fertility in the USSR (Moscow, 1977).

(10) Geoffrey Wheeler, "The Turkic Languages of Soviet Muslim Asia: Russian Linguistic Policy," Middle Eastern Studies 13 (May 1977): 208-217.

(11) Gregory J. Massell believes that the extraordinarily tenacious resistance of a Muslim traditional milieu to direct revolutionary manipulation was the crucial reason for the abandonment of the antifamily campaign. See The Surrogate Proletariat (Princeton, 1974).

(12) The enrollments in higher education per 10,000 people shows a definite increase in favor of the natives:

	1959	1970
Russians	72.0	211.0
Ukrainians	49.6	152.0
Uzbeks	48.2	160.0
Kazakhs	54.7	185.0
Kirgiz	58.0	168.0
Turkmen	57.0	148.0

This compares with France 100, West Germany 73, Sweden 99, United Kingdom 31, Turkey 30, USA 282 per ten thousand for 1966. Allworth, The Nationality Question, p. 90. See also W.K. Medlin et al., Education and Development in Central Asia (Leiden, 1971).

(13) See bibliography on Turkmen by Z.B. Mukhamedova, in Izvestiia Akademii Nauk Turkmenskoi SSR. Seriia obshchestvennykh nauk, 1974, No. 6.

(14) In Turkey there are of course respected publications such as Turk Kulturu (published since 1962) and lesser reviews such as Turk Birligi which publish research and opinion articles mainly on culture and literature designed to appeal to all Turkic peoples. There are also a variety of small periodicals and a rather large number of books dealing with specific Turkic groups in the Soviet Union. See for instance Hasan Oraltay, Kazak Turkleri (Istanbul, 1976); Yusuf Uralgiray, Uzun Gunlerde Oruc (Ankara, 1975); and M. Engin et al., Kazak ve Tatar Turkleri (Istanbul, 1976); and the works published earlier of A. Zeki Velidi Togan, notably Turklugun Makadderati Uzerine (Istanbul, 1970).

(15) Information on the background of this party is in Jacob Landau, Radical Politics in Modern Turkey (Leiden, 1974). For some explanation of the upsurge of the party see my forthcoming review of the book in Middle Eastern Studies. For Turkish-Soviet relations see Kemal H. Karpat et al., Turkey's Foreign Policy in Transition 1950-1974 (Leiden, 1975) and George S. Harris, The Origins of Communism in Turkey (Stanford, California, 1967).

(16) Radio Liberty Dispatch, April 30, 1973. See also W. C. Fletcher, Religion and Soviet Foreign Policy 1945-70 (London, 1973); and Hearings Before the Sub-committee on Europe of the Committee on Foreign Affairs, House of Representatives (Washington, D.C., 1974), pp. 323-328.

(17) See for instance Isa Alptekin, Dogu Turkistan Insanliktan Yardim Istiyor (n.p., 1974).

(18) Ismail Faruqi, "Central Asian Report: Muslims Survive," Impact International, no. 14 (October 27, 1977): 14.

(19) Wheeler, "Islam and the Soviet Union," p. 48.

(20) For instance, in his classical work, Hars ve medeniyet (Culture and Civilization) (Istanbul, 1923), Ziya Gokalp describes the old, rich culture of the Anatolian Turks. "They had national epics known as Oguzname. Of these we can see only twelve pieces in the Dede Korkut book."

(21) I recall a brief encounter in the West with a young Kazakh who occupied a high administrative position in a Soviet university. He expressed a keen desire, if he had the chance, to visit the Istanbul mosques, which he called "the masterpieces of my nation" not in the political but cultural sense. For Turkish interest in Kazakhs see Saadet Cagatay, Kazakca Metinler (Ankara, 1961).

(22) During some of my encounters with Soviet scholars of Turkic origin I was flattered to learn that they had read many of my publications. They were pleased that one of their kinsmen found recognition in the West and thus proved that "Turks can be equal and better than the Russians," since in their eyes the West is superior to the USSR and the Russians. At one of these meetings my communication came under attack by a Russian professor from Moscow University because of my non-Marxist definition of the term "social." At the end of the meeting I was approached by a Turkish lady from the USSR (whom I had not met before) who apologized for the professor's remarks, saying "He is an ignorant dogmatist..." and offered me a pack of Soviet cigarettes and a record as consolation for this unwarranted attack by one of her "bosses," as she called him.

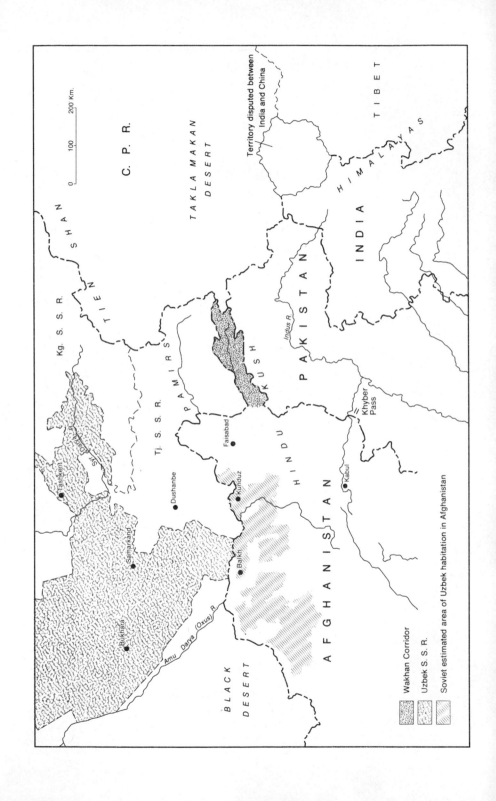

Territory disputed between India and China

C. P. R.

TIEN SHAN

TAKLA MAKAN DESERT

TIBET

Kg. S. S. R.

HIMALAYAS

PAMIRS

HINDU KUSH

PAKISTAN

INDIA

Indus R.

Khyber Pass

Tj. S. S. R.

Faisabad

Kabul

Dushanbe

Kunduz

Tashkent

Syr Darya R.

Samarkand

Balkh

AFGHANISTAN

Bukhara

Amu Darya (Oxus) R.

BLACK DESERT

0   100   200 Km.

Wakhan Corridor

Uzbek S. S. R.

Soviet estimated area of Uzbek habitation in Afghanistan

6
The Uzbeks in Two States: Soviet and Afghan Policies Toward an Ethnic Minority
David C. Montgomery

The Uzbeks, a Turkic-speaking people dwelling in Central Asia, number 11,181,000 by 1973 extimates. The larger part of them (8,025,000) is found in the Uzbek Soviet Socialist Republic (Uzbekistan) of the Soviet Union. Another 1,489,000 live in the Soviet Central Asian republics of Kazakhstan, Turkmenistan, Kirgizia, and Tajikistan. Some 1,649,000 live in northern Afghanistan, while a small number (18,000) live in the western part of the Sinkiang province of the Chinese People's Republic. (1) The 11,000,000 Uzbeks are the second largest Turkic-speaking group in the world (after the 36,000,000 Turks in Turkey); the 9,500,000 Soviet Uzbeks are the third largest Soviet nationality (after the Russians and the Ukrainians) and are the largest non-European Soviet ethnic group.

BEFORE THE REVOLUTION

The early Uzbeks were probably one of the elements in the Turko-Mongolian Golden Horde that dominated Russia and western Siberia from the thirteenth through the fifteenth centuries. The ethnonym Uzbek may have its origin in the name of Uzbek, khan of the Golden Horde from 1313 to 1340. With the breakup of the Horde during the fifteenth century, the nomadic Uzbeks moved southward and by mid-century had established themselves in the lower reaches of the Syr and Amu rivers, from where they challenged the power of the Timurid rulers of Transoxania whom they displaced by the end of the fifteenth century, gaining dominion over the already present Turkic-speaking (Turkmen, Kirgiz, Kazakh) and Iranian-speaking (Tajik) populations. They then adopted much of the Bukhara region's established variant of the Islamic culture - including a Persian literary language, making a large segment of the upper class virtually bilingual. Subsequently, they became increasingly sedentary, engaging mainly in agriculture, but also involving themselves with crafts and commerce.

By the eighteenth century three Uzbek-dominated rigidly Sunni khanates had emerged at Kokand, Bukhara, and Khiva. Centering on ancient oasis cities, these states interacted uneasily with each other and with the nomadic Turkic groups located on the desert steppe to the north and the Afghan highlands to the south. They maintained minimal contact with Shi'ite Iran and distant relations with India, China, and Russia until the third quarter of the nineteenth century when all three khanates were quite rapidly taken over by the Russians. Their confrontation had begun in 1847 and by 1867 a Russian Governor-Generalship of Turkistan had been established at Tashkent which exerted authority right up to the Pamirs. After the takeover, although the Kokand khanate was disbanded in 1876, Bukhara and Khiva remained technically autonomous but actually entirely dependent on the Russians until the revolution of 1917. (2)

Despite the Russian conquest, the Uzbek tribal and court notables and the Islamic clergy continued to dominate an agricultural peasantry in traditional fashion. General literacy remained extremely low, and knowledge of the outside world remained slight. The two generations of tsarist Russian domination did set in motion some currents of change. Especially after the start of the new century, when direct rail connections with European Russia were established, the economy of the area became internationalized. Cotton increasingly became the major cash crop, causing a shift in agricultural labor and landholding relationships. Russian soldiers, bureaucrats, businessmen, and railway workers settled in some of the Uzbek towns. The increasing access to the outside world sparked the introduction of modern and foreign concepts. One manifestation of this new stimulus was the Jadidist educational modernization movement. But on the whole, before 1917, the world of the Uzbeks had only begun to change.

THE ESTABLISHMENT OF SOVIET RULE

In the years before 1914 the tsarist regime became increasingly unpopular among the peoples of Russian Turkistan. (3) During the war itself resentment boiled over. Armed revolt broke out during 1916 as a result of food shortages and an announced policy of conscripting Central Asians into labor battalions.

The February Revolution did not allay this Muslim disaffection from Russia. The Provisional Government of 1917 was unresponsive to nationalist demands from the Central Asian peoples, many of whom had responded initially with favor to talk from Bolsheviks about recognizing national aspirations. Nor did the October Revolution heal the wounds. After the Bolsheviks came to power in Petrograd they tried to preserve as much as possible of the territory of the former tsarist state. Europeans, especially Russians, dominated the new government's apparatus in Central Asia and elsewhere and vigorously sought to suppress nationalist separatist movements.

In Central Asia the Bolsheviks gained control of the Tashkent Soviet in November 1917, and cooperation with native leaders rapidly broke down as a civil war developed almost more on racial than on idealogical lines - though some Europeans resisted the Bolsheviks and some Central Asians sided with them. Native resistance came mainly from the forces of the Bukharan and Khivan khanates, from urban intellectuals - the Jadidist reformers - and from guerilla-type tribal forces known as Basmachis. The Central Asians lacked sufficient modern weapons and unity of action and purpose, rarely cooperating and sometimes fighting with each other. Some of them fought to reassert old privileges; some sought autonomy within a reconstituted Russian Empire; others wanted complete independence; and some engaged in outright brigandage. Of course, not all the Muslims joined in the fighting; a large part of the local population probably attempted to stay apart from either side of the conflict and simply to survive. But resistance was very widespread.

The Bolshevik forces, though based mainly on a European population that was outnumbered twenty to one, were better organized and armed and held their own though at first they were only loosely linked to Petrograd. After reestablishing contact with European Russia in 1919, the Tashkent Soviet was able to achieve increasing success and eventually to defeat the opposing forces. The khanates of Khiva and Bukhara were transmuted in 1920 into "people's republics." Many Muslims then fled to Afghanistan, Iran, and China. The Basmachis of the Fergana Valley (in what had once been Kokand) fought on for some time, but by 1924 the Soviet regime enjoyed a victors' peace.

Moscow used this opportunity to toally restructure Muslim Central Asia. On April 11, 1921, a "Turkistan Autonomous Socialist Republic" was proclaimed which consisted of most of the southern area of the former tsarist Governor-Generalship of Turkistan (much of the northern area had been incorporated into the RSFSR in 1920 as the Kazakh Soviet Socialist Republic). Then, after a period of lenient land, cultural, and economic policies (as well as general war weariness) had weakened native resistance, on December 5, 1924 the Turkistan ASR was reorganized into Turkmen, Kirgiz, and Uzbek Soviet Socialist Republics. The Khivan and Bukharan "people's republics," which had meanwhile in 1923 and 1924 been converted into "Soviet socialist republics," were now (in December 1924) also disbanded and incorporated mainly into the new Uzbekistan, which as a result came to include about 3.5 million Uzbeks (about 72 percent of all Uzbeks).

The motives for this partition of Turkistan into separate nationality republics are varyingly interpreted. Some authorities agree with the official explanations that administrative units based on linguistic nationality lend to efficiency in economic development and also follow naturally from Bolshevik statements recognizing the sovereignty of

national groups. Other authorities take note of the extraordinarily
inefficient shapes of the new republics, and accept the more
Machiavellian view that the partition was designed to thwart Pan-
Turkic and Pan-Islamic projects of the prerevolutionary Jadidists.
Regardless, the reform was decisive for the cultural future of the
native populations. Where formerly there had been Islamic unity, where
language had made virtually no administrative difference, and where
many people were bilingual, a large segment of the population was
compelled to accept an administrative nationality according to one or
another of its tongues.

During the half-century after the organization of the Uzbek SSR
several adminstrative and territorial changes occurred. On May 13,
1925 the Uzbek republic was formally accepted by the Congress of
Soviets of the USSR as one of the constituent republics of the USSR,
but a Tajik autonomous region was set up in its eastern portion. On
December 5, 1929 this became the Tajik SSR, containing two-thirds of
Uzbekistan's 1 million Tajiks. In 1930 the capital of Uzbekistan was
moved from Samarkand to Tashkent. On December 5, 1935 the
Karakalpak Autonomous Republic which had formerly been incorporated
was attached to western Uzbekistan. More recently, on January 26,
1963, in accordance with irrigation development in central Uzbekistan,
a portion of the Hungry Steppe formerly in Kazakhstan was transferred
to Uzbekistan. Over the years there have been frequent internal
changes of administrative boundaries and divisions of administrative
units as the economy developed and the population grew. Many of these
changes were probably motivated primarily by economic efficiency.
For example, the territories transferred recently from Kazakhstan to
Uzbekistan were cotton-growing lands that could be more efficiently
administered within the cotton economy of Uzbekistan. Some changes
tended to weaken the sense that local nationalities control their own
destinies and to reinforce the official view that the boundaries between
republics are losing their former significance. (4)   But none of the
changes has been as significant as the divisive work of 1922 through
1925.

The Educational Revolution

Illiteracy and lack of education were problems attacked early by the
Soviet government in Uzbekistan. Even before the civil war had
quieted, modern, secular educational institutions were being opened,
and the traditional mosque schools were being disallowed. By the mid-
1920s, universities had been created in Samarkand and Tashkent, and
special classes were being established to teach adults all over
Uzbekistan basic reading and writing skills. But the systematic mass
education could not be implemented overnight. It was many years
before educational opportunities were extended to the entire population. Today almost every small village complex has a school system

which provides the compulsory eight years of instruction. Ten-year schools are still being introduced to the towns and villages, though they are standard in the cities. To the qualified Uzbek student, higher-level vocational, technical, professional, and scholarly training is available. By the early 1970s each year approximately 250,000 Uzbek students were finishing technical schools and universities. (5)

The growth of educational opportunity has been paralleled by a growth of literacy. Starting with a literacy rate of less than 4 percent at the time of the revolution, the rate steadily grew until at the present time the Soviet statistics indicate almost total literacy for the area. (6)

In 1943 the Uzbek Academy of Sciences was established. Its many branches include a variety of fields in the areas of physical, biological, mathematical, humanistic, and social sciences. The majority of the higher positions in the administrative structure are held by Uzbeks. Nevertheless, in 1970, despite increasing educational opportunities and definite accomplishments, the Uzbeks had not yet attained representation in the scientific fields proportional to their share of the population of Uzbekistan (65.5 percent). For example, in that year Uzbeks were 48 percent of the scientific workers, 53 percent of the candidates of science, and 52 percent of the doctors of science. Nonetheless the great strides being made in developing a highly qualified, educated establishment are shown by the rapid growth in the number of doctors of science. In 1950 there were 20 Uzbek doctors of science in the republic; in 1960 there were 78; in 1970, 258; and in 1975, 446. Uzbeks increased from 13 percent of the doctors of science in 1950 to 60 percent in 1975. (7)

Instruction at all levels throughout the university is conducted in the Uzbek language, though with each higher level of education more knowledge of the Russian language is needed. At the university level textbooks for many courses are in the Uzbek language, even for such sophisticated topics as nuclear physics. Uzbek students with sufficient attainment and promise have the opportunity for training at the major educational centers in the European part of the Soviet Union. (8)

The Economic and Urban Revolutions

The economy of prerevolutionary Uzbekistan was basically agricultural. Cotton was the major crop and took up approximately half of the sown acreage. This is also the case today. Uzbekistan produces almost two-thirds of the Soviet Union's cotton, and its production rivals that of the United States. But the Soviet regime has also developed industry, primarily light industry, with emphasis on cotton fiber processing, textile weaving, and the manufacture of farm implements and machinery. The evacuation of industrial facilities to Uzbekistan during the Second World War greatly increased the rate of industrialization and brought a large number of European industrial workers, many of whom stayed in Uzbekistan after the war. Recently, electrical and refrigeration equipment plants have been built. The building of hydroelectric plants in the mountainous regions has facilitated industrialization by extending electric power to almost every section of the republic. Similarly, development of the natural gas field in the Bukhara region has provided fuel for industry and homes as well as a surplus to transport by pipeline to European Russia.

The process of industrialization has given many Soviet Uzbeks modern technological skills. These have been applied mainly in the agricultural areas where most of the Uzbeks live, but a growing number of Uzbeks are becoming qualified for industrial and technological positions formerly held for the most part by people of European origin. A numerical appraisal of the labor force in Uzbekistan for 1970 shows the emerging significance of the industrial sector: 1,439,000 persons were employed on state farms and collective farms, and another 132,000 were in machine building and metal working associated with growing, harvesting, transporting, and transforming cotton. In the labor force, 469,000 were classed as industrial workers, and another 139,000 were engaged in light industry. (9)

The spread of industry has not brought about the urbanization of the Uzbeks. In 1924, 79.7 percent of the population of the republic lived in rural areas; over half a century later in 1977, 61.5 percent resided there. The urban population is concentrated in Tashkent Province, where 43.7 percent of Uzbekistan's 5.3 million urban residents live. But Tashkent is heavily russianized. The rising standard of living in the rural areas has helped to keep Uzbeks in the countryside. The rural Uzbek life with its individual courtyards and private plots of land for gardens and livestock and large bonus payments at the end of the cotton harvest is to many Uzbeks preferable to the urban life with its lower-paying industrial or office occupations and residence in small apartments in high-rise buildings. Early in 1978, a high-level Uzbek educator in Tashkent expressed to the author his concern that because so many Uzbeks, even talented university graduates, preferred the rural life-style and were maintaining or seeking employment in the less intensely urbanized areas, Tashkent would become even more russianized. In 1970, that city was already 40.8 percent Russian and only 31.1 percent Uzbek. (10)

Uzbeks did, however, outnumber Russians in the urban population of the republic as a whole in 1970. Russians constituted 33 percent then and Uzbeks, 41 percent. It is important to note, furthermore, that in the next decade the labor shortages in the European industrial zones of the country may well draw off a significant portion of the Europeans from their urban outpost in Central Asia and make urban Uzbekistan a more Uzbek environment. (11) At the same time, the countryside where in 1970 80 percent of the population were Uzbek and only 2 percent Russian, will remain predominanatly Central Asian rather than European. As the author was told in a Tashkent teahouse in 1977, "There are as many Russians in the rural areas of Uzbekistan as there are Jews in all of Uzbekistan."

Control Mechanisms

Though theoretically a voluntary member of the Soviet family of nations, the Uzbek Soviet Socialist Republic is irrevocably attached to the Soviet Union and is under the control of Soviet Russia, which determines the main political, economic, and cultural patterns. Soviet Russian domination of Uzbekistan was established by the events of the Civil War and has been maintained by the apparatus of the Communist Party and the Soviet military. The purges of the Uzbek intellectual and political communities in the 1930s eliminated real and suspected anti-Soviets and nationalists and destroyed a large part of the first generation of local Soviet leaders, many of whom had been inspired by the Jadidist reform movements of the prerevolutionary era.

The administrative bodies of Uzbekistan have been staffed largely by members of the titular nationality, increasingly so during the past several years. Though Uzbeks have been members of the Communist Party since the Revolution, only in recent years have they become a majority of the Party in Uzbekistan. In 1925 the Communist Party of Uzbekistan (CPUz) had 18,351 members, of whom 42.16 percent were Uzbeks and 40.43 percent were Russians. (12) In 1967 the CPUz had 353,841 members, of whom 53.3 percent were Uzbeks and 21.5 percent were Russians. Uzbeks hold three of the five positions in the CPUz Secretariat. (13) The current first secretary, Sharaf Rashidov, an Uzbek, is also a candidate member of the CPSU Politburo.

The republican military units very early were integrated into the Soviet armed forces. After conscription young Uzbeks and other Central Asians generally serve their period of duty away from their home region. The military garrison troops in Uzbekistan and other parts of Central Asia are largely European, as are the border guards. Tashkent is the administrative center of the Turkistan Military District, whose commanding general has always been European. (14) The police, however, are composed mainly of Uzbeks and in 1978 were headed by an Uzbek.

THE NEW UZBEK CULTURE

Educational growth and economic development have been accompanied by great changes in the Uzbek culture. Soviet authorities have worked strenuously to minimize the influence of the Islamic religion on the Uzbeks. (15) During the 1920s most mosques and religious schools were closed and the Islamic clergy was violently persecuted. Civil courts replaced the Seriat courts. Overt religious practices were either discouraged or forbidden, and strident atheistic propaganda was conducted.

Antireligious activity abated during the Second World War, when the regime worked to encourage all possible forms of popular patriotism.

Since the war it has resumed but in the main has taken the form of education and propaganda without physical coercion. Television and radio programming in the Uzbek language features discussions of atheism. Courses in "scientific communism" are part of the higher education curriculum. The promotion of atheism is less than vigorous outside the major urban areas, however. The author was told that in some provincial colleges "scientific communism" courses are irregularly taught because of the lack of appropriate teachers who are usually Russian and do not want to live in the predominantly Uzbek areas. "No true Uzbek would teach such a subject."

Partially to present a favorable image to the Muslim peoples in other lands, the Soviet authorities have permitted some showcase Islamic institutions to exist in Uzbekistan. Among these are a directorate of Islamic affairs in Tashkent and schools of religious instruction in both Bukhara and Tashkent which train a minimal number of clergy to serve the needs of the practicing Muslims of the Soviet Union.

While the overt practice of Islam among the Soviet Uzbeks has been discouraged with some success, Uzbeks to a very great extent still strongly identify with Islam and consider themselves to be Muslims. Theological knowledge is often minimal, but lifecycle rituals such as circumcision are regularly observed in most families, even among the educated urban elite. In many respects Uzbek self-identification with Islam is a second affirmation of their not being Russian. Once, when the author spoke in Uzbek to a seller at the Alaiskii Bazaar in Tashkent, the query immediately followed, "Why do you know the Muslim language?"

The Soviet authorities from the start made efforts to elevate the status of women in Uzbek and other Soviet Muslim societies. The educational and antireligion campaigns were instrumental in raising the status of women. Direct legislation has also helped. Polygamy, the bride price, compulsory wearing of the veil, and other traditional practices have been outlawed. Compulsory education and officially supported women's organizations broadened the social and intellectual horizons of women. The great "Hujum" ("Attack") movement of the late 1920s and early 1930s played a particularly dramatic role in altering women's situation in Uzbek society.

To be sure, certain conservative and traditional attitudes and practices with regard to women linger. Although women are legally "free" to choose their own husband, family approval remains very important in practice. Furthermore, despite the weakening of official religious sanctions against marriage with non-Muslims, marriage between a Muslim woman and a non-Muslim man is still quite rare in Central Asia. (Marriage of an Uzbek man to a Russian or other non-Muslim woman is more common, though still far from typical.) Rural women, in particular, still lead a fairly traditional life, their educational and career attainment often being limited by early marriage and childbearing. Agricultural work brigades are often segregated into male and female units.

On the whole, however, Uzbek society is no longer completely male dominated, and a large number of the women of Uzbekistan are benefiting from participation in education, skilled labor, and the professions. (16) One indicator of the role of women in public life is that in 1976, 34.9 percent of the members of the Supreme Soviet of Uzbekistan were women, most of them Uzbeks. Similarly, 48.1 percent of the members of the local Soviets were women.

A most important aspect of the cultural transformation in Uzbekistan under the Soviet regime was the reform of language and writing. (17) Before the revolution many Uzbek intellectuals had been tending to use Chagatay Turkic written in the Arabic script as their literary language in replacement of the literary Persian of Bukhara. Chagatay gave them a link with the other Turkic-speaking peoples of Central Asia. The reorganization of Soviet Turkistan into separate national republics in 1924 was accompanied by the deliberate abandonment of Chagatay and promulgation of the Tashkent-area dialect as the basis of a new Uzbek literary language, thus causing a greater linguistic separation not only from other Central Asian Turks but also from Uzbeks in Afghanistan and China. In 1929 the Arabic script was replaced by a Latin-based script. A decade later, in 1940, the present Cyrillic-based script was introduced. In the development of modern literary Uzbek an effort has been made to purge the language of many Arabic and Persian words. Many Russian words have entered into the Uzbek language, especially in technical, scientific, and political spheres.

Formal cultural development among the Soviet Uzbeks has proceeded under the official dictum of "national in form, but socialist in content." Cultural affairs are nominally under the direction of the Ministry of Culture in Tashkent, which is headed by an Uzbek and follows guidelines from the central Soviet government in Moscow. Formal Uzbek cultural expression is expected to be secular and to present Islam, when it is mentioned at all, in a negative light. In published folklore more references to Islam have been edited out. Soviet-style modernization is to be lauded. Pre-Soviet history and traditions are to be presented in careful consideration of current ideological trends and the Uzbeks are encouraged to search the non-Turkic and pre-Islamic past of Uzbekistan for their deep roots, but not the older and broader Turkic nomadic and tribal heritage.

Soviet Uzbek literature is under the nominal direction of the Union of Soviet Writers of Uzbekistan, the republic branch of the All-Soviet Writers Union. Publication of books and periodicals in the Uzbek language is copious, as is shown by the following publication figures for 1971: 139 newspapers with a total circulation of 2,753,000 per issue; eighteen magazines with a total circulation of 2,903,000 per issue; and 833 books and brochures with a total printing of 23,630,000 copies. (18) Tsarist and Soviet Russian literatures are extolled as models. Both for fiction and nonfiction the Uzbekistan publishing houses often give

preference to the works of members of the titular nationality. The
works of many Uzbek authors are published in both Uzbek and Russian
language editions.   The Uzbek Academy of Sciences has its own
publishing house, which annually publishes many scholarly books in both
Uzbek and Russian.   In the 1976 to 1978 period a fourteen-volume
Ozbek Soviet Entsiklopediyasi (Uzbek Soviet Encyclopedia) was
published in 50,000 copies.

Although some Uzbek music continues the traditional style, modern
developments based on Western classical and popular patterns have also
appeared.   The national ballet of the Tashkent Ali Shir Nevai theater
presents classical western ballets as well as recent productions based on
native themes.   The opera company has the same varied repertoire.   The
visual arts (painting, sculpture, and architecture) have shown a
continuation of established patterns, or more often a contemporary
stylization of them, as well as imitation of or combination with Soviet
and modern forms.   The Uzbeks produce their own films.   Tashkent
radio currently broadcasts music, news, and sports in the Uzbek,
Russian, and Tajik languages on three frequencies of the middle and
long wave bands.   Each frequency has mixed language broadcasting.

Despite strict governmental control of their culture, the Soviet
Uzbeks have not become russified, though they have become sovietized
and modernized.   They have developed a self-identity that differs from
their identity in pre-Soviet times when their orientation was often more
toward the kinship group, local urban areas, the common Turkic-
speaking heritage, and the broader Islamic community.   Given a
separate administrative status, a distinctive literary language and
orthography, and an official history, the Soviet Uzbeks have acquired
(as interpreted by an outside visitor) a concept of themselves as a
separate nation.   They have, nevertheless, maintained a strong
identification with other Turks and the Islamic world.

Indeed, their archaeological and historical scholarship under the
Soviet regime has given the Uzbek people an increased pride in their
heritage, which they feel is more ancient and more lofty than that of
the Russians.   In addition, the feudal past still lives in the memories of
Uzbek men who were slaves in their youth and of women who were
subject to the stifling cloak of the paranja.   No doubt the irrigation of
extensive tracts of desert by the Soviet regime is viewed as a noble
accomplishment.   The modern skyline of Tashkent and the new Tashkent
subway system are certainly not rejected by the Uzbeks of today.   But
the statement of a French scholar a decade ago is still valid: "After a
century of close contacts with Russia, southern Central Asia seems to
be the last and most secure refuge of the active sense of nationality
among the former Muslim people of the USSR." (19)

ETHNIC RELATIONS

To study the more than 100 ethnic groups that live in Uzbekistan is to gain insight into the difficulty of assessing the relations between the Soviet Uzbeks and the Uzbeks that dwell beyond the Soviet frontiers. Of these many groups the Uzbeks themselves constituted 64 percent of the population in 1970. In that year the Russians were 12.5 percent, Tatars 4.8, Kazakhs 4.6, Tajiks 3.8, Karakalpaks 1.9, Koreans 1.3, Ukrainians 1.0, Jews 1.9, Kirgiz 0.9, Turkmens 0.6, and others 3 percent. (20)

Relations between the majority Uzbeks, the minority Russians, and the other populations are harmonious on the surface. Overt acts of racial discord are less prevalent than in the United States. Schools and housing are "integrated"; the "ethnic neighborhoods" are due to traditional residence patterns and not administrative fiat. Especially in the urban areas, the construction of modern high-rise apartment buildings is creating increased ethnic mixing.

Where national groups are sufficiently concentrated, there are separate schools where the basic language of instruction is Uzbek, Russian, Tajik, Kazakh, Kirgiz, Turkmen, Crimean Tatar, or Karakalpak. The Russian and Uzbek languages are taught in all schools. Russian is taught to Uzbek students from as early as kindergarten. Instruction amounts to a few hours per week through the completion of the middle school. Increasingly, urban middle and upper class Uzbek parents attempt to place their children in Russian language schools, to help them acquire the language skills necessary for success in the broader Soviet society. Due to extracurricular association with Russians and exposure to Russian language mass media, urban Uzbeks usually acquire a good knowledge of the Russian language. Educated upper-class Uzbeks are generally bilingual, having fluency in both their native Uzbek and Russian, and are bicultural, comfortable in and familiar with the Uzbek and Russian Soviet cultures. Rural Uzbeks, on the other hand, frequently do not acquire full fluency in Russian, in large part due to both the scarcity of Russians in the rural areas and inadequacies in the teaching of Russian in the rural schools. Many rural Uzbek men obtain a good working knowledge of Russian only during military service, which is also often the first opportunity that they have to associate directly with Russians and members of other nationalities.

Though the Uzbek language is taught in the Russian schools of Uzbekistan from the third class, few Russians become fluent in Uzbek, particularly in the urban areas. Many Russian students feel that their time could be better spent on mathematics and the sciences. In the urban areas, out-of-class play by Russian children is usually in the Russian language, and in both urban and rural areas there seems to be increasing voluntary social segregation of Russian and local ethnic groups during the teen-age years. The Uzbekistan Russian or European of any socioeconomic level generally has little or no capability in the

Uzbek language and scant familiarity with the Uzbek culture. Those relatively few Russians who are proficient in Uzbek generally reside in the rural areas, or have made an unusual personal effort to learn the Uzbek language.

There is little intermarriage between the European and Central Asian ethnic groups. Intermarriage is more frequent in the urban areas; when it occurs in the rural areas the European woman is expected to adopt the Uzbek culture, including Islam. A rural Central Asian woman who marries a European man is often forced by social pressure to divorce or to move to the city.

Many Russians and Europeans in Uzbekistan, whether they were born there or have immigrated, have a "colonial outpost" mentality, considering their homeland to be the European part of the Soviet Union. They view with discomfort the increasing Uzbek numbers, confidence, competitiveness, and competence, and find increasingly less valid the former stereotype of an Uzbek as being "someone who picks cotton, eats melons, and sings and dances."

The Uzbeks' numerically dominant position in Uzbekistan has engendered tension among the various groups of Muslim heritage. The Uzbeks consider Uzbekistan's land and accomplishments to be mainly their own and are condescending to other Muslim groups. They say, "Their culture is like our Uzbek culture," but not, "Our Uzbek culture is like their culture." Kazakhs and Turkmens, formerly of a nomadic culture that was dependent on trade with the sedentary Uzbeks, have been heard to say, "How can anyone from a merchant background really be honest?" Since Uzbeks often are given preference and priority for jobs and educational placement, non-Uzbeks at times feel discriminated against. In mixed marriages the children are usually registered on their passports as Uzbeks to receive the benefits of the titular nationality. In 1929, when the Tajik SSR was formed from part of Uzbekistan, many of the Tajiks who remained in Uzbek territory registered as Uzbeks to avoid discrimination or the rumored deportation. There has been a gradual Uzbekization of many of the peoples of Muslim heritage in Uzbekistan.

Despite common bonds of the Turkic language and Muslim heritage, many of the Crimean Tatars in Uzbekistan, who were deported there during the Second World War, are actively attempting to preserve their cultural traditions and ethnic identity. The activities of the Crimean Tatars have at times been suppressed by the Soviet Uzbek authorities. Some Crimean Tatar young people, however, in an attempt to live more tranquilly and to advance in Uzbekistan, attempt to pass as Uzbeks.

The Uzbeks are not entirely free from tension among themselves. The Khorasanis in the west (the old Khivan Khanate) and the Ferganis in the east (the old Kokand Khanate) each consider themselves the "purer" Uzbeks. Each group has its own dialect and has a strong tradition of mutual social support. Furthermore, certain families or even clans have great pride in their genealogy and exclusive marriage traditions, considering their lineage superior to that of other Uzbeks. Descent is claimed from early Muslim notables or nomadic aristocracy (the "white bone" tradition).

Another very important source of internal tension developing among the Uzbeks derives from modernist trends. In Tashkent in particular a newly developed russified and urban Uzbek elite dominates the public administration and the mass media and is losing touch with the majority of the Uzbeks in the rural and smaller urban areas. There is much intramarriage in this group, and families frequently obtain special access to educational institutions and jobs. The children of this group often go to Russian language schools, and many are becoming russified in their cultural tastes and goals; they sometimes prefer to speak Russian and have minimal proficiency in Uzbek. Some young Uzbek authors associated with this group write only in Russian. However, this small but developing, new generation of Uzbeks lacks full intimate acceptance either in broader Uzbek or Russian circles.

In conclusion, from the brief remarks above about the intra- and interethnic relationships among the inhabitants of Uzbekistan it may be said that beneath an apparent surface harmony of "Marxist-Leninist friendship among nations" there are many distinct social elements. Attitudes based on differences between East and West, old and new, and language and tradition have contributed to a certain amount of social diversity despite the unifying impulses of both Uzbek nationhood and Soviet patriotism. It is in view of this reality that one must examine the relations between the Soviet Uzbeks and their brothers beyond the frontiers.

THE AFGHAN UZBEKS

More than one million Uzbeks live in Afghanistan, mainly north of the Hindu Kush mountains. They constitute a majority or plurality of the population in the (post-1964) provinces of Fariab, Jozjan, Balkh, Samangan, Kunduz, and Baghlan. The major urban area in the north, Mazar-i-Sharif in Balkh province (the population was approximately 50,000 in 1967, fourth largest in Afghanistan), has a majority Uzbek population. In this region, along with the Uzbeks live lesser numbers of Turkmens, Tajiks, and Pashtuns. For the most part the Afghan Uzbeks do not live along the Amu River border with the Soviet Union. They reside some thirty or more miles to the south where the soil is more suited for agriculture. The intervening sandy wastes are populated by Turkmen nomads. (21)

These Uzbeks have been in northern Afghanistan since the early sixteenth century; they are a branch of the nomadic Uzbek tribes that overthrew the Timurid rulers of Transoxania. During the eighteenth and nineteenth centuries they comprised several petty khanates, tied diplomatically to Kokand and Bukhara, and having relations also with the Qajar dynasty of Iran and the emerging Pashtun kingdom of

Afghanistan south of the Hindu Kush.   These khanates were the precursors of the large estates that still today provide employment for the majority of the Afghan Uzbeks. (22) At the end of the nineteenth century they became part of the kingdom of Afghanistan as a result of an agreement between Russia and England establishing the Amu River as its northern boundary.   The number of Uzbeks in northern Afghanistan increased during the early 1920s with the immigration of as many as .5 million Uzbeks and other Central Asian peoples (Turkmens, Tajiks, etc.) who had fled Soviet authority.

The Afghan Uzbeks are largely sedentary today, living in small towns and villages and engaging in agriculture and stock raising, handicraft, and commercial pursuits.   No Uzbeks are true nomads any longer, but some participate in long-term, extended herding.   The original Uzbek tribal organization has diminished, but tribal identity and knowledge of lineage remains strong, especially among the rural stock-raisers (often seminomads) of more Mongoloid physical type, who have not intermarried over the generations with Iranian groups. Most Uzbeks still refer to themselves by the old tribal names: Harakai, Kamaki, Mangit, Ming, Shesh, Qara, and Taimus. (23)

Through their association (social, political, commercial) with the larger population groups of Afghanistan, many Uzbeks speak the Dari and Pashtu languages. Uzbek, though a minority language of Afghanistan, is often used as a lingua franca among the 400,000 Turkmens and 15,000 Kirgiz who live in the north. (24)   Because of their superior numbers and more progressive sedentary life-style, the Afghan Uzbeks are, to a certain extent, absorbing the other Afghan Turkic groups in the north just as they probably absorbed other pre-Uzbek (pre-sixteenth century) Turkic groups. (25)

Though these Uzbeks are the dominant ethnolinguistic group in their northern part of Afghanistan, they constitute less than ten percent of the total population of the state in which the Iranian-speaking Pashtuns number over eight million and make up about one-half of the inhabitants.   The dominant Pashtuns feel that the country is mainly theirs.   The general tribal orientation of Afghan society, especially among the Pashtuns, has served to keep certain Pashtun lineages in the major political and military positions, even though the trend of Afghan governmental development has been toward extra- or supratribal institutions.   The tribal heritage is not the only factor contributing to ethnic separateness; the rugged terrain and poor surface communications have retarded the development of an integrated national economy. Thus local economic self-sufficiency has been typical and has strengthened local and ethnic particularism among all groups, Pashtun and non-Pashtun alike.

Governmental Ethnic Attitudes and Policies

In general, the Afghan government has had a tolerant, though at times condescending, attitude toward non-Pashtun groups. Modernization was initiated in Afghanistan half a century ago by a group of younger Pashtuns who in some ways can be compared to the Young Turks in the Ottoman Empire, but who were not so ethnocentric. The Young Turks had witnessed the Ottoman state being eaten away by European imperial powers. They perceived the non-Turkic groups of the Balkans and the Caucasus, particularly the Greeks and the Armenians, as tools of foreign states who merited brutal abuse. Afghanistan, in contrast, because of its remoteness was spared the major effects of both imperialistic annexation and minority nationalism. The new Afghanistan arose from tribal chaos, rather than from military disgrace and defeat, and its leaders viewed minorities more as an acquired potential asset than as a burdensome legacy.

The Afghan government has not had a clearly stated ethnic policy, but some general goals have been eliminating tribal localism, promoting social and political integration, developing a modern bureaucratic structure to replace tribal authority, and promoting economic development in non-Pashtun areas. (26) The 1964 constitution (abrogated at the time of the 1973 coup that ended the kingdom and proclaimed a republic) placed no ethnic qualification on citizenship, stating, "that the Afghan nation is composed of all those individuals who possess the citizenship of the state in accordance with the provision of the law and that the word Afghan shall apply to each such individual." (27) Despite this apparent attempt to bring the diverse ethnic groups under one common Afghani umbrella, the official Afghan languages are specified by the same constitution as being Dari and Pashtu, both Iranian languages. Other languages, such as those of the approximately ten percent of the population that is Turkic-speaking (Uzbeks, Turkmens, Kirgiz), have no official status. Of the two official languages, Dari is the most widely used, both in everyday events, administration, and the mass media. There is apparently no publication or broadcasting in languages other than the official Dari and Pashtu. Even native Dari speakers, however, have often been required to learn Pashtu in schools.

In modernizing Afghanistan the civil service and military offer the best chances for employment with upward mobility. Despite laws against nepotism, family, tribal, and ethnic connections are quite important for gaining both an initial position and later advancement. Thus Pashtuns hold the top positions in the civil and military structures, and non-Pashtuns hold a disproportionately smaller number of positions.

The Coup of April 1978

The previous statements about governmental ethnic attitudes and policies must be considered to be generally valid only through the early part of 1978. On April 27 of that year the government of Afghanistan was violently taken over by a military coup led by Lieutenant General Abdul Khadir. President Muhammad Daoud was killed in the fighting, as were numerous other officials of his regime. Three days later a civilian, Nur Mohammad Taraki, emerged as head of the revolutionary council and as prime minister of the newly proclaimed Democratic Republic of Afghanistan. Taraki proclaimed goals of continued and accelerated technical, economic, and social development and a total break with the past. The new government received immediate recognition from the Soviet Union.

As the summer of 1978 progressed, the Taraki government appeared to be taking an increasingly pro-Soviet stance. As the new officialdom became known, seemingly greater numbers were from the non-Pashtun population. Indeed, one of the proclaimed objectives of the new government is greater recognition of the diverse ethnic groups. Within a few months of its accession to power, it gave the ethnic minorities opportunity to publish and broadcast in their own languages. Considering the increased level of Soviet influence in Afghanistan, it would be reasonable to expect that ethnic policies could be greatly influenced by established patterns in the USSR. If such becomes the case, Afghan minorities with counterpart groups in the USSR (Uzbeks, Tajiks, etc.) may achieve unprecedented status in Afghanistan and their opportunities for cultural and educational experiences in the Soviet Union may increase. However, the exact policy and course of the Taraki government was not yet clear to Western observers by the end of 1978.

Education

Though kinship ties are still important for upward mobility, the basic requirements are literacy and education. In a land where the literacy rate is no more than ten percent, only a small segment of the population is available for government service. The literacy required, however, must be in the official languages and the educational system favors the dominant Pashtun group both in location of schools and in provision of scholarships. (28) However, Uzbeks, like Tajiks and other minorities, are often accepted in the schools for higher education in Kabul and on occasion are even sent abroad for advanced training. (29)

The principal modern education facilities are in Kabul, a Pashtun area. Here instruction is in the official languages, particularly Pashtu, or in European languages; textbooks also are in the official languages or in foreign languages. In the state school system in other areas at the middle and higher levels, instruction and texts are in the official Dari and Pashtu languages. In some non-Pashtun areas, basic primary education is offered in the local languages. But as a rule the non-Pashtun student has the problem of first learning the official Afghan language or languages, then getting a basic education (if local facilities exist) to qualify him for the university where usually he must learn a European language or languages. The factors of language and facilities seriously impede non-Pashtuns from working their way into the government apparatus.

Recently special efforts have been made to develop modern educational facilities in the non-Pashtun areas. During the last decade a teachers college and a veterinary school have been established. A branch of the Afghan Literary Society was also recently established which publishes works of Afghan authors (in Pashtu and Dari only, however). The earlier failure to do so can be attributed both to the government's lack of a sense of national purpose and to the practical economics of funding a modern education system in an underdeveloped nation. In the Uzbek area, literacy and educational opportunities have been low. For example, in 1961 in the pre-1964 province of Mazar-i-Sharif the literacy rate was 3.4 percent, much lower than the national average. (30) In the city of Mazar-i-Sharif for years the principal educational facility was the Madrasa Assadiya, a secondary level religious school operated by the municipality. These factors can partially explain the heretofore low upward mobility of the Uzbeks in Afghanistan.

Ethnic Interaction

In addition to promoting educational development in the non-Pashtun areas, the government in Kabul has attempted to integrate the various ethnic groups. An example of this occurred in 1954 and 1955, when over a thousand families were relocated onto new lands in the Nad-i Ali area that had been opened up by irrigation development. Representatives of the various non-Pashtun groups were included to avoid suspicion of ethnic favoritism on the part of the government. Among them were several Uzbek families of Soviet Central Asian origin. The project was a failure, however, due to poor soil conditions, and most of the families left the area. (31) Another avenue of ethnic integration practiced by the Afghan government is military conscription, which not only brings together representatives of the various ethnic groups and provides some technical training, but also takes them away from their own areas for a period of time. A higher level of ethnic interaction has occurred in the meetings of the national assembly. Uzbek delegates participated in the September 1964 meeting to discuss the new constitution, and in the meetings of the national assembly. (32)

When it occurs at all, however, ethnic integration is usually superficial and not on an intimate level. For example, in the Uzbek majority area of northern Afghanistan, though the Uzbek village councils might cooperate with local Tajik and Pashtun village councils about matters of common concern, marriage between members of different ethnic groups is infrequent. (33) When an Uzbek does marry a non-Uzbek, it is more frequently with a member of another Turkic group or with a Tajik than with a Pashtun. (34)

Generally, the Uzbeks, who are a majority in the north, have good relations with the other ethnic groups. One exception is the long-standing tension between the sedentary Uzbeks and small groups of non-

Uzbek nomads. (35) This may be more a cultural problem between two conflicting life-styles than it is an ethnic problem, however. A greater potential for ethnic disharmony exists in the resettlement of Pashtun farmers into northern lands being opened by new irrigation projects, thus lessening the traditional Uzbek majority in the north and creating additional interethnic competition for new job opportunities.

Pashtun dominance is gradually diminishing in Afghanistan, but the minority groups are not yet actively seeking new roles in Afghan society, especially in politics. The minorities have little faith that they can influence high level government policy. Consequently, most minority group political concern is locally oriented. National politics are more the affair of the literate urban elite concentrated in Kabul. (36) Despite the presently prevailing Pashtun dominance, the non-Pashtun groups, including the Uzbeks, find it better to support the central government than to oppose it, since opposition or noncooperation would lessen the traditional degree of autonomy that they enjoy.

In view of factors such as Pashtun dominance, the lack of status for minority languages, and the common Islamic culture, there is a possiblity that the Uzbeks might be gradually afghanized (or pashtunized), yet remain a separate people for many decades because of their tribal and family orientation as well as their regional ethnic concentration.

Afghan-Soviet Relations

The factor that has ultimately determined the relationship between the Soviet and Afghan Uzbeks is Afghanistan's relation to the Soviet Union. The two states share a border approximately 700 miles long. The border terrain runs across arid steppe in the west along the Amu River to the rugged Pamir Mountains in the east. Much of it separates Afghanistan from the Soviet Central Asian republics of Turkmenistan and Tajikistan. But Uzbekistan lies on the border for about one hundred miles on the Amu in the vicinity of the town of Termez.

Relations between Afghanistan and the newly founded Soviet Union were hostile. Afghanistan gave aid to the anti-Soviet Basmachi Muslim nationalist forces.   By 1921, as the Basmachi groups were being defeated by the Red Army, large numbers of Uzbeks and other Central Asian Muslims moved southward into northern Afghanistan. Among the refugees was the Uzbek Emir of Bukhara, Sayyid Alim Khan of the Mangit tribe. With the waning of Basmachi fortunes in that year, a treaty of friendship was signed between Afghanistan and the Soviet Union, and as a sign of good will, the Afghan government withdrew its direct support for the Basmachi groups operating across the border. (37) Then, with the suppression of the autonomous political entities of Bukhara and Khiva, the Afghans cooled toward the Soviet Union, disheartened that these entities would no longer remain as border buffer states.

Northern Afghanistan thus remained as a refuge and base of operations for the anti-Soviet Basmachi forces composed of refugees and concerned local residents of the Turkmen, Uzbek, and Tajik groups. Despite a 1926 Soviet-Afghan nonaggression treaty, anti-Soviet activities centered in the Uzbek area of Afghanistan for several years. In 1929, when a civil war raged in Afghanistan after a Tajik-led group attempted to overthrow King Amanullah, the Soviet Union sent an armed force with aircraft into northern Afghanistan, ostensibly to support the king. The Soviet forces passed through Mazar-i-Sharif and later in the same year withdrew. The Soviet intervention had two seeming purposes: first, to make the Afghan king indebted to the USSR for their support; and second, to move against Basmachi units in the Uzbek area. The latter may have been the weightier reason, for in 1930 a Soviet army unit again penetrated 40 miles into northern Afghanistan in pursuit of Basmachis, whose activities had increased among Central Asians after forced collectivization had begun. (38)   Not until a neutrality treaty had been signed between the USSR and Afghanistan in 1931 did the Afghan government move on its own to restrain the remaining Basmachi groups in the north.

Throughout the 1930s Afghanistan remained cool in its relations to the Soviet Union. The suppression of Islam in Soviet Central Asia was an influencing factor. When the Second World War began, Afghanistan announced its neutrality but prudently reduced German influence within its borders, having seen the fate of neutral Iran which had been invaded and occupied by British and Russian forces. In the course of the war some Uzbeks and members of other Central Asian nationalities crossed from the USSR into Afghanistan.

The end of the war saw another increase in tension between Afghanistan and the Soviet Union. One source of the tension was the disputed possession of several islands in the Amu River. Another was the attempt by the Soviet Union to gain influence over the transborder nationalities in northern Afghanistan. The border dispute was resolved in 1946, but Soviet attempts to subvert the nationalities of the north lasted longer. Between 1945 and 1949, small groups of Soviet provocateurs crossed into Afghanistan. Soviet Uzbeks tried to proselytize among the Afghan Uzbeks. Quite often, however, Afghan Uzbeks turned in their surprised Soviet-oriented fellow tribesmen to the Afghan authorities. This may be explained by the fact that many Afghan Uzbeks (Tajiks and Turkmens also) were either Basmachis or sons of Basmachis. Others knew about the 1930s collectivization program in Soviet Central Asia. Also, by not cooperating with the Soviet bordercrossers, the northern ethnic groups denied a further excuse to the Pashtuns to disturb their relatively independent ways. (39)

In the late 1950s, however, Afghan-Soviet relations warmed up. This was in part due to the Pashtunistan dispute and to the competitive offering of development funds and economic aid by the USSR and the United States. Since that time Afghanistan has stayed ideologically neutral in the superpower competition but has been inclined toward the

Soviet Union for the larger portion of its economic aid. Since the mid-1950s, the Soviet Union has taken up approximately half of Afghanistan's export-import trade and has provided almost two-thirds of its development funding. Since the mid-1960s the Soviet Union has also been the major supplier of military equipment to Afghanistan. (40) The April 1978 coup that overthrew the government of Daoud and installed the Taraki government has resulted in a greater shift of Afghanistan toward the Soviet Union.

A particular focus of Soviet development funding in Afghanistan has been the area north of the Hindu Kush mountain range. Soviet aid has centered on developing natural resources, improving communications, and building industry. Surveys have been made of mineral resources and exploitation has increased. Soviet geological teams explored for oil in the Mazar-i-Sharif region during the late 1960s, and a pipeline has been constructed to ship natural gas from Jozjan province to the Soviet Union. In Mazar-i-Sharif a fertilizer plant and a thermal power plant have been built with Soviet aid. Also in Mazar-i-Sharif a grain storage facility has been built with Soviet aid and at the Amu River port of Sher Khan, petroleum storage facilities have been erected. Soviet construction teams have built an airport capable of handling jet aircraft at Mazar-i-Sharif, and roads crossing the USSR border have been paved. Over these roads cotton grown in the north on farms using agricultural techniques modeled after practices in Uzbekistan and Tajikistan is trucked to Tashkent in Uzbekistan for processing. (41)

In its activities in Afghanistan, the Soviet Union has used Central Asian Muslims as part of the staffs for diplomatic and technical missions. (42) The Soviet personnel in Afghanistan, no matter what their ethnic background, have been instructed to stress the ethnic and cultural affinities between the Muslims of Afghanistan and those in Soviet Central Asia. (43) Along with attempting to form personal contacts between its Afghanistan-based Soviet Muslims and similar Afghan ethnic groupings, the Soviet Union beams Uzbek-language broadcasts from Tashkent to northern Afghanistan. These programs, carrying music and commentary, are popular because Afghan radio does not broadcast in Uzbek. Also, some Uzbek television from Termez on the Amu River can be received. (44) The Soviet-Afghan border is fenced and carefully patrolled to prevent smuggling and other unauthorized border crossings. But, whatever the intent, Moscow now makes friendly overtures to transborder ethnic groups in Afghanistan.

Soviet Uzbek Views of the Diaspora

Because of Soviet control of the mass media, the mass of the Soviet Uzbeks may be only faintly aware of the Afghan Uzbeks. Although they may know that many of their relatives or friends fled to Afghanistan in the 1920s, they may have little information about the fate of these refugees or about the kind of life that Afghan Uzbeks may lead.

Furthermore, despite a sense of Muslim consciousness that gives them a sense of distinctiveness from Russians and other non-Muslims, the mass of the Uzbeks probably consider themselves an integral, contributing, and vital part of the Soviet Union. Uzbek contributions to the Great Patriotic War (World War II) are often recalled. Many young Uzbeks have served in Soviet army units along the Chinese border. Moreover, the tales of the poor life in China told by Turkic-speaking refugees from Sinkiang remind the Uzbeks and other Soviet Central Asians of the value of their Soviet connection. Separatist thoughts, if still harbored by the Uzbek masses, are no doubt of a wistful or hypothetical nature.

Uzbeks who are educated within the Soviet Union probably know more. Surely they also are well aware of the great material benefits of being part of the Soviet Union and of the much lower standard of living in the Muslim states beyond the borders. In 1969 the author was told by an Uzbek university instructor:

> I have heard our own propaganda about how people in Afghanistan, Iran and Turkey live and I have also talked with students from these countries. I realize that perhaps our people do not live as well as some people in these countries, but I also know that our people do not live as poorly as many people in these countries. Would independence have been worth the poverty, disease, and ignorance that is still found there? (45)

But these self-conscious Uzbeks may also have doubts. The Soviet Union has invested sufficient resources in the modernization of Uzbekistan to integrate the region into the national economy. The image of Uzbekistan as a "cotton colony" of Russia is changing because of the growing diversity of the economy of Uzbekistan and the growing importance of the Central Asian populations to the Soviet labor force. Yet Central Asia was forcibly annexed to Russia and the Soviet Union. Soviet Uzbeks do differ from Russians in culture, language, and race. Their identity as Uzbeks is officially recognized and is reinforced by cultural policies and administrative boundaries. Moreover, the pride that educated Soviet Uzbeks take in their achievements during the Soviet era is in a sense not so much a measure of their appreciation for the help given by their European brothers, as of their need to view their progress as their very own creation. Prosperity and a continuing degree of cultural tolerance by the Russians may keep Soviet Uzbeks satisfied with, or at least acquiescent to, their status in the Soviet Union. But they will remain aware of their distinctiveness.

One should note, moreover, that the importance of the Soviet Uzbeks does not lie solely in their present and potential numbers. They are an important link for the Soviet Union with the non-European, particularly Muslim peoples elsewhere in Asia. In part due to Tashkent's role as an international airline junction, Uzbekistan has been portrayed to the non-European world as a showcase of Soviet-style development. Many "Third World" students study in the higher education institutions of Tashkent. Older specialists from these areas are brought to Uzbekistan for advanced training. The Soviet government apparently considers that these "Third Worlders" would be more comfortable in Uzbekistan with its large non-European population than in Moscow and other European parts of the Soviet Union. In addition to educational activities, non-Europeans are attracted to cultural festivals such as literary and film conferences.

Since the all-union government will no doubt continue to cultivate a positive image among the non-European world, Uzbekistan will continue to have an important role in Soviet development and propaganda. It follows that educated Soviet Uzbeks will not be allowed to stop thinking altogether of their brothers outside the boundaries of the present republic. Because of the tensions that exist below the surface of Uzbek society, the nationalism of the educated Soviet Uzbeks will probably not be perfectly egalitarian. But on the other hand, it will probably not die.

Afghan Uzbek Views of the Soviet Union

Undoubtedly the people of northern Afghanistan appreciate the material improvements that Soviet activity has brought to Afghanistan. However, among many Uzbeks there is a legacy of hostility toward the USSR as the result of personal or family experiences with the anti-Soviet Basmachi movement of the 1920s. The Russian-led secularization of the Central Asian Muslim peoples has tended also to tarnish the Soviet Union's image among the conservative and traditional Afghan Uzbek leadership, among other Afghan groups having transborder ties, and among the Muslim peoples in general. (46)

Though at the present the Afghan Uzbeks appear to have little interest in joining with the more numerous Soviet Uzbeks, the Soviet Uzbek community in the future could appear increasingly attractive to a younger generation of Afghan Uzbeks. Two circumstances might bring this about. First, as the Afghan Uzbeks become more literate and educated, they will increasingly want upward social and economic mobility. If Pashtun dominance of the social, economic, and governmental structure of Afghanistan continues, and if economic growth lags behind the growth in the number of trained and qualified Uzbeks, the underemployed Uzbeks may look with increasing admiration at the full employment, modernized economy of the Soviet Uzbeks to the north and thus be increasingly receptive to influences from across the border. Second, if Pashtuns continue to migrate to the newly opened lands in the north, the long-established majority status of the Uzbeks there will be jeopardized and may raise concern among the Afghan Uzbeks about their future. In such a circumstance the major group of Uzbeks in the Soviet Union could appear increasingly as a source of ethnic security. (47) A more modernized and educated Afghan Uzbek community under cultural, economic, and residential pressure from a Pashtun majority could overcome the recollection of past Soviet acts and earn an admiration for the USSR's economic opportunity and relative ethnic tolerance. (48)

One should not forget, however, that the Afghan Uzbeks, while differing linguistically and sometimes racially from the dominant Pashtun group, retain a Muslim culture that is somewhat similar to that of the Pashtuns. They have no separate legal status as a group; their language is not officially recognized. But they are accorded the same formal rights as citizens that are nominally accorded to all Muslim individuals in Afghan society. This is an integrating factor in Afghanistan which, unless there is a radical revolution, should not be disregarded.

CONCLUSION: UZBEKS ACROSS THE BORDERS

Both the Soviet and Afghan Uzbeks have a strong sense of awareness as peoples separate from the numerically dominant groups in their countries. Both constitute an ethnic majority in their main areas of residence, and both enjoy a degree of autonomy, though constrained by the central governments. But neither group constitutes more than ten percent of the total population of the state in which it resides. Both are dominated by an ethnic group that comprises approximately half the population. These are the main factors that might lead the Uzbeks someday to develop a sense of common purpose, expressed perhaps in demands for political unification or for Uzbek autonomy in Central Asia.

The Soviet and Afghan Uzbeks still share many social and spiritual values. Should either group seek today to increase its contacts with the other, it would still find much that is familiar across the border. But the dynamic forces of the Soviet system are affecting Soviet Uzbek life to the very core. With the passage of time, what may be termed "traditional" Uzbek culture will be found ever more exclusively in Afghanistan and not in the USSR. This growing divergence between the two groups of Uzbeks could provide the basis either for a reaching northward by Afghan Uzbeks for the better lot that has befallen their Soviet brethren, or a reaching southward by Soviet Uzbeks for their roots in rural Afghanistan, but it may inhibit any striving for a perfect unity of fate for the Uzbek people.

The developing social policies of the Taraki government may greatly alter the relations among the ethnic groups within Afghanistan and may produce new patterns of interaction between the peoples of Afghanistan and ethnically related groups in the Soviet Union. What has been written here is in a sense retrospective. At this writing the exact policies and practices of the new government are not fully known to western observers.

NOTES

(1) These figures were supplied by Richard V. Weekes, editor of the forthcoming An Ethnographic Survey of the Muslim World, which is to be published by Greenwood Press in 1978. They have been used by the author in his short essay on the Uzbeks to appear in that work. The figures for the Afghan Uzbeks are approximate because there has been no accurate census in Afghanistan; however, all sources that have been consulted for this study state that there are "more than a million." This appears to be an estimate from approximately 1960; if this is so, and a three percent annual growth is assumed from 1959 or 1960, then 1,649,000 is a reasonable estimate of the current population.

(2) Summaries of tsarist rule in Central Asia can be found in the chapters by Helene Carrere d'Encausse in Central Asia: A Century of Russian Rule, Edward Allworth, ed. (New York, 1967), Chaps. 4 and 5; and in Seymour Becker, Russia's Protectorates in Central Asia. Bukhara and Khiva 1865-1924 (Cambridge, Mass., 1968).

(3) See Carrere d'Encausse, op. cit., Chaps. 8-10.

(4) That the boundaries between Soviet republics are losing their former significance was noted in the official pronouncement on nationality relations in the Third Party Program adopted at the Twenty-Second Congress of the Communist Party of the Soviet Union. See XXII S"ezd kommunisticheskoi partii Sovetskogo Soiuza, 17-31 Oktiabria 1961 goda: stenograficheskii otchet (Moscow, 1962), vol. 3, p. 312.

(5) James Critchlow, "Uzbeks and Russians," Canadian Slavonic Papers 17, nos. 2 and 3, 1976, p. 368.

(6) Uzbekskaia sovetskaia sotsialisticheskaia respublika (Tashkent, 1977), p. 135. This appears to be disputed by Allworth in Central Asia, p. 376, where he indicates a literacy rate of 51.0 percent in 1959 for the 9-49 age group.

(7) A Valiev, Oktiabr', kul'tura, intelligentsiia (Tashkent, 1977), p. 133.

(8) A discussion of the development of modern education in Uzbekistan can be found in William K. Medlin, Education and Development in Central Asia: A Case Study on Social Change in Uzbekistan (Leiden, 1971).

(9) Donald S. Carlisle, "Uzbekistan and the Uzbeks," Handbook of Major Soviet Nationalities, Zev Katz et al., eds. (New York, 1977), p. 284. A discussion of economic development in Uzbekistan and other parts of Central Asia can be found in Alec Nove and J.A. Newth, The Soviet Middle East: A Communist Model for Development (New York, 1966).

(10) Ts. S. U., Itogi vsesoiunoi perepisi naseleniia 1970 goda (Moscow, 1973), vol. 4, p. 218. Other figures for 1970 given in this essay are derived from the same source.

(11) The prospects for outmigration of Russians and local nationalities from Central Asia are explored in Michael Rywkin, "The Political Implications of Demographic and Industrial Developments in Soviet Central Asia," paper presented at the annual meeting of the American Association for the Advancement of Slavic Studies, Columbus, Ohio, October 13, 1978. For a provocative view of the prospects for population shift among Soviet Central Asian nationalities, see Robert A. Lewis, Richard H. Rowland, and Ralph S. Clem, Nationality and Population Change in Russia and the USSR (New York, 1976), esp. pp. 354-383.

(12) Uzbekskaia sovetskaia sotsialisticheskaia respublika, p. 190.

(13) Carlisle, "Uzbekistan and the Uzbeks," pp. 290-292.

(14) Krasnoznamennyi Turkestanskii (Moskva, 1976), pp. 429-435.

(15) A discussion of how Islam has fared in the Soviet Union can be found in Alexandre Bennigsen and Chantal Lemercier-Quelquejay, Islam in the Soviet Union (New York, 1967).

(16) A discussion of early Soviet policies toward women is found in Gregory J. Massell, The Surrogate Proletariat: Moslem Women and Revolutionary Strategies in Soviet Central Asia, 1919-1929 (Princeton, 1974).

(17) Edward Allworth discusses Soviet language policies for Central Asia in his Uzbek Literary Politics (The Hague, 1964).

(18) Carlisle, "Uzbekistan and the Uzbeks," p. 299.

(19) Helene Carrere d'Encausse, "The Republics Lose Their Independence," in Allworth, ed., Central Asia, p. 265.

(20) Carlisle, "Uzbekistan and the Uzbeks," pp. 290-292.

(21) A map showing the distribution of ethnic groups in Afghanistan can be found on page 36 of Donald N. Wilber's Afghanistan (New Haven, 1962); a map showing the provinces of Afghanistan can be found on page 12 of Area Handbook for Afghanistan, DA Pamphlet no. 550-65 (Washington, D.C.) by Harvey H. Smith et al.

(22) Smith, Area Handbook, p. 75.

(23) Louis Dupree, Afghanistan (Princeton, 1973), p. 61.

(24) Smith, Area Handbook, p. 82.

(25) Wilber, Afghanistan, p. 49.

(26) Smith, Area Handbook, pp. 61-62.

(27) Ibid., p. 63.

(28) Ibid., p. 128.

(29) Wilber, Afghanistan, p. 54.

(30) Dupree, Afghanistan, p. 248. Approximately the same rate prevailed among Soviet Uzbeks at the time of the Russian Revolution.

(31) Smith, Area Handbook, p. 269.

(32) Dupree, Afghanistan, p. 567.

(33) Smith, Area Handbook, p. 99.

(34) Wilber, Afghanistan, pp. 54 and 82.

(35) Louis Dupree, ed., Afghanistan in the 1970s (New York, 1974), p. 137.

(36) Smith, Area Handbook, p. 199.

(37) Similar treaties were signed by the Soviet Union during the same year with Turkey and Iran as steps toward securing its southern borders.

(38) Wilber, Afghanistan, pp. 21-22.

(39) Dupree, Afghanistan, p. 512. The infiltration attempt by Soviet Central Asians into northern Afghanistan was but one phase of a general effort by the Soviet Union at the end of the Second World War to acquire transborder ethnic areas. Among the areas that were subject to political and propaganda efforts were Turkish Armenia, Kurdistan, Iranian Azerbaijan, the Iranian Turkmens, Sinkiang, Tuva, and southern Sakhalin. More about this topic can be found in works such as: Gunther Wiehe Nollau and Hans Jurgen, Russia's South Flank (New York, 1963); John J. Stephan, The Kurile Islands: Russo-Japanese Frontier in the Pacific (Oxford, 1974); and Allen S. Whiting, Sinkiang: Pawn or Pivot (East Lansing, 1958). Also see the chapters by June Teufel Dreyer, Gerard Libaridian, Eden Naby and S. Enders Wimbush in this volume.

(40) By coincidence in 1956 Sayyid Alim Khan, the former Uzbek Emir of Bukhara, died in Kabul. It is possible that the death of this refugee from the USSR symbolically freed Afghanistan from hospitality obligations, so that relations with the USSR could then become warmer.

(41) Dupree, Afghanistan, p. 520.

(42) Soviet Muslims are used in many Middle Eastern posts. The ethnic identity of those used in Afghanistan has not been exactly determined, but it would seem that English-speaking Tajiks, if they exist, would be best suited, since they already speak an Iranian language related to Dari and Pashtu. Uzbeks would have linguistic access to a smaller part of the Afghan population and could be used

only in the northern Uzbek area. Dupree indicates that the regular Soviet diplomatic personnel in Afghanistan appear to have no great knowledge of the Afghan languages. See Dupree, Afghanistan, p. 527.

(43) There have been several cultural delegations of Soviet Turks and Uzbeks to transborder areas where Turkic-speaking peoples reside. For example, during 1940 a group from the Uzbek Writers Union went to Herat in Afghanistan to seek manuscripts and background information about the fifteenth century poet Ali Shir Nevai in conjunction with the planned Ali Shir Nevai festival. During the Soviet occupation of northern Iran in World War Two, Uzbek and other Soviet Turkic cultural delegations visited the Turkic-speaking areas of Iran. In 1955 a delegation of Soviet Turks and Uzbeks visited the Turkic areas of Sinkiang.

(44) Dupree, Afghanistan in the 1970s, p. 234.

(45) David C. Montgomery, "An American Student in Tashkent," Asian Affairs 59 (New Series vol. 3), part 1 (February 1972), p. 38.

(46) The Afghan Uzbek negative attitudes toward the secularization of Soviet Central Asian society may in part be conditioned by the fact that in Mazar-i-Sharif stands a venerated Islamic shrine reputed to be the tomb of Ali Muhammad's son-in-law and the fourth caliph of Islam.

(47) Perhaps there is an analogy here to the Mongols of the Inner Mongolian Autonomous Region of the Chinese People's Republic and their attitude toward the Mongols of the Mongolian People's Republic or the attitude of the Kazakhs and Uighurs of the Sinkiang province of the PRC toward related groups in the Soviet Union.

(48) The Soviet Union has been attempting to use Uzbekistan as an example of a Muslim society that has been modernized according to Soviet and Marxist-Leninist principles. The effectiveness of this propaganda on other Muslim peoples is difficult to gauge. An extreme negative reaction is perhaps illustrated by a remark made by Kadafi of Libya who at a conference of Muslim states a few years ago objected to the seating of a delegation from India, stating that India was "as much a Muslim country as Uzbekistan."

7 Ethnic Relations under Closed Frontier Conditions: Northeast Badakhshan

Nazif Shahrani

The tribal and ethnic heterogeneity of Afghanistan is not a recent discovery. For centuries chronic ethnic and tribal strife have constituted the history of Afghanistan as well as the entire area of Western and Central Asia. Both external and internal political-historical developments during the past few decades, however, have had a profound effect upon interethnic, intraethnic, and tribal relationships. Externally, the closing of the Soviet Union frontier in 1917 and the Chinese frontier in 1949 (following the Communist revolutions) brought about the complete severance of social, economic, and cultural intercourse between the peoples of Russian and Chinese Turkistan and those of Afghan Turkistan. The border closures also resulted in territorial losses to small ethnic communities and their consequent spatial confinement to extremely marginal lands stretched along the newly closed boundaries. Internally, the centralized political and military organization of Afghanistan has for the first time developed a commitment to forging a unified nation-state. As a result, all population groups, whether traditionally powerful or weak, have been brought under the direct rule of the politically dominant Pashtun ethnic group who are generally supported by outside (international) forces in maintaining their authority over the rest of the country.

Little is known about the sociological effects of the recently imposed closed frontier conditions, or the impact of strong, centralized government authority upon the many different communities that have been subjected to these new socioecological constraints. This paper will examine some aspects of the changing nature of the ethnic identities and interethnic and intertribal relationships in northern Afghanistan in general and the extreme northeastern frontier regions of Badakhshan in particular - the Wakhan Corridor area, wedged between the frontiers of the Soviet Union, China, and Pakistan. (1)

For the purpose of this discussion ethnicity refers to culturally

174

distinct categories of people who display common bonds based on shared historical experiences, congruent or similar value orientation, linguistic affinity, religious-sectarian ideology, socioculturally significant phenotypic attributes or territory, past or present. Members of one such population generally express their distinctiveness from others through visible symbolic means and sociopolitical action. One of the basic reasons for the emergence and continued existence of culturally defined population aggregates in pluralistic societies is their usefulness as a means of adaptation for individuals and collectivities within a changing social and economic environment. The bases of ethnic solidarity are, therefore, dynamic and subject to redefinition and reorganization according to the needs of the ethnic group. The genesis and development of ethnic processes in Afghanistan are perhaps best understood through an anthropologically informed historical account.

ESTABLISHMENT OF AFGHAN TURKISTAN

The predominantly Turkic territories between the Amu Darya (Oxus) and the combined Hindu Kush and Kuh-i-Baba mountain range, stretching from Maimana to Badakhshan, were added to the newly created independent Pashtun state of Afghanistan during the early years of the reign of Ahmad Shah Durrani (1747-1772). The territory had been part of the Persian Nadir Afshar's Empire, and Ahmad Shah received help in his bid for the establishment of the new state of Afghanistan from a native soldier of fortune, an Uzbek named Haji Khan, his one time comrade-in-arms in Nadir Shah Afshar's army. (2) Consequently, the annexation was relatively bloodless.

The northern area, which later became known as Afghan Turkistan (or Turkistan-i-Afghani), was then composed of a number of principalities, namely those of Maimana, Andkhui, Sar-i-Pul, Shiberghan, Balkh, Khulm, Kunduz, and Badakhshan. In return for Haji Khan's support and allegiance, Ahmad Shah made him the Wali (ruler or governor) of two of them (Maimana and Balkh) "on the simple condition that he should furnish certain military aid at call." (3) After the death of Haji Khan, his son, Jan Khan, retained control of both Maimana and Balkh for some years. Then in 1793 Balkh and the neighboring principality of Aqchah were seized by the Emir of Bukhara, Shah Murad.

Meanwhile, toward the end of the reign of Ahmad Shah's son, Timur Shah of Kabul (1772-1793), and while he was preoccupied with the Sind and Kashmir disturbances, Quwat Khan (a former soldier who had taken part in the Indian expedition in the armies of Timur Shah) seized power in Kunduz, proclaiming independence from the Kabul monarchy. (4) This set the stage for nearly a century of local political intrigue and jockeying for power among the Uzbek and Tajik khans and mirs of the northern regions. These factional struggles were based (just as were those of the Afghan territories south of the Hindu Kush) on the principles of segmentary opposition of kinship and ethnicity, and were always characterized by tyranny, intrigue, and tragedy. But unlike the south, the Pashtun were not deeply involved. These were intertribal struggles among various Turkic groups, the Tajiks, and other minority populations (e.g., Wakhi, Shighni) to the north of the Hindu Kush.

The center of political gravity in Afghan Turkistan was Kunduz, and its ruling group were members of the Qataghan tribe of Uzbeks. Among them succession to political leadership (as well as the temptation for individual power holders to seek greater influence) followed the same patterns as among the Saddozai and Barakzai tribes of Pashtun in the south. Political ascendency was, for the most part, a function of the personal skills and ability of individual contenders in first securing a following from among their own kinsmen, tribal, and ethnic members. Therefore access to political leadership, as well as retention of political influence, was subject to profound uncertainties. For example, P.B. Lord reports that

> Revolutions amongst the Uzbeks are frequent and at times apparently causeless. I never have been able to ascertain why it was that Kooat [Quwat] Khan [1792?], whose praises they to this day recite should one morning have found his hall of audience deserted.... Not a man had come to pay his respects; and the chief terrified by this most unequivocal mark of oriental revolt, mounted horse and issuing from a back gate of the fort of Kundooz, attempted to make his escape in the direction of Khana-abad. His enemies however had no intention he should get off so easily. He was pursued, overtaken, brought back and given into the hands of Mahomed Shah, Meer [Mir] of Budukshan [Badakhshan], whose father he had slain, with free permission to use him as he pleased.... He led his captive to the Sung-i-novishtah about a mile from the city, where with but little ceremony his head was struck off....

Lord tells later that:

> Alla Verdee Khan Tas had highly distinguished himself as a partizan warrior on the occasion of the advance of Tymoor Shah against the King of Bokhara [1793]. He was now [1800] by the unanimous voice of his countrymen, named chief of the Kutaghuns, and immediately took possession of Kundooz.... The greater part of his reign was spent in a series of aggressions on the inhabitants of Budukshan whom he brought to acknowledge his power. He then turned his arms against Bulkh and ravaged all the surrounding country.... From this he marched to Hissar which he plundered, but here his career terminated. A body of troops sent against him by Meer Hyder defeated his army ... having taken Alla Verdee himself prisoner, quickly cut off his head. To him succeeded Kutta Khan, son of Kooat Khan. (5)

A change came in 1818 with the accession at Kunduz of Murad Beg, also an Uzbek of the Qataghan tribe. The immediate ancestors of

Murad Beg had been forced to retreat from Kunduz some years earlier to a small district of Rustaq, where Murad Beg's father, Darab, had become tributary to the Mir of Badakhshan. Murad Beg and his four able brothers are reported to have deplored such a state of submission to a Tajik state. However, at the death of their father (1815), Murad Beg declared his independence from the Mir of Badakhshan and his intention to assert his power over the rest of Turkistan. By 1818 he and his brothers were able to extend their dominion over Kunduz and its dependencies, and in order to maintain it the four brothers agreed on a division of the territory to be ruled by each.

In 1821 the ruler of Badakhshan, Mirza Kalan, waged war against Murad Beg. However, Murad Beg and his brothers defeated the Badakhshi armies in Taliqan and pursued them to their capital city of Faizabad. While in Faizabad, Murad Beg forced Mirzu Kalan

> ... to present himself as a suppliant in his camp. He however on this occasion treated him with leniency, merely exacting a moderate tribute in lapis lazuli, rubies and slaves, forbidding the Meer [Mir] to enter Fyzabad [Faizabad] , his capital town, and assigning him in lieu of it a residence at a small fort in Kishm.... [T] heir forced submission was quickly thrown off, when they found attention of the conqueror withdrawn to other quarters, but like all Tajik tribes, they depended more on the strength of their [spatial] position, or other adventitious circumstances than on their personal courage.... Four times they rebelled, and as many times were overthrown, the terms granted them being ... more and more severe, until at last enraged at their obstinacy, Mahomed Murad Beg, at the head of 12,000 men, entered their territory on occasion of their last rebellion, ... seized Fyzabad, ... which he razed to the ground.... He further seized their Meer, took him with him, and has since held him as a sort of prisoner at large at his court. But his most deadly revenge was taken by driving before him no less than 20,000 families, whom he transplanted from the beautiful hills and valleys of Budukshun to the fens of Kunduz and Huzrut Imam, in which they have from year to year pined and languished, and died, so that of all the great number between four and five thousand could now with difficulty be collected. (6)

Meanwhile the power struggle in the western states of Turkistan was not much different. It is reported that when Haji Kahn's son, Jan Khan, the ruler of Maimana, died around 1790

> ... His death was followed by a series of domestic tragedies, and popular revolutions, which furnish a curious picture of the restless plots and intrigues which seem to have prevailed in these remote states, just as they prevailed at Kabul, Kandahar, and Bokhara. Jan Khan left several sons. One obtained the petty throne of Maemana by blinding an elder brother; but after some years he was overthrown

by a popular insurrection and put to death. Then a younger brother, named Ahmad Khan, reigned from 1798 to 1810, and was in like manner put to death by the people of Maemana. A nephew of Ahmad Khan, named Alah Yar Khan, was next placed upon the throne, and reigned from 1810 to 1826.... (7)

Centralized political organization in Afghan Turkistan was achieved by Murad Beg of Kunduz, after 1815, but at his death in 1840 the region again became subject to the plague of political intrigue and disorganization. Finally, in midcentury the Kabul government began to appoint its own governors to the various strategic towns where they maintained a degree of indirect control over the population. However, the influence of the Kabul government and of the Pashtun in Turkistan remained tenuous, at least until the later part of the reign of Amir Abdur Rahman (1880-1901). In general in the nineteenth century in northern Afghanistan, the prolonged political dominance of any single group over the entire territory was thus not achieved. Petty local leaders demanded allegiance from the leaders of any subjugated groups but did not attempt to assimilate members of minority groups. Conversely, the subjects of these states did not claim any rights, demand any privileges, or have any expectations from their rulers, and none were extended. In fact, during times of peace the relationship between the center and the periphery was more a matter of political stalemate than of active administrative control by a central authority.

Today's spatial distribution of ethnic enclaves throughout the area, and thus their access to resources, clearly reflects the relative political strength of the various groups in these conflicts of the past century. On the one hand, Uzbek and other Turkic-speaking groups which were politically strong inhabit the low lying fertile central valley floors throughout most of Turkistan. In Badakhshan, likewise, a number of Uzbek tribes and some Sunni Tajiks jointly occupy some of the most productive valleys (e.g., the valleys of Kishm, Argu, Darayim, Khash, Jirm, and Baharak). Other relatively fertile but narrow river valleys of the upper Kukcha river and its tributaries are claimed by the Sunni Tajiks. On the other hand, the politically weak Tajik-speaking Sunni Hazara are found in the higher reaches of these central valleys. The Ismailite Wakhi, Ishkashimi, Sanglechi, Kurani, Munjani, Darwazi, and Shighni, all of whom are distinct population categories without political clout, inhabit comparatively marginal and less productive lands in the upper reaches of the Amu Darya (Oxus) and the headwaters of the Kukcha and its tributaries, the Yumgan and Warduj rivulets. (8)

The ethnic and tribal political processes of nineteenth-century Afghan Turkistan had two notable characteristics. First, they were not in the long run internecine. The ethnonym "Turk" applied to all those who spoke Turki or Turk teli (Turkic language) and who were members of one of the following tribal groups: Uzbek, Turkmen, Kazakh, or Kirgiz. In addition to their own version of the Turkic language, members of all groups were able to understand and converse in the literary form of Turk teli. They also collectively identified with Turki speakers to the north and west of the Oxus, as well as those of Eastern Turkistan. Generally, in spite of intertribal conflicts, they rallied as a collective political force against non-Turkic populations. As a dominant political group they occupied the most extensive and fertile agricultural lands and pasturage in Turkistan and controlled all the major strategic trade centers and trade routes leading into or out of Turkistan. Therefore in the conflicts we have described, defeat, however violent, did not mean ethnic demise or destruction.

Moreover, no defeat was seen as final. The various khanates of Turkistan all lacked a centrally organized administrative structure. Political influence outside the tribal territory was achieved and maintained by either actual use of military force or the threat of it. Consequently, to avoid or to decrease the possibility of loss of life and destruction of property when threatened with a military attack, the weaker political community exercised one of two choices: it retreated to a more distant and less hospitable environment or it submitted to the rule of tyranny and showed allegiance by payments of tribute in the form of goods, money, valuables, and slaves. In neither case did it give up the expectation of a dowran (turn to rule and be free) through rebellion, for there was a common belief that political power never remains permanently with any single ethnic group, tribe, or family and that all groups or families will one day have an opportunity to exercise their share of political authority. In other words, both political dominance and subservience are transient. This belief is succinctly expressed in a Kirgiz-Kazakh proverb: "Eluu jilda el jangirat" [A nation regenerates in fifty years]. (9) These characteristics of the ethnic and tribal conflicts of the past have had a profound effect on the ways the people of the region have adapted to subsequent political developments.

Turkistan Under Kabul's Rule

In 1884, four years after the beginning of the reign of Amir Abdur Rahman, all of Afghan Turkistan, including Badakhshan, was subdued and brought under the control of the Kingdom of Kabul. Abdur Rahman's methods of tribal and ethnic pacification were not radically different from those practiced in the area by rulers who preceded him, which included (among other things) deportation of leading households to the capital or to distant territories, and in some instances summary execution to eliminate any potential threat. But he also had an ideology of creating a politically and culturally unified Afghanistan, free of tribalism and "feudalism." Furthermore, with the help of a relatively efficient police and administrative organization and standing army, Amir Abdur Rahman for the first time instituted direct rule of the territories of northern Afghanistan under the Kingdom of Afghanistan. It was during this period that all of Afghanistan's northern borders, including the Wakhan Corridor and the Afghan Pamirs, were delineated and recognized by Russia, British India, and Afghanistan. Recognition of these new boundaries marked the beginning of an attempt to isolate the Turkic populations of the region from the larger Turkic political community of Central Asia across the Oxus and the Pamirs, which later led to the effectual cultural and socioeconomic isolation of the Afghan Turks. (10)

The peoples of Afghan Turkistan accepted the authority of the new Kabul government without much resistance, with the exception of minor revolts in Maimana (1882), Shighnan and Roshan (1882) and Badakhshan (1889). (11)   This lack of reaction on the part of Turkistanis and Badakhshis was due, I believe, to two facts: the prevailing Kabul authority put an end to the chronic warfare in the area that had sapped the human resources of the inhabitants, and the terms of submission to the alien political authority were about the same as to the local khans - payment of taxes and a show of allegiance. For many small minority ethnic groups Pashtun merely replaced Turkic or Tajik sovereignty over them. In addition, the relationship between the local population and the state of Afghanistan continued on the same basis as with the indigenous Turko-Tajik khanates of the earlier period. Although the subjects were obliged to pay taxes and other tributes to the government, they did not have any rights or claims on the political authority in charge. The character of this relationship was one of passive submission and not active political support.

Indeed, this general attitude of inactive participation on the part of the populations of the northern provinces (then known as Afghan Turkistan) in the political processes of the country continued through the reigns of Amir Habibullah, Amir Amanullah, King Nadir Shah, and the early part of the reign of King Zahir Shah. Needless to say, during the half century after the death of Amir Abdur Rahman (1901) the authority of the central government grew stronger. (12)

In these circumstances many population changes took place. First there was a significant Pashtun incursion. Abdur Rahman relied on Pashtun support and provided the Pashtun ample incentives to settle in the north.   The first large-scale Pashtun immigration into the northwestern territories of Afghan Turkistan occurred during the 1890's when Amir Abdur Rahman persuaded his political rivals, the Ghilzai Pashtun pastoral nomadic tribesmen, to occupy the region. By 1910 some Pashtuns and Pashtu-speaking Baluchi herders had reached the Kunduz areas in central Turkistan.   More Pashtun maldar (nomadic herders) arrived in Turkistan during the 1930s and 1940s and began taking their herds through long seasonal migrations to the Lake Shiwa region of Badakhshan and other high pastures on the northern slopes of the Hindu Kush mountains. The incursion of large numbers of Pashtun nomads resulted in the displacement of some Uzbek and Tajik communities and alienation of their agricultural and pasture lands, which had a tremendous impact on the nature of interethnic relations in the area. (13)

Furthermore, Pashtun colonies, made up of military and administrative personnel and their families, had been established in Turkistan prior to the turn of this century in nearly all major towns, including Faizabad, the capital city of Badakhshan province, as well as some rural areas. These early official colonies, with an ever increasing number of Pashtun military and civilian officials who either received land grants from the government or bought public land and invited their kinsmen and tribal members to join them, later developed into sizable communities within towns known as Deh Afghanan or Guzar-i-Afghani, as in the case of Faizabad. Such settlements in rural areas were usually referred to by the tribal name of the settlers. (14) It should also be pointed out that until the early 1950s, all military and police officers and most civilian officials (plus their entourage) in the northern provinces were exclusively from among Pashtun or Tajik from the south of the Hindu Kush. Consequently, in addition to the Pashtun colony in Faizabad there is a sizable Pashtun settlement in Baharak, as well as a smaller one in Ishkashim at the entrance to the Wakhan Corridor. Both of these areas are located in militarily strategic areas and have relatively fertile land.

A large number of Turkic (Uzbek, Turkmen, Kazakh, and Kirgiz) and Tajik populations also immigrated from north of the Oxus into Afghan Turkistan during the 1920s and 1930s following the Soviet Communist take-over of the Central Asian khanates. (15) Among them, a group of some 2,000 Kirgiz herders left their traditional pasturage territories to take permanent refuge in the Afghan Pamirs. Prior to this flight and the consequent permanent year-round confinement on the "roof of the world," these Kirgiz had little contact with the people of Badakhshan and the inhabitants of Wakhan. However, they have reluctantly had to establish relations with a number of ethnically distinctive communities under the new conditions in Badakhshan. The circumstances surrounding the Kirgiz entry into Badakhshan were considerably different from those of the Pashtun who came to the province. Nevertheless, both groups had one thing in common. They were culturally distinct populations who had not had extensive contact with the resident populations of the area and who had to create a niche for themselves within their new socioeconomic and political-ecological environment.

NATIONALITY POLICIES IN AFGHANISTAN

International and national political developments in Afghanistan have had a substantial influence on the processes of adaptation of both Kirgiz and Pashtun groups in Badakhshan during the past several decades. To begin with, the imposition of closed border policies by the Soviet Union and Communist China has effectively ended all the traditional socioeconomic and direct cultural ties that the Kirgiz and other Turkic groups enjoyed with the larger ethnic community in Turkic Central Asia.

Soviet nationalities policy attempted to weaken existing Pan-Turkic identity by forging separate "national" identities for each linguistic group within the larger community of Turkic speakers. This policy has had a negative impact indirectly upon the Kirgiz as well as other Turkic populations in Afghanistan. A significant aspect of Soviet nationalities policy was the abolition of the use of Turki or Turk teli, written in Arabic characters, as the common literary form and as a medium of instruction in Soviet Central Asia. Instead, in the late 1930s (after a period in which the languages were given Latin scripts) different Turkic and non-Turkic languages were given Cyrillic-based alphabets. As a result of such language policies in the Soviet Union and later in Chinese Turkistan, the production of large amounts of material in Turki, mainly for readers in Turkic Central Asia and published by presses in northern India, came to a complete halt. The peoples of Afghan Turkistan had depended upon the north Indian Turki publications for much of their educational and literary materials.

The consequence of these developments for the Turkic-speaking populations in northern Afghanistan has been not only a loss of social contact with the larger Turkic populations of Central Asia, but also the severance of contact with the historical heritage of literary Turkic languages and cultural traditions. Radio broadcasts in a number of different Turkic languages from Soviet Central Asian Republics over the past several decades have provided the only means of contact for the peoples of Afghan Turkistan with the spoken languages and oral traditions of the peoples to the north of the Oxus. (16)

The government of Afghanistan has never formulated anything like the so-called "Soviet Nationalities Policy." On the contrary, it has consistently de-emphasized the presence of minority groups in the country and has taken measures to undermine larger ethnic and regional identities and allegiances. (17) For example, the Afghan government dropped the use of the term Turkistan, replacing it by the phrase manatiq-i-Shamal (northern regions), and divided the area a number of times for administrative purposes, each time assigning new names to various provinces. Whether intentionally or not, this policy has helped to weaken the broader ethnic and regional identities of the populations in the north. This unwritten policy, initiated by the Afghan government in its attempt to create a modernized nation state and coupled with the lack of availability of traditional and modern Turkic literature and education in Afghanistan, has effectively fragmented the traditional collective identities of "Turkistani" and "Turk" into the Soviet created ethnonyms Uzbek, Kirgiz, Turkmen, Kazakh, and Karakalpak. Thus the Kirgiz who settled in the Afghan Pamirs (like other Turkic refugees in other parts of the country) were not only faced with the disintegration of a larger political identity, but were also stripped of all national privileges in the context of the new Pashtun-dominated state of Afghanistan. They were further affected by their physical isolation from other Turkic-speaking communities in northern Afghanistan; they also had to cope with the extremely marginal economic conditions in the high Pamirs.

In marked contrast, the Pashtun population that settled in Badakhshan represented the dominant central authorities and enjoyed all the privileges and resources that the new nation-state could offer. These included education (military and civilian), access to public office, cash income, access to reclaimed government land, and a variety of other strategic resources and services not easily available to members of other ethnic groups. This practice by the governing power accorded with the conventional rules of political dynamics in this part of the world - the powerful have the right to exploit and the weak must submit, perish, or flee. Flight, however, is no longer an option since the takeover of Turkic Central Asia by the Soviet Union and China.

While the notion of civil and human rights for the subjugated may have been entertained by individual rulers in Turkistan or Afghanistan, no such rights existed, even in principle, until the promulgation of the first Constitution of Afghanistan (Nizamnamah-ye-Asasi-e-Daulat-e-'Aliyah-e-Afghanistan) under the guidance of Amir Amanullah in 1923. This document for the first time spelled out "the General Rights of the Subjects of Afghanistan" in Articles 8 through 24, and the spirit of the law proclaimed equality of all citizens of the state. (18)   Later constitutions (1931 and 1964) also retained quite idealistic statements about civil equality.   However, as Dupree has stated, "Until recently, these rights [of Afghan subjects] were more violated than perpetuated." (19)

Most rights and services that were granted to the citizens of the country on the basis of national laws were extended at differential rates to different ethnic populations residing in different parts of the country.   For example, until the 1950s educational services in Badakhshan and other non-Pashtun or non-Tajik areas were introduced at an extremely slow pace to a limited area. The medium of instruction was always Persian or Pashtu, and in some cases Turkic-speaking children living in predominantly Tajiki-speaking areas were instructed in Pashtu, a practice that still continues in some areas of Badakhshan. (20) Most students from the northern provinces allowed to pursue secondary education in Kabul boarding schools were permitted to enter only vocational schools. Perhaps more significant was the fact that until about 1958 no students from Badakhshan of any ethnic origin were admitted to the military school that trained officers for the Afghan Army. This restriction was removed only after the central government had sufficiently strengthened its military base.

Similarly, health care and other social services in Badakhshan are introduced slowly compared to other parts of the country.   There has been virtually no appreciable public investment in any kind of economic development anywhere in the province, despite the fact that the economy of the province suffered considerably because of the closure of trade routes to Chinese Turkistan.   Many Uzbek and Tajik caravan traders from the province experienced severe financial losses, as well as the loss of social and political status, as a result of the closure of borders. Badakhshan province has remained the least developed in Afghanistan and the regional economy is increasingly drained by a flood of nonessential but expensive consumer goods from the outside.

NEW TRADE RELATIONS IN BADAKHSHAN

Improved roads and market demands for raw materials, together with the termination of regional trade with Chinese Turkistan, created particularly favorable conditions for the influx of traders from trading centers in other parts of the country. Most successful of these entrepreneurs are Pashtun and Tajik immigrants from areas south of the Hindu Kush. The newcomers are virtually in control of the truck and bus transportation system throughout Badakhshan. In addition, a small group of Pashtun have dominated the used clothing market, the tea trade, and the only commercial export-import company in Badakhshan.

Unlike the Pashtun nomads and officials, the penetration of Pashtun traders into Badakhshan has not been limited to market towns or summer pastures. On the contrary, during the past decade their presence has been felt everywhere. Very enterprising Pashtun itinerant traders have entered the area of Wakhan and the Afghan Pamirs and their impact on the local economy as well as interethnic politics has been marked. Pashtun are, however, not the only outside traders operating in the area. A number of Uzbek and Tajik itinerant traders, from the villages and towns of central Badakhshan, also frequented these frontier regions even before the arrival of their Pashtun competitors. The transactions among the ethnically diverse traders and Wakhi and Kirgiz inhabitants of the Corridor under the current political and economic conditions are of interest here for two reasons. They represent new forms of socioecological adaptation and interethnic competition for economic resources, mainly through trade and exchange rather than armed struggle; and they permit an examination of interethnic relations at the local level under the new conditions, and the consequent ethnic claims to differential statuses as reflected through exchange systems among members of different cultural categories.

Kirgiz speak a language of the same name, Kirgiz. They adhere to the Hanafi school of Sunni Islam and are relatively conservative practitioners of their belief. The Kirgiz have inhabited the high valleys of the Afghan Pamirs (altitudes of from 13,000 to 16,000 feet) for half a century. Despite loss of much of their traditional pastoral territory and of their socioeconomic and cultural ties with other Turkic communities of Central Asia, they have managed to retain a pastoral nomadic life in the high Pamirs. (21)

Wakhi are the indigenous inhabitants of the Upper Oxus valley (altitudes of 9,500 to 11,500 feet) and are mixed farmers and herders. They speak Wakhi, an archaic Indo-Iranian language, and are adherents to an Ismaili sect of Shi'a Islam. They refer to themselves as Kheek and their features are Iranian in comparison to the more Mongolian appearance of the Kirgiz. (22)

The itinerant traders operating in this region are rural and urban based individuals from the outside. Some have become permanent residents of Wakhan and have acquired large land holdings in the area. The majority of the approximately 35 traders are from central areas of Badakhshan and are either Tajik or Uzbek speakers. About ten Pashtun traders come from a village near Jalalabad. The Pashtun all seem to be related by kinship and marriage and a few of them are in partnership. All of these outside traders admit to having been less successful in their economic ventures in their original community, and their success in Wakhan and the Pamirs varies greatly from one to another. All the traders are Sunni. They have varying degrees of competence in the Wakhi and Kirgiz vernaculars.

The traders maintain regular and direct contact with Kirgiz and Wakhi, and they also have firsthand knowledge of the regional and market demands for agricultural and pastoral products. Successful traders seem to be those who have made full and effective use of local, regional, and national political and economic realities to further their own interests. They are not only the economic middlemen linking primary producers with national market economies, but are also agents of social change and an important force for the development of the Kirgiz pastoral nomadic and Wakhi agropastoral subsistence systems, which ultimately perpetuate the ethnic identity and separate communities of the Kirgiz and Wakhi inhabitants of this frontier region.

Itinerant traders of all ethnic origins have a significant role in organizing and perpetuating a triadic network of trade and exchange relationships involving the Kirgiz and Wakhi in the larger regional and national economy. In this process the traders maintain strict control over the supply, type, and amount of different market goods as well as of the selection of pastoral and agricultural products acceptable in exchange for market goods. Traders have also fostered need and dependency among farmers for market goods and have relied on the use of credit or delayed exchange rather than direct and immediate exchange to maximize their profits. (23) The choice of commodities brought into or taken out of the area is influenced most significantly by bulk, weight, and the margin of profit to the trader. As a result, selection of imported market goods disproportionately favors harmful "luxury" items such as tea and opium.

Among the traders, the Pashtun have been the major suppliers of these two items, particularly of tea. In their economic exchange with Wakhi, Pashtun traders determine prices and terms of credit; on occasion, they induce Wakhi to buy their goods by means of threats or deception. The traders generally have the cooperation and tacit approval of government officials, because of ethnic association, kinship relationships, or bribery. While the problems between Wakhi and Pashtun traders could be brought to the courts, the Wakhi generally meet Pashtun demands. Pashtun superiority over the Wakhi is further demonstrated by the fact that a number of Pashtun have taken wives from Wakhi, bought Wakhi land, and settled in the area; but the reverse never happens.

The economic and social interaction between Pashtun traders and the Kirgiz is somewhat different. In economic transactions with the Kirgiz, Pashtun traders operate on the basis of uniform rates and terms of credit, regardless of the social position or the place of residence of the individual Kirgiz. This is generally due to the strength of the Kirgiz kin-based local political organization and the absence of Afghan government administrators in the Pamirs. The Kirgiz khan often negotiates the exchange values of commodities with the traders, and once settled the rates are followed by all traders. Disputes are rarely taken to government officials but are generally resolved through the local political leaders - khan, be, or aksakal. There have been no cases of exchange of women between Kirgiz and Pashtun, and the likelihood seems remote.

Uzbek and Tajik traders operate on low budgets, and most of them deal mainly in trinkets and opium, although they may obtain some tea on credit from their Pashtun counterparts. Their attitude toward Wakhi is contemptuous, but in their dealings with them they do not generally resort to threats or engage in deceit. However, different rates and terms of credit are available to individuals on the basis of social position and rapport with the trader. Generally, their interaction is amiable. Tajiks and Uzbeks from Badakhshan, traders and others, have married Wakhi women; but no Uzbek or Tajik women have been given to Wakhi men. The Wakhi, together with their neighbors the Kirgiz, have twice elected an Uzbek trader, who lives in Wakhan, to the Afghan Parliament as their representative during the latter part of the 1960s.

Uzbek and Tajik trade and social relations with Kirgiz are on an equal footing. Some of them (especially Uzbek traders) have established permanent trade partnerships with individual Kirgiz households and enjoy a great deal of help and respect. They obey the rule of uniform rates of exchange and terms of credit. Any conflict of interest is resolved through negotiation and the use of local mediators such as the khan. Violence and dependence on the courts is rare. Both Uzbek and Tajik traders have married Kirgiz women, and although no women from either group have been given to the Kirgiz, there are no cultural objections on either side.

Status differences between Uzbek and Tajik are extremely difficult to detect at present in Wakhan or in other parts of Badakhshan. Numerous forms of exchange, including political support and exchange of women, are carried on without reservation by either side. Pashtun, on the contrary, claim a higher status than both Tajik and Uzbek, which can be seen in some exchanges. Pashtun have married both Tajik and Uzbek women but marriage of Pashtun women in Badakhshan to Tajik or Uzbek men, although not unheard of, is rare.

Perhaps the most significant status differences are observed in exchanges between Kirgiz and Wakhi. The Kirgiz refer to Wakhi as Sart (a derogatory term) and regard them as nonbelievers. Feelings of contempt are mutual, yet both groups have developed an economic dependence on one another. The Kirgiz, who cannot produce their own cereals in their high altitude habitat, depend on Wakhi for grain, obtained either directly or indirectly through the traders. The Wakhi, on the other hand, depend on Kirgiz for animals and animal products, both for subsistence or for paying the traders who offer better exchange rates for pastoral products than for agricultural produce.

Wakhi and Kirgiz, who had very little contact with each other prior to the closure of the Soviet and Chinese borders, have had to establish close socioeconomic ties with each other. Both groups travel freely to each other's territory for trade, and they exchange a variety of agricultural, pastoral and, at times, market goods. However, members of each group conduct themselves on these occasions in ways that communicate attitudes about their status claims vis-a-vis each other. While economic exchange moves both ways on the basis of market principles, other forms of exchange are quite assymetric. For example, while the Wakhi eat food cooked by the Kirgiz, Kirgiz rarely eat with Wakhi. Kirgiz often spend months during winter in Wakhi territory on trading trips, spending most of the time in Wakhi households. Neverthe-less, Kirgiz eat nothing cooked by Wakhi, except tea. Kirgiz hire both Wakhi men and women to perform menial tasks for them, but a Kirgiz will never be found working for a Wakhi.

Conflicts between the two groups are rarely, if ever, taken to court staffed by Pashtun and others from outside the corridor. Instead, they are resolved through negotiation or by Kirgiz threats of aggression. I have encountered situations, however, where the Wakhi have been accused of initiating aggression against individual Kirgiz, generally in Wakhi territory. Exchange of women, or even the suggestion of sexual relations with Wakhi women, outrages Kirgiz males; giving a Kirgiz woman to a Wakhi is unthinkable.

Perhaps the most symbolic expression of the sharp value contrast Kirgiz see between themselves and their neighbors is demonstrated in an episode which I recorded during my field work. An old Kirgiz man died while in Wakhan on a trading journey in the winter of 1973. Such a situation had not arisen before. His kinsmen and companions refused to bury him in Wakhan, "the territory of nonbelievers." Instead, they transported the corpse on horseback to the Pamirs, a journey of four days, so the man could be properly buried in Muslim soil.

CONCLUSION

On the basis of our discussion a number of points may be emphasized. First, historically the dynamics of local political processes as well as of social and economic intercourse in northeastern Afghanistan have been dominated by ethnic and tribal conflicts and competition for power, privilege, and access to strategic resources. Second, allocation of social services and economic development projects are, at present, governed by a set of rules based on an idiom of segmentary kinship principles, as well as on ethnicity and spatial distance of the periphery from the center. Third, the traditional petty states of Turkistan as well as the early Afghan monarchies operated on the principles of exploitation of subjects by rulers, where subjects had no rights and could make no demands on the state. Reaction, or expression of discontent, was by means of retreat or revolt whenever possible. These options, however, became impossible in the modern Afghan state due to the increasingly strong military support base, created with the help of foreign governments, and the prevailing condition of closed borders. Therefore, for a long time the traditional outlet for ethnic or tribal discontent has been absent, but no alternative mode of expression has yet developed. Finally, the submission of the Turkic and other minority groups to the rule of dominant Pashtun authority has been realized; and the larger ethnic and regional identities of Turk and Turkistani have effectively weakened.   With the increasing spread of education in all parts of the country, however, attitudes are changing and the expression of demands for rights and privileges along ethnic lines as in the Western model may, of course, come.

NOTES

(1) This paper is based on data collected during the author's doctoral dissertation research in the Wakhan Corridor and the Afghan Pamirs (1972-1974).   The research was supported by the Foreign Area Fellowship Program of the Joint Committee of the Social Science Research Council and the American Council of Learned Societies, and by the Wenner-Gren Foundation for Anthropological Research. A version of this paper was presented in a symposium on "Ethnic Process and Intergroup Relations in Afghanistan" at the Eleventh Annual Meeting of the Middle East Studies Association, New York 1977.

(2) See Charles M. MacGregor, ed., Central Asia, Part II: A Contribution Towards the Better Knowledge of the Topography, Ethnology, Resources and History of Afghanistan (Calcutta, 1871), p. 142; Sir Alexander Burnes, Lieut. Robert Leech, Percival B. Lord, and John Wood, Reports and Papers, Political, Geographical and Commercial in Scinde, Afghanistan and Adjacent Countries (Calcutta, 1839), p. 98.

(3) MacGregor, op. cit., p. 142.

(4) Burnes, op. cit., p. 98.   For an earlier general description of various ethnic populations, the nature of their social and political organization, estimated numbers, political status, military capabilities, spatial distribution, modes of subsistence, and development of

the Pashtun (Pathan or Afghan) monarchy see: Mountstuart
Elphinstone, An Account of the Kingdom of Caubul (1939, 3rd
edition reprinted with introduction by Sir Olaf Caroe, London - New
York, 1972); Sir Alexander Burnes, Cabool: Being a Personal
Narrative of a Journey to and Residence in that City in the Years
1836-7 and 8 (London, 1842); George P. Tate, The Kingdom of
Afghanistan: A Historical Sketch (1911 edition reprinted by D.H.
Publishing House, Delhi, 1973); Sir Olaf Caroe, The Pathans: 550
B.C. to A.D. 1957 (London, 1958); George B. Scott, Afghan and
Pathan: A Sketch (London, 1929).

(5) Burnes, op. cit., pp. 98-99.

(6) Ibid., pp. 101-102. Also see John Wood, A Personal Narrative of a
Journey to the Source of the River Oxus, (London, first published in
1841, 2nd edition 1872).   Wood's travels took place during the
lifetime of Mohammed Murad Beg of Kunduz.   His narrative,
however, should be read with caution since at times it sounds not
only purely conjectural but expresses strong feelings of dislike
towards certain groups in the area and their way of life. Also see
Burhanuddin Kushkaki, Rahnuma-i Qataghan Wa Badakhshan [Guide
to Qataghan and Badakhshan] (Kabul, 1923 in Persian), pp. 162-173.
Kushkaki's work represents the only reliable indigenous account
containing comprehensive ethnographic information and ethnic
population composition and distribution about the provinces of
Qataghan (present-day Baghlan, Kunduz, and Takhar provinces) and
Badakhshan.   Partial translation of this work appears in Gunnar
Jarring "On the Distribution of Turk Tribes in Afghanistan: An
Attempt at a Preliminary Classification" Lund Universities
Arsskrift, N.F. Ard. 1, Bd. 35, Nr. 4. (Lund, 1939). Also see Ludwig
W. Adamec, ed., Historical and Political Gazetteer of Afghanistan, 6
vols. (Graz, Austria, 1972-73).

(7) MacGregor, op. cit., pp. 142-143.

(8) See Kushkaki, op. cit.   Similar spatial distributions of ethnic
populations in central Afghanistan, the Bamian Valley, and adjacent
areas are reported by Robert Canfield, "The Ecology of Rural Ethnic
Groups and the Spatial Dimension of Power," American Anthro-
pologist, vol. 75 (1973), pp. 1511-1528; and Robert Canfield, Faction
and Conversion in Plural Society: Religious Alignment in the Hindu
Kush, University of Michigan Museum of Anthropology, Anthropological Paper No. 50 (Ann Arbor, 1973).   It is certain that the
same patterns of population distribution and allocation of resources
prevail in other parts of the country on both macro- and microen-
vironmental scales.

(9) Cited in Edward Allworth, ed., The Nationality Question in Soviet
Central Asia (New York, 1973), p. 3.

(10) For accounts of Russo-Afghan and Anglo-Afghan relations see: Theo F. Rodenbough, Afghanistan the Anglo-Russian Frontier Question: A Series of Political Papers (London, 1874); Munawar Khan, Anglo-Afghan Relations: 1798-1878 (Peshawar, 1964); Sir W. Kerr Fraser-Tytler, Afghanistan: A Study of Political Development in Central and Southern Asia (3rd edition revised by M. Gillett, London, 1967). For a more recent, and a very well documented analysis of Afghanistan's foreign relations see: Ludwig W. Adamec, Afghanistan, 1900-1923: A Diplomatic History (Berkeley, Calif., 1967); and Ludwig W. Adamec, Afghanistan's Foreign Affairs to the Mid-Twentieth Century: Relations with the U.S.S.R., Germany, and Britain (Tucson, Arizona, 1974).

(11) See Louis Dupree, Afghanistan (Princeton, 1973), p. 419. For accounts of the life of Amir Abdur Rahman ("The Iron Amir") and his pacification methods and efforts see: Sultan Mohammed Khan Munshi, ed., The Life of Abdur Rahman: Amir of Afghanistan (London, 1900 in 2 volumes); John A. Gray, At the Court of the Amir: A Narrative (London, 1895).

(12) For an excellent analytical history of Afghanistan see Varton Gregorian, The Emergence of Modern Afghanistan: Politics of Reform and Modernization 1800-1946 (Stanford, 1969). For a more general treatment of the history of political dynamics see Donald Wilber, Afghanistan, it's people, it's society, it's culture (New Haven, 1962); Harvey H. Smith et al., eds., Area Handbook for Afghanistan, 4th edition (Washington, 1973); and Richard Newell, The Politics of Afghanistan (Ithaca, 1972). For collections of essays dealing with various aspects of life in Afghanistan see: George Grassmuck, Ludwig Adamec, and Frances H. Irwin, eds., Afghanistan: Some New Approaches (Ann Arbor, 1969); Louis Dupree and Lenet Albert, eds., Afghanistan in the 1970s (New York and London, 1974).

(13) For details, see Hasan Kakar, Afghanistan: A Study in Internal Political Developments: 1800-1896 (Lahor, 1971); Nancy Tapper, "The Advent of Pashtun Maldars in North-western Afghanistan," Bulletin of the School of Oriental and African Studies, University of London 36 (1973): 54-79; and Louis Dupree, "Settlement and Migration Patterns in Afghanistan: A Tentative Statement," Modern Asian Studies 9 (1975): 397-413. For an account of Pashtun incursions into Hazarajat region in Central Afghanistan see Klaus Ferdinand, "Nomad Expansion and Commerce in Central Afghanistan," in Folk 4 (1962): 123-159. For accounts of Pashtun nomadic pastoralist expansion in Baghlan, Kunduz, and Badakhshan provinces see: Thomas Barfield, "Pastoralism and Pakhtun Immigration in Northeast Afghanistan," in Jon Anderson and Richard F. Strand, eds., Ethnic Processes and Intergroup Relations in Afghanistan, Occasional Papers of the Asia Society (New York, in press); and Asen Balikci, "The Nomadic Family in Transition," presented at

Conference on Rural Life in Afghanistan: (University of
Nebraska at Omaha, September 23-26, 1976).

(14) See Kushkaki, op. cit., pp. 174-177.

(15) See Dupree, "Settlement and Migration Patterns," p. 405. Also see
Barfield, op. cit., and Balikci, op. cit.

(16) Afghanistan Radio did not broadcast in any of the Turkic languages
spoken in the country until 1972. After a long parliamentary debate,
a forty-five minute program in Uzbek and Turkmen was introduced
as part of minority "national languages programs" of Radio Afghanistan. The program was a definite success with northern audiences.
For the first time it also created a dialogue on the air between the
peoples of Afghan Turkistan and Soviet Central Asia. In 1974, much
to the dismay of everyone in the region, the entire "national
languages program" of Radio Afghanistan was inexplicably abolished
by the Daoud regime.

(17) See Shafie Rahel, Cultural Policy in Afghanistan (Paris, 1975).
This booklet, put out by UNESCO, depicts the "cultural policies" of
the late President Daoud's regime, and as a statement of policy it is
very general, vague, and uninformative.

(18) See Leon B. Poullada, Reform and Rebellion in Afghanistan, 1919-
1929 (Ithaca, New York, 1973), pp. 297-289.

(19) Dupree, Afghanistan, p. 466.

(20) For an early documentation of this fact see: UNESCO, Report of
the Mission to Afghanistan (Paris, 1952). In addition, all school
textbooks and popular histories published in Afghanistan emphasize,
and often exaggerate, the role of Pashtun in the development of
political events in the region. On the other hand, the role of Turkic-
speaking and other minority groups in the history of the area is
frequently ignored, misrepresented, or presented in such a manner as
to convey erroneous, negative images of their part in political
processes. Consequently, despite alleged equality of Afghan
citizens, Afghan school children are told that Afghanistan is
primarily the product of Pashtun efforts. The negative psychological and sociological effects of this intentional or unintentional
practice by Afghan educators upon the identity formation of non-
Pashtun youth is undoubtedly enormous. Until the 1960s, for
instance, Turkic-speaking school children denied their Turkic identity and tried to pass as Tajik whenever possible, a practice
encouraged and accepted by school officials. Unfortunately, it
seems unlikely that the content of school textbooks and histories
published in Afghanistan will be corrected.

(21) See M. Nazif Shahrani, "Kirghiz Pastoralists of the Afghan Pamirs:
An Ecological and Ethnographic Overview," Folk 18 (1976): 129-143;
M. Nazif Shahrani, "Kirghiz Pastoral Nomads of the Afghan Pamirs:

A Study in Ecological and Intra-cultural Adaptation," Ph.D. dissertation, University of Washington, Seattle (1976); M. Nazif Shahrani, "The Retention of Pastoralism among the Kirghiz of the Afghan Pamirs," in James F. Fisher, ed., Himalayan Anthropology: The Indo-Tibetan Interface (The Hague, in press); and M. Nazif Shahrani, The Kirghiz and Wakhi of Afghanistan: Adaptation to Closed Frontiers (Seattle, in press). For earlier reports about the Kirghiz in the Pamirs of Afghanistan see: Gabriel Bonvalot, Through the Heart of Asia: Over the Pamirs to India, translated by C.B. Pitman (London, 1889); The Earl of Dunmore, The Pamirs, 2 vols. (London, 1893); Jean Shor, After You, Marco Polo (New York, 1955); and Francis Younghusband, The Heart of a Continent: A Narrative of Travels in Manchuria, Across the Gobi Desert, through the Himalayas, the Pamirs and Chitral, 1884-1894, 2nd edition (London, 1896).

(22) For additional information on the Wakhi see: Shahrani, The Kirghiz and Wakhi of Afghanistan; Wood, A Personal Narrative; and Ole Olufsen, Through the Unknown Pamirs: The Second Danish Pamir Expedition 1898-99 (New York, 1969).

(23) See Shahrani, The Kirghiz and Wakhi of Afghanistan, chap. 8.

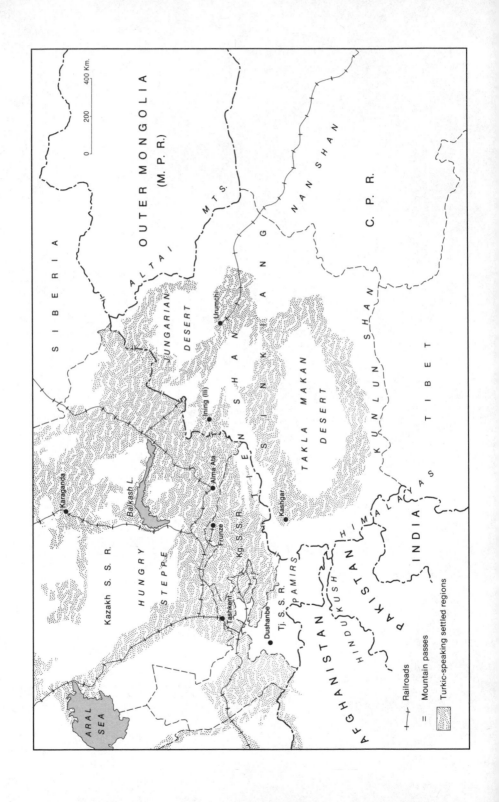

8 Ethnic Minorities in the Sino-Soviet Dispute

June Teufel Dreyer

THE PROTAGONISTS

The Sino-Soviet frontier in Central Asia is an artificial boundary which divides several minority groups. This paper will focus on two of these groups, the Kazakhs and Uighurs, and their relations with their fellow Turkic Muslim peoples and with the Soviet and Chinese governments.

There are approximately 5 million Uighurs and 700,000 Kazakhs in China, most of them living in Sinkiang province, (1) which is contiguous to the Soviet republic of Kazakhstan. According to the 1970 Soviet census, there are 173,000 Uighurs and nearly 5.3 million Kazakhs in the USSR. Both Soviet and Chinese Uighurs and Kazakhs are minority groups not only in relation to the populations of their own countries (China has an estimated 900 million people and the Soviet Union 250 million), but even in the provinces in which they live. Sinkiang has a population of approximately 11 million and Kazakhstan, 12.13 million. However, the importance of the Uighurs and Kazakhs lies not in their numbers but in their interactions with the other minority peoples of the area, and in the strategic roles of these groups for the Soviet and Chinese leaderships. The position of these minority peoples becomes much more impressive if viewed in this light. The combined minority peoples of the four Soviet Central Asian republics account for 59 percent of the total population thereof, and those of China's Sinkiang province, for over 60 percent.

The ethnic mosaic of Central Asia is complex, formed over many centuries of nomadic migration and the rise and fall of invading warrior tribes. The emergent picture is one of constant reshuffling of alignments and of a steppe constantly in flux. Both Uighurs and Kazakhs are Turkic Muslim peoples, though the modern-day Uighurs are predominantly sedentary agriculturists while the Kazakhs are nomadic herders. The Uighurs first appear as a clearly separate people in records dating from the fourth century A.D. By the eighth century, they had created a large empire in what is now the Mongolian People's Republic but were themselves conquered by another tribe, the Kirgiz, during the following century. Many of the defeated Uighurs dispersed throughout Central Asia, with a certain amount of intermarriage and intermingling with other steppe people resulting. A large number of Uighurs entered what is now Sinkiang province in 840 A.D., and soon established their dominance of the oasis areas characteristic of southern Sinkiang.

The word Kazakh first appears during the fifteenth century. Of Turkish origin, it derives from a term meaning a masterless person or freebooter, and came by extension to refer to nomads as well. The Kazakhs are closely related to other Central Asian Muslim peoples, particularly to the Kirgiz and Uzbeks. Curiously, the traditional nobilities of the Kazakhs and these other groups trace their origins to Genghis Khan, a Mongol. While the accuracy of historical records, and particularly of genealogical tables, from this period is often diluted by fanciful embellishment, it would appear that the Mongol conquests of the thirteenth century effected a fundamental redistribution of the separate nomadic groups of the Central Asian steppe. In the following centuries, the culture of the Kazakhs, Kirgiz, and Uzbeks was formed. Because of this, different ethnic groups may have the same ancestor. Whether the presence of the ancestor in several different genealogical tables is genuine or fictive is often less important than that the table is credible to the groups involved. Normally these kinship groups were loosely organized and spread over extensive areas. Unless united under a single leader, such as Genghis Khan, they did not pose a large-scale threat to more centralized governmental systems. However kinship, real or imaginary, often manifested itself in cooperation in time of hostilities, and even resulted in a certain amount of crossing of ethnic lines. (2)   In addition to the potential binding force of kinship, cooperation has also been facilitated by the Muslim faith common to most of these groups. The Islamic admonition to join together in time of holy war was usually accepted enthusiastically by most of these peoples, even when the cause was tenuously related to religion. Their location in the paths of two expanding empires provided the peoples of Central Asia with many causes for uprising.

THE COURSE OF EMPIRE

Imperial China had traditionally claimed jurisdiction over Central Asia but in fact rarely exercised it. Chinese civilization was based on sedentary agriculture, and the mountainous, arid cold of much of Central Asia did not attract Han Chinese settlers. Except for a small area in which moderate climatic conditions prevailed, the territory referred to rather vaguely in Chinese sources as "the Western Regions" could not be considered part of either the Chinese cultural or administrative sphere. A few caravan routes traversed the area from earliest times, allowing trade between Han (3) dynasty China and imperial Rome, but the hazards of the route combined with the anticommercial bias of official Confucian philosophy to limit the effects of this contact. It would be difficult to consider Central Asia an integral part of the Chinese economy. Culturally, since the inhabitants of these lands did not partake of Han civilization, they were regarded by the Han Chinese as barbarians. The expert horsemanship and martial skills that characterized their life-styles frequently threatened Han culture.

These people could be, and several times were, conquered by Chinese armies, but garrisoning such far-flung areas was difficult and expensive. One device to reduce the problem of maintaining armed forces in distant areas was the military agricultural colony. Soldiers were charged with raising their own food and were expected to form self-sufficient outposts of the empire. Though ingenious, the scheme had several drawbacks, not least of which was that soldiers tended to marry local women and eventually became assimilated by the very people they had been sent to subdue. In general, Chinese policy toward these and other border peoples aimed at control rather than absorption. The inhabitants were permitted to maintain their traditional life-styles and cultures as long as they did not disturb the order and peace of empire.

Shortly after the Kazakhs began to appear as a separate people, the Russian Empire began to expand eastward. In 1689, China ceded 93,000 square miles of its Central Asian domains to the tsar's government, and in 1727 the Treaty of Kiakhta gave Russia an additional 40,000 square miles. In the years to come the once-powerful Ch'ing dynasty became progressively enfeebled and unable to repel the demands of foreign powers. By the Treaty of Aigun in 1858 the land on the left bank of the Amur River down to the Ussuri became Russian territory and in 1860, the Treaty of Peking enabled Russia to annex 133,000 square miles of land east of the Ussuri to the Pacific. (4) The Ch'ing government bitterly resented these cessions. Together with other concessions that had to be made to various foreign countries, they came to be referred to as the "unequal treaties." That these settlements were forced on an unwilling government forms the basis for the present-day Chinese government's claim to large portions of Kazakhstan and other parts of Soviet Central Asia.

One result of tsarist expansion was the colonization of Kazakhstan by peasants from European Russia. The Russian government originally maintained restrictions on migration but, on realizing its value, began to offer attractive inducements to settlers. Their arrival aroused considerable resentment among the Kazakhs, whose numbers were then estimated at three million. (5) The nomads had pastured their herds over large portions of the steppe. Russian colonization took land away from grazing and denied many Kazakhs the use of their traditional winter camps. Many of them fled south, to land still held by China.

The increasing weakness of the Ch'ing dynasty led to more than the cession of territory to Russia. The efficient and relatively honest governors and officials the Chinese government sent to the Western Regions soon after it had reconquered the area in 1759 were gradually replaced with greedy and less competent administrators who oppressed the peoples under their charge and aroused their hostility. This corruption and the arrival of the Kazakhs, whom the Russian government could claim were the subjects of the tsar, played into Russian hands.

Accumulated grievances against the Ch'ing government flared into a Muslim rebellion in 1862, which eventually encompassed the entire Chinese northwest. In 1865, a Turkic Muslim named Yakub Beg took advantage of the rebellion to set up an independent state; tacit support from Russia helped Yakub Beg to maintain his position. (6) However, in the attendant chaos, Russia's trade was disrupted and its consulates burned. A substantial number of refugees fled to Russia. Seeing a territorial opportunity in this as well as a way to reassert its trading position, Russia moved into the rich Ili Valley, in Kazakh territory, and annexed it. The enfeebled Ch'ing dynasty, in a costly campaign that it could ill afford, finally defeated the northwest Muslim rebellion and destroyed Yakub Beg's state. The subsequent Chinese demand that Russia withdraw from Ili led to a major diplomatic confrontation between the two states. Eventually a convention was signed providing for Russian withdrawal on China's cession of some territory west of Ili, its granting of special trading concessions in nearby areas, and the payment of a 9 million ruble indemnity to cover Russia's expenses in "administering" Ili. (7)

Fearful of further Russian moves, the Ch'ing government decided to incorporate what had been the Western Regions into the regular administrative system of China. In 1896 it was formally created a province with the name Sinkiang, or "New Territory."

In the following years, the tsarist government attempted to cope with mounting domestic problems, an expensive and ultimately humiliating war with Japan, and international intrigues on its European borders. But the colonization of Kazakhstan continued. Between 1896 and 1916 more than 1.4 million new settlers poured into Kazakhstan and implanted a strong Russian presence there. Its economy became firmly tied to that of European Russia, which it supplied with meat, hides, and dairy products. (8)

Further escalation of tensions between China and Russia over Central Asia were limited by domestic difficulties that prevented each state from consolidating its hold over its Central Asian domains. In 1911 the Ch'ing dynasty fell and was replaced by a series of warlord governments that were preoccupied with quarrels with other warlords. In Russia a 1916 decree ordering Kazakhs, who were traditionally exempt from military service, to be drafted to help fight in World War I caused a bloody rebellion that further weakened the faltering tsarist government. During the ensuing disruptions on the steppe, additional numbers of Kazakhs fled to Sinkiang, over which even Chiang Kai-shek's Kuomintang (KMT) government, which assumed power in 1928, was unable to exercise more than nominal control. (9)

THE 1917 REVOLUTION AND ITS
EFFECTS ON CENTRAL ASIA

The success of the Bolshevik revolution that began in Russia in 1917 changed the power equation in Central Asia in favor of the newly formed Soviet Union. The new government's success did not come easily, and its relations with the non-Russian peoples of the former tsarist empire were among its more difficult problems. In the Bolshevik Party's first bid for the support of these peoples, called minority nationalities in Marxist parlance, it had promised self-determination to all who wished it. After the consolidation of its power, however, the Party came to view self-determination as "profoundly counterrevolutionary" and ruthlessly suppressed such movements. The Kazakhs' Alash Orda provisional government was one of the victims, and a bitter anti-Bolshevik struggle took place in which many Kazakhs joined the White Army of Admiral Kolchak. (10)   The economy of the area was badly affected. In the Kazakh province of Semirechie, livestock decreased by 51.7 percent during the three years between 1917 and 1920. (11) In 1920 and 1921 the Kazakh areas were hit by famine. The Kazakhs were more seriously affected than the Russian colonists; their herds had been depleted in the fighting and they did not receive their fair share of the emergency food supplies sent in by the new government. An estimated one million persons died of hunger and related diseases in 1921 alone, and a necessary preoccupation with sheer survival reduced the Kazakhs' organized resistance to the Bolshevik government. (12)

In contrast to the tsarist government's relatively cautious attitude toward altering the traditional life styles of its Central Asian subjects, the Soviet government promoted rapid change. Although Kazakhstan was designated an "autonomous socialist republic" in 1920 and given the constitutional right to secede from the USSR, its non-Russian inhabitants actually had very little to say about the governance of their area, and it was clear that any attempts to exercise the right to secede would be regarded as counter-revolutionary. Measures were introduced to force the nomads to settle down, to destroy tribal and kinship ties that might facilitate resistance to the new government, to promote agriculture as an alternative to pastoralism, and to introduce the Kazakhs, Uighurs, and other Central Asian peoples to the Russian language and Marxist ideology. While motivated by a desire to improve the lives of Central Asian peoples as well as to facilitate the new government's control of the area, the reforms were not perceived as improvements by many of those affected. The fictional autonomy was

patently obvious to all.   The Kazakh and Uighur intelligentsia,
influential despite their small numbers, was irked by the introduction of
a new script that the government alleged would suit the nationalities'
needs better than the traditional Arabic script.   They would have
preferred a system devised by Crimean Tatar Ismail Bey Gaspirali
(1851-1914), which would have been suitable for all Turkic peoples, and
they especially viewed the Soviet government's choice (in 1938) of a
Cyrillic script as an attempt to separate them from these other
peoples. (13)

In addition, there was a cultural contradiction between the Soviet
leadership's implicit belief that agriculture was a more desirable way of
life and the nomads' attachment to their animals and to a peripatetic
mode of existence.   A collectivization program begun in 1928 was
carried out without adequate planning and far in advance of collectivization in Russian areas.   Forced into collectives where grazing was
often insufficient, thousands of Kazakhs watched their herds starve.
Others killed their animals and tried to escape.   Some fled to
Afghanistan, others to China.   The Kazakh population of the USSR fell
by almost 900,000 between 1926 and 1939, and there was a sharp drop in
numbers of animals as well. (14)   Soviet policies were the worse in their
effect on the Central Asian minorities because they were administered
through the local Russian-colonist elite.   As described by Richard Pipes,
this group

> utilized the Soviet government and party machines to intensify the
> economic and political exploitation of the native population.   The
> Revolution, therefore, brought to the Moslem areas not an abolition
> of colonialism, but colonialism in a new and much more oppressive
> form....   The classes which in Russia proper constituted the lower
> orders of society formed in the eastern borderlands a privileged
> order, which itself was engaged in exploitation and oppression. (15)

The situation of the Kazakhs and Uighurs, like that of other Soviet
nationalities, has improved since the death of Stalin, though not enough
to eliminate discontents.   Khrushchev's reforms in higher education
allowed a higher percentage of Kazakhs, Uighurs, and most other
nationalities to attend universities and to take advantage of better job
opportunities.   Standards of living in Central Asia have improved
markedly.   Locally situated factories turn out desired consumer goods.
The Soviet housing shortage is a lesser problem in Central Asia than in
European Russia, as is the supply of fresh meat, milk, and vegetables.
There is a Kazakh member of the Politburo. (16)

But the results of raised living standards and two generations of
pressure have not made significant numbers of Turkic Muslims into
either committed Soviet citizens or assimilated Russians.   Nomadism
has survived, albeit in a modified form.   It has been pointed out that
although Soviet propaganda describes nomads as "roving" (otgonnyi)
rather than nomadic (kochevoi), and describes herders as "specialists

skilled in the care of livestock" and the nomadic family as a "brigade" with each member holding an official title, the end result continues to be pastoral nomads moving seasonally in family groups to find grazing for their animals. (17)

A recent study concludes that the Turkic Muslim peoples have been extraordinarily resistant to linguistic assimilation. This is true even of persons who have been exposed to Russians for long periods of time. The linguistic russification level of urbanized Kazakh communities who have had over two centuries of extensive contact with Russians was only 3.2 percent in 1959; that for rural Kazakhs was even lower, 2.7 percent. (18) Interestingly, the 1970 Soviet census listed a slightly higher percentage of Uighurs reporting Uighur as their native language than in the previous census of 1959 (88.5 percent versus 85.0 percent). That for Kazakhs remained almost exactly the same as in 1959. (19) Similar figures are reported for other Central Asian minorities, tending to support the conclusion that "the effect of exposure to Russians on the russification of Muslims is exceedingly small." (20) An American student in Tashkent in 1970 was told by a recent Russian arrival that at first it was hard for him to believe that Russian rule extended to Central Asia. (21)

A Western social scientist, analyzing the significantly higher rates of population increase among Central Asian minorities than among Russians, describes these peoples as pursuing la vengeance des berceaux - getting even through the cradle, or compensating for heavy in-migration to their homelands and some assimilation losses through a high birth rate. In Kazakhstan the percentage of the school-age population that is Muslim is significantly higher than the Muslim percentage of the total population of the province, even though children of the Muslim minorities, particularly female children, are more likely to drop out of school than Russian children. That available labor now seems to be directed at Siberia rather than Kazakhstan makes russification still less likely. (22) Nonetheless, Russian dissident Andrei Sakharov has pointed out that Soviet prisons are filled with ethnic dissidents. (23)

Activities of the Soviet and Chinese
Communist Parties in Sinkiang

While the Soviet government was extending and consolidating its power over the former tsarist domains in Central Asia, it did not lose interest in those Central Asian territories still nominally under Chinese control. At this point it is necessary to backtrack again to 1917 in order to examine the situation in Sinkiang during the years following the October revolution.

When the Bolshevik government assumed power in Russia, it issued a declaration abrogating the unequal treaties concluded during the tsarist era. However, none of the land obtained thereunder was returned to

China, and by the 1930s the Soviet Union was proving even more interested in Sinkiang than had tsarist Russia. The warlord of Sinkiang, Sheng Shih-ts'ai, was concerned with maintaining his independence from the government of China, then headed by Chiang Kai-shek, and the Soviet Union provided financial assistance that helped Sheng in this endeavor. In return, the Soviet Union received a privileged position in Sinkiang. Soviet geologists explored the province's rich natural resources, Soviet engineers surveyed railways, and Soviet pilots manned Sinkiang's air routes.

Propaganda activities aimed at forming a pro-Soviet communist party. The atmosphere in Sinkiang was for the most part distinctly unfriendly to the Chinese Communist Party (CCP). In 1934, when the beleaguered CCP fled its Kiangsi Soviet base to escape annihilation by Chiang Kai-shek's forces, it wandered about for many months in search of a reasonably safe haven. The USSR, ostensibly its fraternal socialist ally and adviser, never told the CCP of its position in Sinkiang. An ex-CCP leader who later defected has speculated that this was because Stalin had designs on Sinkiang and wished to exclude Chinese influence of any sort from the province. (24)

In 1938, Sheng, seemingly attempting to gain a degree of independence from the USSR by playing off the Soviet and Chinese parties against one another, welcomed several CCP advisers into his government and even announced his intention to join the CCP. A few years later, however, alleging their involvement in a plot against him, he had them arrested and executed. Mao Tse-tung's brother, Mao Tse-min, was among these martyrs to Chinese Communist concern with Sinkiang.

When, due to its involvement in World War II, the USSR could no longer sustain its aid to Sinkiang and, in fact, appeared to Sheng Shih-ts'ai as if it might be losing the war, Sheng began mending fences with Chiang Kai-shek's KMT government. Accepting a cabinet-level position in Chungking, Sheng left Sinkiang, and the KMT was able to choose its first governor of the province. Sinkiang's non-Han groups were not pleased by the reassertion of Chinese control, and the new administration of the province proved neither tactful nor honest. Han settlers were arriving and would presumably occupy minorities' lands; a Han army stationed there had to be provisioned and paid, and the province's economy was deteriorating.

Meanwhile the Soviet Union took the offensive in World War II and, miffed at losing its position in Sinkiang, reasserted its interest there. Because the previous government-to-province special relationship failed, the USSR began to work through Sinkiang's aggrieved non-Han groups. Sympathetic Soviet agents provided dissident ethnic group leaders with financial aid and advice, and a major rebellion ensued. A multiethnic alliance representing Uighurs, Kazakhs, Kirgiz, Russians and others cooperated in establishing an independent state, the East Turkistan Republic, with its capital at Ining in the predominantly Kazakh territory bordering Soviet Kazakhstan. Its leader Ahmejan was a Uighur, though the ETR's mainstay was its Kazakh cavalry, commanded by Osman Bator. At one point the rebel cavalry threatened the provincial capital of Urumchi. (25) That they pulled back only when the Soviet Union, having offered its services as mediator, advised them to do so seems to indicate the movement's dependence on the USSR. The abundant evidence of KMT mismanagement makes it clear, however, that the Soviet Union was exploiting existing grievances rather than creating them.

At the end of the war with Japan, Chiang Kai-shek's KMT government was amenable to compromise, especially since the Sinkiang rebellion was tying down troops and materiel Chiang wished to use in his battle with the Chinese Communist Party. Eventually a compromise was worked out, providing for increased minority representation in government and a greater degree of autonomy for the province. Burhan, a Tatar who had managed to create a certain amount of rapport with all sides, was made governor. The troops of the ETR would remain undispersed as a partial guarantee that the KMT would observe its part of the bargain, and a KMT garrison also remained in Sinkiang.

As Chiang Kai-shek lost his battle with the CCP, the Soviet Union not only failed to aid the CCP but actually entered into publicly announced negotiations with the KMT. Although the exact bargaining terms were not revealed, the Soviet Union was clearly offering Chiang arms, which surely would have been used against the CCP, in return for some form of control over Sinkiang. (26) Eventually the CCP's military success foreclosed this option. By the late summer of 1949 the Communist armies had been victorious in most of the rest of China and were pressing hard on Sinkiang. At this point virtually the entire provincial government of Sinkiang, from governor Burhan on down, and including most of those who had been leaders of the ETR, defected to the CCP en masse.

Thus Singkiang, with its large Turkic Muslim majority (estimated at that time at 75 percent Uighur, 10 percent Kazakh, and less than 6 percent Han) formally became part of the Chinese People's Republic. Exactly how the province's leadership had been persuaded to defect is not known. However, in addition to the certainty of CCP takeover regardless of their wishes, the provincial leaders were surely influenced by promises that Sinkiang would receive autonomous status (the content of this autonomy probably somewhat ambiguous), that there would be concessions to the ethnic groups and their cultures, and that the leadership role of the present elite would continue. This last the CCP did not have to make good on in several significant cases; the plane carrying most of the high-ranking ETR leaders, including Ahmejan, crashed mysteriously en route to a conference in Peking. The Chinese did not release news of the disaster until many months later, thus fanning speculation that the crash might not have been accidental. (27) The only remaining ETR leader of note was Saifudin, a young Moscow-trained Uighur who then spoke Chinese rather poorly. He had been engaged in fomenting anti-Han riots in Sinkiang during the early 1940s, had been Minister of Education in the ETR government, and was a member of the Communist Party of the Soviet Union.

Saifudin was not the only reminder of the Soviet Union's privileged position in Sinkiang. Beginning its political career as an international outcast, the new Chinese People's Republic was forced to turn to the USSR for help. Negotitations over a treaty dragged on for many months, leading observers to conclude that the Soviet Union was driving a hard bargain. The full provisions of what would become the Sino-Soviet Treaty of 1950 were not announced by either side, but are known to have included a special consular position for the USSR in Sinkiang, plus joint exploration of Sinkiang's resources and the creation of joint stock companies to exploit those resources. (28)

The Chinese did not send People's Liberation Army (PLA) work teams (29) to the three predominantly Kazakh districts in December 1949 when such teams were sent to the rest of Sinkiang, explaining that "conditions were as yet unsettled" in those areas. (30) But the work teams did appear in the three districts in the latter half of 1950, after the Sino-Soviet Treaty was signed (on March 27). One may speculate that the "unsettled conditions" may therefore have included the unsettled question of who should administer the three districts, and that the USSR was arguing for jurisdiction over them. Certainly the Soviet Union retained an influential position in the three districts. When, toward the end of 1950, the organs of local power in Ili, Tacheng, and Tarbagatai were "reorganized," the Administrative Control Boards that replaced them included many Kazakhs and Uighurs who had been members of, or sympathetic to, the ETR government (though a Han Chinese generally held the final decision-making power). In urban areas of the three districts, the pro-Soviet minority intelligentsia remained in power and was not generally made to undergo intensive ideological remolding or reform. The local clan headman structure was left largely unaltered as well, except for those who overtly resisted the new government. Osman Bator, whose Kazakh cavalry had been so important to the success of the ETR, was one such holdout. He fled south, where eventually he was captured and executed. As for Saifudin, while he was in Moscow helping to negotiate the 1950 treaty, it was announced from Peking that he had become a member of the CCP and that he had resigned from the CPSU.

In 1951 a purge, probably undertaken in connection with the "three-anti" campaign then being conducted in the rest of China, reportedly removed pro-Soviet figures in the minority areas and in 1953 a large-scale pacification and re-education campaign was conducted. In 1954 the official New China News Agency (NCNA) explained that "it was only after all this that the entire Kazakh people returned to the fold of the ancestral land." (31)

In general, however, strenuous efforts were made to conceal any differences between the Chinese and Soviet governments over the Central Asian lands. The Sino-Soviet frontier was referred to as "Friendship Border," and Kazakhs and Uighurs crossed it frequently in both directions to graze their herds and to visit kinfolk.   Soviet technicians were lavishly praised in the Chinese press for the selfless way in which they were helping their socialist neighbor to develop its resources, and Soviet ethnographers worked with the Han Chinese among Sinkiang's minorities. (32) Soviet aid helped build a railroad connecting Lanchow, capital of China's Kansu province, with Urumchi, the capital of Sinkiang.   It was planned to continue the line on through Ili, from which it would ultimately reach the Soviet border.   According to that plan, the USSR would extend the terminus of its Turk-Sib railroad from Aktogai to the border, and the two lines would connect at a new town, Druzhba [Friendship] .

To avoid antagonizing the minorities and risking the reinforcement of any pro-Soviet tendencies they might have, Chinese policy was cautious and followed a modified Soviet model.   "Land" reform was carried out under slogans such as "herdowners and [poorer] herders both profit" and "no struggle, no liquidation, no division of property." Chinese state trading organs offered relatively high prices for herders' products.   While presented as evidence of the CPR's high regard for its minority nationalities and its desire to ensure their prosperity, this was also a way for the new government to gain control in the herding areas by linking them with the Chinese market system, and to re-direct trade away from the USSR as well.   Lenient attitudes were also taken toward most religious practices, even toward polygamy.

In 1954 Khrushchev visited Peking, hoping to obtain Chinese support in his bid to succeed Stalin.   He did earn this support, but not before the Chinese exacted a quid pro quo.   Khrushchev agreed, among other things, to terminate the joint stock companies in Sinkiang.   Soviet influence, however, remained in the form of advisers, technicians, and the need to order equipment and spare parts from the USSR.   The Chinese also announced that Uighur, Kazakh, and the other Turkic Muslim languages would henceforth be written with Cyrillic script. Because many of the intelligentsia of these minorities had been educated in the Soviet Union and were already acquainted with Cyrillic, this was understandable.   However, the use of Cyrillic in writing Uighur and Kazakh also created a bond between these Chinese minorities and their fellow Uighurs and Kazakhs in the USSR, while creating a linguistic distance between the Chinese minorities and the Han majority in China.   Sheng Shih-ts'ai, from his vantage point in Taiwan, later recalled his own misgivings when his Soviet advisers repeatedly declared that "the peoples along the Sino-Soviet frontier are all brethren.   The racially related peoples will one day be united as citizens of the same nation." (33)   It is inconceivable that the leaders of the CPR would not have seen the implications of allowing Cyrillic to replace Arabic in Sinkiang, and the fact that this decision was announced at all (34) is indicative of the degree to which the Chinese government felt it necessary to placate the Soviet Union at this time.

A month after Khrushchev's visit to China the Ili Kazakh Autonomous Chou was created, encompassing the three predominantly

Kazakh districts of the former ETR and, like the ETR, having its capital at Ining. The chairperson was a Kazakh and there were Uighur and Kazakh vice-chairpersons, but there was also significant (and presumably more powerful) representation from regular units of the Chinese People's Liberation Army (PLA) and from the Sinkiang Production and Construction Corps. The latter, with its motto "on the one shoulder a rifle, on the other a hoe," was intended to garrison the area while helping local people to develop their economy. The possibility of American and other imperialist intervention always existed, and there were surely ways in which the local economy could be improved. But it was also possible for the Soviet Union to view the Production and Construction Corps as guarding the border against it. And the local people, noting the large number of persons in the corps and their preoccupation with agriculture, as opposed to animal husbandry, could see the corps as yet another Han Chinese plan to usurp their lands, to turn the nomads into sedentary agriculturalists, and to assimilate them. The corps also bore an uncomfortable resemblance to the military agricultural colonies of imperial China, whose minorities policies were regularly and vehemently denounced by Mao. In 1956 there began a large-scale transfer of Han Chinese into Sinkiang, with many of them being absorbed into the corps or onto newly-created state farms.

Curiously, and very much at variance with the practice elsewhere in China, the Ili Chou's creation in 1954 and Sinkiang's reconstitution as the Sinkiang Uighur Autonomous Region (SUAR) during the following year occurred despite the fact that elections in 14 counties of Ili Chou could not be held until 1956.

Also in 1956 the party began a major investigation of its policies toward minority nationalities. This was carried on at the same time that persons throughout China were encouraged to voice their opinions of socialism in a campaign to "let a hundred flowers bloom, let a hundred schools of thought contend." The results, as they became known in 1957, were profoundly disquieting to Party leaders. Among the Uighurs, Kazakhs, and other Sinkiang minorities the campaign revealed lurking preferences for the Soviet Union over China; often strongly-voiced preferences for an independent Kazakh, Uighur, or Turkic state; and the repeated conviction that were ETR leader Ahmejan still alive, he would be most dissatisfied with what had become of the autonomy he thought he had been promised. There were also charges that the Han were exploiting the minorities and demands that they leave Sinkiang en masse. (35)

Saifudin, who had been made governor of the SUAR in 1955, attempted to refute these charges in the expected ways - Sinkiang had "always" been part of China, the Han were sacrificing themselves to build a better Sinkiang, and there was sufficient wealth in the province for all. Those who thought otherwise were either counterrevolutionaries or had been duped by counterrevolutionaries. (36) As might be anticipated, many of the hundred flowers were found to be poisonous weeds; Uighurs and Kazakhs who had voiced them were now removed from office and sent for "reform through labor." These included, among others, the talented young poet Kazhykumar Shabdanov, Jahoda, the head of the Ili Kazakh Autonomous Chou, the vice-director of the Chou's propaganda department, and the president of its People's Court. (37) Significantly, Zunin Taipov, a former leader of the ETR army who had been absorbed into the Chinese military, was removed as well.

Public mention of the pro-Soviet predilections of those purged was muted in order to avoid a confrontation with the Soviet Union. But the anti-Soviet aspect of the antirightist campaign is sworn to by later refugees into the Soviet Union and one may legitimately read it into the Chinese criticisms of local nationalism in Sinkiang. The pro-Uighur, pro-Kazakh, and Pan-Turkic sentiments that the CCP attacked openly, and the nostalgic recollections of Ahmejan, Osman Bator, and the ETR that it simply suppressed, all obviously reminded the Chinese leadership of Soviet machinations in Sinkiang. Moreover, the example of Mongolia was constantly in view. There the Soviet Union had successfully encouraged "local nationalists" to set up a state "independent" of China, which in practice was almost completely dependent on Soviet aid and trade. Hence local nationalism in Sinkiang, while not identical to pro-Sovietism, is perceived by the Chinese leadership as having a high degree of overlap with it.

THE SINKIANG MINORITIES AND THE
SINO-SOVIET DISPUTE, 1958-1976

In 1958 China began the Great Leap Forward which represented a sharp break from the social, economic, and ideological policies it had pursued during the previous nine years. There were many reasons behind the launching of the Great Leap, and why it was begun at this particular time. Among the more important were the growing conviction among an influential segment of the Chinese leadership that continued adherence to the Soviet model would be detrimental to China's development, and the feeling that the Soviet Union had abandoned its commitment to true Marxism. Communes encompassing many tens of thousands of persons were created, the use of material incentives in production was sharply curtailed, and there was large-scale confiscation of private property. The relative tolerance accorded to minority nationalities' languages, customs, and life-styles under the influence of the Soviet model was also ended.

During this campaign the Uighurs, Kazakhs, and other minorities of Sinkiang were expected, among other things, to contribute their animals to the communes, to learn Han Chinese, to adopt Han cultural forms, and to give up various "decadent" customs including polygamy. Communes were generally not established in Uighur and Kazakh areas until several months after they had been set up in much of the rest of

China, by which time their major deficiencies had become known. Although there is some evidence that these later established communes were created in a somewhat modified form, their effects were as dysfunctional as in other areas of China. Production fell drastically, and there was widespread hunger and dissatisfaction with both the economic and social policies of the Great Leap Forward. In 1958 and 1959 there were rumors of small-scale uprisings in Sinkiang. (38)

The Soviet leadership was evidently contemptuous of these Chinese policies and annoyed at the repudiation of the USSR's model that the Great Leap represented. In 1959, Khrushchev publicly criticized the communes and the Soviet press treated China's ensuing economic difficulties with smug "concern." In 1960 all Soviet technicians still remaining in China were abruptly withdrawn. Increasingly, outsiders could observe the strains in the Sino-Soviet relationship. Finally, in 1962, a combination of intense minority dissatisfaction with Chinese rule in Sinkiang and growing hostility between the Soviet and Chinese leaderships provided the backdrop for conflict in the border areas.

This began with an incident that we must reconstruct from circumstantial evidence because the Chinese have published little about it. In 1964, in his lengthy report to the National People's Congress, Chou En-lai admitted:

> In 1962, under the instigation and direct direction of external forces, a group of the most reactionary protagonists of local nationalism staged a traitorous counterrevolutionary rebellion in Ining, Sinkiang, and incited and organized the flight to foreign territory of a large number of people near the frontier. Under the leadership of the Party, the people of all the fraternal nationalities in Sinkiang resolutely crushed these subversive and traitorous activities. (39)

Meanwhile, the Soviet side published a graphic "eyewitness" account:

> Forty residents of Ili Kazakh Province [sic] went to the local Party committee for permission to leave for the USSR. But there the [authorities] did not even want to listen to them. And when more than 2,000 persons gathered before the Party Committee building, bursts of machine-gun fire from the windows lashed the crowd. From the military district headquarters, which was across the street, they also opened fire, shooting people in the back. Ordinary people - shepherds, farmers - cursing the maniacs mad with thirst for power, fell, mowed down by a scythe of lead.

> The crowd scattered. Only several dozen bodies of men, women, old men and children remained lying before the windows of the Party Committee building as testimony to the bankruptcy of the nationalities policy pursued by the Chinese leaders, as a reproach to their unclean conscience.

And after this, they call themselves Communists! After all, one of the chief perpetrators of the crime, Chang Shu-chi, Secretary of the Ili-Kazakh Party Committee, was not even censured; he is at liberty and occupies a high post. Who knows, perhaps he will again arrange a "bloody Sunday" somewhere in the outlying nationality districts. (40)

However different their emphases, these official Chinese and Soviet accounts agree on the essence of the story. In May 1962, a demonstration of some size apparently took place in front of CCP headquarters in the Ili Kazakh Autonomous Chou, during which the demonstrators were fired upon and several dozen Uighurs and Kazakhs were killed. The background of this massacre may probably be found in discontent caused by the culturally repressive social policies introduced during the Great Leap Forward, the critical economic situation that followed the Great Leap, and a belief among the Sinkiang minority groups that Han residents received preferential treatment in the allocation of food and other rationed commodities.

We know also that by 1962 on the southeast coast of China authorities were allowing those citizens who wished to leave for Hong Kong to do so, presumably thus reducing the task of enforcing social order and easing pressure on China's scarce food resources. For a time, the authorities in Sinkiang seem to have followed a similar policy, allowing Uighurs and Kazakhs to leave for the Soviet Union. Subsequently, however, they began to worry about the large size of the migrant population, about the fact that the emigrants were taking their herds with them, and about the uses to which the now openly hostile Soviet Union could put the refugees. Chinese officials also discovered that Soviet consular authorities had been issuing thousands of false Soviet passports to those who wished them. For such reasons it appears that they ordered the exodus halted, to the annoyance of many would-be emigrants, and the demonstration and massacre resulted. (41)

News of the massacre spread quickly, resulting in rioting and disorder in other parts of Sinkiang. The Chinese suspected the Soviet Union of having fomented the incident (which indeed closely resembled the incidents preceding the formation of the ETR two decades before), while the Russian press used it to "prove" the repressive, racist nature of Chinese policy toward its non-Han peoples. An ongoing public confrontation between China and the Soviet Union resulted, which has had important repercussions for the political, economic, and cultural lives of the minority peoples of both sides of the border.

Both sides complain of border incursions by planes, troops, and, ostensibly, private citizens. (42) Only once has fighting on any significant scale been reported from the Sinkiang/Kazakhstan area. In August 1969 there were clashes involving several hundred Chinese and Soviet troops, with causualties on both sides. The Chinese accused the Soviet Union of sending helicopters, tanks, armored vehicles, and several hundred troops two kilometers into the Chinese side of the

border, where they were repelled. The Chinese Foreign Ministry's note
charged that larger numbers of troops and vehicles were being
assembled to provoke even larger conflicts in the future. (43)   The
Soviet Ministry of Foreign Affairs replied that the Chinese authorities
had been "deliberately exacerbating" the border situation for several
months and had purposely provoked both this and a previous clash in the
Ussuri River area. That the Chinese soldiers were equipped with movie
cameras was held indicative that the Chinese attacks were planned, (44)
and captured documents were released which purported to prove
Chinese guilt. (45)   More recently, however, an analyst of the United
States Central Intelligence Agency has taken the position that while the
Chinese did indeed provoke the Amur/Ussuri confrontation, the one in
Sinkiang was perpetrated by the Soviet side. (46)

A smaller-scale confrontation on the Sinkiang border occurred in
March 1974 when a Soviet helicopter landed inside Chinese territory at
Altai and was seized by the Chinese.   The Soviet Foreign Ministry
protested that the vehicle had been sent to pick up a seriously ill
serviceman who was in urgent need of hospitalization but that it had
lost its bearings and made a forced landing, in what proved to be China,
when its fuel supply ran out. (47)   The Chinese Foreign Ministry's reply
formally accused the USSR of "cook [ing] up a bunch of lies to cover
the crime," noting that the helicopter carried neither medical personnel
nor medical equipment, but did possess arms, ammunition, and recon-
naissance equipment. Documents on board had indicated that the crew
was on a "special mission"; moreover, this intrusion was not an isolated
incident. (48) Mass rallies were held throughout Sinkiang in which the
participants accused the Soviet Union of carrying out provocations,
planning a large-scale invasion, and wishing to add to the 560,000 square
kilometers they had already "stolen" from Sinkiang (49) (a reference to
the treaty of 1881).   Despite the Soviet Union's threat of "serious
consequences" if the helicopter and crew were not returned, the
confrontation gradually subsided. More than two and a half years later
the helicopter and its crew were returned with a statement explaining
that "investigation has established the veracity of the Soviet crew's
contention that they crossed into Chinese territory unintention-
ally." (50)   In both Soviet and Chinese accounts of the 1969 and 1974
incidents indigenous ethnic names among the personnel mentioned are
conspicuously lacking, leading one to conclude that each side considers
border defense in the area too important to be left to the natives. The
Chinese side did belatedly note that "people of all nationalities" had
helped in apprehending the Soviet helicopter and paraded one of them,
variously referred to as Chiyatapieke and Muyatapiehko, at National
Day rallies in Peking several months later where he declared that "the
militia and people of various nationalities ... are not to be bullied." (51)

Most Sino-Soviet confrontations on the Sinkiang border were not as
spectacular, though carrying no less potential for rapid escalation.   A
more typical situation was described by one Soviet army man in 1968:

A fisherman comes, sticks a pole with Mao's portrait on it in the snow and begins to dig a hole. We explain that it is forbidden to cross the border. We escort him back. The next day 20 fishermen come. Three have nets and each one has a booklet of quotations. They wave them around so that fishing will be better. We escort them back to the border. About 500 people are brought to the border. There are women and children among them. They organize a rally and beat drums. They are loaded on trucks and head for the Soviet shore. Our fellows stand in a chain. The trucks race at them, intending to frighten them. Nothing happens, and they go away. [Then] they come with streamers: quotations are attached to stocks and there are iron pipes on top of the sticks. Again our men form a wall. Their people put the quotations in their pockets and start swinging the sticks. Never mind, we drove them away. (52)

It is highly likely that mutual accusations of infiltration, subversion, and sabotage activities contain substantial elements of truth.

Although the physical presence of the minority peoples is scarcely noticeable in these post-1962 confrontations, propaganda channels for both parties to the dispute have sought to fill in the gaps with lengthy discussions of the feelings of Kazakhs and Uighurs on each side of the border. The 1962 incident touched off a major media "war," with both China and the Soviet Union increasing their minority language broadcasting to areas where transborder reception is possible. The Soviets were immeasurably aided in this by the appearance in the Soviet Union of leading Kazakhs and Uighurs who had been imprisoned or purged by the Chinese government, many of them during the antirightist campaign. Just how they made their escape has never been made clear, but it is plain that they are of great value to the Soviet Union as propagandists.

Uighur, Kazakh, and Kirgiz programs beamed from Tashkent, Alma Ata, and Frunze were instituted in 1964 and expanded in 1967. Special correspondents from TASS, Kazakhstanskaia Pravda, and others joined the refugee newscasters, who could truthfully claim to have seen both sides of the border. Much of the content of the programs seems to present a factually accurate description of the situation in Sinkiang, presumably in order to establish the credibility of the broadcasts. Other themes, however, include the material advantages of life for Kazakhs, Uighurs, and others in the USSR; the higher level of labor-saving technology available; and the greater cultural freedom and diversity allowed there. The broadcasts frequently hark back to the Ili revolt of 1944, the founding of the ETR, the historical independence of the Turkic Muslim peoples, and their praiseworthy struggle to maintain this independence, the 1962 incident, and other items with similarly subversive content. Sympathy is expressed for those who are being persecuted by the Chinese authorities for having relatives in the Soviet Union or who are suspected of proautonomy or pro-Soviet feelings. (53)

A few examples may serve to transmit the flavor of these broadcasts. Zunin Taipov, the former head of the ETR army, reported from his new home in Kazakhstan:

> ... [H]ow many bitter stories have I heard from my fellow countryman about those who have remained behind the cordon, who have not yet succeeded in returning home! ... [H] ow bitter it is to realize that thousands of my brothers, Uighurs and Kazakhs, Kirgiz and Mongols, have remained there, beyond the barricade, and are being subjected today to incredible persecution and repression.... Peking does not hide its intention of "sinifying" Sinkiang. (54)

A correspondent for Kazakhstanskaia Pravda added:

> It seems almost unbelievable that one is standing on the farthest limit of the motherland. The windows of the neat houses on the collective-farm village face through the poplars onto the empty village road, the wire fences and a narrow control strip. Just below it is the grassy bank of a small ordinary river ... and yellow mountains rising like a wall. On their table-flat tops one sees bright patches of crops that have not been harvested.
>
> "They'll be there 'til the snow flies," the collective farm chairman said to me, pointing across to the other side. "Even if they are tiny plots, no one can do much by hand, with sickles and rollers. And especially this year."
>
> "Why?"
>
> "The Chinese authorities ordered all the Kazakhs and Uighurs out of our part of the border area into the interior of the country. Do you see that over there?"
>
> Yes, I did see the adobe ruins of some resettlement just to the right, at the foot of the mountains.
>
> Why, I wondered, did they have to chase from their native haunts hundreds of peaceful people - farmers and herdsmen - and destroy their houses?
>
> "Why?" the chairman asked in astonishment. "They were afraid. They were beside themselves to show how badly the Kazakhs and the Uighurs were living here in the Soviet Union. And every day, from morning to night a showcase of life was visible over here. They could look and compare."
>
> The borderland collective farm we were talking about is a middling one in the production administration, but it long ago finished grain mowing and it was now harvesting a rich corn crop. It was typical that all the field work here was mechanized. The output per corn-harvesting combine had reached record levels.
>
> Naturally, our neighbors saw all this. They saw it and, of course,

they made comparisons.   Frankly, the comparisons were not flattering to the Chinese authorities.   Just last year dozens of families - representatives of the so-called "national minorities" - fled across the border here into the Soviet Union.   These people were wasted with hunger and were dressed and shod in all sorts of unthinkable rags and foot bindings.   The Chinese border guards fired at them, but they kept on coming.   Many of them are now working on the collective farm.   From now on they will work not from fear but from conscience.   They were given outright grants and helped to build houses.

I talked to some of these people.   Among them were those with relatives and friends on the other side.   For this reason alone I shall not give their names in this account.   It is known that the Chinese authorities, extending their anti-Soviet campaign further and further, have, in their mad fury, undertaken to persecute the Kazakhs and Uighurs living in the Chinese People's Republic.

Obviously they put their prison camp on the border also for purposes of visual propaganda.   From the pastures of the collective farm one could see with the naked eye little chained figures moving huge stones to clear a road into the mountains.

"My brother might be there," said an old shepherd peering out with eyes as sharp as an eagle's.   For more than six months he had had no news from the other side.   He had spent almost all his life in Western China....   Was he in one of the people's communes?   Yet, but just as before, he saw nothing but the tattered yurt and the herds of sheep.   He had to tend a flock of 600 by himself.   It was no easier for the peasants in the "commune."   Just try living for a long time in a barracks where life is measured by the ringing of a gong, and where you march in ranks from field to field!

I looked at the shepherd in his fine fox-fur cloak and his sheepskin hat (it is now wintry cold high in the mountains) and I found myself thinking: "How many years did this man waste in vain?..." (55)

The passages quoted above, like many other Soviet propaganda releases, clearly imply that the minorities' sympathetic kin, backed by the Soviet government, are ready to welcome their Chinese relatives to the Soviet Union.   A Western journalist who visited Alma Ata in 1976 noted the publication there of a thrice-weekly paper called Yeni Khaiat [New Life] for the refugees.   Interestingly, it employs Arabic script since, its editor explained, Soviet authorities discovered that the refugees had difficulty adjusting to the Cyrillic-based script used by other Turkic-Muslim language newspapers published in the USSR.   It should be noted that the Soviet authorities probably had other reasons for not using the Latin-based alphabet that the Chinese introduced in 1960 after the break with the USSR.

Yeni Khaiat's editor claimed that over 100,000 persons had crossed the border (Chinese sources say 60,000) and that they had been provided with food, clothing, and medical attention and eventually settled on collective farms; most have apparently continued as sheep herders. (56) To enhance the contrast between its picture of the cultural genocide of minorities in China and their happy life in the USSR, the Soviet Union has also allocated funds to refurbish Islamic monuments, including Tamerlane's tomb, (57) and has also published multivolume compendia on Uighur, Kazakh, and other nationality heritages. This effort to contrast the USSR's appreciation of its indigenous Muslim cultures with Chinese denigration thereof was no doubt reinforced by the Soviet desire for friendly relations with Muslim countries of the Middle East.

The Chinese Communists have countered by accusing the USSR of being a "big prison for nationalities," (58) of forcing the nationalities to learn Russian - this last juxtaposed with a quotation from Lenin on linguistic diversity (59) - and of exploiting its nationality republics. Chinese analysts were delighted to note that while a 1974 edition of the book Problems of the CPSU Economic Policy and Reclamation of Virgin Lands in Kazakhstan quoted Party leader Leonid Brezhnev as saying "We must spare no expenditure to carry out material encouragement, for such expenditure will bring returns a hundredfold," a 1976 reprint had deleted these words, thus showing the deliberately "exploitative nature of the Brezhnev government." (60)

Just how seriously each party takes the propaganda efforts of the other is unclear, though neither has exerted much effort to jam its antagonist's broadcasts. In 1964 Saifudin publicly accused the USSR of using radio transmissions to "spread lies and slander attacking the leadership of the CCP and to distort the history of Sinkiang in an effort to undermine the unity of the Chinese people of all nationalities," and thus seemed concerned enough to issue the statement. (61)

In 1967 Ivan Spivanhov, Deputy Chief Editor of Kazakhstanskaia Pravda, was quoted as saying that Chinese broadcasts "beam in hot and strong" but that "few people take any notice. It is so rude and clumsy." (62) The efforts made to answer Chinese charges, however, may indicate a somewhat less nonchalant attitude. China's claim to much of Soviet Central Asia on the grounds that "many hundreds of years ago, Chinese troops came to these parts and the Chinese emperor once used to collect tribute from the local inhabitants" was termed

childish.... [O] ne could say that England was French territory because it was once the domain of a Duke of Normandy, or that France is an English possession since during the Hundred Years' War it was almost completely conquered by England ... or that the boundary of the CPR passes only along the line of the Great Wall, less than 100 kilometers from Peking: the boundary of China did once pass there, the wall being evidence of this. (63)

The Soviet Union also reacted sharply to evidence of collaboration between the CPR and Ukrainian separatists, (64) and answered Chinese charges that Kazakhstan was being exploited:

> ... [T]he republics are no longer divided into agrarian and industrial or raw-material and processing republics.... The Party has consistently carried out Lenin's behest in the economic and cultural fields and in all spheres of social life; without this it would have been impossible to strengthen the mutual trust of the working people of all nationalities, to put an end to their alienation and to bring about unprecedented cohesion among the peoples of the USSR....
> [T]his special feature of our Party's nationalities policy is reflected, in particular, in the Law on the USSR State Budget for 1972.... ·`[A]lmost all the money from all-Union turnover tax receipts from the territory of [five] republics will be deducted into these republics' state budgets, while the Kazakh Republic's budget will receive 100 percent of these funds. In addition, Kazakhstan will receive a large subsidy from the Union budget - more than 456,000,000 rubles. (65)

Izvestiia also announced plans to publish a ten-volume dictionary of the Kazakh language (66) and a multivolume Kazakh Soviet encyclopedia. (67) There was renewed evidence in civil defense in Kazakhstan, (68) and Brezhnev personally made highly touted visits to the republic in 1970 and 1972. (69)

Chinese media have attempted to refute Soviet charges of cultural repression with lengthy articles discussing the exact numbers of pamphlets, books, and texts printed in Uighur, Kazakh, Mongolian, Kirgiz, and Sibo, "publication of which has had considerable use in developing the languages and literatures of the various nationalities, enriching their culture and accelerating the progress of the socialist revolution and reconstruction in Sinkiang." (70) A post-Cultural Revolution attempt to renew pressure on these minorities to use the Latin alphabet was carried out at the same time that many of China's non-Sinkiang minority groups were being urged to study Han (71); apparently it was considered sufficient to separate Chinese Uighurs and Kazakhs from their Soviet counterparts on the basis of script.

The death of Mao's heir-apparent, Lin Piao, coincided with a further liberalizing of attitudes toward minorities. Uighurs and Kazakhs were reportedly adapting the new revolutionary operas introduced under the aegis of Mao's wife to their own languages and art forms, and were receiving more consumer goods manufactured to the specifications of their customs and traditions. (72) A protege of Lin Piao, who had become First Party Secretary of the Sinkiang Uighur Autonomous Region after the Cultural Revolution, was removed from office and replaced by Saifudin, thus placing a minority group member in charge of the SUAR for the first time since 1949. Other Uighurs and Kazakhs were given prestigious, although not necessarily influential, positions in government and party, and a campaign began to recruit more of them into leadership positions at lower levels of society. (73)

Chinese propaganda tended to treat the 1962 incident as if it were instigated by the Soviet Union and as constituting one more sad proof that the USSR was following in the footsteps of its tsarist predecessors. Russia's explanation of the nineteenth century territorial cessions was flatly rejected: the lands obtained thereunder should have been returned, presumably with their inhabitants as well.   A news report, supposedly emanating from NCNA which circulated in the capitals of several African states implied that the peoples of Soviet Central Asia desired to "enter into a close union with China." (74)

Thus, while the Soviet side has been less overtly fearful of the effect of Chinese propaganda than the Chinese have seemed of Soviet propaganda, both parties have attempted to answer each other's charges and have accompanied these refutations by actions significantly liberalizing policies toward minorities.

Nonetheless, neither side remains certain of the loyalties of its minorities.   Within a few years of one another, two books were published in the Soviet Union to disprove "falsifiers of history who claimed that Soviet rule was established artificially and against the wishes of the populations of Central Asia and Kazakhstan." (75)   At approximately the same time, a Soviet journal commented that although

> ... there is no socio-economic basis in the USSR for nationalistic ideology .... survivals of nationalism and chauvinism still persist in the minds of some people. They are viable and are often combined with religious survivals and, "what is particularly dangerous, are capable of reviving relatively rapidly under certain conditions." Difficulties in inter-national relations are encountered where there were violations of the national policy under the Stalin personality cult.... [N]ationalistically minded and religious elements are speculating on the mistakes of the past and trying to kindle nationalist dissension and spread national mistrust. (76)

A few years later, several Kirgiz scholars were severely criticized for various "errors," including the assertion that even if a nationality's demands for separation and political self-determination conflict with the interests of the nation, no one has a right to intervene forcibly in the nation's internal life and to "correct" its errors. Another view that was officially declared mistaken was historians' treatment of attempts (in the 1920s) to establish a separate Mountain Province in the Turkistan Autonomous Republic as the desire of the Kirgiz people to set up an independent state:

> Everyone knows that this proposal was advanced by bourgeois nationalists, in opposition to the fundamental interests of the Kirghiz people. The proposal was rejected by the Bolshevik Party and its proponents were removed from their posts and expelled from the Party. (77)

In China the media react with almost frenetic joy at each new archaeological find in Sinkiang that links that province with China proper. A rally is held with banners and headlines proclaiming, for example, that "T'ang [Dynasty] Relics Prove Sinkiang Historically Part of China." Rally leaders dutifully reiterate the most recent twist in the Party line, and explain that these latest discoveries will give the lie to "nationalistically-minded internal splitters" and to the "Soviet revisionist new tsars" who wish to separate Sinkiang from the ancestral land. (78)

The group accompanying James Schlesinger to China recently has testified to their Chinese hosts' extreme nervousness while guiding the American guests through Sinkiang. In a newspaper account admittedly modified for diplomatic reasons, one visitor writes

A Caucasian (i.e., non-Han Chinese) waiter in Sinkiang ... reacts stiffly to a Chinese "hsieh-hsieh" and warmly to an English "thank you." ... Or take the crowds in Ining, less than 50 miles from the Soviet border. As our caravan goes from stop to stop, the crowds on the streets grow, until at last the local citizens virtually climb into the cars. The crowds are nearly all Kazakh and Uighur, though the town is supposed to be half Chinese. They break into almost joyous applause at every wave. Our hosts from Peking grow testier than at any other point in the trip. A few nights later they are relaxed in their reaction to a large crowd in Huhehot. In the second crowd, the faces were yellow and the mood merely curious. In the first, the mood stirred by American faces was implicitly anti-Chinese. (79)

A West German magazine has published the story of two recent refugees from China to the Soviet Union, one a Kazakh and the other a Kirgiz. On apprehension, both had been placed in a Soviet prison where a fellow prisoner, an ethnic Russian hostile to the Soviet government and familiar with the cruelties of the Gulag Archipelago, was amazed to learn that they were happy with their new lot. He quoted one as saying, "I have a bunk, a light bulb in the cell, we get food every day, even fish. What else do I need?" (80) Members of the Schlesinger party mentioned earlier have confided that their Chinese hosts seemed surprised by the relatively low standards of living in Sinkiang, speculating that the Chinese guides were shocked by the discrepancy between reality and what their own propaganda had led them to believe. (81)

CONCLUSIONS

It has been shown that the principal factors in the internationalization of the Turkic Muslim question were the hostilities between the two host countries and the deteriorating economic conditions in China during the late 1950s and early 1960s. The many references in Chinese media to local nationalism over the entire decade of the 1950s make it clear that

Kazakh and Uighur dissatisfaction with Chinese Communist rule existed prior to the catalyzing incident of May 1962, but that due to the appearance of Sino-Soviet friendship, the public manifestation of these dissatisfactions was muted.

The exact nature of Kazakh and Uighur demands on the Chinese government has never been made clear. There are references to separatism, implying an independent Sinkiang; to joining together with other Turkic Muslims (some of whom would undoubtedly come from Soviet Kazakhstan) in a larger separate state; to demands for the greater autonomy of Sinkiang within the Chinese state, some of them including demands for the Han Chinese to leave Sinkiang and others simply asking that they relinquish their commanding positions in the province's economic and administrative infrastructure.

Whether or not Soviet intrigues were behind the May 1962 incident, as the Chinese side charges, the Soviet side hastened to make use of Kazakh and Uighur dissatisfaction thereafter. Championing the cause of China's Turkic Muslim peoples, it sought to contrast the economic hardship and cultural repression on the Chinese side of the border with the much better situation on the Soviet side. The Soviet Kazakhs and other Central Asian minorities seem to have profited as a result, being granted various cultural and material benefits in an effort to provide suitable anti-Chinese propaganda. Because the Chinese leaders have perceived it as necessary to refute Soviet charges, Chinese Kazakhs and Uighurs have benefited as well. Compilations have been made of folksongs, and resources have been transferred to Sinkiang via a preferential revenue redistribution plan that has returned more money to the province than is collected there. This has allowed the construction of mining and other industries and aided in raising living standards. There has been an increase in the number of Uighurs and Kazakhs in leadership positions in the SUAR.

While Chinese and Soviet Kazakhs and Uighurs have gained leverage over their respective governments as a result of the Sino-Soviet situation, there are limits to how far either government can be manipulated. Past experience has shown that overzealous catering to minority cultures simply reinforces the continued perception of ethnic separatism and prevents the drawing together of peoples that each of the two countries desires. Moreover, the granting of more autonomy may lead to subsequent demands for separatism. In addition, the more liberal policies of China and the USSR are probably looked upon with justifiable skepticism by minorities on both sides of the border. In some instances the liberality of a pronouncement may be tempered by other words spoken in a different context. In other instances, the policies are known to be subject to rapid reversal. For example, Leonid Brezhnev, on presenting the Order of Friendship of Peoples to Kazakhstan, says: "In speaking about the new historic community of peoples, we certainly do not mean that national differences are already disappearing in our country or, all the more, that a merging of nations has taken place. All nations and nationalities populating the Soviet Union retain their

features, national character traits, language and their best traditions." (82)   But one must understand this in the context of other
statements, such as: "The peoples of the Caucasus had a custom in
ancient times: The warriors mixed drops of their blood in a common
bowl and were bound together forever by ties of brotherhood, honor and
glory.   The Union of Soviet Socialist Republics became this blood
brotherhood for us, a brotherhood of peoples.   Since then, this
brotherhood has become our sun. Cherish the sun, people!" (83) Chinese
minorities have become familiar with "soft line" policies toward the
retention of their customs and languages changing virtually overnight
with the launching of new mass campaigns or shifts in leadership, as
occurred during the Great Leap Forward and the Cultural Revolution. (84)

Given the higher degree of ideological orthodoxy demanded and
lower living standards prevailing on the Chinese side, the Soviet Union
would probably enjoy an advantage in any contest between the two
states for the loyalties of the Central Asian peoples. Still, for reasons
discussed earlier, the Soviet Union cannot be fully certain of the
loyalties of its own minorities. There is evidence that certain Soviet
minorities might actually welcome the Chinese. A Soviet dissident
reports that "In our Central Asian cities I and many others have often
heard the cry: 'Just wait till the Chinese come, they'll show you what's
what!' This is said as a rule by moderately educated people who cannot
be unaware of what the arrival of the Chinese would entail for
them...." (85) Moreover, recent Chinese efforts to raise living standards
in Sinkiang, to co-opt more Uighurs and Kazakhs into the province's
elite, and to relax some of the more culturally repressive aspects of the
past make it unlikely that the Soviet Union will decide to employ the
incitement of China's Kazakhs and Uighurs in any large-scale way.
Anti-Chinese propaganda and infiltration directed toward Sinkiang will
probably continue on a small scale, in an attempt to impress the
Chinese side with the potentially damaging effects of a larger-scale
effort. The probability that the Soviet Union does not intend to support
Chinese Kazakh separatism or autonomy in any meaningful way, when
added to the ever-larger Han Chinese presence in Sinkiang (and Russian
presence in Kazakhstan), makes it highly unlikely that those Turkic
Muslims in Central Asia who desire a separate state will ever see their
wish fulfilled. The most feasible scenario for the creation of such a
state would entail a major destabilization of the present equilibrium on
the border, such as a Sino-Soviet war. This possibility has already
occurred to at least one Soviet citizen; the dissident Russian intellectual Andrei Amalrik has written.

Simultaneously   [with the Russian middle class becoming increasingly anti-Soviet government and extremist organizations
playing a greater role] the nationalist tendencies of the non-
Russian peoples of the USSR will intensify sharply, first in the Baltic
area and along the Volga.

In many cases, party officials among the various nationalities may become proponents of such tendencies and their reasoning will be "Let Russian Ivan solve his own problems." They will aim for national separatism for still another reason: if they can fend off the growing general chaos, they will be able to preserve their own privileged positions. (86)

Amalrik's vision is apocalyptic and does not discuss the probable outcome of a collapse. Recently even he has revised his timetable and does not envision the dismemberment of the Soviet Union by his original target date of 1984. (87) Moreover, his hostility toward the Soviet Union may lead him to overstate its weaknesses. Given the unlikely eventuality of a Sino-Soviet war and the resurfacing of autonomy demands, there is a high probability that the Soviet Union would win and might, as part of the settlement, detach Sinkiang from China and establish it as an autonomous state, even though it would be highly dependent on the Soviet Union for its continued existence. At first glance, given the Soviet Union's mixed record of relations with its own Central Asian minorities, the effort might not seem worth the potential gains. On the other hand, the example of the Mongolian People's Republic may indicate that the venture is indeed worthwhile. The MPR is, and Sinkiang could be, a buffer state between the Soviet Union and China. The MPR is rich in minerals and has been usefully integrated into the Soviet economy; Sinkiang could be also. Moreover, though Mongolians would probably under other circumstances wish a higher degree of international maneuverability, their actions indicate that they strongly prefer an independence circumscribed by the Soviet Union to the risk of inclusion within the Chinese state. Thus there are very real prospects for gain for the Soviet Union in such a situation.

Chinese foreign policymakers have shown themselves to be highly skilled and fully cognizant of the realities of, and limitations on, Chinese power. The existence of the MPR is a constant reminder of what may happen in Sinkiang. It is therefore probable that the Chinese side will do its utmost to prevent an escalation of Sino-Soviet violence. The influx of Han to Sinkiang, and specifically to the border areas including Ili, (88) will probably continue insofar as the local economy can absorb the immigrants. Sinkiang's minorities will be treated carefully to diffuse resentments through the granting of some privileges while not courting the minorities to such a degree that further demands for separatism will be encouraged.

Of course Sino-Soviet armed struggle is but one of several possible scenarios that might rekindle hopes for separatism in Sinkiang and/or Kazakhstan. It is conceivable, for example, that such a minority group uprising might occur independently of any impetus from Peking or Moscow. Here the social mobilization phenomenon may be of crucial importance. In destroying the traditionally loose knit kinship groups of the Central Asian peoples, in giving them a common written language, making them literate, and drawing them into factories and mass organizations, the Chinese and Soviet governments may inadvertently be creating the preconditions for large-scale well-organized resistance to their respective rulers, rather than the small-scale and loosely organized hostilities they have successfully coped with so far.

It is difficult to tell how much genuine feeling Kazakhs and Uighurs have for their kinfolk across the Sino-Soviet borders, but the constant reminder by both sides (particularly by the Soviet Union) that they are indeed one people would surely reinforce such common feelings that do exist, and may even create them where they do not. This may spark desires for irredentism that operate independently of official Chinese or Soviet wishes.

At present, however, these possibilities remain remote and the outlook seems to portend a continuation of low-level resistance that may occasionally be exacerbated by local economic shortages or a misguided or misinterpreted order from Peking or Moscow. There seems little probability of either an escalation or a solution to the Turkic Muslim question.

NOTES

(1) Peking Review (cited henceforth as PR) 19, no. 22 (May 28, 1976): 28. Other Chinese population figures are, unless otherwise specified, drawn from John S. Aird, Population Estimates for the Provinces of the People's Republic of China: 1953 to 1974, International Population Reports, Series P-95, No. 73, United States Department of Commerce, 1974. Soviet population data are, unless otherwise specified, drawn from the 1970 census as reported in the Current Digest of the Soviet Press (cited henceforth as CDSP) 23, no. 16 (1971): 14-18.

(2) Lawrence Krader, Peoples of Central Asia (Bloomington, Ind., 1963), p. 193. See also Alfred E. Hudson, "Kazakh Social Structure," Yale University Publications in Anthropology, no. 20 (1938; reprint ed., New York, 1964).

(3) The Han dynasty, commonly divided into Former or Western Han (206 B.C.-23 A.D.) and later Eastern Han (25-220 A.D.) is regarded as one of China's most glorious, and gave its name to the majority (94 percent of the present-day population) ethnic group of the country.

(4) W.A. Douglas Jackson, The Russo-Chinese Borderlands (Princeton, 1962), pp. 112-113, 116.

(5) George J. Demko, The Russian Colonization of Kazakhstan, 1896-1916 (Bloomington, Indiana, 1969), pp. 121-122.

(6) Yuan Tsing, "Yakub Bey and the Moslem Rebellion in Chinese Turkestan," Central Asiatic Journal 6, no. 2 (1961): 154.

(7) Immanuel C.Y. Hsu, The Ili Crisis: A Study of Sino-Russian Diplomacy 1871-1881 (Oxford, 1965), pp. 186-187.

(8) Demko, op. cit., p. 182.

(9) Elizabeth E. Bacon, Central Asians Under Russian Rule (Ithaca, 1966), pp. 116-117. See also Richard Pipes, The Formation of the Soviet Union (Cambridge, Mass., 1964), p. 83.

(10) Pipes, op. cit., pp. 108, 172-173.

(11) Bacon, op. cit., p. 117.

(12) Pipes, op. cit., p. 174.

(13) Bacon, op. cit., p. 114.

(14) Ibid., p. 118.

(15) Pipes, op. cit., p. 191.

(16) Ann Sheehy, "The Central Asian Republics," Conflict Studies no. 30 (December 1972): 13-27.

(17) Bacon, op. cit., pp. 119-120.

(18) Brian Silver, "Social Mobilization and the Russification of Soviet Nationalities," American Political Science Review 68, no. 1 (1974): 63.

(19) CDSP, op. cit., p. 16.

(20) Silver, op. cit., p. 62.

(21) David C. Montgomery, "An American Student in Tashkent," Asian Affairs (February 1972), p. 37.

(22) Rein Taagepera, "National Differences Within Soviet Demographic Trends," Soviet Studies 20, no. 4 (1969): 478, 481, 489.

(23) Andrei Sakharov, Sakharov Speaks (New York, 1974), p. 43.

(24) Allen S. Whiting and Sheng Shih-ts'ai, Sinkiang: Pawn or Pivot? (East Lansing, Michigan, 1958), p. 54.

(25) Excellent accounts of this period may be found in Whiting and Sheng, op. cit., and also in Owen Lattimore, Pivot of Asia (Boston, 1950).

(26) New York Times (cited henceforth as NYT), February 1, 1959, p. 1; February 2, 1959, p. 18; February 6, 1959, sec. 4, p. 1; March 22, 1959, p. 22.

(27) Whiting and Sheng, op. cit., pp. 142-143.

(28) Ibid., p. 86.

(29) Work teams were charged with unifying and mobilizing the masses, helping in the formation of peasants and herders' associations,

preparing for the establishment of local representative organs, and similar organizational "spade-work." In addition, they engaged in propaganda and indoctrination work, the recruitment and training of cadres, and the "guidance" of local-level mass campaigns.

(30) K.F. Kotov, Autonomy of Local Nationalities in the Chinese People's Republic (Moscow, 1956); trans. in United States Department of Commerce, Joint Publications Research Service (cited henceforth as JPRS), no. 3547, p. 56.

(31) New China News Agency (cited henceforth as NCNA), Lanchow, May 6, 1954, quoted in Whiting and Sheng, op. cit., p. 144.

(32) See, e.g., Kotov's report cited in note 30 above; and S.I. Bruk, "Ethnic Composition and and Distribution of the Population in the Sinkiang-Uighur Autonomous Region of the People's Republic of China," Sovetskaia Etnografiia no. 2 (1956), trans. in JPRS, no. 16,030.

(33) Whiting and Sheng, op. cit., p. 168.

(34) There is no evidence that the decision to use Cyrillic was actually implemented on a significant scale, though the break with the USSR and China's development of its own Latin-based pin-yin system as a standard orthography for all the linguistic groups occurred too soon after the decision to use Cyrillic to draw any meaningful conclusions from this.

(35) Bruk, op. cit., p. 16.

(36) Saifudin, speech to the Party Committee of the SUAR, December 16, 1957, Peking Radio, December 25, 1957.

(37) Li Hui-yu, "The Ili Autonomous Chou Has Very Extensive Powers; Why Do the Local Nationalists Say It Has No Powers?" Ili jih-pao, August 30, 1958, quoted in George Moseley, A Sino-Soviet Cultural Frontier: The Ili Kazakh Autonomous Chou (Cambridge, Mass., 1966), p. 68.

(38) Ibid., pp. 107-110.

(39) Chou En-lai, "Report on the Work of the Government," speech to the First Session of the Third National People's Congress, December 30, 1964, trans. in United States Consulate General, Hong Kong, Survey of the China Mainland Press (cited henceforth as SCMP), no. 3370, p. 12.

(40) Zunin Taipov, "Eyewitness Account: On the Other Side of the Barricade," Kazakhstanskaia Pravda September 29, 1963, p. 4; CDSP 15, no. 38 (1963): 16; see also A. Mirov, "Sinkiang Tragedy," Literaturnaia Gazeta, May 7, 1969; CDSP 21, no. 19 (1969): 5-6.

(41) "China Said to Send Troops to Sinkiang," NYT, April 16, 1964, p. 6, quoting a Belorussian refugee interviewed in Hong Kong; Moseley, Sino-Soviet Cultural Frontier, p. 108.

(42) See, e.g., "The Chinese Ministry of Foreign Affairs" protest to the Soviet Union (NCNA, September 17, 1968), and the Soviet Union's reply "Provocative Fabrication of the CPR Ministry of Foreign Affairs," Izvestiia, November 2, 1968; CDSP 20, no. 43 (1968): 42.

(43) PR 12, no. 33 (1969): 3.

(44) S. Borzenko et al., "On Stony Hill," Pravda, August 16, 1969, p. 6; CDSP 21, no. 33 (1969): 4.

(45) Published in both Pravda and Izvestiia, September 11, 1969; CDSP 21, no. 37 (1969): 8-9.

(46) Roger Glenn Brown, "Chinese Politics and American Foreign Policy," Foreign Policy no. 23 (Summer 1976): 3-23.

(47) Text of note in Pravda, March 21, 1974, p. 9; CDSP 26, no. 12 (1974): 4.

(48) NCNA (Peking), March 23, 1974; SCMP no. 3585, p. 66.

(49) See, e.g., Urumchi Radio (Sinkiang), March 28, 1974, in United States Foreign Broadcast Information Service, China (hereafter cited as FBIS-CHI), no. 62 (1974): A1-A3.

(50) TASS, December 27, 1976; CDSP 28, no. 52 (1976): 14.

(51) Peking Radio, October 1, 1974; FBIS-CHI no. 192 (October 17, 1974): D6; FBIS-CHI no. 201 (1974): A4.

(52) "That's How It Is On the Border," Pravda, March 12, 1969, p. 6; CDSP 21, no. 11 (1969): 3. This particular incident occurred on the Ussuri border, on the northeast China/southeast Soviet border. It has been included because, although the participants were fisherfolk, whereas on the Sinkiang/Kazakhstan border they are typically sheepherders, it represents a composite picture of elements reported in similar confrontations there.

(53) Gretchen S. Brainerd, "Soviets Intensify Propaganda to Moslem Nationalities in China," Radio Liberty Dispatch, February 14, 1972, pp. 1-4.

(54) Taipov, op. cit., CDSP 21, no. 19 (1969): 5.

(55) O. Matskevich, "Along the Border," Kazakhstanskaia Pravda, September 24, 1963; CDSP 15, no. 38 (1963): 17-18.

(56) Christopher S. Wren, "Kazakhstan Beckons Refugees From China," NYT, April 24, 1976, p. 8.

(57) Hedrick Smith, "Tamerlane Stirs Soviet Controversy," NYT, June 2, 1974, p. 2.

(58) "Soviet People's Struggle Against New Tsars," PR 19, no. 46 (November 12, 1976): 21-22.

(59) "Analysis of Soviet Revisionists' Policy of 'National Rapprochement," PR 17, no. 29 (July 19, 1974): 18-20.

(60) "Soviet Social Imperialism Pursues a Policy of National Oppression," PR 19, no. 22 (May 28, 1976): 19-23.

(61) NCNA (Urumchi), April 28, 1964.

(62) Brainerd, op. cit., p. 2.

(63) Pravda, September 2, 1964; CDSP 16, no. 34 (1964): 4-5.

(64) M. Panchuk, "The Chinese Splitters and the Ukrainian Nationalists," Rabochaia Gazeta, February 27, 1972; CDSP 24, no. 8 (1972): 13-14. For a representative sample of Chinese propaganda in favor of the Ukrainian nationalists, see NCNA (Peking), October 15, 1974; FBIS-CHI no. 201 (1974): A1

(65) E. Bagramov, "The Drawing Together of Nationalities is a Law of Communist Construction," Pravda, June 22, 1972; CDSP 24, no. 25 (1972): 10-11.

(66) Izvestiia, November 23, 1972, p. 5; CDSP 24, no. 47 (1972): 23.

(67) Izvestiia, May 12, 1972; CDSP 24, no. 19 (1972): 26. The effect of showing the Soviet Union's encouragement of nationality cultures may have been somewhat diluted by the newspaper's observation that the encyclopedia's first entry was that of Abas, "the great Kazakh poet and educator, whose ardent dream was to educate his people and bring them closer to Russian culture."

(68) V. Totov, "Our Common Duty," Pravda, August 14, 1972; CDSP 24, no. 33 (1972): 6-7.

(69) See CDSP 22, no. 35 (1970): 1-8 and CDSP 24, no. 35 (1972): 6-7 for accounts of Brezhnev's visits.

(70) Kuang-ming jih-pao [Bright Daily] , October 23, 1963; JPRS no. 22, 246, p. 91-95.

(71) Contrast Jen-min jih-pao [People's Daily] , August 22, 1971, with Urumchi Radio, December 10, 1970.

(72) Urumchi Radio, October 9, 1974.

(73) NCNA (Urumchi), May 17, 1972, SCMP no. 5143, p. 22-23.

(74) TASS, April 21, 1969; CDSP 21, no. 34 (1969): 19. TASS's evident anger at this, plus Russian fears of the potentially subversive effects of such statements, make it unlikely that the NCNA report was a Soviet fabrication.

(75) Khamid Inoiatov, Central Asia and Kazakhstan Before and After the October Revolution, trans. by D. Fidlon (Moscow, 1966); and I.I. Mints, The Triumph of Soviet Rule in Central Asia and Kazakhstan

(Tashkent, 1967), reviewed in Pravda, November 22, 1967, p. 3; CDSP 19, no. 47 (1967): 22.

(76) L.M. Drobizheva, "On the Social Homogeneity of the Republics and the Development of National Relations in the USSR," Istoriia SSSR no. 1 (1967); CDSP 19, no. 18 (1967): 28-29.

(77) D. Malabaev and M. Dzhanuzakov, "Protect and Strengthen Our Great Fraternity," Sovetskaia Kirgizia, December 7, 1972, p. 3; CDSP 25, no. 12 (1973): 17.

(78) Urumchi Radio, March 16, 1976; FBIS-CHI no. 54 (1975): E5.

(79) Robert L. Bartley, "In China, Trust What You Feel," Wall Street Journal, October 1, 1976, p. 10.

(80) A. Uchitel, "Escape to an Adjacent Cell," Possev, no. 2 (1976), quoted in Freedom at Issue, September-October, 1976, p. 10.

(81) Information available to the author.

(82) Quoted in E. Tadevosian, "A State Based on the Friendship of Peoples," Izvestiia, January 23, 1974, p. 3; CDSP 26, no. 4 (1974): 28.

(83) Leonid Gurunts, "Cherish the Sun, People," Pravda, May 3, 1968, p. 3; CDSP 20, no. 18 (1968): 23.

(84) See June Teufel Dreyer, China's Forty Millions (Cambridge, Mass., 1976), for a more general examination of the shifts in policies toward minorities under the CPR.

(85) Igor Shafarevich, "Separation or Reconciliation? The Nationalities Question in the USSR," in Alexander Solzhenitsyn et al., From Under the Rubble (Boston, 1974) p. 88.

(86) Andrei Amalrik, Will the Soviet Union Survive Until 1984? (New York, 1970), p. 63.

(87) Raymond H. Anderson, "Author Sees Soviet Lasting Beyond '84," NYT, December 12, 1976, p. 8.

(88) Outer Mongolia had a very small proportion of Han Chinese residents in 1911 when it severed its relationship with China. This is one aspect in which its position is quite different from that of Sinkiang now. The Chinese government has been reticent in giving an exact breakdown of the population of Sinkiang, but Soviet sources estimate that the Han proportion of Sinkiang has increased from 3 percent in 1949 to almost 45 percent in 1966. See T. Rakhimov, "The Great-Power Policy of Mao Tse-tung and His Group on the Nationalities Question," Kommunist no. 7 (May, 1967): 114-119; CDSP 19, no. 20 (1967): 3-4. Given the large-scale population transfers into Sinkiang since the Cultural Revolution, the 45 percent figure (which this author considers plausible) would be significantly higher now, perhaps by as much as 10 percent.

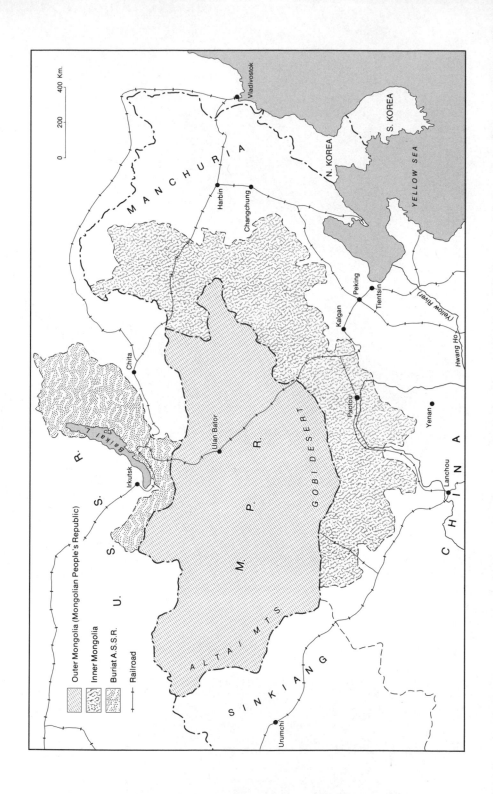

9 The Failure of a Self-Determination Movement: The Inner Mongolian Case

Sechin Jagchid

Mongolia, prior to the Manchu-Ch'ing Dynasty (1644-1911), was not considered even by the Chinese to be part of the Middle Kingdom. This land north of the Great Wall was viewed as a wasteland of the Northern Barbarians (Pei-man), and the Chinese people, far from recognizing the nomads as fellow countrymen, saw them as barbaric enemies. A mass of historical records demonstrates that the Chinese traditionally have favored a policy that severed all contact with these non-Chinese people. The following record, written by the great historian Pan Ku of the Han Dynasty (206 B.C. - 200 A.D.), exemplifies the mainstream of Chinese thought toward Mongolia until the end of the Ming Dynasty (1368-1644).

> As for clothing, costume, food and language, the barbarians are entirely different from the Middle Kingdom. . . . Mountains, valleys and the great desert separate them from us. This barrier which lies between the interior and the alien was made by heaven and earth. Therefore, the sage rulers considered them as beasts and neither established contact with them nor subjugated them. . . . The land is impossible to cultivate and the people are impossible to rule as subjects. Therefore, they are always to be considered as outsiders and never as citizens. Our administration and teaching have never reached their people. . . . Punish them when they intrude and guard against them when they retreat. Receive them when they offer tribute as a sign of admiration for our righteousness. Restrain them continually; make it appear that all the blame is on their side. This is the proper policy of the sage rulers toward the barbarians. (1)

Neither did the nomads to the north at any time recognize themselves as a people of the Chinese "Middle Kingdom." Mongolia and China were first brought under one sovereignty by the Mongol Emperor Kubilai Khan (r. 1260-1294) and then again more permanently by the Manchu rulers of the Ch'ing Dynasty (1644-1911). Neither Kubilai nor the Manchus were Chinese in a strict historical ethnic and cultural sense, and the Manchu rulers referred to the Mongols as wai-fan or fan-pu ("outside subordinates" or "subordinate tribes") to distinguish them from the nei-ti or Chinese proper.

North and west of Mongolia are vast open steppe lands which were once grazing fields and hunting grounds of the nomadic peoples of the Altaic ethnic family. (2) For centuries they served as a route for the expansion of nomadic power based in Mongolia into Central Asia and further west. They were also a refuge for the nomadic peoples during military assaults by their agricultural neighbors in China. Under the Mongolian Empire these steppe lands became the territories or ulus (states) of the Genghisids. Following the Empire's decline, however, the expansion of Muscovy brought many of these lands into Russian hands. By the latter part of the seventeenth century Mongolia was sandwiched politically between the Manchu Ch'ing Empire in China and Tsarist Russia to the west. Long the cradle of powerful inner-Asian nomadic empires and the base of their expansion, Mongolia now began to suffer from its landlocked position.

From the time of Genghis Khan (r. 1206-1227), Mongolian society had gradually abandoned clan-lineage institutions in favor of quasi-feudalistic organization. This organization was established on the basis of a feudal-lord (noyan) and underling (arad or khariyad) relationship. However, it differed from the agricultural feudalism in China that was based on a lord and land (fief) relationship. Originally, the entire nomadic feudalistic unit could migrate long distances to better grazing fields. After the Mongols came under the rule of the Manchus, these alien rulers shrewdly divided the original Mongolian units into much smaller fragments, naming them khushighun (or khushuun, banner). In order to diminish the striking power of a nomadic people, they reduced the mobility of the Mongols. They did this by designating part of a grazing field as a notogh (fief) for each tribal lord and his people, thus confining the Mongols to a limited area. As a result, tribalism, localism, and separatism emerged among the Mongols. Several banners were put together as a chighulghan (league), and under the banner there were the somuns (arrows). A banner became a feudalistic, self-ruling unit of Mongolian local administration, subject to Manchu manipulation.

Furthermore, following its subjugation to the Manchus, Mongolia was politically divided into "inner" and "outer" administrations (jasagh) that eventually created the popular designations, Inner Mongolia and Outer Mongolia. The Mongols themselves, however, usually use the term aru (back) instead of outer and obor (bosom) instead of inner. This Mongol usage clearly expresses the notion that Mongolia is one body, back and bosom being only different sides of the same entity.

When they first assumed power over China, the Manchus treated the Mongols as common allies against the Chinese, and both Manchuria and Mongolia were forbidden to Chinese immigrants. Toward the latter part of the eighteenth century, however, with the sinicization of the Manchu rulers and the growing threat of Russian expansion toward Asia, the Manchu Ch'ing court altered its original policy and encouraged Chinese settlers to immigrate to Mongolia in order to eliminate the power vacuum that was so tempting to the Russians. At that time China, faced with the problem of limited arable land and a seemingly limitless population growth, was beset with famines and rebellions. Subsequently, the impact of Western imperialism caused both economic and political crises in China which in turn further enhanced the instability and poverty of the people. In a sense the plans to promote the migration of Chinese to border lands such as Mongolia were therefore for China one-stone, two-birds policies intended to ease population pressures and to assimilate the Mongols, as well as to restrain further Russian expansion.

The settlement of the Chinese and their cultivation of Mongolian land forced the Mongols out to more arid and less suitable grazing fields, severely damaging the Mongols economically. Furthermore, with the onslaught of Chinese settlers, Chinese governmental adminstration penetrated into Mongolian territory, creating conflict between traditional Mongol political organizations and Chinese institutions. The outpouring of Chinese into Mongolia threatened the existence of the Mongols as a nation economically, politically, and culturally. Eventually this threat became the chief justification for the independence movement of Outer Mongolia after 1911 and the self-determination movement of Inner Mongolia that climaxed in the 1930s and 1940s. The latter is the subject of this paper.

THE BEGINNINGS OF THE
SELF-DETERMINATION MOVEMENT

Even before the collapse of the Manchu Dynasty in 1911 and the emergence of the Republic of China, there were stirrings of "modernism" in Inner Mongolia. These are especially associated with Prince Gungsangnorbu (1871-1931), a leader of the Kharachin Mongols of eastern Inner Mongolia. (3) Aware of Mongolia's isolation from virtually all other parts of the world except Tibet, conscious of her cultural "backwardness," and fearing the impact of the political and economic decay of China, this prince began late in the nineteenth century to establish schools. He sent some students to study in Japan, and began implementing moderate changes of traditional ways in spite of the fact that he was under heavy pressure not to do so from the Manchu rulers in Peking and the Manchu-Chinese governors and magistrates along the Mongolian border. His measures for the first time stimulated what we may call nationalistic feelings and a desire for change among some younger generation Mongols.

During the chaos after 1911, following the establishment of the Republic of China, Prince Gungsangnorbu went further to seek Japan's support for an Inner Mongolian independence movement. His political effort failed because of the changing situation in China and a problem of the power balance among the world powers in Asia. Furthermore, the very close proximity of eastern Inner Mongolia to Peking made an escape from the Chinese sphere of influence next to impossible. But meanwhile events acquired a momentum of their own. The emergence of Chinese warlordism added greatly to popular distress in Inner Mongolia. The warlords ignored the Mongolian quasi-feudalistic, self-governing "league" and "banner" system and forcefully imposed a Chinese style of local government, sheng (province) and hsien (county), on Mongol territory. They precipitated the emergence of what was known as "Mongolian banditism" (Meng-fei), (4) exposed the impotence of the Mongolian feudal lords, and showed the inadequacy of the entire feudal system. Meanwhile Chinese settlers were encouraged to continue encroachment on Mongolian grazing lands and Mongol herdsmen were driven deeper into the desert. Mongols who resisted these measures and fought for their own right of existence were killed or exiled. As a result, people who had contacts with the Chinese began to liberate themselves from the old traditional feudalistic attitudes. This, on one hand, undermined the unity and the power of the leagues and banners. On the other hand it was a step forward toward social reform and created a desire for greater unification of all the Mongols.

In addition to these changes the original pastoral economy suffered from the pressure of the Chinese agricultural and commercial economy. Some Mongols who were living along the borderland moved farther north. Others adopted Chinese methods and began to cultivate land, but no matter whether they migrated to the north or remained in their own homeland, ecnomically they had to struggle for survival against Chinese pressure.

All this increased the national consciousness of many Inner Mongols and their concern for their identity as a people different from the Chinese in religion, culture, way of life, language, political organization, and history. They looked down on the Chinese and referred to them as muu Kitad (bad Chinese) or khara Kitad (black or uncultured Chinese), a counterpart to the Chinese view of the Mongols as "stinky Tatars" (sao Ta-tzu).

This sort of range of ethnic and psychological solidarity grew as the republican Chinese developed a policy of assimilation (t'ung-hua). Even in the Tumed region of Koke-khota (present Huhe-hot) in Inner Mongolia, where by the 1920s the vastly outnumbered Mongols had already lost their language and writing system, a sense of Mongolian identity survived. Ulanfu, (5) a leading Mongol Communist purged as a Mongol nationalist during the Cultural Revolution, was from this Tumed region.

Mongolian consciousness varied over time. As has been mentioned before, from the latter part of the last century and the earlier two decades of this century the Inner Mongols used direct military action and bloodshed to express fury against the Manchu-Chinese domination. Chinese authorities reported this type of rioting and mass rebellion as the actions of "Mongolian bandits." These movements were not well organized nor firmly politically oriented. Most of the leaders had no thoughts of independence. Only in 1912 did Prince Gungsangnorbu advocate Inner Mongolian independence and seek assistance from outside. Other leaders only desired to maintain the status quo with no further Chinese intervention. Even Gungsangnorbu only considered the restoration of the Manchu-Ch'ing Dynasty.

Sun Yat-sen's doctrine of national self-determination brought a change. In the fourth article of his Chien-kuo ta-kang (Outline of National Construction) (1924) Sun Yat-sen declared that the government must assist weak and small nationalities in the state and enable them to carry out self-determination and self-rule. The Mongolian intelligentsia became more articulate and a Pan-Mongolian movement developed. Then, in 1924, the Outer Mongolian independence movement led to the establishment of the Mongolian People's Republic, and the launching of socialist revolution there. (6) This produced an enormous change in outlook in the entire Mongolian world and provided particular hope to radical, modern-thinking young people in Inner Mongolia.

In the middle of the 1920s a group under Pai-yun-ti (7) decided that the greatest hindrance to Mongolian liberation was not external oppression by Chinese authorities but the actions of reactionary Mongolians. Therefore, instead of fighting Chinese authorities, this group fought for social reform inside Mongolian society. Accordingly, they organized an Inner Mongolian People's Revolutionary Party (also known as the Inner Mongolian Kuomintang) with the assistance of Sun Yat-sen and his Kuomintang in Canton, of Dambadorji and his Mongolian People's Revolutionary Party in Ulan Bator, and of the Third (Communist) International. The purpose of this party was threefold: to abolish Inner Mongolian feudalism, to fight against Chinese warlords in Inner Mongolia and North China, and to implement self-rule and democracy. Although it was not a publicly stated goal, one of the chief purposes of the party was gradually to unify Outer and Inner Mongolia. This revolutionary movement failed largely because it became too involved with internal Chinese struggles and because of opposition by conservative Mongol leaders. The movement did, however, open the eyes of many Inner Mongolian intellectuals to the cause of national liberation and social reform. Some of them went to Ulan Bator and the Soviet Union to work more directly for Inner-Mongolian independence, unification with the Mongolian People's Republic, and social revolution.

After the Kuomintang's northern campaign of 1928, many Inner-Mongolian leaders petitioned the national government to carry out Sun Yat-sen's progressive declaration regarding minority nationalities. One of them, Wu-ho-ling, organized a party to fight for Mongolian self-rule under Chinese sovereignty through peaceful legal steps. (8) This moderate idea was reasonable. In 1931 the national government in Nanking promulgated an "Organizational Law of the Mongolian leagues, tribes, and banners" to guarantee Mongolian self-rule in their own land. (9) This limited measure did not satisfy Mongol demands for a change of the oppressive actions of the local Chinese warlords, however, and failed because the Chinese local warlords did not accept the decisions made by the central government. Its failure opened the way for the founding of the Inner Mongolian Autonomous Movement.

After the Japanese occupation of Manchuria and Inner Mongolia in 1931, eastern Inner Mongolia was organized into the so-called "Hsingan provinces" and exercised self-rule outside the ordinary Chinese administration of Manchukuo. In 1933 both conservative and liberal Mongol leaders, taking advantage of the Japanese invasion, gathered under the leadership of Prince Demchugdungrub (10) to organize a Mongolian Autonomous Movement for the purpose of gaining self-determination. The attitude of the Prince and his followers was comparatively complicated. First, they did not believe that the Chinese authorities would grant any kind of autonomy unless they were forced to; therefore they chose a hostile and uncooperative attitude toward them. In the camp of this movement were radicals and conservatives, pro-Japanese and pro-Chinese, Soviet- or MPR-trained and Chinese-trained elements. All had a common purpose in fighting first for self-rule. Secondly, though some in the movement preferred the social status quo and others did not, all realized that change and social reform were inevitable. And third, the movement's policy was not limited to the self-rule of Inner Mongolia only; its ultimate hope was the independence of Mongolia as a whole. The main difference in goals between this group and the later group after the war led by Ulanfu was the demand for independence. Ulanfu's group followed the line of Chinese Communists - willingly or perforce - and strongly emphasized that the main target was social revolution, not a separatist movement against the Chinese regime.

Following the outbreak of the Second Sino-Japanese War in 1937, part of Inner Mongolia was reorganized into the Mongolian Autonomous State (Mongghol-un obosuben jasakhu ulus) and became known in Chinese as the Mengchiang government. The Demchugdungrub group consequently came to be seen in Chungking as a Japanese puppet organization. In fact it was purely a Mongolian initiative.

THE CRISIS OF 1945

Rapid changes occurred in Inner Mongolia between 1912 and 1945. In addition to their political awakening and demand for self-rule, the Mongolian leaders paid great attention to general education. Schools were established and young intellectuals were sent to the large cities in China and Japan to study. In eastern Inner Mongolia the traditional quasi-feudalistic institution was abolished in the 1930s. Though western Inner Mongolia was somewhat behind the eastern part, social reforms began to take place there also. Khorishiya (cooperatives) were organized to protect the economy of the herdsmen, and the number of the llamas was reduced. Both in the east and the west the occupations of the Mongols began to change. In addition to herdsmen there emerged farmers, soldiers, public servants, handicraft workers, and intellectuals.

Because so many real changes had taken place, the defeat of Japanese militarism and the incursion of Russian and Outer Mongolian forces into Inner Mongolia in 1945 led many Inner Mongolian leaders to hope for the unification of Mongolia and gave them renewed enthusiasm for self-determination.   But to Inner Mongol pleas for a unified Mongolia the MPR forces now responded with propagandistic statements, chastising them for not following the same socialistic course as their northern brothers and challenging them to make their resolve to do so.   Unfortunately for the Inner Mongolians, an agreement had been signed by Stalin, Roosevelt, and Churchill on February 11, 1945.   It says that "The status quo in Outer Mongolia (The Mongolian People's Republic) shall be preserved." And it states: "It is understood that the agreement concerning Outer Mongolia . . . referred to above will require concurrence of Generalissimo Chiang Kai-shek.   The President will take measures in order to obtain this concurrence on advice from Marshal Stalin." (11)   This agreement led to the Sino-Soviet Treaty signed in Moscow on August 14, 1945 (just after the Soviet declaration of war on Japan), to a plebiscite in Outer Mongolia on October 20, 1945, and to the Kuomintang government's subsequent relinquishment of Chinese claims to sovereignty over Outer Mongolia.   The Yalta agreement effectively ended the possibility of Mongolia's reunification by obtaining international recognition of the partition of Mongolia.

In 1945, during the process of liberation, leaders of eastern Inner Mongolia organized an "Eastern Mongolian Autonomous Government." Leaders of western Inner Mongolia formerly under Japanese occupation organized an "Inner Mongolian Liberation Committee" that later altered its name to the "Inner Mongolian Government."   Prince Demchug-dungrub went to Chungking to negotiate with Chiang Kai-shek and the Chinese Government for an Inner Mongolian autonomous status like that of Canada and Australia in the British Commonwealth. (12) In addition to the Prince, Mongolian leaders in the Kuomintang Party petitioned for the restoration of the unified Mongolian autonomous institutions that had been established after the Autonomous Movement of 1933.

At this point we must mention that towards the national problem (min-tsu wen-ti) the view of the Mongols (and other national minorities in China) was (and still is) quite different from the view of the Chinese. The basic demand of the Mongols toward the National Government and Kuomintang Party in 1945 was to be recognized as a nation, for which the Chinese word is min-tsu.   However, the Chinese authorities wanted to use the word tsung-tsu instead, which means only a branch of the original nationality (min-tsu).   They emphasized that China is one nation (min-tsu) and that is the Chinese nation, Chung-hua min-tsu, while the Mongols, Tibetans, Uighurs, and so forth are merely the branches (tsung-tsu) of the great Chinese nationality.   Therefore they said that China is different from those countries which are troubled by nationality conflicts, and that China had no such problem.   They used this reasoning in order to reduce the importance or the eminence of Mongolian (or of other peoples') desires for national self-determination, turning it into a second-class, internal, minor problem of a branch nationality that should not be recognized as a problem of national separation or independence. The term tsung-tsu was not acceptable to the leaders of the Mongols and other nationalities. Consequently some other terms began to devleop, such as jo-hsiao min-tsu (the weak and small nationalities), pien-chiang min-tsu (the nationalities of the border regions), and shao-shu min-tsu (the national minorities). Of the three terms the Mongols and other peoples preferred the last, shao-shu min-tsu.

In Nanking in the winter of 1946, during meetings of the National Constitutional Assembly, the Mongolian delegates' demand for establishment of a unified national organization and Mongolian autonomy was rejected. However, a limited or divide local self-government system for Mongolia was passed by the Assembly. (13) In 1948 when the first session of the National Assembly was held in Nanking, the Mongolian delegates again demanded national autonomy under a unified administrative structure and again were turned down. During this time the local governors of the border provinces were becoming increasingly aggressive, refusing to abide by the existing law code for Mongolia and trying to subject all Inner Mongolian administration to their rule. In the end all the Inner Mongolian moves failed in their purpose because of the opposition of the Chinese border provinces' warlords and officials, men such as Fu Tso-Yi (14) and Hsiung Shih-hui. (15) Meanwhile the Chinese Communist Party entered the scene.

The Chinese Communists had initially adhered to Lenin's principles toward minority nationalities and in 1922 announced that they supported the right of self-determination for Mongolia, Tibet, and Chinese Turkistan. (16) In 1931 the Chinese Soviet constitution had recognized the right of self-determination for the minorities inside China, and the right of each minority to separate from China and to establish its own free country. Mao Tse-tung himself, in December 1939, published a liberal view in his article "Chinese Revolution and Chinese Communist Party." The first section, entitled "The Chinese Nation" [Chung-hua min-tsu], greatly emphasized the oneness of China; (17) but Mao did not use the term tsung-tsu, and he did acknowledge that China is a country of many significant national minorities (shao-shu min-tsu).

After the Communist power center moved from Kiangsi Province to Yenan in northern Shensi Province, the Chinese Communists had actual contact with the southern Ordos banners of the Yeke-juu League south of the great bend of the Yellow River and thus began dealing with the Mongols in reality. In 1945, faced with the defeat of Japan and the Russian occupation of Manchuria and Inner Mongolia, the Chinese Communists welcomed the chance to expand their influence in Inner Mongolia. The Mongolian member of the CCP leadership, Ulanfu, and his group utilized the organization of the "Inner Mongolian Government" to establish a power base. Then they absorbed the "Eastern Mongolian Autonomous Government." Finally, in May of 1947, they established an "Inner Mongolian Autonomous Region."

All this time the Communists struggled against the Kuomintang to win the confidence and support of other minorities in China as well as of the Inner Mongols. When the Inner Mongolian demands were turned down by the National Government in 1946, the Communists proclaimed that they would provide minority rights not allowed by the Kuomintang. They would, for example, allow the Mongols and other minorities regional autonomy in their own territories. The Communists labeled the Kuomintang's policy toward the minority nationalities as "great Chinese chauvinism" (ta Han-tsu chu-i), a type of propaganda that greatly appealed to the Mongols. Through the manipulation of the term shao-shu min-tsu the Communists won a lot of sympathy from the Mongols and other national minorities. Many of the Inner Mongolian leaders began to turn to the Communists.

As Mao's forces moved from success to success in the spring of 1949, Prince Demchugdungrub proceeded to Alashan in the western corner of Inner Mongolia where he gathered many anti-Communist Mongol leaders in a conference to discuss the future of Inner Mongolia. By May they had organized a provisional government and declared autonomy. But the movement was abortive, although in Canton the National Government unenthusiastically took official notice of what had happened. (18) As the Communists approached victory in China, some members of the Mongol leadership proposed that the Alashan government should flee via Tibet, establish a Mongolian government in exile, and there seek justice by way of world opinion. But the plan failed for lack of time and because of opposition within the leadership by a few conservatives and several who preferred surrender to the Communists. Alashan was finally occupied by the Communists, Prince Demchugdungrub escaped to the Mongolian People's Republic, and the Inner Mongolian independence movement collapsed. (19)

Under Communist Rule

From the beginning of this century the national consciousness of the Inner Mongols and their desire for self-determination became ever more intense, as seen from the foregoing narrative. At the time of the Communist unification of China, the Mongol desires were widely recognized and could not be neglected by the Communist leaders. Particularly during the Sino-Russian honeymoon period of the early 1950s, the Mongolian People's Republic was one of the warmest members of the "fraternal brotherhood" and Inner Mongolia was a "land of peace and safety." Consequently, in order to earn the confidence of the Inner Mongols, the Chinese Communist leaders decided to allow the Inner Mongols more autonomy than they had enjoyed in the past.

In the 1930s the Communists had recognized the right of the Mongols, the Tibetans, and others to self-determination and the freedom to establish their own countries as separate from China. Now they allowed the Inner Mongols to unify themselves into one administrative entity, at the same time abolishing all Chinese border provinces formerly established on Inner Mongolian territory. However, the Communist leaders did not follow through with their earlier promise entirely.

In their constitution of 1954 the Chinese Communists projected China as a country of many nationalities. All nationalities, they claimed are equal and there should be no discrimination against or oppression of them. Any behavior that might be damaging to the unity of all nationalities was prohibited. All nationalities were to have the freedom to develop and use their own languages and scripts and to maintain or change their own culture and institutions. In the territories of the minority nationalities autonomy should be practiced, but all autonomous districts were at the same time considered indivisible parts of the People's Republic of China. (20) The Chinese Communists also proclaimed that all nationalities of China had already been unified into one great family of freedom and equality in order to develop friendship, love, and mutual cooperation. Official policy was to unify all nationalities in China as a foundation for antiimperialism, anti-chauvinism, antilocal nationalism, and to suppress the people's common enemies within each nationality. (21)

On the one hand the Chinese Communists made concessions to national minorities - including the Inner Mongols - who had desired autonomy, but on the other hand they thus clearly blocked any kind of separatist movement. Leaders who encouraged nationalism among their people were accused of harboring local-nationalistic sentiments, a crime meriting liquidation. Many advocates of Inner Mongolian self-determination were removed from public office and purged from the Party.

Meanwhile, right after the "liberation," all the original league and banner systems were reorganized. Although the old names remained they were no longer traditional Mongolian units. Many of the Chinese hsien (counties), which were established by the warlords and Kuomin-tang authorities, continued to exist and some larger ones were promoted to shih (cities). The "provinces" were abolished because of the establishment of the Autonomous Region. But this turned out to be very similar to a province. Before 1949 a major objective of the local warlords and governors in these border provinces had been dissolution of the Mongol administrative units as a measure for furthering assimila-tion. Before, strong Mongol opposition had blocked this reform. Now the Chinese Communists pressed it through.

At first the Chinese Communists promised the protection of the Mongolian grazing fields, and they agreed not to emphasize class struggle among the Mongols. They also allowed Inner Mongolian leaders to learn the cultural patterns of Outer Mongolia. They put away the traditional Mongolian script and adopted the Cyrillic alphabet in an attempt to bring both the written and spoken language closer to that of the Outer Mongols.

Schools were established and publications increased. Yet education and enlightenment worked not only for the Chinese Communists and their doctrines; it also encouraged the forbidden rise of Mongolian nationalism.   Ulanfu, at first merely an instrument of the Chinese through whom they governed the Mongols, began gradually to recognize his own Mongolian heritage, to increase the power of the Mongols in the autonomous region, and to prevent the flow of Chinese immigrants into Mongolia.   This change in Ulanfu's views and approach to Mongolian development proved in the long run unwelcome to the Chinese leaders in Peking.   In the 1960s, therefore, during the great Proletarian Cultural Revolution, Ulanfu and his group were accused of trying to establish a separate kingdom inside the People's Republic and they were all purged. The adoption of the Outer Mongolian writing system was construed as the greatest "crime" Ulanfu committed.

From that time until the present, the leading officials of the Party, government, and military in the Inner Mongolian Autonomous Region have been Chinese.   Furthermore, the land of the Inner Mongolian Autonomous Region has been fragmented.   Except for its middle part, known during the Japanese occupation as <u>Meng-chiang</u> (Mongolian Territory) and which remained as the Autonomous Region, all other territories were relegated again to the administration of Chinese provinces.   Consequently, 733,000 square kilometers of territory were taken from the Mongolian Autonomous Region that originally occupied 1,183,000 square kilometers of land.   Today Inner Mongolia contains only 450,000 square kilometers, and its military affairs are under the direct control of the Peking Military Zone that confronts the Soviets' formidable power over the border in the Mongolian People's Republic.

As a result of the Cultural Revolution, the people in the old Mongolian banners were organized into people's communes and brigades. The Mongolian grazing fields were opened even more to Chinese settlers, and Chinese herdsmen even appeared in the so-called pastoral zones.   Chinese "construction corps" poured into Mongolia as did deported intellectuals.   As a result, the Mongols are a minority group in the inner part of their own country.   Before the Communist occupation, the Chinese majority was concentrated in the cities of the Mongol-Chinese frontier zones.   After the Communist occupation, however, the Chinese spread throughout Mongolia.   Even the leaders of the communes and brigades are today interspersed with Chinese.

ASSIMILATION OR SURVIVAL

China is a country of more than sixty nationalities, with the Chinese comprising 94 percent and the minorities only 6 percent.   The total population of the People's Republic is believed to be more than eight hundred million.   The number of Mongols is probably just over one and a half million.   The population of the present Inner Mongolian Autonomous Region is about 6,240,000, the Mongol population comprising no more than 420,000.   The ratio of Mongols to Chinese settlers even in the early

1960s was 1 to 12. (22)   As a result of various types of social
engineering by Peking, Mongols in Inner Mongolia will find it very
difficult to escape assimilation.

On January 17, 1975, the Chinese Communists published a new
constitution which states: "The People's Republic of China is a unitary
multinational state.   The areas where regional national autonomy is
exercised are all inalienable parts of the People's Republic of China.
All the nationalities are equal.   Big-nationality chauvinism and local-
nationality chauvinism must be opposed.   All the nationalities have the
freedom to use their own spoken and written languages."   It reads
further: "The organs of self-government of national autonomous areas,
apart from exercising the functions and powers of local organs of
state. . . may exercise autonomy within the limits of their authority as
prescribed by law.   The higher organs of state shall fully safeguard the
exercise of autonomy by the organs of self-government of national
autonomous areas and actively support the minority nationalities in
carrying out the socialist revolution and socialist construction." (23)   In
reality the power of autonomy of these national minorities is less
protected than under the old constitution of 1954 and the possibility of
self-determination has become more remote than ever.

The term "Chinese integration" is often in reality merely a disguise
for a word long since forbidden in Communist terminology, assimilation.
Assimilation (t'ung-hua) is a symbol of chauvinism and a great crime
that was committed by precommunist "Chinese chauvinists" (ta-Han-tsu
chu-i che).   Regardless of the circumstances, it is quite unlikely that
Chinese Communist leaders will ever officially recognize that their
party and government have carried out any policy of integration or
assimilation.

With regard to culture, the Chinese Communists prohibited the Inner
Mongols from using the Cyrillic script and instead reintroduced the old
writing system.   Prior to the Cultural Revolution many kinds of
literature and historical words were published, whereas now Mongol
publications are largely limited to translations of Mao's works and party
instructions.   No encouragement is given to the Mongolian translation of
new terminologies; Chinese terms are transliterated into the Mongolian
script.   As a result, the number of words borrowed from Chinese is
continually increasing within the Mongolian vocabulary.   In the yurts of
today's Mongols, Chinese language slogans are common.

None of Mongolia's economic activities has escaped the involvement
of Chinese immigrants.   Formerly, animal husbandry was managed
solely by Mongols, but now Chinese participation is high.   Chinese work
together with Mongols on all farms and other productive centers.
Huhehot (Koke-khota), the capital of the region, has now been
devleoped into a center of light industry with a largely Chinese labor
force.   The Dabusun-Nor (Salt-Lake) of Ujumuchin supplies the salt for
North China.   The iron ore of Bayanoboo, the coal of Badghar (Ta-
ch'ing-shan), and the water of the Yellow River have made Paotou a
center for heavy industry in the People's Republic.   The railway that

traverses Inner Mongolia from the north to south is the shortest land route from Moscow to Peking, and the railway crossing the region from east to west is the main link between Peking and Chinese Turkistan. All of these economic and military factors, tightly controlled by the Chinese, suggest that China is methodically absorbing Inner Mongolia.

Inner Mongolia, since the turn of this century, has become a very sensitive area politically. The policies exercised here by the Chinese were once the model for policies toward other minorities. Also, because of Inner Mongolia's "betweenland" position, the success or failure of Chinese policy there will undoubtedly influence the attitude of the Mongols and other minorities in the Soviet camp. The earlier Chinese Communist policy of moderation toward Inner Mongolia was a result of Sino-Soviet friendship. The present policy is in part a result of the Sino-Soviet split. Even though the future relationship between China and Russia may change, it is not likely that Inner Mongolia's unfortunate condition created by present Chinese Communist domestic policy will change. It must be remembered, however, that though Chinese power can prevent communication between Inner Mongolia and the Mongolian People's Republic, Peking has no way of rooting out the emotional ties of a people on one side of the Gobi Desert for their brothers on the other side.

The majority of those people living along the entire length of the Sino-Soviet border are neither Chinese nor Russian but are, like the Mongols, members of minority nationalities of the Altaic ethnic group. Consequently, the policy of the Chinese Communists does not only affect the attitude of the Mongols in the MPR but also the minority nationalities in Siberia and Central Asia. Similarly, the Soviet Union's policy toward minorities within its realm influences the non-Chinese peoples in the CPR. This may explain why both Peking and Moscow are so quick to publicize the oppressions and injustices in each other's national minority policy. For instance, the most common attack from the Soviet side is the criticism of Maoist, great Chinese chauvinism and the contention that the so-called Inner Mongolian Autonomous Region is not self-ruled by the Mongols but is ruled by the Chinese. The Chinese usually attack Soviet colonialism and economic extortion in the Mongolian People's Republic and the high-handed policy of the Soviet Union towards its own minorities. (24)

At present the official attitude of the Chinese Communist Party towards the national minority problems could be identified with an important instruction of Mao Tse-tung, "On Ten Great Relationships (Lun shih ta kuan-hsi)," in which Mao considered "The Relationship Between the Chinese (Han) and Other National Minorities" as the sixth most important matter of the party and the state:

> As for the relationship between the Chinese and the national minorities, our policy is comparatively stable and comparatively acceptable to the national minorities. We emphasized opposition against great-Chinese chauvinism and also opposition against local nationalism. However, this is the general idea but not the key point.

. . .In our country the land occupied by the national minorities is large; however, in population the Chinese occupy ninety-four percent. . . .But who has more land? The national minorities occupy fifty to sixty percent of the land. . . .The national minorities are entitled to say "The land is large and the resources are splendid." At least for the national minorities the underground resources are 'splendid' to them. . . . The Chinese reactionary rulers had created all kinds of alienation among our nationalities and had brow-beaten the national minorities. The influence created by this type of situation is difficult to wipe out even among the laboring people.... Therefore. . . we should . . .carry out education for the proletarian nationalities policy and constantly check the relationship between the Chinese and other national minorities. . . .In the Soviet Union, the Russian relationship with other national minorities is very abnormal. We have to take it as a lesson. (25)

By reading this document carefully, one realizes that the opposition toward great-Chinese chauvinism and local nationalism - especially Chinese chauvinism - is no longer to be emphasized. The key point is the utilization of the land and the mineral resources of the national minorities to fit the needs of Greater China. Traditional national prejudice still exists. The official way to wipe out this prejudice is to carry out the so-called proletarian or Maoist nationality policy, turning national disharmony between the Chinese and the non-Chinese peoples into hatred against the "class enemies" of their own nationality. In other words, minorities are to be integrated or assimilated into one greater nationality under the umbrella of proletarian class struggle. Since the ratio of the land and population is so different, the immigration of the Chinese surplus population into Inner Mongolia is inevitable. The criticism of the Russian policy toward their national minorities will open a further dispute on Soviet national minority policy and can be used as a weapon of psychological warfare to win the sympathy of those national minorities under the Russian shadow.

This instruction was given on the occasion of the Enlarged Meeting of the Political Bureau of the Chinese Communist Party held in 1956, and was only published by the Red Flag in January 1977. Some experts studied this document carefully and discovered that this section on the nationality problem was originally the seventh item but is now the sixth. More words were added to the original which had been published as a secret document and only circulated in a limited number of copies. (26) Why did Hua Kao-feng edit and publish this in this critical period of political instability? (27) Do the changes that he made in this section indicate the importance and the existence of nationality problems in the PRC? Although these questions can only be answered when the dust settles, the main guidelines of the policy toward the Inner Mongols and other national minorities by this post-Mao regime are suggested by the publication of this document.

NOTES

(1) Pan Ku, "The Account of Hsiung-nu," Han-shu (Po-na edition) 94, sect. 2, p. 32 a-b.

(2) For the following, see Owen Lattimore, Inner Asian Frontiers of China (reprint, Boston, 1962); and Robert A. Rupen, Mongols of the Twentieth Century (Bloomington, Indiana, 1964), vol. 1.

(3) Sechin Jagchid, "Prince Gungsangnorbu--Forerunner of Inner Mongolian Modernization," will be published in Zentralasiatische Studien (Bonn), no. 12 (1978).

(4) Sechin Jagchid, "An Interpretation of 'Mongol Bandits'" Paper delivered at the nineteenth meeting of the Permanent International Altistic Conference, Helsinki, June 1976.

(5) Paul Hyer, "Ulanfu and Inner Mongolian Autonomy Under the Chinese People's Republic," Mongolian Society Bulletin 8 (1969): 24-62.

(6) On the revolution in Mongolia, see Rupen, Mongols of the Twentieth Century, vol. 1; and George G. S. Murphy, Soviet Mongolia (Berkeley and Los Angeles, 1966).

(7) Pai-yun-ti is also known by his Mongolian name Buyantai. For the following see Howard H. Boorman (ed.), Biographical Dictionary of Republic of China (New York, 1967), vol. 1, pp. 6-9.

(8) In 1928, Wu-ho-ling (Unenbayin) organized the Mongolian Delegation Group and proceeded from Peiping to Nanking to petition for Mongolian self-rule. See Boorman, Biographical Dictionary, Vol. 3, pp. 353-356.

(9) "The Organizational Law of Mongolian Leagues, Tribes and Banners," was a resolution of a Mongolian Conference held in Nanking, 1930. The law was officially promulgated by the National Government in January 1931.

(10) Paul Hyer, "Demchugdungrub: Nationalist Leader in Inner Mongolia's Confrontation with China and Japan." Paper delivered at the Thirtieth World Congress of Orientalists, Mexico City, August 1976 and published in the proceedings.

(11) "Agreement Regarding Entry of the Soviet Union into the War against Japan," in Foreign Relations of the United States - The Conferences at Malta and Yalta, Diplomatic Papers (Washington, 1955), p. 984.

(12) Personal conversation of the author with Prince Demchugdungrub, January 1946.

(13) See "The Constitution of the Republic of China" (1947), Articles 119 and 168.

(14) After the war, Fu Tso-yi was the governor of the Suiyuan Province and commander of the Twelfth War Zone including the three provinces of Suiyuan, Chahar, and Jehol that covered most of Inner Mongolia.

(15) Hsiung Shih-hui was Director of the Office of the Chairman of the Military Committee in the Northeast, a transitional agency set up by the Central Government over territories formerly occupied by Japan, which contained the Mongolian territories of eastern Inner Mongolia.

(16) For the following, see Kenichi Hatano, Chukoku kyosanto shi (History of the Chinese Communist Party), (Tokyo, 1961), vol. 1, pp. 43, 580, 610-612; Wu Hsi-hsien, "Nei Meng-ku hsing-cheng ch'u-yu to yen-pien" (Changes in the Inner-Mongolian Administrative Districts), Fei-chin yueh-pao (Taipei) 19, nos. 2, 3 (August and September 1976); and Tsao Po-i, Chiang-hsi Su-wei-ai chih chien-li chi-ch'i peng-k'vei, 1931-1934 (The Rise and Fall of the Chinese Soviet in Kiangsi, 1931-1934) (Taipei, 1969), pp. 101-122.

(17) Mao Tse-tung, "Chung-kuo Ke-min ho Chung-Kuo Kung-ch'an-tang," in Mao Tse-tung hsuan-chi (The Selected Works of Mao Tse-tung), 10th ed. (Peking, 1969), vol. 2, pp. 584-586.

(18) Chun-yu pei-an.

(19) Prince Demchugdungrub was subsequently extradited by the MPR to Communist China. He died in 1968 or 1970.

(20) "The Constitution of the People's Republic of China" (1954), Article 3.

(21) Ibid., introduction.

(22) Meng-tsang-wei-yuan-hui (Mongolian-Tibetan Affairs Commission), Nei-meng fei-ch'ing kai-k'uang chi-ch'i yen-pan (The General Situation and Study of the Communist Activities in Inner Mongolia) (Taipei, 1961), p. 39; Ti-t'u ch'u-pan-she, Chung-hua jen-min kung-ho-kuo fen-sheng ti-t'u-chi (A Collection of the Maps of the Provinces of the PRC) (Peking, 1972), p. 23; Stephen Osofsky, "Soviet Criticism of China's National Minorities Policy," Asian Survey 14, no. 10 (1974): 913.

(23) "The Constitution of the People's Republic of China" (Peking, 1975), Articles 4 and 24.

(24) Tursun Rakhimov, "China's Nationalities and Maoist Policy" New World Review 42, no. 2 (1974); "Minority Nationalism in the Soviet Union as seen by Peking People's Daily," article published June 24, 1969, by the Radio Liberty Committee, New York.

(25) Mao Tse-tung, "Lun shih ta Kuan-hsi," (On the Ten Great Relationships), Hung-chi (The Red Flag), January 1977, pp. 3-4. The original date is April 4, 1956.

(26) See Chang Ching-li, "Hua-fei ts'uan-kai 'Lun shih ta kuan-hsi' chih yen-hsi" (An Analytic Study of Hua Kao-feng's Changes on the Ten Great Relationships), <u>Fei-ching yueh-pao</u> 19, no. 8 (1977): 21-26.

(27) Hua Kao-feng was officially authorized by the Party to edit and publish the works of Mao Tse-tung after the latter's death.

10 A Conversation with Owen Lattimore
William O. McCagg, Jr.

McCagg:	You've been watching ethnic inland Asia for almost sixty years. Do you think we're any nearer an understanding today than when you started?
Lattimore:	Let me reply out of history. Toward the end of the nineteenth century there was an enterprise to lay a land telegraph line which would cross over from Alaska into northern Siberia and connect the United States with Europe via Russia. This was later abandoned when the Atlantic cable was successfully laid, but in the meantime explorers were sent out to prospect the line and one of them was a man named George Kennan, whose cousin, twice removed, is the latter-day American Soviet expert. Kennan came home and published an "adventures on the frontier" book entitled <u>Tent Life in Siberia</u>. (1) It was, on the whole, very friendly to the Russians, and it became a best-seller.
McCagg:	Very friendly to the natives, too?
Lattimore:	Oh, yes, friendly to the Russians partly because of their good handling of the natives. But my point is that this same Kennan later in life published as expose of the tsarist criminal and political exile system in Siberia which was very anti-tsarist, and this also was popular in America. (2) The change was symptomatic. Until the end of the nineteenth-century Americans traveling in the areas of tsarist conquest in Asia rather generally saw the Russians as accomplishing a civilizing mission comparable to their own. Eugene Schuyler, for example, who wrote a classic work in the seventies entitled <u>Turkistan</u>, was favorably impressed

by Russian efforts to abolish slavery and the slave trade in such Central Asian Khanates as Bukhara and Khiva, and therefore depicted them in Central Asia as bringing a higher culture to a backward area. (3) There was lingering anti-British feeling in this too. You find favorable comparisons in this Russian expansionism to the British "imperialist" subjection of relatively advanced cultures in India. But the overriding view was that the eastward moving Russian "pioneers" would reach the Pacific from their side, and the westward moving American pioneers would build out to the other side of the Pacific, and then the two sides would meet in friendship - that kind of thing. Then in the years before Kennan's second book, Siberia and the Exile System, for a lot of extraneous reasons Americans changed their attitudes. The great pogroms of the 1880s started thousands and thousands of Jewish refugees on the road to America with tales of cruelty, hardship, and oppression. The Open Door issue came up in China. The United States started making arrangements with other powers which premised competitive commerce entering Asia from the sea. The Russians were approaching China from the landward side and penetrating Manchuria. The Russians were assumed to be after territory, whereas Americans thought they themselves stood for the integrity of China. Russia now appeared to the Americans as a menace looming up on the Pacific, and the Open Door Treaties in fact expressed the first American (or Anglo-American) "containment of Russia" policy. It was the Japanese who were now seen as imposing a bit of discipline and law and order in Eastern Asia.

Kennan's second book helped influence this new mood in America but it wasn't the only factor any more than his first book was. I think the mood became a great deal more than the influence, so to speak, and this is what is relevant to the question you asked about the literature on inland Asia. It wasn't just in America in the nineteenth century that mood overpowered the evidence. Remember how the British were afraid that the Russians were going to come all the way into Afghanistan and threaten the borders of India, whereas the Russians were equally afraid that the British were going to swallow up Afghanistan and stand on the borders of Central Asia and also Persia. When explorers such as Armenius Vambery and Curzon wrote about their adventures they did their bit to fan these suspicions, but their testimonies in no way account for the lasting quality of the myths. In the twentieth century too, over and over again, one sees this same kind of thing. During the second World War there was that great upsurge of pro-Russian feeling; in the 1950s and 1960s a comparable anti-Chinese feeling. Your "Ethnic Frontiers" conference may bear a certain relationship to the Nixon-Mao rapprochement and the detente with Brezhnev's Soviet Union.

McCagg: But don't you find a completely new scientific knowledge of inner Asia emerging in your lifetime, and a completely new set of attitudes towards the natives? I'd say that your own books are landmarks of this change, and what about Marxism and the Russian and Chinese revolutions?

Lattimore: Ah, well, of course, Marx regarded all the peoples of Asia as victims of imperialism; but he also thought that the British and French opium wars were a useful bashing of the despotic Manchu dynasty. Lenin portrayed the colonial possessions of the European powers as the Achilles heel of imperialism. He predicted that with the support and encouragement of a successful revolution in European Russia the Asian colonial peoples would carry out successful revolutions of their own. Today it's unfashionable to say anything good about Stalin, but he of course decreed respect for the territory, the cultures, and the languages of minority peoples on Russia's frontiers. One has to look at the results in a certain perspective. You may say that this was only on paper, but still there was more education under Stalin, from primary school to university, than in any Western colony in Asia, and more publication into languages of minority peoples.

              I remember apropos a book by Edward H. Parker, quite famous early in the century, when it was new, called A Thousand Years of the Tatars. (4) This was a history of China from the perspective of its landward frontier. It represented a new approach. The author even extracted from China's own chronicles his references to the eastern Huns or Hsiung-nu down through history. But the book is a curiosity today, because Parker's mind had been formed by his time, when respect for the military was just about universal. His attitude was that the Mongols and their predecessors in Central Asia were rude and barbarous people, but dammit, they were soldiers! Whereas the Chinese were soft, pliable, easily conquered. Fine culture, yes, but no soldiers. What this book really said was that the Chinese are a people who have always been conquered. In the past it was done from the landward side, but now we're in the twentieth century: let's see what lessons of conquest can be applied from the seaward side. It was never expressly put that way, but that is the impression you get reading it.

I won't say that the Soviets' new attitudes are the same as those of the tsars, but as I mentioned earlier, there's a basis in Russian history for an intelligent modern handling of the problem of the national minorities in Asia. Don't forget that when the great Russian surge eastwards into Siberia and Central Asia began in the sixteenth century, the tsars saw to it that the income from these new territories should flow directly into the state treasury and not, as in their European territories, into the pockets of a landlord class. Hence free peasants instead of serfs in Siberia. There was also a pronounced policy of "we can use some of those native peoples." And I don't suppose there's ever been an imperialism which did so much to finance science. The tsars were interested in "what is there? What can we get out of these new domains?" Consequently, they sent out all sorts of geological, botanical, geographical, and linguistic expeditions to investigate the East. At first, of course, they had to hire their scientists, or most of them, from Europe. But then they began to develop a Russian scientific intelligentsia, and in the nineteenth century one finds a Buriat Mongol intelligentsia trained in Russia. There was a famous Buriat scholar, Doryi Banzarov (1822-1855), for example, who worked through the medieval reports about Mongolia using Latin, plus Russian, German, French, English and Mongol sources. He was also well-grounded in Sanskrit and Manchu. It is tragic that he died at the age of only 33, but he has had many learned successors. (5)

McCagg: Didn't the Portuguese, the Dutch, and even the French all frequently adopt a "make use of the native peoples" policy, conspicuously not "racist," as they moved in the sixteenth, seventeenth and eighteenth centuries into what we know as "the Third World"?

Lattimore: So did the British sometimes. They used Indians in India at certain levels of the imperial civil service. They raised Indians up to certain levels of their army officer corps.

McCagg: As the Russians did the Kazakhs.

Lattimore: But I think that with the Russians a non-Russian could
               rise to much higher levels than a native could in the
               British service. Maybe this was because in southern
               Russia for centuries before modern times there was an
               ebb and flow of power, with Slavs sometimes under
               Turkic rule as well as Turkics sometimes ruled by
               Slavs. For the Russians power was power, whereas the
               British went by race, though they considered some
               peoples more reliable than others. There was a famous
               case when the Russians were first making contact with
               the Manchu Empire. A chieftain named Gantimur
               elected to join their side. The Manchus tried to get
               him handed back as a traitor. The Russians insisted
               that he was a political refuge and not a criminal, and
               refused to hand him over - this sounds nice today! So
               he stayed in Russia, founded a family, and in the siege
               of Port Arthur in 1904 to 1905 a descendant with the
               rank of Prince Gantimur headed a band of Cossacks
               which broke through the Japanese lines and got away
               safely - became a Russian national hero. This sort of
               passage of upper-class "native" Asians into the Russian
               gentry was perfectly normal; and nothing like it
               existed among the British.

               There's another story I always love reported by an
               English Protestant missionary who visited the Buriat
               region. The church being part of the state in old
               Russia, it was in the local Russian Orthodox churches
               that the birth, marriage and death records were kept -
               the basis for population statistics. He recalls visiting
               such a church and seeing an entry: "So-and-so born on
               this date, a Buriat, baptized on this date, a Russian."

               Getting back to the question of whether Soviet
               Marxism has brought about a radically new Russian
               understanding of the "native" question in Asia, though,
               let me tell a story. In 1937 my wife and I were on our
               way from Greece to Egypt on an Italian steamer. We
               found on board a crowd of pilgrims making a journey to
               Mecca. We learned they were from Sinkiang. I didn't
               know any Turkish, but a number of them spoke
               excellent Chinese and they were delighted that they
               had found someone to talk to. It turned out that they
               had come from Sinkiang overland through the Soviet
               Union, then across the Black Sea. This was the first
               pilgrimage which had been possible for many years.
               They had still encountered trouble on the Turkish end;
               there was a cholera scare, and they were not allowed

to land in Turkey. But the Soviet-Sinkiang frontier was for once open, and in the Soviet Union they had been issued passports which were inscribed "peasant." Peasant! It was quite obvious that they were really rich landlords who were accompanied by serfs. I asked them how they liked the Soviet Union and they replied that it was marvelous. Also, I was curious how they were able to travel around, what kind of money they were using. One of them reached into the breast of his gown and pulled out a bag of gold dust. Why hadn't this been confiscated? They answered that the Russians are "democratic," and when asked they defined "democratic" as "favorable to Muslims." Certainly the Soviet revolution brought a more constructive official treatment of the "native" problem in Soviet Asia than ever before. It made the tsarist treatment of the national minorities seem at least heavy-handed, if not malevolent.

McCagg: Let's attack this question of modern understandings of inner Asia from another direction. Marxists tell us that we may comprehend virtually any sort of social grouping if we look first of all at the economic system and then identify its stage of economic development, its economic classes, and so forth. Even at the Soviet-Asian Ethnic Frontiers Conference, where most of us were non-Marxists, we all spoke of Mongol, Kazakh, Armenian "bourgeoisies," "peasantries," "landlord classes," etc., as if they all were comparable. But isn't there a certain danger in using these labels, which after all are taken from western European experience? Do you feel we can escape our western prejudices?

Lattimore: Again, an anecdote! One time in 1930 I was on a river steamer going down the Sungari River to the Amur in search of a fragmented ancient tribe related to the Manchu. It was spring, when the ice had just melted. The winter before there had been that celebrated winter war in which the Chinese authorities of the Northeast tried to take complete control of the Chinese Eastern Railway, and the Soviets had responded with a military intervention. A great many villagers of Heilung Kiang and Kirin had fled and many of them were now returning to their homes. I was the only foreigner on the boat. I had a little cabin on the deck with a big window and the crowd gathered around to inspect me. They knew I spoke Chinese, but that didn't inhibit them at all from discussing me within my hearing. They were pointing out in what ways I

resembled an American and in what I resembled a
Russian. One young fellow went off and came back
with his grandmother, and said to her: "Come and look
at the American." She said: "That is no American,
that is a Russian. He has a nose like a brute. And look
at his horrible green eyes! He's a Russian, all right!"
But everyone said, "No, no!" and they explained that I
wasn't a Russian, that America was a separate
country, that it lay across the ocean, and so on.
"Well," the old lady said, "you say it is an independent
country. What does that mean? You mean that they
don't belong to the Russians?" "No, no, they don't
belong to the Russians," they said. "And they don't
belong to the Japanese?" "They're independent. They
don't belong to anyone." Well, finally the old lady got
it. She puzzled a little bit. Then she said: "If they
don't belong to the Russians, and they don't belong to
the Japanese, and they don't belong to us, then are we
afraid of them, or they afraid of us?"

It is often said of the Chinese peasant in the past
that he had no political instincts, that if he were not
over-taxed, he didn't want any change in life. Even
today one frequently hears that the Mongols before
1921 were a traditional society, that the revolution
was artificially made in Russia and then exported full-
blown to Mongolia, and all that kind of tripe. It just
isn't true. People are people, no matter how "primi-
tive." There are differences, of course. One of the
most interesting conversations I can recall was with a
Yakut reindeer herdsman. We started talking on a
professional level about the differences between migration with herds of reindeer and migration with
flocks of sheep. But there are comparabilities, too.
Nomad societies, which in history have been based on
the management of livestock, are different from
agriculturally based societies, and consequently there
are certain things comparable between Muslim Arabs
and formerly Buddhist Mongols. Likewise, one may say
of the Mongols - the people I know best - that before
the revolution they lacked a bourgeoisie because the
"bourgeois functions" were carried out by Chinese -
and once the Chinese departed, the class was gone too.
In America we go about saying such things deviously,
because sometimes if you refer to "classes" in history,
you're labelled as a Marxist or under Marxist influence.
So we talk about "group interests" and "factional
interests," etc. But classes were not invented by
Marx. If you go back and read Gibbon's Decline and

Fall of the Roman Empire, you'll find he was not at all shocked by the idea of class as an element in politics. And, in inner Asian history, you find that there was not just Russian conquest, or Chinese conquest, but commercial interests - for example in Khiva and Bukhara - which welcomed Russian takeover because it promoted them.   And in tsarist times it is quite clear that Russian expansion into Siberia favored the growth of new entrepreneurial "middle classes" in some of the more advanced statelets, and of "intelligentsias" in others.

McCagg: OK, this is acceptable terminology for certain generalized communications, but when you try to be scientific, don't you find that the differences are greater than the similarities? You yourself are always telling anecdotes.

Lattimore: The key question is how you go about getting the information. Today many outsiders start in a university.   They get a sociological training in theory and methodology, and then off they go into the field with a list of questions to be asked.   Questionnaires and quantification are great producers of Ph.Ds, but sometimes they don't throw much light on the inner workings of a society. I talk about classes among the Mongols, but I never in my life went up to a Mongol, notebook in hand, and asked, "What was your bourgeoisie like?" To get a glimpse of what is real to the members of a society, you have to be very careful, and let the system emerge almost by itself.

I remember once in Mongolia, a few years ago there was a crowd of people and they were talking with my Mongol traveling companion, who had been in China. They were all anxious to know, "What is really going on in China?" When they finished with him, they said, "Who's this foreigner you've got in tow?" And the man said, "Oh, that's quite simple. He speaks Mongol; ask him yourself." So they formed a circle and stuck me in the middle and said, "We've never heard of such a thing as an American who speaks Mongol. Kindly explain."   So I told them about how I first came in contact with Mongols and decided to learn the language and travel among them. I didn't notice it until the end, but by the time I'd finished, the older people there were in tears because they said, "Here is a man who knew Mongolia in the old days. He knew the sufferings of our people and he tried to tell people about it. This shows he's a human being, he takes a human interest in us." This led to a long, revealing talk. Then when we broke up, the younger people started swarming around, and they said, "What is your profession?" I said, "I'm a retired professor." "Ah," they said, "that's a lot of money." I said, "Yes, but it doesn't cover things like medical expenses, educating my grandchildren, that kind of thing, you see." So they talked and then said, "Our system compares pretty well with yours." Now if I had gone among these people with a questionnaire, and said to various older people, "What was it like in the old days?" the reaction would have been: "What would this foreigner like to hear?" or conversely, "What would it be better for this foreigner not to hear?" and they would have given me convenient answers.

McCagg: Do you think there is such a thing as national character?

Lattimore: Yes, I think so, but it's very difficult to pin down and its manifestations will vary from individual to individual and from time to time. For example, early in the century the Mongols were involved in an attempt to break away from China and out of a situation in which the Chinese were regarded as blood-sucking imperialists. You could call it a rebellion rather than a revolution, but at that time anti-Chinese feeling seemed almost a matter of Mongol national character. But that's gone. Now, the Mongols don't want to be ruled by China, but they are quite content that the Chinese should be Chinese as long as the Mongols can be Mongols. The old attitude arose just because the Chinese were always someone to be feared.

What you can talk about and define is conscious-ness. A minute ago I was speaking of those old people practically weeping over the old days. Those were not good old days, but bad old days. This was not a romanticization. There was a bad old time which the youngsters knew nothing about, and the old people were saying, "Here is a foreigner, of all people, who knew and understood the bad old days." A bond of sympathy emerged from the common awareness. The same way, the young people didn't know anything about the old days, but were aware of "our system."

McCagg: You mean that what the youngsters are conscious of is completely detached from past reality?

Lattimore: This is very complicated. We in the West sit on the outside of Asia trying to classify facts that we get chiefly out of printed material. Some of us get the opportunity for more or less short visits there, we talk to people who have come from there, and so on. We try to sort out everything into categories and this leads to a neglect of the most fantastic variation within the categories.

To illustrate the point: One day in the Moscow airport, I went into the breakfast room and saw a chap who looked Mongol. I went and sat down with him and addressed him in Mongol. He replied with one or two polite phrases and then got up and went away. I thought he was afraid of being reported for talking to a foreigner. But no, not a bit. He went over to another table and spoke to an older man who then came over, took his place, and said, "The kid you were talking to is a Kalmuk, we both are. At the time of the deportation (1943) the kid was too young and he doesn't remember his native tongue. I was old enough and didn't lose it." Now they were both eligible for repatriation. I asked whether they were on their way to the Kalmuk Autonomous Region on the Volga. He said, "The kid is, but not I. During the deportation I qualified as an engineer in Tashkent and now I have a good job. I go to all kinds of good places all over the Soviet Union. I'm not going back to that silly rural life." Consciousness doesn't always mean language, and vice versa! Another example: In 1968 I was with a group of Mongols near the Chinese frontier. We were listening to a broadcast from Chinese territory which was in beautiful Mongol. But you should have seen the expression on their faces. The whole thing was Mao Tse-tung this and Mao Tse-tung that - cult of personality - and my companions were resenting it intensely. "We've been through all that. Don't try it on us again" was their reaction. Propaganda of this sort was absolutely self-defeating.

Maybe the best way to discuss what young people retain from the culture of the past is to refer to the debate about the impact of Bolshevism on Islam. I think you can contrast the survival of Christianity among the Russians with the weakness of Islam today in Central Asia. I think the reason is that in Christian communities children get their first acquaintance with religion from mothers and grandmothers. In Islam women have always been in an inferior position. They've been excluded from the mosques, etc., and children - boys - are not indoctrinated with the religion until they get to school when they reach the age of puberty. You can abolish or secularize a schooling system more easily than mothers and grand-mothers!

This is one aspect of the question, but it's impor-tant to recognize another. As Professor Karpat stressed at your conference, there is nothing in Islam that prohibits political radicalism, and in numerous Islamic communities today there are movements which are extremely radical, and even leftist. Professor Fletcher of Harvard is doing some extremely interest-ing research on the Sufi mystic sects. He believes that all the movements of political modernization in Islam are generally traceable to the secret or semisecret Sufi sects, which have often been persecuted, of course, by the orthodox. There is a Japanese scholar, Professor Shinotu Iwamura, who also, confirms this. During the Japanese occupation of Inner Mongolia he studied the Muslims, mostly traders and caravan men, and found that all the modern political ideas among the Chinese Muslims came from the Sufi in Iran and not from the pilgrimages to Mecca. The transmission of a culture is thus very subtle indeed and cannot be expressed just in terms of the literal carry-over from one generation to the next.

McCagg: But in Mongolia there has been a particularly radical change - a smashing break with the Buddhist past - hasn't there?

Lattimore: I always like to refer back to the destruction of the monasteries in England under Henry VIII. A great deal of beautiful art was destroyed then, a great many manuscripts were lost, and a long period followed before people brought up in the new Protestant tradition could read the ecclesiastical history of medieval England in an impartial way. This is true of many parts of continental Europe also. Revolutionary attacks on cultural monuments are not just a Bolshevik phenomenon.

McCagg: But in Mongolia wasn't the smashing of the bad old culture much more definitive than in Western Europe during the Reformation, or even in Russia after the revolution of 1917? The old culture was tribal, and therefore more fragile.

Lattimore: Don't underestimate the old culture! It was not "tribal" and had not been for centuries. A Mongol knew his tribal ancestry, but he also knew that he was a Mongol, just as a Scottish Highlander knows his clan, but also knows that he is a Scotsman. I must admit that in the past I have used "tribe" and "tribal" in ways that could be misleading. It was nineteenth century foreign travelers who passed off the Mongols as dirty, ignorant, and diseased, and so forth. Manichaeanism, Nestorian Christianity, later Buddhism all had reflections in Mongolia long before the great Mongol Empire of the 13th century. There were learned Mongol scholars in the past. The Buddhist period was very important culturally. The great monastic repositories of prerevolutionary Mongolia had encyclopedic compositions which covered medicine, botany, and all sorts of things. I've just been reading about how certain lost Sanskrit tests are partly preserved in Mongolian translations.

But there is a fair question here, and I think that part of the answer lies in the intense nationalism of the new regime. There's an unending argument among Marxists about what sort of nationalism is tolerable and praiseworthy, and what is "bourgeois." But this is dying down, and meanwhile precisely because of what 19th century foreigners used to say, the new regime in Mongolia feels obliged to prove that Mongolia did have a culture. There's an enormous amount of work being done, for example, on folklore and legend for the recovery, if not of hard historical data, at least of evidence illustrating what various periods of history were like.

McCagg: Is there a tendency to build up a cult of the Mongolian warriors of the past?

Lattimore: No, the warriors tend to be discounted. Today's Mongols point out - correctly enough - that the Mongol fighters were never just plunderers and robbers, in fact that the nomads in history usually preferred trade to robbery. This was as true, incidentally, of the Germanic barbarians on the frontiers of the Roman Empire as of the Turko-Mongol barbarians on the edge of the Asian civilizations. There are great possibilities for historical research here. The Chinese under the new Marxist regime, for example, are very much interested in what they call the "periods of sprouts of capitalism" in Chinese history. They wonder why these sprouts always withered, instead of developing into full-grown capitalism. My feeling is that if you investigate the chronology, you will find that the "periods of sprouts of capitalism" were periods in which parts of northern China were invaded and ruled by tribal peoples. Take the celebrated period of the Southern Sung Empire in the twelfth and thirteenth centuries. The Sung were paying enormous tribute then to the barbarians in the north: hundreds of thousands of ounces of silver, hundreds of thousands of rolls of silk per year. This gave the barbarians great purchasing power, particularly since they sold the silk further into western Asia. If they weren't allowed to buy things with their wealth they tended to make trouble, and consequently the Chinese social culture, which usually downgraded merchants, came to give merchants much more elbow room. The Sung period became a period of "capitalist sprouts."

And you can even explain the barbarian invasions in such terms. Tribal Mongols could be immensely wealthy in horses, cows, sheep, camels, etc. They could have far more than they could possibly consume. But the Chinese demand for beef and mutton was rather low. They preferred pork. Further the Chinese made their clothes of cotton and silk, not wool. So, when China for one reason or another stopped purchasing the steppe products, there existed an immediate pressure on the richer tribesmen to turn from buying and selling to robbery and invasion. In this framework barbarians do not represent simply conquest for plunder: they represent commercial exchange and the development of modern economic relationships.

McCagg: The Mongolians are making a great thing of this nowadays?

Lattimore: They're beginning to, they're beginning to. And there's another factor which encourages the new regime to recover parts of the culture of the past. This is that Buddhism in Asia today is a peace religion. It seems to favor detente, to be against colonialism, to afford links with other Asian nations which are useful to the regime's foreign policy. Even the Soviet Union is taking advantage of these aspects of Buddhism. For example, I saw in Buriatia a new Buddhist monastery, or at least a temple, being built. They'd actually brought all the way from India a slip of the sacred Bo tree (ficus religiosa), under which the Buddha is said to have achieved enlightenment. They planted it in a specially heated glass building. Similar things are happening in Mongolia. Today there is a new seminary in Ulan Bator for the training of young priests. They are reopening or even building monasteries, which incidentally make good tourist attractions. And they're sending Mongolian Buddhists to other parts of Asia to make contact with Buddhist organizations abroad.

McCagg: Isn't the political situation in Mongolia in many respects anomalous? A tribal society has managed to acquire independent statehood between the Soviet Union and China, and consequently it has a Communist regime of its own to protect, or recreate its culture from the past. It strikes me that most of the inner Asian peoples are in greater danger of being squashed.

Lattimore: Well, again there are all sorts of different problems involved here and they go right back to the beginning when the Russian and Chinese Empires were first coming together. As soon as the Manchus established themselves in Peking in the 17th century they became aware of a new danger in the frontier regions of the north. But their information was imperfect. One name for the Russians was transmitted by the northern Siberian tribes in a form originally taken from Finnish, and reached Peking as "Lo-ch'a," which was handy, as it could be written with the two Chinese characters used to transcribe the Buddhist term rakcha, "a demon." Another name came along a more southerly route via Mongolia. Since it is difficult for Mongols to pronounce "r" at the beginning of a word, they tend to put a vowel in front of a foreign word beginning with "r." In this way "Russ" became "Oros," and in its Chinese pronunciation, "Nge-lo-ssu." The result was that for a time the Manchus thought they were faced with two different savage peoples out there. Border peoples can often exploit the ignorance or failure to agree with overland states. Look at the North-West Frontier of British India, where the "tribal problem" survives as the Pashtun controversy between Pakistan and Afghanistan. Nor should one forget the old Scottish Border saying, "Elliots and Armstrongs ride thieves all."

Now another very important point. The Russians, as they expanded, were intent upon settling; and if the character and state of development of the tribes they encountered allowed, they sometimes smothered them just as the white men smothered the American Indians. (Alcohol was used by Chinese, Russians, and the white man in North America alike as the barter commodity which had the highest purchasing power and also rotted the society of the "savages" who bought it with

valuable furs, etc.) But then they met the Buriats who
were already a people of mixed culture. They were
not simply herders and hunters. They had agriculture
which was quite developed and a sophisticated irrigation system. Their engineering was not Chinese, but
Central Asian, and must have come in with the Turks
in the seventh century A.D. The Buriats were,
moreover, already in a state of rapid social transformation, like the Russians themselves, developing a
new entrepreneurial class. Now for the Buriats,
submission to the new Manchu Empire to the East
would have meant definite deterioration, because the
Chinese only understood replacing nomadism with
agriculture. The Russians, on the other hand, as I
mentioned earlier, were innovators. They had a policy
of "make use of the natives." "Incorporate the
natives" would in fact be a better term, I think. After
some initial armed clashes, the two decided to get
along. As Soviet writers say, this was not just a
question of the Buriats choosing the lesser evil: for
the Russians, as for the Buriats, there were positive
advantages in joining together. Jumping up in time a
bit, at the end of the nineteenth century when the
Russians began importing American farm machinery,
the agents of the American companies were often
Buriats. And I can remember in the 1920s the first
modern dairy in Tientsin - the first controlled dairy
where the milk was pasteurized and safe to drink - was
started by Buriats.

McCagg: Do you find this pattern among other Soviet nationalities east of the Urals?

Lattimore: In very different degrees. It depends upon how far the
class structure of the particular people you are
studying had been transformed at the time of the
absorption by the Russians. But what you do find even
west of the Urals is that it was rare for the entire
minority people to be against the Russians. Often part
of the intelligentsia of peoples in an early stage of
development said: "Ah. This is our opportunity to
take the lead, to liberate our people from the
disadvantages they have suffered under the old regime." You find, to use a later example, that the
Ukrainians, who provided some of the most bitter last-
ditch nationalistic opponents of the Russian revolution,
also provided some of the most simon-pure, devoted,
internationalistic Marxist-Leninists. There are other
such cases.

This brings up the whole great question of assimilation. The Chinese accuse the Russians of forcible assimilation of the minorities and the Russians accuse the Chinese of the same thing. But we are really facing here an historical process. The Russians don't need to forbid the use of any minority language nor do the Chinese, because it works the other way - if you want a better career in the Soviet Union you learn Russian, same thing in China. This is something that applies to any small nation. A Dutchman or a Dane, if he wants to get into the big time in physics or mathematics cannot stop with Dutch or Danish. He has to acquire one of the world languages. You may work for the survival of the Breton or the Welsh languages; but Lloyd George went on to a brilliant career because of his eloquence in English. Among the Soviet and Chinese minorities, it's the reward as much as the repression which is significant. Apropos, I remember several years ago in the capital of Buriatia I was talking to the local "Mayor Daley." We were exchanging polite information about our families, and I asked what his children did. He replied, "Oh, it's hell being a father these days. My daughter goes to the Buriat language school, and she gets onto me because my Buriat is full of Russianisms. My son goes to the Russian language school, and he is down on me too because I don't have either English or German as a supplementary language. I just can't deal with them."

McCagg:

Still, it strikes me that with the population pressures of today and the "total" character of the Soviet and Chinese states, the outlook is pretty depressing for the little peoples.

Lattimore:

I tend to look back to something that has been much neglected by historians: the self-limitation of empires, a contradiction of the simple Marxist theory that empires are insatiable. In Eastern Asia one finds a classic example in the period when the Russians and the Chinese were first coming into contact. The Chinese were then moving into new lands. But China was still operating according to the traditional notion that she herself produced everything necessary for civilized life. Foreign trade was seen as unnecessary, and foreign relations with inner Asia, Mongolia, and so forth, were permitted for political, not economic reasons. Peking sent out expeditions in all directions to see if there was any possibility of recurring disturbances on the frontier. Some went all the way up to the Amur and left a stone marker which the present-day Chinese see as quite important. But this stone and others were in the nature of "Kilroy was here."

The same way, there were Russians in tsarist times who wanted to go into Sinkiang, Russians who wanted to go into Mongolia, but they were always called back by Petersburg, which realized the dangers of over-expansion and recognized also a line of diminishing returns beyond which anything you took would cost more in imperial maintenance than it produced in terms of new income. Likewise, there was a "forward group" of British in India who said, "Why not go on in and take Afghanistan?" and London had to pull them back. Today's ordinary construction is that the Soviets went into Mongolia after 1921 imperialistically. Actually they were worried about Ungern-Sternberg, the "Mad Baron," who was trying to use Mongolia as a counter-revolutionary base. They actually bargained with the Chinese. Twice they asked the Chinese for joint action, and it was only when the Chinese refused that they intervened.

This same thing is at work today. The Chinese, for example, are an overwhelming majority compared with the Tibetans, the Uighurs of Sinkiang, the Mongols of Inner Mongolia, etc., but this does not mean that they are systematically trying to drown these peoples. In fact, the Chinese are trying to limit the growth of the Chinese population through birth control, but do not direct the family limitation propaganda at any of the minorities because they want to tell them - and the rest of the world - that the minorities are free under socialism to increase, to multiply, to enjoy the earth. Likewise, I read not long ago about the waning position of the Great Russians in the population spectrum of the Soviet Union, and the increasing numbers, propor-tionately and absolutely, of the non-Russian peoples.

McCagg: The author went on to say that the Russians were scared stiff of this.

Lattimore: Which I doubt, for there's always the matter of the omnipresent confrontation between the Soviet Union and China, if you want to call it that. I'm a maverick on this subject. Back in the days when all people "knew" that China was totally controlled by Moscow, I said "Nuts," and today when people say that the gap between the Soviet Union and China is so great that it can never be bridged, I say "Nuts." One thing you have to concede to both Russians and Chinese is that they have excellent systems of contemporary education. You may have totalitarianism, but if you're educating lots of people, you can't stop them from thinking. And I take it for granted that in an intelligentsia as large as the Russian or the Chinese intelligentsias there are some people on both sides who are thinking and arguing that the other is not so far off on certain points, subjects, or methods - this even during periods of apparent antagonism between the two states. In other words, you must always bear in mind the elements of possible adjustment and harmonization, as well as the elements of confrontation.

Still, there's no doubt that two different great states do exist and that the peoples we are discussing are in between them. I've lived long enough to see the results. In 1927, for example, my wife and I were traveling in Sinkiang. At that time material conditions of life were pretty tough in the Soviet Union. Many Kazakhs and Kirgiz from the Soviet side were coming over to the Chinese side, where life was easier. Quite recently, there have been reports of the Kazakhs in particular crossing back into Soviet territory. These would be the sons and grandsons of the people I knew half a century ago. The Chinese interpretation is that the Soviets are using subversive propaganda to tempt these people across the line. My assumption, pending proof to the contrary, is that in the turmoil of the Cultural Revolution Kazakhs have been saying, "Well, let's give it a try on the other side, where conditions are more settled and stable."

Then again, in 1972 when I was in Inner Mongolia, I was told not by Mongols, but by Chinese, that "of course in Outer Mongolia, in the People's Republic, they are new serfs of the new tsars. The Russians are taking over everything, and Mongolia is becoming one vast cattle ranch run by the Russians. We're getting refugees crossing the frontier all the time." My mind went back to several years before, when I'd been down near the frontier in the Mongolian People's Republic, and we were talking about this and that, and they said to me, "We don't graze right up to the frontier either, in order to avoid frontier incidents." And I said, "Well, are there any refugees, defectors, coming over from the Chinese side?" They said, "Very few. The frontier is extremely strictly guarded." And I said, "Any traffic the other way - any people from your side going over to the Chinese side?" And the man looked at me and he said, "I thought you were the man who was supposed to know us Mongols. What Mongol here in a country which we run would want to go over to the other side to be run by Chinese?"

McCagg:

It keeps ringing in my mind that all those peoples might just want out.

Lattimore:

What does that mean? Russia is going to be there for a long time, China is going to be there a long time. The way things stand today, if the regime in either one were to be overthrown, it would give way not to an anti-Marxist regime, or a weak, democratic, and tolerant regime, but to a new sort of Marxist dictatorship. I remember talking some years back to a Yakut reindeer herder who was very funny on the subject of a government experiment in improving the quality of life for the herdsmen. "They were sorry for us," he said, "because we had to camp in tents when migrating from our winter quarters to our summer pastures in the miserable spring weather, which is the worst weather of the year. So they built a string of 'migration stations,' suitably spaced, with log cabins for the people and corrals for the deer. What they didn't know is that reindeer moss does not replace itself every year, like the grass on a sheep pasture. It takes several years. So a string of log cabins and corrals is no use at all, because you have to follow a different route each year."

Now, a man like that is not "wanting out." He thinks his government makes mistakes, but is trying to make life better. Therefore, what has to be done is to improve the government's expertise and match it more and more efficiently to the production needs of each region.

Next, extend this kind of thinking to a country like Mongolia, which is not part of the Soviet Union. Unfortunately it seems impossible to cure our newspapers of saying Mongolia is "squeezed between two giants." I have always said that if you are and always have been on one side, then you are not "squeezed between." Mongols - and the more educated they are the more likely they are to express it clearly - put it this way. From 1911 to 1921 Mongolian semi-independence was made possible by tsarist Russian support; but tsarist Russia would not support full independence. Since full de facto independence in 1921, recognized by China at the end of the war,

Mongolia has benefited continuously from association with the Soviet Union and later COMECON. Conclusion: the Soviet Union is better than tsarist Russia, and association with the Soviet Union and COMECON is the essential guarantee of continuing Mongolian progress and prosperity. What reason would the Mongolian Peoples Republic have for "wanting out" or for "playing China against the Soviet Union"?

Returning to minorities within the Soviet Union and within China, why should they "want out"? Where would they go? The question can be answered by asking another question. Do American blacks, American Navahos, and Pueblo Indians "want out"? What all such minorities want is recognition of their right to be proud of themselves plus a fair shake, a fair chance, within the larger, general community. They don't want out: they want up. And if there is competition among various countries and different systems in helping them move upward, so much the better.

NOTES

(1) George Kennan, Tent Life in Siberia, and Adventures Among the Koreks, and Other Tribes in Kamchatka and Northern Asia (New York: G.P. Putnam and Sons, 1874).

(2) George Kennan, Siberia and the Exile System, 2 vols. (London: J.R. Osgood, McIlwain and Co., 1891).

(3) Eugene Schuyler, Turkistan: Notes of a Journey in Russian Turkistan, Khokand, Bukhara and Kuldja, 2 vols. (New York: Scribner, Armstrong and Co., 1877).

(4) Edward H. Parker, A Thousand Years of the Tatars, 2nd rev. ed. (New York: Knopf, 1926; orig. ed. Stringham, 1896).

(5) Istoriia Buriat-Mongol'skoi ASSR, 2 vols. (Ulan Ude, 1954), vol. 1, pp. 263 ff.

Author Index

Subject Index

About the Contributors

DR. WILLIAM O. McCAGG, JR. is a Professor of History and Director of the Russian and East European Studies Program at Michigan State University. He is the author of An Atlas of Russian and East European History (Praeger, 1967), with Arthur Adams and Ian Matley; Jewish Nobles and Geniuses in Modern Hungary (Columbia University Press, 1972); and Stalin Embattled, 1943-1948 (Wayne State University, 1978).

DR. BRIAN D. SILVER is an Associate Professor of Political Science, Michigan State University. Primarily interested in comparative politics and Soviet political and social processes, he has published articles on Soviet ethnic relations in Slavic Review, Soviet Studies, Demography, and American Political Science Review.

DR. JUNE TEUFEL DREYER is Professor of Political Science and Chairperson of the Center for Advanced International Studies at the University of Miami in Coral Gables, Florida. She is a specialist on national minority problems in China, she has published China's Forty Millions (Harvard University Press, 1976), and is Northeast Region Editor for Edwin A. Winkler, A Provincial Handbook for China (Stanford University Press, 1977).

DR. ALAN W. FISHER, Professor of History at Michigan State University, is an authority on Russian and Ottoman history and the author of The Russian Annexation of the Crimea, 1772-1783 (Cambridge University Press, 1970) and History of the Crimean Tatars (Hoover Institute, 1978).

DR. SECHIN JAGCHID is Professor of History and Asian Studies, Brigham Young University. From the late 1950s until 1972 he was

Professor of Mongolian History, Language, and Literature at both the National Chengchi University and the National Taiwan University at Taipei, Taiwan. From 1969 until 1971 he was Secretary General of the Chinese Historical Association and National Research Professor, National Science Committee at Taipei. He has published a two-volume study of Mongolian history, Meng-ku chih chin-hsi (Taipei, 1955), and a book on the north Asian nomadic peoples and the agricultural Chinese, Pei-ya yu-mu-min-tsu yu chung-yuan nung-yeh-min-tsu chien ti ho-ping, chan-cheng yu Mao-i chih kuan-hsii (Taipei, 1973).

DR. KEMAL H. KARPAT is Professor of Middle East Studies in the Department of History and Chairman of the Middle East Studies Program, University of Wisconsin (Madison). He is the author of several books including Turkey's Politics: The Transition to a Multi-Party System (Princeton, 1959); Political and Social Thought in the Contemporary Middle East (Praeger, 1964); Social Change and Politics in Turkey (Brill, 1973); An Inquiry Into the Social Foundations of Nationalism in the Ottoman State (Princeton, 1973); Turkey's Foreign Policy in Transition (Brill, 1975); The Gecekondu, Rural Migration and Urbanization (New York, 1976).

DR. OWEN LATTIMORE is a world-renowned scholar of Chinese and Mongolian studies. Since 1963 he has been Professor of Chinese Studies and Director of the Hayter Center of Chinese Studies at the University of Leeds. Dr. Lattimore has published The Desert Road to Turkestan (Little, Brown, and Co., 1929), Studies in Frontier History (Oxford University Press, 1962), Inner Asian Frontiers of China (2nd ed., American Geographical Society, 1951), Nomads and Commissars: Mongolia Revisited (Oxford University Press, 1962), Pivot of Asia: Sinkiang and the Inner Asian Frontiers of China and Russia (Little, Brown, and Co., 1950), and Nationalism and Revolution in Mongolia (Oxford University Press, 1955).

DR. GERARD J. LIBARIDIAN is Assistant Professor of Armenian History and Culture and Chairman of the Department of Armenology at the American Armenian International College at La Verne, California. He earned his Ph.D. in history from UCLA, where he wrote his dissertation entitled "Ideological Developments Within the Armenian Liberation Movement, 1885-1908."

DR. DAVID C. MONTGOMERY is Associate Professor of History, Brigham Young University. He has published a book entitled Mongolian Newspaper Reader (Indiana University Press, 1969).

DR. EDEN NABY is an Assistant Professor, Department of History, Pahlavi University in Shiraz, Iran. She has written Tajikistan with Richard Frye (forthcoming, Stanford University Press).

DR. NAZIF SHAHRANI is a visiting Assistant Professor of Anthropology, University of Nevada-Reno. A native of Badakhshan, Afghanistan, he studied at Kabul University and was a postdoctoral Research Fellow at the Center for Middle Eastern Studies at Harvard University. He has done ethnographic research in the Wakhan Corridor and the Afghan Pamirs, and his publications include The Kirghiz and Wakhi of Afghanistan: Adaptation to Closed Frontiers (Seattle, University of Washington Press, in press).

DR. S. ENDERS WIMBUSH wrote his dissertation on Contemporary Great Russian Nationalism: Real Dilemmas of the Dominant National Group in a Multi-National State. In 1975 and 1976 he did research at Moscow State University, and he is co-author, with Alexandre Bennigsen, Muslim National Communism in the Soviet Union: A Revolutionary Strategy for the Colonial World (Chicago: University of Chicago Press, 1979).   Dr. Wimbush currently works for the Rand Corporation in Santa Monica, California.

Pergamon Policy Studies